THE DEATH OF DESIRE

A stunning exploration of the relation between desire and psychopathology, *The Death of Desire* is a unique synthesis of the work of Laing, Freud, Nietzsche, and Heidegger that renders their often difficult concepts brilliantly accessible to and usable by psychotherapists of all persuasions. In bridging a critical gap between phenomenology and psychoanalysis, M. Guy Thompson, one of the leading existential psychoanalysts of our time, firmly re-situates the unconscious – what Freud called "the lost continent of repressed desires" – in phenomenology. In so doing, he provides us with the richest, most compelling phenomenological treatment of the unconscious to date and also makes Freud's theory of the unconscious newly comprehensible.

In this revised and updated second edition to the original published in 1985, M. Guy Thompson takes us inside his soul-searching seven-year apprenticeship with radical psychiatrist R. D. Laing and his cohorts as it unfolded in counterculture London of the 1970s. This *rite de passage* culminates with a four-year sojourn inside one of Laing's post-Kingsley Hall asylums, where Laing's unorthodox conception of treatment dispenses with conventional boundaries between "doctor" and "patient." In this unprecedented exploration, Thompson reveals the secret to Laing's astonishing alternative to conventional psychiatric and psychoanalytic treatment schemes.

Movingly written and deeply personal, Thompson shows why the very concept of "mental illness" is a misnomer and why sanity and madness should be understood instead as inherently puzzling stratagems that we devise in order to protect ourselves from intolerable mental anguish. *The Death of Desire* offers a provocative and challenging reappraisal of depth psychotherapy from an existential perspective that will be of interest to psychoanalysts, psychotherapists, philosophers, social scientists, and students of the human condition.

M. Guy Thompson, Ph.D. is a Personal and Supervising Analyst at the Psychoanalytic Institute of Northern California and Adjunct Professor at the California Institute of Integral Studies, San Francisco. His most recent book, *The Legacy of R. D. Laing* (2015), is also published by Routledge. Dr. Thompson is the author of numerous books and journal articles on psychoanalysis, phenomenology, and schizophrenia. He lives in Marin County, California.

"In our medicalized age of diagnosis and disease, we have forgotten what it means to be a person. In this superb book, M. Guy Thompson returns psychoanalysis to its existential origins. Offering a sophisticated and shrewd exegesis of the phenomenology of desire and pathos, he humanizes suffering and situates therapy within a moral framework of embracing experience. Thompson succeeds brilliantly in advancing an authentic discourse on the human condition."

—**Jon Mills**, PsyD, PhD, ABPP, author of *Inventing God*.

"Written with great clarity, insight and precision, this new, substantially revised edition of *The Death of Desire* by M. Guy Thompson invites its readers to reconsider their views on sanity and madness and the inter-connected role that each plays in our becoming who we are. Thompson's intent throughout is both radical and explicit: to excise from our understanding of madness all medically-attuned notions of pathology and, instead, to 'return it to where it belongs: the everyday agony and ecstasy of living, in all its attendant mystery and complexity.' This is a challenge whose boldness is matched by its urgent necessity. Whatever the stance taken towards the debate, I can't think of any mental health professional who will not benefit from reading this book."

—**Professor Ernesto Spinelli**, ES Associates, London, UK.

"A compelling exploration of the madness in sanity and sanity in madness in existential depth psychological keys. Thompson, heavily influenced by R. D. Laing, amplifies links between existential and psychoanalytic insights in this fervent probe of the human condition. Whether or not you agree with particular points, your appreciation for who we are and what we are up against will grow. A much needed affirmation of the human spirit in all its vicissitudes."

—**Michael Eigen**, Ph.D., author of *Image, Sense, Infinities, and Everyday Life*.

"M. Guy Thompson's revised edition of *The Death of Desire* is a clarion call for love – or 'being with' – as the crux of psychological and psychiatric care. Interwoven with keen scholarly insights and compelling personal anecdotes, this volume provides a rare window into Thompson's many years as student and later colleague of psychiatric maverick R. D. Laing. Through both case vignette and personal observation, Thompson builds a powerful case for sanity (or the nurturance of desire, authenticity, and responsibility) in a maddening, sanity-depleted world. This book is probably more relevant now, given today's machine-mediated, medicalized ethos, than it was 30 years ago when the first edition was published. I couldn't recommend it more highly."

—**Kirk Schneider**, Ph.D., author of *Existential-Humanistic Therapy, Awakening to Awe* and *The Polarized Mind*.

"*The Death of Desire* is alive with the spirit of Laing with whom Dr. Thompson trained and worked. Laing would have loved this revised edition even more than the original. This wonderful book provides a unique, absorbing and insightful exploration into the varieties of human experience and how best to live today.

Dr. Thompson's open-ended, open hearted, and creative approach reflects his thoroughly existential philosophical approach to psychoanalysis. The book brilliantly illuminates crucial questions about love, authenticity, therapy, sanity and madness."

—**Douglas Kirsner**, Ph.D., Emeritus Professor, Deakin University,
Melbourne; Honorary Member, American Psychoanalytic Association.

"Michael Guy Thompson, in this important work, provides a much needed and updated interweaving of existentialism and psychoanalysis. Building on how both Laing and Lacan attempted to rescue Freud from sanitised, often behavioural misunderstandings, Freud as well as Laing are treated as both existentialists and psychoanalysts. The result is a very readable exploration, highly recommended for both the general reader and experienced therapist interested in the relationship between desire and the human condition."

—**Del Loewenthal**, Existential-analytic psychotherapist, Professor of
Psychotherapy and Counselling, University of Roehampton, UK,
author of *Existential Psychotherapy and Counselling after Postmodernism*.

"In *The Death of Desire*, M. Guy Thompson takes the reader on a fascinating journey through the landscapes of psychoanalysis and existentialism. His search is for a deeper and more complete understanding of sanity and madness. Thompson provides a vivid and compelling depiction of key writings from Freud, Laing, Nietzsche and Heidegger; and shows how their works all form part of a single, unified landscape, at the heart of which is the need for love. This is the patient's need to experience love in their life, which allows for the actualisation of their authentic possibilities; and the therapist's capacity to facilitate this process through a caring, loving sympathy. This book is a valuable source of ideas and inspiration for therapists of all orientations, and particularly those working at the borders between existential and psychoanalytic therapies."

—**Mick Cooper**, Professor of Psychology, University of Roehampton,
Author of *Existential Therapies*, 2nd revised edition

"In this wise, intellectually rich and deeply thoughtful book, M. Guy Thompson explores the central, complex and paradoxical role that human desire plays in life, love and madness. Building upon foundational Freudian premises, and synthesizing profound insights derived from Nietzsche, Heidegger, Laing, and with his own clinical experience, Thompson provides a compelling and deeply compassionate perspective on the human condition and the process of healing. In this new edition of his classic book, Thompson incorporates a detailed account of his own apprenticeship with R. D. Laing and grounds his thinking in a deeply personal memoir of a monumentally important and often misunderstood experiment in the treatment of psychotic and schizophrenic patients. The Death of Desire breathes new life into R. D. Laing's legacy, at a time when our culture is in desperate need of it."

—**Jeremy Safran**, Ph.D., Chair and Professor of Psychology,
The New School for Social Research, New York

THE DEATH OF DESIRE

An existential study in sanity and madness

Second Edition

M. Guy Thompson

Routledge
Taylor & Francis Group

LONDON AND NEW YORK

Second edition published 2017
by Routledge
2 Park Square, Milton Park, Abingdon, Oxon OX14 4RN

and by Routledge
711 Third Avenue, New York, NY 10017

Routledge is an imprint of the Taylor & Francis Group, an informa business

First edition published by New York University Press, 1985.

British Library Cataloguing in Publication Data
A catalogue record for this book is available from the British Library

Library of Congress Cataloging-in-Publication Data
Names: Thompson, M. Guy, 1947– author.
Title: The death of desire : an existential study in sanity and madness /
    M. Guy Thompson.
Description: 2nd edition. | Milton Park, Abingdon, Oxon ; New York, NY :
    Routledge, 2017. | Includes bibliographical references and index.
Identifiers: LCCN 2016006769 | ISBN 9781138790216 (hbk : alk. paper) |
    ISBN 9781138790223 (pbk. : alk. paper) | ISBN 9781315764337
    (ebk : alk. paper)
Subjects: LCSH: Psychology, Pathological. | Desire. | Psychoanalysis. |
    Freud, Sigmund, 1856–1939. | Phenomenological psychology.
Classification: LCC RC454.4 .T47 2017 | DDC 616.89/17—dc23
LC record available at https://lccn.loc.gov/2016006769

ISBN: 978-1-138-79021-6 (hbk)
ISBN: 978-1-138-79022-3 (pbk)
ISBN: 978-1-315-76433-7 (ebk)

Typeset in Bembo
Apex CoVantage, LLC

Printed and bound in Great Britain by
TJ International Ltd, Padstow, Cornwall

For Alex and Dashiell

Those who restrain desire do so because theirs is weak enough to be restrained, and being restrained it by degrees becomes passive, till it is only the shadow of desire.
—William Blake, *The Marriage of Heaven and Hell*

There is always some madness in love, but there is also some reason in madness.
—Friedrich Nietzsche, *Notebooks*

CONTENTS

Preface to the second edition   *xi*
Preface to the first edition   *xvi*
Acknowledgments   *xix*

1   The myth of mental illness   1

2   That discreet object of desire   21

3   *Ressentiment*: toward an existential paradigm for
    symptom formation   45

4   Deciphering "psychopathology"   69

5   What to make of an incidence of incomprehensible madness
    (or a clinical case not so easy to diagnose)   98

6   The unobjectionable transference   121

7   Love and madness   143

8   On sanity   174

Concluding postscript   *201*
Index   *203*

PREFACE TO THE SECOND EDITION

This book has been extensively revised, without being changed in any fundamental way. It remains an attempt to understand the role of desire in sanity and madness, from an existential perspective. Thirty years have passed since the first edition of this book was published. As one would expect, my thinking has significantly evolved during that time. I have endeavored to update this edition with my current thinking while remaining faithful to the original. The reader will have to judge for him- or herself the degree to which this effort has been successful.

The most significant difference between this and the first edition is suggested in the revised subtitle. The term psychopathology has been replaced with "sanity and madness." Perhaps a brief word about this change will prove helpful.

When I wrote the first edition to this book, I employed the term psychopathology in the subtitle because that is the term typically taken to mean all that is wrong with a person who undertakes therapy. Why, indeed, do people seek therapy and what do they hope to change about themselves by undertaking it? As I explain in this edition, psychopathology is a psychiatric term modified from the medical term, pathology, connoting a medical disease of one type or another. I have never understood psychopathology to connote a "disease" of the mind or of anything else, but as a metaphor for something that has gone wrong in the manner by which a person conducts his or her life. The term psychopathology implies a problem with a person's psyche or mind, but that is far too narrow to denote the problem one confronts when determining why someone is suffering from mental and emotional anguish. We employ the terms mental as well as emotional interchangeably when referring to this or that psychopathological condition because we know intuitively that such problems are never strictly "mental." Nor are they simply emotional. The kinds of problems patients bring with them to therapy are always expressed in the peculiar types of thinking, sometimes of a tortuous nature, they are burdened with. Their emotions, whether anxiety, depression, or anger, also dominate their attention, to a greater or lesser degree. But these are merely symptomatic of the underlying condition, which is neither mental nor emotional, but existential. It is the way a person conducts his or her life that is askew, not the thoughts or feelings they have about it.

I originally employed psychopathology in the subtitle because I assumed at the time that anyone reading that book would take this term metaphorically, not literally as a "disease of the mind." That was then. Thirty years hence, I can no longer take this for granted. The dominance of the medical metaphor in contemporary culture has increased even further. It seems today that everyone likes to regard anything that ails them as a medical condition of one kind or other. Even psychoanalysts are prone to this folly. Thirty years ago, if you imbibed marijuana to alter your consciousness, you were getting high. Today marijuana is increasingly defined as medicine. When you imbibe it you are no longer altering your consciousness, you are medicating whatever "condition" that you happen to suffer. It appears that any form of suffering is medical in nature. This didn't happen overnight, but it speaks to a sea-change in our society's perception about the nature of sanity and madness. We have come to believe that virtually any form of mental, emotional, or existential malaise can be branded a medical condition which, once diagnosed, can be treated accordingly. It shouldn't surprise us that the treatment of choice is medication, not of the cannabis variety but the type of psychotropic drugs zealously pedaled by the psychiatric/psychopharmacological industry. This has effectively wended its way into the lives of virtually every person in America, and it is spreading.

Thirty years ago, I took it for granted that most people seeking therapy didn't assume that the reason they sought it was because they were afflicted with a medical condition. They probably thought that they weren't as self-aware as they wanted or needed to be in the conduct of their lives, especially their relationships, and wanted to know themselves better. Today I'm not so sure. The above may continue to motivate people to seek therapy, but they are more likely to assume that their relationship problems, for example, are also medical in nature, and that medication may be useful in coping with their emotions. This is how pervasive the erstwhile medical metaphor has become, and how the metaphorical aspect of this term – psycho-pathology – is no longer taken metaphorically, but literally.

This is the reason I changed my subtitle to "an existential study in sanity and madness." I feel that today I need to spell this out, that what I am talking about is not a medical condition of any kind, but rather an existential question: What is the nature of sanity, what is the nature of madness, and how do these polarities of our all too human condition intersect to make us the person you or I have become? By situating my exploration of the relation between desire and sanity and madness I hope to remove the concept of madness (occasioning all forms of mental and emotional distress) from any vestige of pathological and medical connotations, and return it to where it belongs: the everyday agony and ecstasy of living, in all its attendant mystery and complexity.

This book was originally, as it is today, an attempt to bridge a fundamental fissure between the existential and psychoanalytic traditions, each of which is surprisingly hostile to the other. Though there have been valiant attempts to bridge this gap (Cannon, 1991; Frie, 2003; Strenger, 2011; Atwood and Stolorow, 2014), there remains an effective "no man's land" between the two disciplines. Analysts dismiss existentialists as un-analytic and existentialists regard analysts as obtuse and impersonal. I have found neither to be the case. I have always felt at home in both traditions and have written two books, *The Truth About Freud's Technique* (1994) and *The Ethic of Honesty* (2004), to demonstrate how well-wedded they truly are.[1]

No doubt this has something to do with my relationship with R. D. Laing, who exercised an enormous impact on my intellectual and clinical development. Laing was both a psychoanalyst and existentialist, and helped me see the common ground between the two disciplines. My former analyst, Hugh Crawford, was especially instrumental in my recognizing Freud as an existentialist. Freud was not a philosopher, but he read philosophers voraciously and the fruit of their wisdom pervades the corpus of his thinking. The first existential analysts, including Ludwig Binswanger and Medard Boss, understood this and integrated Freud into their conceptions of therapy. Today Freud has become anathema to a new generation of existential therapists who have formed short-sighted opinions about the psychoanalytic tradition and its relation to existential philosophy.

Freud is also important to existentialists because he was the first anti-psychiatrist. Though Freud relied on the extant psychiatric and diagnostic language of his day, and even contributed to it, the moment he concluded that neurosis is not a disease that afflicts some individuals and not others, but part and parcel an aspect of the human condition, Freud dispensed with psychiatry and its medical moorings.[2] Freud believed that neurosis and even psychosis are necessary aspects of every human being's make-up and that they speak to our sometimes successful but usually imperfect efforts at self-healing. Moreover, he concluded that our personalities are riddled with strategies that are hardly sane but so pervasive that he termed them the "psychopathology of everyday life." Our minds are always at work fending off objectionable thoughts, feelings, and realizations that we are incapable of entertaining at the time we first experience them, a self-defensive "mechanism," as Freud would say in one of his least articulate moments. As Laing noted, the so-called defense mechanisms that pervade psychoanalytic thinking are nothing more than strategies that the mind orchestrates to live in an unlivable situation, by contorting ourselves into mental gymnastics, or knots, that help mitigate the anxiety that underlies them, but at a cost. They render us senseless. Psychotherapy is nothing more than a method of untying these knots, then embracing the anguish we were previously incapable of surmounting. There is nothing medical about this, and Freud knew it. If nothing else, this insight alone makes Freud the most important existential psychoanalyst in history.

Perhaps the antipathy with which contemporary analysts regard philosophy, especially existential philosophy, has something to do with the opposition between the two traditions, even their hostility to Freud. The chasm between existentialists and psychoanalysts is beginning to recede, in part thanks to the existential psychoanalysts I referenced earlier. But there is much that remains to be done if a genuine reconciliation between these two disciplines is to be realized. As far as I can tell, the existential therapists who reject Freud outright are either too lazy to read him, or sorely misunderstand his take on the human condition. For those interested in reconsidering their position, I hope this book will serve as an inspiration.

This brings me to another difference between the two editions of this book. The current one is far more autobiographical than the first. Because the earlier edition was used as my doctoral dissertation (at The Wright Institute in Berkeley), its style of presentation was unashamedly academic. With this constraint behind me, this version is more personal and, hopefully, accessible. I have written it with a minimum of jargon and with a view to showing how the decade I spent studying with Laing helped shape the contours of my perspective on both psychoanalysis and philosophy. In effect, this book is the epigraph of a journey that I undertook in my twenties, and culminated in becoming the man I am today, warts and all.

As with the first edition of this book, an important motive in writing this revision is to explore further the relationship between desire and mental anguish. Following Freud, I view our desires as fundamental to our occasions of happiness and misery, and so decisive in our lives that we have no choice but to reckon with them. Unlike Freud, I do not see desire as essentially sexual in nature, but existential. This doesn't mean that sex is unimportant. I agree with Freud that sexual pleasure and its complement, repression, are far more pervasive in our lives than many of us are willing to suppose. I explore the nature of desire in Chapter Two, and argue that if desire is the fulcrum of our human condition, then the chronic ambivalence we are often besotted with is the most pervasive incidence of the madness we share. We think we can mitigate the trouble our desires get us into by repressing them, and hedge our bets accordingly. This results in a kind of double-mindedness that Kierkegaard speaks of, where I am neither here nor there, embracing neither this nor that, thus becoming, in the words of John Lennon, a Nowhere Man. The only cure for this condition is a heavy dose of self-honesty and courage, and it is this task that psychotherapy, especially psychoanalysis, undertakes to perform.

As with any undertaking, I have many to thank for the second edition of this book. First and foremost, I want to thank my literary agent, William Stranger, who persuaded me that a second edition of this work was warranted, and in turn convinced Routledge to publish it. Bill is more than an agent, but a loyal and stalwart friend who has helped me in innumerable ways. I owe him a debt of gratitude. A debt of thanks I also want to express to my friends and colleagues, Jon Mills and Doug Kirsner, for their unstinting support in this project, and for all their help in its realization. I also want to thank the many former students and friends who taught me so much over the past thirty years, to whom I owe whatever wisdom I may have accrued since the first edition of this book was published. Finally, I want to especially thank my editor at Routledge, Kate Hawes, for her warmth, diligence, and charm, and for believing in this project, as well as her assistant, Charles Bath, for all his help and support.

M. Guy Thompson

Notes

1 I have also published numerous journal articles and chapters in anthologies devoted to integrating psychoanalysis and existential-phenomenology. For a full list of these articles see *www.mguythompson.com*.
2 Freud devoted a book, *The Question of Lay Analysis* (1926), to arguing that a background in medicine was irrelevant to training as a psychoanalyst, and that the study of literature and history were far more relevant and useful.

References

Atwood, G. and Stolorow, R. (2014) *Structures of subjectivity: Explorations in psychoanalytic phenomenology and contextualism* (Psychoanalytic Inquiry Book Series). Revised, 2nd Edition. London and New York: Routledge.

Cannon, B. (1991) *Sartre and psychoanalysis: An existentialist challenge to clinical metatheory.* Lawrence: University Press of Kansas.

Freud, S. (1953–1973) *The standard edition of the complete psychological works of Sigmund Freud.* 24 volumes. Edited and translated by J. Strachey. London: Hogarth Press. (Referred to in subsequent references as *Standard Edition.*)

Freud, S. (1926) *The question of lay analysis. Standard Edition*, 20:179–258. London: Hogarth Press, 1959.

Frie, R. (2003) *Understanding experience: Psychotherapy and postmodernism.* London and New York: Routledge.

Strenger, C. (2011) *The fear of insignificance: Searching for meaning in the twenty-first century.* New York: Palgrave Macmillan.

Thompson, M. Guy (1994) *The truth about Freud's technique: The encounter with the real.* New York and London: New York University Press.

Thompson, M. Guy (2004) *The ethic of honesty: The fundamental rule of psychoanalysis.* Amsterdam and New York: Rodopi.

PREFACE TO THE FIRST EDITION

This book is a study of desire in psychopathology and its cure in psychoanalysis. Its purpose is to make psychoanalysis comprehensible, so the reader will have to judge for himself the success or failure of this aim. I would prefer, however, to be judged on what this book is intended to achieve and not on what it is not intended to. This book is not intended to provide an inventory of so-called mental disorders, but rather to get to the root of what is manifest when pathos is ascribed specifically to the human condition, which is to say, the condition of man himself.

This work is theoretical and, as such, is intended to provide a way to understand human suffering as well as the unique task of the psychotherapist when he encounters, in his charge, the weight of this suffering. In the main, I have tried to demonstrate the efficacy of this study from cases readily available in the literature, cases that have been discussed by numerous authors already. In choosing this course I hope this work provides an opportunity to compare my approach to psychoanalysis with those of others, an opportunity that would not be so feasible were I to rely on cases from my own practice.

A further purpose is to provide, in terms relatively free of jargon, an account of some forms of psychopathology, specifically neurosis, psychosis, and perversions. A brief statement about my intentions will, I hope, avoid misunderstanding.

In reviewing the major concepts of Freudian theory, I have attempted to bridge a gap between phenomenology and psychoanalysis, which is to say, between phenomenologists who, in my opinion, have failed to account for the Freudian unconscious, and those psychoanalysts who have been unable to render the theory of the unconscious comprehensible. In trying to situate the significance of desire in psychoanalysis from a phenomenological perspective, I believe this work to be the first of its kind. In order to do this, I have abandoned Freud's conception of desire rooted, as it were, in the fulcrum of the body, and replaced it with Hegel's, which conceives it in terms of the subject's appeal for recognition, in terms of the lack at the heart of man's being. Viewed from this perspective, psychoanalysis is in turn conceived as an undertaking that aims at the realization of desire and not merely its satisfaction, which is to say, its adaptation. I have thus defined man as the ensemble of his desires and, alternately, psychopathology as the subversion, that is, the deadening, of those desires.

The reader will recognize numerous authors cited from the phenomenological tradition in this work, yet it is not the direct application of any of them. While I have relied extensively on the theories of Hegel, Sartre, Heidegger, Scheler, Merleau-Ponty, Laing, and Lacan, my views express important points of divergence with each of them. That being said, it is to the phenomenological tradition that I own my greatest intellectual indebtedness. Moreover, it is psychoanalysis that is my calling, and it is to Freud that I ultimately turn to for my clinical inspiration. In my reading of psychoanalysis I have tried to situate my thought squarely in the Freudian tradition, and to return to that tradition by elaborating a conception of the unconscious in a language that endeavors to be clear and to the point, and yet, not so easy to grasp. Many of Freud's earliest insights into the human condition have been lost due to the vocabulary that housed them, and due to the ideas themselves and their more disturbing implications.

Admittedly, the view that Freud's most radical notions about human nature have been repressed or distorted is nothing new. R. D. Laing, Jacques Lacan, and others have been making this claim for decades. That this message has, in the main, fallen on deaf ears is not altogether surprising. Laing's attacks on conventional psychiatric treatment and Lacan's insistence that every psychoanalyst since Freud has misunderstood him could hardly be expected to endear them to the hearts and minds of their colleagues. This argument does not rest on whether to follow Freud or to reject him, but whether we have managed to understand him in the first place. Further, having understood him, if only in an approximate way, what are we to make of the tortuous vocabulary he has left us?

Beneath the sometimes amusing and oftentimes confusing terminology of the various schools and fashions of psychoanalysis, there emerges a somewhat unsettling thought that the more disturbing elements of Freud's earlier work – his critique of unconscious subjectivity and the irrepressible perversity of desire – have been tamed or altogether rejected by many of his followers, including the object relations theorists in Britain and the ego psychologists in the United States. If there is any validity in the taming of these theories, then it is precisely those theories that we must turn to in order to see what is there, which is a return to Freud himself.

Laing and Lacan, each in his own bombastic style, have tried to rescue Freud from the grasp of increasingly behavioristic interpretations of his message, interpreters who on the other extreme have taken his biological metaphors too literally. While Lacan emphasized his debt to Hegelian dialectics and Saussurian linguistic theory, Laing pointed to the potential corruptive power that inhabits the family constellation – all in the name of love. On the one hand, Lacan is telling us that humans are vastly more complex and unknowable than we are ready to admit, while, on the other, Laing is reminding us of our inherent human cruelty, the truth of which each of us must bear. Not a popular message, but one that is beating at the heart of the Freudian vision of man. If these truths seem so hard to face, what price must we bear if we continue to ignore them?

My aim in this book has been to point to desire as the foundation of the human condition and to locate this desire at the heart of the unconscious, an unconscious that, after having been situated in phenomenology, reveals the nature of interpersonal relations. If my task has been less than successful, I have no one to blame but myself. I would add that while my questioning of psychoanalysis falls within a tradition occasioned by both Laing and Lacan, my theories are not derivative of either of them. They belong to no one but me.

I would like to express my deepest gratitude to R. D. Laing, John Heaton, and the late Hugh Crawford, from whom I received my psychoanalytic training at the Philadelphia Association in London from 1973 to 1980. It is to them that I owe the greatest measure of my analytic education. This book is the culmination of the seven years I worked with Laing and his cohorts and for that I am immeasurably grateful. The views in this study were discussed with more individuals than I can conveniently list, but I would like to thank particularly Douglas Kirsner, Chris Oakley, Steve Gans, Robin Cooper, Martin Grotjahn, Alan Swope, Ben Tong, David Cooper, and especially Dr. Leo Goldberger and my editor at New York University Press, Kitty Moore, for their support and encouragement.

M. Guy Thompson
July 1985

ACKNOWLEDGMENTS

Portions of Chapter One were presented at the *R. D. Laing in the Twenty-First Century Symposium* convened at Wagner College, Staten Island, New York, on October 14, 2013.

A portion of Chapter Five appeared in *Contemporary Psychoanalysis*, Volume 33, No. 4, 1997, in "The Fidelity to Experience in R. D. Laing's Treatment Philosophy." Reprinted by permission of Taylor and Francis LLC, The William Alanson White Institute, and The William Alanson White Psychoanalytic Society.

A portion of Chapter Six appeared in *Psychotherapy in Australia*, Volume 17, No. 1, 2010, in "The Demise of the Person in the Psychoanalytic Situation." Reprinted by kind permission of the journal.

1

THE MYTH OF MENTAL ILLNESS

Psychiatry is unique in several respects. It is the only branch of medicine that treats people physically in the absence of any known physical pathology. It is the only branch of medicine that 'treats' conduct alone, in the absence of symptoms and signs of illness of the usual kind. It is the only branch of medicine that treats people against their will, in any way it likes, if it deems it necessary. It is the only branch of medicine that imprisons patients, if judged expedient.

Laing, 1985, pp. 2–3

With these provocative words, spoken in 1985, the same year the first edition of this book was published, R. D. Laing succinctly summarized the anomaly that psychiatry presents us with today in its mission to treat so-called disorders of the mind as though mental anguish is a sickness comparable to cancer, tuberculosis, or measles. Indeed, the concept of mental illness is so common that few can even imagine that this very term may well epitomize an error in our thinking, even a fallacy. Yet, as we embark on a brave new century, there is increasing dissatisfaction with psychiatric treatment in general, and the concept of psychopathology to which it adheres in particular. In order to glean a little insight into this most controversial of subject matters, I begin this study with a review of how we typically employ the term psychopathology and its more popular derivative, mental illness.

Perhaps no one since Freud has been more determined to get to the bottom of what this concept entails than R. D. Laing, the inspiration for this book. What exactly did Laing, the titular father of so-call anti-psychiatry,[1] have to say about the matter? This is not such a simple question to explore because Laing was patently dubious about this concept and avoided using it in his many publications. In *The Politics of Experience* (1967) Laing questioned whether schizophrenia, the form of psychopathology he is most identified with, even exists. Yet many of the people who Laing saw in psychotherapy suffered miserably, and sought him out in the hope that he might relieve them of the most unbearable anguish imaginable, where others had failed. What, exactly, Laing was hoping to relieve them *of*, if not a psychopathological condition? Surely, if there is such a *bona fide* activity as psychotherapy (i.e., the "treatment of the mind"), then there must be some condition or state, however we opt to label it, that the therapeutic process presumably relieves. What else is the one person, the patient, paying the other person, the therapist, to do, if not treat a pathological condition?

I will never forget when Thomas Szasz, the author of *The Myth of Mental Illness* (1961), in the 1970s accused Laing of betraying the cause of anti-psychiatry (though Szasz hated this term) because Laing was treating patients whom he deemed mentally ill, despite his condemnation of psychiatry for engaging in the same practice. Szasz accused Laing of wanting it both ways, on the one hand to condemn psychiatry for treating a condition whose existence (Laing believed) was dubious at best, while on the other hand advocating his own treatment for such conditions at Kingsley Hall, the experimental therapy center that Laing established in London in 1965. Szasz built his career around the notion that mental illness is a myth, that there is no such thing as an "illness" of the mind, and that psychiatry had orchestrated a hoax by insisting that mental illness does exist and that psychiatrists are engaged in treating it with relative success. Szasz argued that Laing was merely advocating a more benign form of treatment than, say, drugs, lobotomy, or electric shock, but that he was advocating *treatment* nonetheless and, by it, perpetuating the same hoax as the psychiatrists whom Laing roundly condemned. The gauntlet that Szasz threw down was nothing if not direct: "Do you believe in psychopathology or not? And if you do not, then what is it exactly you claim to be treating, if not mental illness?"

In fact Laing did not believe in psychopathology, or mental illness, but he took a more nuanced and less polemical approach to the problem than did Szasz. Whereas Szasz insisted that the entire structure of psychiatry, including its psychological derivative, psychotherapy (which for the most part is conducted by non-medical practitioners), should be abolished, Laing believed that however flawed psychiatry is, we still need it, or something like it, to help those people who need someone to relieve them of their unremitting emotional and mental distress, especially those who were labeled schizophrenic (a population that few therapists outside of psychiatry are interested in helping). Laing took issue with the way these people were being helped, not with the fact that they needed help, even if what they needed help with is not, strictly speaking, a mental illness. Though this distinction is not so easy to articulate, I hope to bring some clarity to the problem.

Let me begin with the term itself. The word psycho-pathology derives from the medical term *pathology*, which in turn derives from the Greek *pathos*, meaning suffering. The term was also employed by the Greeks to connote passions or feelings more generally. The first psychotherapists were physicians and the term psychiatry, which was only coined in the nineteenth century, became the medical specialty of doctors whose mandate was to treat the psyche or the soul, or as we say today, the mind. Laing's first book, *The Divided Self* (1960), was his most concerted effort to show why psychiatrists, and for the most part psychoanalysts, have misunderstood the kind of suffering that people labeled schizophrenic, say, experience, and why psychiatric nomenclature does little to help us understand the phenomena so labeled. If what psychiatrists believe they are treating is, as Laing suggested, not schizophrenia, or *any* form of psychopathology, then what is it they are treating? And why do we, whether psychiatrists, psychologists, psychoanalysts, or lay psychotherapists, still refer to the conversations we conduct with our patients as *treatment*, or its derivative, *psychotherapy*?

In order to ponder these questions I want to explore whether the conversations we employ with our patients, though not specifically *medical* in nature, may nonetheless be termed a form of "therapy." The subtitle Laing assigned to *The Divided Self* was "an existential study in sanity and madness," the same subtitle I have chosen for this book. Neither Laing's book nor mine is an existential study in *psychopathology*. Why is this distinction important? Are madness and psychopathology not the same thing? In order to answer this question, I want to take a look at what Laing set out to accomplish in that study, why he calls it an *existential* study, specifically, and how this classic work laid the foundation for what would eventually evolve into *anti-psychiatry*.

As Laing says in the preface to that work, this book is "a study of schizoid and schizophrenic persons," and its basic goal "is to make madness, and the process of going mad, comprehensible" (1960, p. 9). At the outset, the diagnostic language Laing employs is readily familiar to every psychiatrist and psychoanalyst who works with this population. Terms such as psychotic, schizoid, schizophrenic, paranoid − all standard nosological entities with which therapists the world over are familiar − proliferate throughout this book. He is speaking *their* language, so to speak, but the meaning he assigns these terms is anything but ordinary. Laing explains that he has never been particularly skillful in recognizing the diagnostic categories that are standard in every psychiatric diagnostic manual in the world, including the *Diagnostic and Statistical Manual* (*DSM*), which is the bible of the mental health community in America. Laing had trouble recognizing the subtle nuances that are supposed to distinguish, for example, the various types of schizophrenia, of which there are several, or even what distinguishes them from other forms of psychosis, including paranoia, bipolar disorder (previously manic depressive syndrome), or dementia.

None of these terms is written in stone. In fact, they are constantly changing and undergo revision in every new edition of the *DSM*, currently in its fifth edition. So what is Laing saying? Is he suggesting he is simply too stupid to understand the complexity of these entities? I don't think so. Rather, he is suggesting that because there is no agreement in the psychiatric community as to how to recognize these symptoms and the mental illnesses they purport to classify, it is impossible to take them literally, or even seriously. No two practitioners agree on how to diagnose a person, and given the never-ending revisions to these categories, currently numbering in the hundreds, practitioners often change their own minds as to how to recognize what it is they are supposed to be diagnosing and treating. This is hardly the science it is alleged to be.

What did Laing conclude from this disarray in categorization? That there is no such thing as "mental illness," or psychopathology, so no wonder there is no agreement as to what *it* is. When a doctor sets out to diagnose a typical medical illness, he customarily looks for physical symptoms in his patient. The color or tone of one's skin, dilation of the pupils, body temperature, and so on may indicate an abnormality. Additional tests may be administered that examine the blood or urine, and if that fails to provide conclusive results, perhaps x-rays, CAT scans, EKGs, heart stress tests, mammograms – all ways of examining the chemistry or interior of the body – may be utilized in order to hone in on what is malfunctioning. For so-called psychiatric symptoms, however, such tests will be useless, because no one has ever been able to locate the symptoms of psychopathology inside or on the surface of the body. Even an examination of the brain, which is now the darling of neuropsychiatrists and neuropsychoanalysts, has yet to locate the presence of any form of mental or emotional disturbance that we can label a mental illness. (Ironically, organic conditions such as Alzheimer's or drug-induced psychosis are not labeled "mental illnesses," because they *are* specifically organic in nature, meaning they can be detected inside the brain or because there is a direct correlation between ingesting a drug and the resulting psychotic symptom.)

When seeking signs of mental illness, what we are able to examine, according to the *DSM*, is the *behavior* of the person being diagnosed, whether, for example that person is suffering from delusions or hallucinations, confusion, disorganization, incoherent speech, withdrawal, flights of fancy, or depression, anxiety, dissociation or maladaptation, or perhaps a persistently elevated, expansive, or irritable mood, and so on. This list is hardly inclusive, but what all these symptoms share in common is that they refer to experiences that *everyone* has, at one time or another, some more than others, some less. Even delusions and hallucinations, the gold standard for schizophrenia, are common in dreams, and not that uncommon when we are awake. Yet most people who exhibit or experience these so-called symptoms are never subjected to a formal diagnosis or treated for them. So why is it that some people are and some people are not? Why are some people deemed crazy and others sane, when they exhibit the same symptoms?

Laing argued that diagnosis of a mental illness contradicts accepted medical procedure. Diagnoses of mental disorders, for example, are made on the basis of *behavior or conduct*. Examination and ancillary tests that traditionally precede diagnosis of viable pathologies occur *after* the diagnosis of a mental disorder has been rendered, not prior to such diagnosis. This is why psychiatry is founded on a false epistemology: illness diagnosed by conduct, but "treated" biologically. The principal mode of treating psychotic conditions today is not psychotherapy, but "medication." Medication is typically prescribed for a medical illness or condition, so why is it prescribed for *mental* illnesses that do not really exist? Why are drugs used to treat people who do not suffer from a *bona fide* medical condition? There is nothing about drugs, inherently, that possess medicinal properties, though some do. Drugs were around a long time before they were adopted by medicine, and most of the drugs we use today are not the kind you need a prescription for, and do not claim to "medicate" illness. Alcohol, marijuana, opium and its derivatives, coffee, sugar, tea, tobacco are only some of the traditional mind-altering drugs that nearly all cultures throughout history have employed. For what purpose? For the most part, to reduce anxieties, and perhaps the tedium of an unsatisfying life or a stressful occurrence. In a word, to feel better. There is nothing wrong with this. Drugs have always been used to enhance our lives, though some in desperation have erred in believing they can be used to obliterate their problems or because the weight of their problems has become unbearable. We label such people "addicts." What distinguishes the drugs they become addicted to from the kind promoted by psychiatry is that street drugs are used episodically, when the need arises, usually prompted by anxiety, or the wish to have an adventure. Prescription drugs, such as Prozac, Paxil, Zoloft, Wellbutrin, Thorazine, Haldol, Risperdal, Zyprexa, Clozapine, Abilify, Lithium, Adderall, or Xanax are employed variously for depression, psychosis, manic episodes, attention deficit disorder, or anxiety and are ingested daily (or more frequently) in order to remain in the nervous system, *continuously*. Whereas street drugs are ingested in *response* to anxiety or boredom, prescription drugs are ingested to *prevent* such feelings from arising, or to keep them in check. Virtually all drugs, if ingested habitually, are addictive, including those prescribed by a doctor. In other words, we grow to depend on them, and then take them for granted. They become a part of who we are.

What all these drugs share in common, whether prescribed, recreational, even spiritual, is not that they are good for treating a medical condition, but that they are capable of altering our *states of consciousness*, depending on the state of consciousness we want to alter, and to what degree it may be distressing. We like to say that alcoholics are self-medicating their depression or anxiety, but in fact they are not *medicating* anything. They are simply using a drug to mitigate their suffering whenever they feel unable to cope with it. Again, there is nothing wrong with this, nothing immoral or sick about it. Because we all draw the line somewhere, some of us are able to handle a lot more anxiety than the next person, and some of us are fairly astute at solving our problems before they get out of control. We don't know why some people manage the stress and strain of everyday life more ably than others. Extreme situations such as assault or catastrophic loss may be temporarily intolerable, but whatever the root cause or causes may be, we are always left with a choice when confronted with such feelings. We can either examine why life is making us so anxious and adjust our behavior accordingly, or we can render ourselves senseless with this or that drug. What do we gain by calling these problems incidents of mental illness? I don't think one has to ponder that question for very long in order to arrive at the answer. There is a colossal and highly lucrative drug industry that makes enormous amounts of revenue selling so-called remedies to an unwary public that doesn't know any better. This is nothing new. The desperate have been victimized by unscrupulous vendors throughout history. We have simply become more sly about it, and more sophisticated.

What about medicating people who suffer from suicidal depression, whose lives are in the balance? After all, the singular purpose of medical treatment is to prolong life, in some cases to save it from serious medical conditions such as cancer or heart failure. Most medical treatments are designed to simply ease suffering or hasten the body's natural healing, as with bacterial infection or viruses, a wound or bone fracture. How should we respond to people whose lives are in danger because they threaten to kill themselves, or have already tried to? It is an interesting anomaly that if I assault someone with a view to killing him it is a criminal act, but if I attempt or want to assault *myself* it is a medical emergency that calls for psychiatric intervention. Why?

The only thing cancer and attempted suicide have in common is that in both cases one's life is in danger. Yet, psychotherapy has nothing to do with prolonging life, only examining it with a view to improving it, if that. The suicidal patient, however, raises the controversial question as to whether it is right to forcibly medicate (i.e., drug) a person who threatens to kill himself in order to save his life, even if such interventions are against his will. Currently, the only rationale we have for such forced "treatment" is that, a) his life is in jeopardy, and b) we feel compelled to treat him forcibly because he has lost his senses, for only a person who is stark raving mad, or overwhelmed with catastrophic grief, would consider killing himself. Or so we imagine. It is patently obvious that this justification for preventing suicide is not literally concerned with "medicating" an "illness." It is simply a way of coercing a person to stay alive, if only temporarily, whether that person wants his life saved or not, with the hope that in time that person will recover from his depression and no longer wish to kill himself. The nature of our democracy is such that we are prevented from stopping a person from killing himself unless it is deemed a mental illness that can be forcibly "treated." This is a contradiction: we don't want people stopping *us* from doing what we please with our bodies, but we don't want *them* offing themselves because we find it too disturbing, so we label it an illness in order to have it both ways.

A similar controversy in the psychiatric community is forcibly treating (which is to say, drugging) a person who is behaving in an overtly crazy and threatening manner, when this behavior is perceived a threat to *others*. Now we are talking about someone assaulting, not himself, but another person. Ordinarily, this is deemed a criminal act for which a person may be arrested and prosecuted. But if the arresting officer deems the perpetrator to be not of sound mind, in other words, crazy, then the officer may elect to take that person to a mental hospital for treatment instead of a jail for incarceration. In fact, that person will effectively be incarcerated at the hospital, but instead of a jail cell he will be given drugs that will render him so senseless he will no longer be a threat to anyone. At that point he will follow the same course of treatment as the suicidal patient. This is the kind of situation that drove Szasz crazy. Even if a person who is momentarily mad and behaving unpredictably is not literally mentally ill, we have a duty to protect others from such people, don't we? If not jail or mental hospital, then where? That is the sixty-four-thousand-dollar question. There is no third alternative, given the way our society is currently structured. No one else besides the psychiatrist is mandated to help. But it is a slippery slope, and it doesn't take much to abuse the enormous power that doctors are given when we don't know what else to do with such situations.

These are only some of the questions that Laing alluded to in *The Divided Self*, but he never arrived at a conclusive answer as to how to solve them. In matters of the mind, the act of diagnosis can just as often be a political as a medical ceremonial. I don't believe that we will ever succeed in understanding such phenomena as long as we persist in looking at people from an alienating, and alienated, point of view. It is the *way* we look at each other, the way psychiatrists and psychoanalysts typically see a patient when they look at him or her, that is the crux of the problem. The reason Laing called *The Divided Self* an existential study instead of, say, a psychiatric, or psychoanalytic, or even psychological, study is because the existential lens is a supremely *personal* way of looking at people, a person-to-person manner of regarding others and recognizing them, as Harry Stack Sullivan once said, as more human than nonhuman. This is another way of saying that the person, or patient, I am treating is not a sick person, but someone *like me*. It is the fact that he is just like me that makes it possible for me to understand and empathize with him in the first place.

Laing began writing *The Divided Self* while working at a mental hospital in Glasgow, when he was still in his twenties. It doesn't sound like he had an opportunity to do much psychotherapy there, but he did have lots of time to hang out with the patients under his charge, all of them diagnosed schizophrenic. Instead of looking for symptoms of recognizable forms of psychopathology, Laing sought instead to simply talk to his patients, as he was fond of saying, "man to man," and to listen to what they had to tell him. What he heard, which he recounts in *The Divided Self*, is nothing short of amazing. They told him stories about their lives, their belief systems and experiences, the things that worried them, and the things they thought about, day in and day out. They were sharing with him, not their pathology, but their *existential* situations. The thing I remember standing out for me when I first read this book was that I felt he was talking to *me*. This, from what I have subsequently gathered from others, is not an unusual experience. It is this reaction that has made this book the classic that it is.

Instead of trying to determine what makes "us," the sane ones, so different from "them," the ones that are crazy, Laing sought to explore what we share in common. Laing used the term schizoid – common in Britain but only marginally employed in the United States – to depict a state of affairs that lies at the heart of every person labeled schizophrenic, as well as many who are not so schizophrenic, in fact all of us to varying degrees. The common thread is this: that the person so labeled, in his or her personal experience, suffers from a peculiar problem in relation to others. *He cannot tolerate getting too close to other people, but paradoxically cannot tolerate being alone either.*

This is a terrible dilemma to be faced with. Most of us either hate to be alone and throw ourselves into the social milieu with others (Jung would have called them extroverts), or we cannot bear social situations and opt instead to spend most of our time by ourselves, or with one other person at most. These more introverted, private individuals may be gifted writers or artists or scientists or psychotherapists, well suited to their relative isolation, whereas the extroverts among us make excellent politicians or salesmen or actors or any number of other callings that entail contact with others. We tend to incline in one direction or the other, and either may be a perfectly viable way of existing and living a happy and desirable, contented life. Some are good at both, the so-called ambivert. The person who is schizoid, however, doesn't excel at either. He cannot tolerate isolation, nor can he get genuinely close to others. He is caught in a vise, a kind of quiet hell that is rife with unrelenting anxiety, what Laing calls *ontological insecurity*. Simply existing is a serious and persistent problem for him. Intimacy is such a source of consternation that in his relations with others this person must, in effect, hide himself behind a mask by pretending to be somebody else, by erecting a "false self" and living incognito among others, like a spy in a cold war drama. In speaking of a person this way we are not really diagnosing him, we are simply describing what it is like to be him. He is not a sick person, *per se*, but he is living inauthentically, which means he has become alienated from himself.

Laing characterized ontological *security* as a state of feeling at home in one's self and the world. Most of us, for example, experience ourselves as alive, real, worthwhile, and having a purpose in life. He distinguished this more healthy condition from that of ontological *insecurity*. Here we no longer take our aliveness for granted, but find ourselves trying to feel real and searching for a sense of identity, which we feel is missing. This characterizes the typical state of the schizoid personality which, to some degree, may happen to anyone in crisis, so the schizoid condition is something we all experience from time to time.

The ontologically insecure person suffers unremitting, even catastrophic, anxiety. Laing proposed three such types of anxiety: engulfment, implosion, and petrification. We typically associate engulfment, which is characterized by a dread of intimate relationships, with schizophrenia. Because the schizophrenic fears that intimacy with others will cause him to lose his autonomy, his typical method of coping with such anxiety is to isolate himself from others. Though this only serves to make him feel even more lonely and alienated, it may be preferable to the feeling of implosion, the feeling that the world will obliterate what is left of one's fragile sense of identity. The third type of ontological anxiety Laing calls petrification, feeling objectified by others. Laing believed that this condition is so common that it may be deemed universal, though most of us are so busy trying to conform that we hardly question it. What all three share in common is the sense of danger encountered in intimate relations. The ontologically secure person seeks such intimacy, whereas the ontologically insecure person avoids it.

Laing makes a careful distinction between the kind of person who struggles with schizoid character traits and the kind of person who gets labeled schizophrenic. The so-called schizophrenic is at the extreme end of the spectrum, though it is notoriously difficult to generalize about this for reasons we have discussed already. It is often impossible for a person who is beset with schizophrenia, whose world is collapsing around him, to work at a job or enjoy satisfying, sexual relationships. The reason is due to the extreme anxiety that close proximity to others, which is a given with jobs or sexual relationships, requires. We all find the work environment stressful, but the person who struggles with paranoia often finds these stresses and strains intolerable, even when numbed with medication. Better to avoid such relationships altogether than to risk being at the mercy of someone else. Even one's relation with a therapist may be too much to bear. When fearing engulfment, for example, the simple experience of feeling understood, loved, or acknowledged by another may feel too dangerous to risk. There are exceptions to this, though – people so diagnosed who are managing, more or less, perhaps the consequence of having found a way to accommodate long-term psychotherapy – but even with that caveat intimacy can be a persistent and unremitting problem. The schizoid person shares a similar repulsion to intimacy, but is much better, as Sartre would have said,[2] at *acting the part* of an employee, lover, or spouse, and can often function perfectly well in work situations where the expectation of intimacy is mitigated. If work is the only milieu in which he is comfortable he may become a *workaholic*, and complain about the very condition that he thrives in. The problem is that there is always a part of him that holds back, that struggles with paranoid worries about the power he believes others enjoy at his expense. This is the kind of person who, like the typical neurotic, is more likely to seek therapy and, in time, possibly benefit from it, by becoming more courageous in his social relationships and less alienated from himself. Laing wondered if the schizoid condition is, for all intents and purposes, the *normal* condition in our present age, due to the extraordinary alienation we all suffer, in this relatively new, twentieth century (and now twenty-first century) norm. We will explore this complicated, existential question in the chapters that follow.

When I first read this I couldn't help but wonder how many of us are really all that comfortable being alone, and how many of us are truly at ease in our relationships with others, which is to say, free from anxiety? Isn't this a problem, for example, that psychotherapists, a relatively quiet group of people, typically share with their patients, with whom they must identify in order to be effective? Psychotherapy is a fabricated relationship thats purpose is to achieve uncommon intimacy with another person, while placing extraordinary constraints on it, conducted by two people who, to a considerable degree, get close to others, shall we say, reluctantly. Isn't this rather like the lame leading the blind? Laing didn't think so, but he was acutely aware of the paradox, of how wounded a person must be to even want to spend all his professional time in the company of people who are beset with problems.

Laing was not the first to recognize this paradox. Nor was he the first to accuse psychiatrists of employing means of helping others that are for the most part ineffectual. For that, Sigmund Freud would have to be credited, arguably the first anti-psychiatrist. Freud was a neurologist, not a psychiatrist, and he was scathing in his commentary about the psychiatrists of his day who, Freud believed, knew nothing about why their patients suffered and how to help them (Freud, 1916–1917, pp. 243–256; Thompson, 1994). Freud believed that people develop symptoms of hysteria and neuroses, or worse, because they have been traumatized by unrequited love in their childhoods. He was the first to recognize the powerful effect that our parents, in fact all our relationships, have on us and how our capacity to love is also the source of the most profound suffering. Freud was also the first to recognize that our demand for love is unremitting and insatiable, no matter how much we get, and that we are most vulnerable when at the mercy of the people we love.

Yet Freud was not interested in the kind of person Laing described in *The Divided Self*, because he did not believe that a person who suffers from psychotic anxiety is capable of attaching himself to the psychotherapist who is treating him. Freud was correct in recognizing how vulnerable such people are, but mistaken in his prognosis about their capacity to change or benefit from therapy. It has been argued that Laing accomplished for the so-called schizophrenic what Freud accomplished for the neurotic: a way of establishing an intimate relationship with them that may, *in itself,* serve as a vehicle for healing. Freud was unhappy with the brutal way that the hysterics of his day, mostly women, were typically treated, and even less happy with the prevailing conception of psychopathology. Unlike psychiatrists, Freud did not believe in an us versus them mentality. He did not believe, for example, that some people are neurotic and that some people are perfectly healthy. He believed that *all of us* are neurotic to varying degrees and that neurosis (about which I will say more later) is an essential aspect of the human condition. He also believed that neurotics may, on occasion, become psychotic if pushed far enough. So if everyone is neurotic and curing us of neurosis is not on the table, then what is psychotherapy good for?

Freud was never able to definitively answer this question, at least not as definitively as we would like, but he believed it could help.[3] If you read between the lines, you can't help concluding that Freud viewed anxiety, and the forms of alienation that Laing was so good at describing, as an essential aspect of our human condition. What we call "ill" versus "healthy" or "crazy" versus "sane" is not so black and white, but a matter of degrees. If all of us are neurotic, and on some occasions even psychotic, some more, some less than others, then all of us are also healthy, which is to say *sane*, to varying degrees. Though he was reluctant to admit it, Freud rejected the concept of psychopathology as it is commonly understood, *and replaced it with an existential perspective that emphasized the management of anxiety as an inescapable aspect of living.*

Freud's invention of psychoanalysis was a huge step forward in treating people we think of as nuts, or crazy, as human beings like ourselves. But once it was embraced by psychiatrists, psychoanalysis became yet one more weapon – and in America a very popular one – in the war on mental illness. Whereas psychiatrists had depersonalized the relationship between doctor and patient by pretending it wasn't the person, but rather his illness, that was being treated, psychoanalysts depersonalized the treatment relationship by insisting it wasn't the person who was responsible for his condition, but his *unconscious*. Though psychoanalysis made extraordinary gains in humanizing the treatment relationship over prevailing psychiatric practices, Laing believed both disciplines seem strangely incapable of formulating a genuinely symmetrical therapy relationship between equals. There have been notable exceptions to this, and Laing himself stood proudly on the shoulders of practitioners like Fairbairn, Sullivan, Fromm-Reichmann, Winnicott, and other psychiatrists and psychoanalysts who advocated a more personal way of treating their patients, not treating them for illnesses, but treating them like they would want to be treated themselves, which is to say, with compassion, were they in a similar predicament. As Laing was fond of saying, treatment isn't something you administer to someone, but rather how you treat each other.

This isn't to say that Laing was advocating simply being nicer, or kinder, to his patients, as though that alone is sufficient for gaining a discernable benefit from therapy. Instead, his concern was with being more real, or authentic, with them – in effect, more honest. That is considerably more difficult than just being nice. You can feign being nice to people, but you can't feign being honest. This, he believed, could only happen if we stop objectifying our patients into diagnostic categories that only serve to alienate them from us. Perhaps the model that best exemplifies what Laing advocated is not a relationship between therapist and patient, *per se*, or parent and child, but one between friends. After all, friends confide in each other, and confiding is an essential aspect of what therapy entails. The problem is that our friends don't have the time to help us with our problems, or the inclination. In one of his more mischievous moments Laing suggested that therapists might as well call themselves prostitutes (Evans, 1976, p. 36), because what patients are buying is not treatment, *per se*, but a *relationship*. Whether we think of ourselves as friends or prostitutes to our patients, or neither, Laing didn't have a problem with calling the people who paid to see him his "patients," any more than he objected to calling what they were doing "therapy," both undeniably medical terms. But isn't this inconsistent with what Laing has been saying about the myth of psychopathology?

Whatever problem Laing had with the institution of psychiatry, he never had a problem with being a *doctor*. He was proud of his medical training, and while such training is not necessary to practice psychotherapy, he thought it was as good a preparation as any from which to enter the field. After all, what doctors share in common is that they want to help people. This is also what therapists want to do. Laing was fond of pointing out that the word therapy is etymologically cognate with the term *attention* or attendant. In ancient Egypt a religious cult called the *Therapeutae* were attendants to the divine, the first psychotherapists.[4] So the term predates the subsequent medical appropriation of it by the Greeks. *If we take the term literally, a therapist is simply a person who is attentive, or pays attention to the matter at hand, the suffering of his patient.* Similarly, a patient is literally a person who "patiently" bears his suffering without complaint, because by assuming the role of patient he is doing something about it. The term doesn't necessarily refer to someone in *medical* treatment because the kind of suffering is not specific, or explicit. Laing concluded that if you put these two terms together you get one person, the therapist, who is attentive to the other person's, or patient's, suffering. To what end? Hopefully, such attention, with enough patience, good will, and most importantly, time, will lead to something, to a point where the patient no longer requires such attention and can get along perfectly well without it. This is something that Thomas Szasz never understood. He seemed more interested in the legalities of the issue than he was with helping people.

According to Michel Foucault (1965), a close friend of Laing's, the history of madness and how society reacted to it is checkered at best. Historically, people who acted crazy were thought to be possessed, either by evil spirits or by the gods, and sought to expiate this condition through shamanistic sacrifice. From at least the early Greek period, physicians entered the picture and took a crack at helping those who were deranged with herbs and the like in order to calm them down. Though they were not deemed to be suffering from a medical condition, it was hoped that drugs may have a soothing effect. Then, in the fifth-century bc Greece, Hippocrates introduced a novel explanation for madness, the first evidence of what we now call the medical model, which held that mental problems were due to natural, bodily causes. Hippocratic healers believed there were imbalances in the brain, and thought they might correct them with drugs.

This was not the only remedy the Greeks came up with. In fourth-century bc Greece, another view, the Epicurean model, was introduced. The Epicureans attributed madness to spiritual anguish, a consequence of the universal fear of death. They also believed that mental anguish was neither a medical or spiritual condition but caused by poor choices and the failure to resolve the inevitable conflict between appetite and responsibility. Akin to Buddhists, Epicureans thought that excessive desire results in anguish, so the path to recovery is devotion to a life of contemplative, healthy practices, such as gardening and living in the company of fellow travelers. By living together in friendship, Epicureans believed that even the mad could come to know a life of peace and tranquility. But by the time of the Ecclesiastical State of the Middle Ages and the early modern period, the belief in evil spirits reemerged. Jesus himself was cited as a source of this view. He had been a firm believer in demons and frequently cast them out of the afflicted. The Church insisted that witches, possessed by the devil, as well as Jews and heretics, were responsible for mental abnormality because all of them were possessed and damned to hell. The favored treatment for this condition was exorcism or, when that failed, burning at the stake in the belief consumption by fire would save their souls.

In the fifteenth century, a completely different approach emerged in the Bethlem Royal Hospital in London (nicknamed "Bedlam") to accommodate the lunatics who were running rampant in the streets. These poor souls were not actually "treated" for a medical condition, but given respite from living a dangerous life on the streets. "Hospitals," from the Middle English *hospitale*, or hospitality, were not necessarily medical treatment centers in those days but rather ports in a storm for those who needed lodging. By the seventeenth century and the rise of the *bourgeoisie* Europeans began to feel unsafe with the crazy people in their midst, who wandered freely in the streets (not unlike the homeless people who wander about our cities). Foucault points out that this was when they began to confine them as a means of protection, just as lepers had been confined earlier. Not surprisingly, such confinement made them even crazier and their jailors began chaining them to the walls of lunatic asylums (formerly leprosariums) they had been cast into. They soon developed diseases, which only accelerated their problems further until the French physician, Philippe Pinel, was brought in to attend to their resulting *medical* maladies. Pinel couldn't help but observe that the way they were being treated was inhuman. He argued they should instead be treated compassionately, as sick people, who deserved the kind of attention and consideration any sick person had come to expect. It was then, according to Foucault, that the modern world collectively decided that mad people were indeed "mentally ill." This designation, as we all know, has stuck.

This was a remarkable step forward in treating such people as human beings who warranted society's help, but it also initiated the slippery slope that occasioned the birth of psychiatry and, with it, the diagnostic universe we now live in. Laing was proud of being a physician, but he recognized that we now find ourselves in an historical quandary. Like the Europe that invented the Lunatic Asylum, our society feels the need to protect itself from crazy people, some of whom are undeniably dangerous and capable of violence, even murder, but most of whom are perfectly harmless, and even more vulnerable than you or me. When violence does erupt, if it does, someone needs to make the call: Is the person in question crazy enough to lose, if only temporarily, his constitutional rights and be confined to treatment, which is to say, "medication," that renders him senseless or worse, against his will? Whether we like it or not, that task has been assigned to psychiatrists, and it has given them enormous power over those they deem dangerous, whether to themselves or others. Laing had no ready or easy remedy to this problem, but believed that all of us are implicated in it. It comes down to how tolerant we are prepared to be with people whose mental stability is erratic and disturbing to be around.

Laing never formulated an overarching theory of psychopathology to replace the edifice that psychiatry and psychoanalysis have built. For the most part, his focus was on schizoid phenomena and schizophrenia, not as specific diagnostic categories but, like Freud's conception of neurosis, as a metaphor for varieties of mental anguish that compromise our ability to develop satisfying relationships with others. As the subtitle of *The Divided Self* suggests, Laing was more comfortable thinking in terms of sanity and madness than psychopathology. So what does it actually mean to be crazy? And what does it mean to be sane?

These terms lack precise definition when compared, say, with the plethora of diagnostic categories in the *DSM*. Because they are used colloquially, as a manner of speaking, it is up to each of us, individually, to determine how to employ them. It seems to me that the essence of what it means to be crazy, in the way this term is ordinarily used, can be broken down into three components, the combination of which will tell us how crazy a given person may be. The first concerns how someone exercises his or her judgment; the second concerns how agitated that person may be; and the third concerns the lengths a given person will go to mitigate anxiety.

Our use of judgment is probably the most critical of the three, because it determines how we make sense of things, including the situation we are facing at a given moment. After all, improving one's judgment is a principal goal of psychotherapy. The judgment of a person suffering a manic episode, for example, is said to be seriously compromised, but so is that of a person who suffers from acute paranoia or hallucinations. Our judgment is where we live, and there's no escaping it, though we can improve it if, and only if, we have the presence of mind to realize that we cannot trust it. Yet, who gets to decide whether a given person's judgment is impaired or sound? If I judge that I need help in improving my judgment and take my plight to a therapist, can I trust the judgment of that therapist over my own? I'm not going to get much out of therapy if I am unable to trust his or her judgment, but who is to say that my therapist's judgment is more sound than mine is? How can I render such a judgment about my therapist if, say, I don't trust *my own* judgment? This is a problem, and one that makes therapy almost, but not necessarily, impossible. This dilemma introduces into the equation the problem of risk, that any time we embark on therapy we are taking a chance with the therapist we select to help us. Sometimes we choose foolishly and sometimes we are lucky to have found someone we can, in fact, learn to trust. I believe it was Ernest Hemingway who asked: "How can you tell if you can trust someone? By trusting him!"

A person's judgment is for the most part a private affair. The person who is crazed is often in a state of agitation, which others can't help but notice. It is this state that usually makes my judgments public, when, for example, I am about to leap off a tall building, or assault someone for no discernable reason. This is the prototypical image we all have of the crazy person, who is acting crazy, and often in a manner that not only gets our attention, but frightens us, because we don't know what he is going to do next. Each of us has been crazed at some time or other, but the moment usually passes before any real damage has been done. If it persists, that is a different matter, and things can quickly spiral out of control. This is when I am most likely to be taken to jail or a mental hospital, whether I want to be taken there or not.

The third way I may feel or appear crazed concerns what psychoanalysts call defense mechanisms,[5] the mind-games I employ to mitigate my anxiety. This was the issue that Laing was most concerned with in *The Divided Self*, evidenced in the so-called schizoid person. We notice his defenses in the way he engages social space. As we noted earlier, this is a person who cannot tolerate being isolated from or being intimate with others because either position makes him intolerably anxious, so he walks a tightrope somewhere in the middle where he feels the least amount of anxiety, but still too much to navigate his relationships effectively, which is to say satisfactorily, in a way that he can live with. Much of what we do to cope with our anxieties doesn't appear crazy to others and doesn't feel crazy to ourselves, and works for us, more or less. It is the most severe states of anxiety, such as ontological insecurity, that are the most problematic and result in extreme measures to mitigate, such as catatonic withdrawal.

Not all states of craziness occasion distress. Schizophrenia and schizoid states generally elicit various degrees of anxiety and the unpleasant, even haunting, sense of distress that drives one into treatment. We feel distressed when we have reached the end of our tether and can no longer cope. When we arrive at this point we need help, and we turn to others to assist us. Manic states are usually contrary to this, because the person experiencing a manic episode doesn't typically feel distressed. He usually feels the opposite: he feels excited, happy, alive. The world is a wonderful place, and he is the master of it. This would appear to be the ideal state to be in. After all, don't we all aspire to happiness, even giddiness, as a measure of how content we are with our lives? Feeling good *is* good, isn't it?

Unfortunately, it isn't that simple. We cannot always rely on our feelings to tell us when we are behaving in a sane way or a way that is nuts. It is easy to determine when we feel bad that we are in a bad way. But feeling good does not always indicate that things are well in the world. The manic state depicts a person who often *feels* good, but has lost all sense of proportion and self-control. In a word, his judgment has become seriously impaired, compounded by the complication that he doesn't know it. The reason bipolar disorder was once called manic depression is because when a person experiences a manic episode, it doesn't last. Before long, it reaches a terminus, and then gives way to profound, sometimes suicidal, depression. One way of understanding this phenomenon is to regard the manic "high" as a *defense against depression* and its accompanying anxiety. It is a sort of denial, an escape from an unacceptable or intolerable development in one's life (such as divorce or other catastrophic loss). Manic episodes often occasion intense sexual activity, profligate spending, in short, unreasonable and highly risky, almost always self-destructive but extremely pleasurable behavior.

If you happen to know someone who is exhibiting such behavior, you may also note that this person is not being "herself," and you soon realize that something is the matter. But if you do not know this person, and meet her for the first time when in the throes of this episode, you might think of her as a perfectly interesting, charismatic, even exciting person to be with. Given the intensity of this person's libido, you might even fall in love with her. Don't be fooled. This behavior is nothing more than a mask, intended to camouflage the underlying anguish which, for whatever reason, this person cannot, in her current state, handle, or even concede.

People suffering from manic episodes are not the most promising candidates for psychotherapy. The reason is simple. They do not feel that they need help, so why should they seek it? If a family member tries to persuade them to see someone, they will often resist, because they feel perfectly fine. How do you reach a person who is incapable of self-doubt, who is under the illusion that everything is okay in the world, when you can see that they are behaving as though they have lost their mind? Not very easily, if at all. Yet not everyone who suffers a manic episode enjoys the experience. They may feel agitated, anxious, or angry, but the thing they have in common with the person who relishes it is that they, too, are impervious to therapeutic intervention. Just because a person acts crazy doesn't mean he recognizes it and accepts your judgment over his. A person who does not want help and does not seek it cannot, by definition, benefit from psychotherapy. He may, however, and often does, respond to "medication." And how motivated is this person to voluntarily take this medication when he doesn't believe there is anything the matter with him? I am confidant you can guess the answer to that.

Even under the best of circumstances, determining what it means to be crazy, and who can be deemed crazy, is not so simple. Sometimes a person who is behaving in a way that you think is crazy just so happens to feel crazy himself and doesn't like the experience one bit. Sometimes that person, behaving the same way, feels that there is nothing the matter with him. How do you convince a person, who does *not* believe he is crazy, that he is? This dilemma sometimes comes down to just how much craziness a given society is willing to tolerate amongst its citizens, and how much is acceptable, as long as it isn't harming anyone. Some cultures are more tolerant than others, some less. This is where the psychological leaks into the political, the place where we are confronted with how tolerant we are of our fellow human beings, despite their obvious eccentricities.

If these criteria offer a rough and ready means of discerning what it means for me, or you, to be crazy, what does it mean to be sane? It would more or less approximate the opposite of feeling crazy. Our judgment would be sound, relatively speaking; our use of defensive maneuvers would be minimal because we would bear our anxieties with relative ease; and we would not find ourselves in a state of panic or agitation, but one of serenity, at peace with ourselves and the world. When we weigh the two, there are no crazy people, or sane people. Every one of us goes from one state to the other over the spectrum of our lives and oftentimes in the course of a single day. By this definition, all of us have been crazy, and will be, no matter how sane we are most of the time. If this were not so there would be no way for a psychotherapist to connect with or empathize with a person who has been diagnosed, say, schizophrenic. *We can only help people with problems we ourselves can relate to, and have experienced ourselves.* This doesn't mean that one has to be schizophrenic in order to empathize with someone who is, but the underlying experience that all persons diagnosed schizophrenic suffer is something we all share in common, a profound sense of *alienation.* Not everyone is in touch with their alienation, and for the most part we mask it, but every psychotherapist worth his salt is acutely aware of his own. This is all it takes to recognize a fellow traveler who, by the grace of God, may, under different circumstances, be me.

What about the genetic theory? It is commonplace to believe that "mental illness" runs in families, so it must be genetically inherited, from one generation to the next, right? There is no denying that many of these diagnostic entities, including schizophrenia, bipolar disorder, and depression do show up with remarkable regularity among family members. So how does that happen? It is quite possible that temperaments, predispositions, and certain character traits are somehow "passed on" from *some* fathers, to *some* sons, but not others, in ways we simply cannot explain. We have no way of knowing if some of these traits or characteristics are discreetly modeled and adopted by regular contact with a parental figure, in other words, environmentally. Perhaps some of us are born with greater sensitivity to our environment than the next person, and this sensitivity, while it may predispose some, under certain environmental triggers, to become artists or thinkers, may predispose others, with different triggers, to become psychotic. But even if some are genetically transmitted, why call them *mental illnesses*? Do we regard political dynasties, that tend to run in families, genetically transmitted? Is the Irish proclivity to drink and literature, which I share, a mental illness? I don't think so.

I have yet to find a satisfactory etiological theory of what causes us to become neurotic, or psychotic, or just plain crazy, though I readily favor the environmental thesis over the biological. Neither model, however, is entirely compelling and, like the good sceptic I aspire to be, it seems to me that our mental states and what accounts for them are for the most part a mystery, and may always be. We may never know why this person is crazier than the next person, or why, in fact, all of us are crazy in some contexts and not in others. It seems that some people are capable of driving others crazy, but there are those who appear to be perfectly capable of becoming crazy on their own. Laing believed that common deception is a problem, but difficult to recognize.[6] The bottom line, given the inherent ambiguity of the situation we are in, is to proceed cautiously, with a degree of humility, in how we treat such people when we meet them.

This is because, when all is said and done, our principal concern as psychotherapists, psychoanalysts, clinicians – whatever we call ourselves – is not explanatory, but *ethical*. What is the right way to treat people who are the most vulnerable members of our society? Whenever Laing addressed this topic, whether in writing or in public, he often invoked the Golden Rule. How would you, if you lost your wits, fell apart with grief or consternation, want to be treated by those who have you at their mercy? When the shoe is on the other foot, shouldn't you treat them the way you would like to be treated yourself? It is impossible to separate our thinking about psychopathology, about sanity and madness, from our work as psychotherapists. If I met a mad person on the street who is threatening me, I would defend myself without hesitation and, if need be, ask the police to confine that person. But if you made an appointment to see me, as a potential therapist, no matter how crazy you are, and want my help, and you do not try to assault me, that is another matter. And that is the matter that concerns all of us, for the most part, over the course of our careers. How to meet another person in dire straits, whether you are that person's therapist, family, or friend, and how to treat that person in such a way that, in the tradition of the Hippocratic oath, you add no further harm to that person than he or she has already suffered.

Over the course of history, every culture has grappled with what to make of madness, and how to address it. Every culture has names for madness, and they have fluctuated and been modified from epoch to epoch. There is something inherently scary about the loss of one's mind, whether another person's, or my own. When cultures were dominated by religious beliefs, it stands to reason that madness was interpreted through this lens. If you were mad, you might have been touched by the gods, or angels, and were accorded due reverence and respect. Or, in another context and another era, you might have been possessed by the devil, or demons, or be a demon yourself in disguise, or a witch. In that case you would have been treated harshly, perhaps mercilessly, and cruelly. Or a mad person may have been treated as an eccentric, someone to be neither feared nor revered. You might have been placed on a Ship of Fools and simply escorted to the next port of call, and let them deal with you. Most recently, we have opted for the medical argument, that the madman is ill, sick in the head, and logically, if you are ill there must be a treatment that will make you well.

It has been difficult, until Freud, to think of madness as simply a state of mind. Stripped of the medical metaphor, we seek explanations into the nature of sanity and madness, what they are comprised of, and how to best be with them. Freud was a doctor, and despite his genius for seeing things that the rest of us missed, he was wedded to the medical metaphor because it provided a ready explanatory vocabulary with which everyone was familiar. The alternative to medicine and science, he feared, would be something more mystical, which Freud had sympathy for but was convinced it would be rejected as quackery. This was because mysticism was too closely tied to religion, and we know what religions have done with madness through the centuries. Post-Freud, there have been other efforts to find alternative metaphors for how to depict the search for sanity that all psychotherapies aspire to. One is the educational metaphor. We simply need to *learn* more about ourselves and, armed with knowledge, use it as wisely as we are able. This metaphor has appealed to some psychoanalysts, though they continue to call themselves mental health professionals and work under a clinical license. Another, potentially more radical, metaphor is the philosophical one. In this view, Socrates was the first therapist, and what he was treating among the philosophers he encountered was their ignorance and obvious confusion. Based on that metaphor, we are all seeking wisdom, which we may equate with relative sanity. Therapy in this context emphasizes our capacity to reflect on our lives and follow the example of history's greatest philosophers. The existential analysts in Europe who identified with those philosophers and were preoccupied with the human condition and its ailments, wedded philosophy to psychoanalysis but retained the medical metaphor initiated by Freud.

More recently we find some therapists who rely more or less exclusively on philosophy as their paradigm, with no mention of explicit "clinical" considerations in the nomenclature they profess. In Great Britain, where psychotherapy and psychoanalysis are not included in the mental health template, it is possible to experiment with such paradigms because there is no mandatory licensure *as* a mental health practitioner in order to practice the kind of therapy one is drawn to. In other cultures, like the United States, psychotherapy is aligned with the mental health paradigm, which makes it impossible to call oneself a "therapist" without a clinical license. In this case, call it what you will, but to be a therapist and charge someone money to have conversations with them, with a view to relieving their suffering, ensconces you in the medical metaphor, whether you like it or not. The only alternative is to come up with a new paradigm that rejects the medical metaphor entirely. There are some philosophers in the United States who are doing just that, who claim they are not "treating" anyone for anything, just charging their clients for edifying conversations of a philosophical nature. As you might expect, finding clients for such a calling is challenging. More realistic is the emergence of *life coaching*. Under this convention you can sell your time any way you see fit. All that is needed is vigorous marketing, and there is no shortage of demand for helping people sort out the messes that their life often occasions. This option, however, is hardly lucrative. Yet another metaphor is the *spiritual crisis*, or emergency. Many psychotherapists and psychoanalysts have found Buddhism to be a helpful discipline to complement more conventional approaches to therapy, and understanding what madness is. Some of these practitioners have opted out of the medical paradigm altogether by couching their work as a spiritual quest, with all its attendant dangers and risks. Though most therapists identified with the so-called transpersonal movement are licensed, medical-model therapists, some are not and work more or less "off the grid," which is to say, without clinical licensure. But by doing so they are breaking the law.

I have to admit that I find all these alternative metaphors unsatisfactory, at least for me. Despite its shortcomings, which a lot of this book is about, I find the medical *metaphor* convenient, despite its hazards. So long as we treat it as a metaphor, I think it can continue to be viable, even preferable over the other alternatives. Besides, our culture is deeply embedded in this metaphor and to abandon it by replacing it with something original would take another cultural revolution of the kind Freud initiated a century ago. Though medical practitioners have largely abandoned psychotherapy for the more lucrative practice of dispensing drugs, doctors are undeniably suited for the role of *helping* people in dire straits. They are not unique in this, but serve as admirable role models. It is a pity that psychiatry, as a branch of medicine, is so inept at enlisting the medical tradition in order to genuinely help people who are crazy.

In the chapters that follow I will examine various aspects of what we customarily label incidents of psychopathology. I retain, for the most part, the medical metaphor and conventional psychoanalytic way of characterizing these phenomena, by relying, for the most part, on broad distinctions between neurosis and psychosis. The former suffers from the weight of his or her desires, the latter from the demands of social reality. The rest should be self-explanatory. I will now turn to the role that desire plays in a life that is worth living, and the ways that desire may lead us astray.

Notes

1 In fact, it was Laing's close associate in the 1960s, David Cooper, who coined the term and made it popular in his 1967 book, *Psychiatry and Anti-Psychiatry* (1967). The term was more political than descriptive, which served Cooper's radical motives well, but detracted from Laing's concern to focus his efforts on developing a more humane treatment of persons suffering from debilitating mental and emotional distress, especially schizophrenia. Laing initially went along with the label, but as Cooper became increasingly disenchanted with any form of treatment, humane or otherwise, and more politically active, he and Laing parted ways, at which point Laing pointedly rejected the label. Cooper eventually settled in Paris where he occupied the center of the now-established anti-psychiatry *movement* that included Felix Guattari in France, Franco Basaglia in Italy, as well as others who shared in common a loathing for *bourgeois* values and a passion for Marxist ideology and the burgeoning protest movement. Despite all of Laing's efforts to distance himself from this label, he nevertheless remained on good terms with his Continental cohorts, all of whom looked to him as their leader, due no doubt to Laing's incredible fame and charisma which served, if only indirectly, to legitimize their movement! Today, Laing's argument that he was never an anti-psychiatrist has become a rather moot point, now that the term has much wider usage than when Laing was still alive. For all intents and purposes, Laing is regarded as the instigator and champion of any effort to question psychiatric orthodoxy and the involuntary incarceration and treatment of the mentally ill.
2 See Sartre's *magnum opus*, *Being and Nothingness* (1943/1954) in the section on Bad Faith, for a lucid description of this form of interpersonal subterfuge.

3 For Freud's most succinct thoughts about treatment outcomes, see Freud (1937) and Thompson (1994).
4 For a lucid discussion of these ancient therapists, see Meier (1967).
5 Sullivan hated the term and used "security operations" instead – hardly an improvement! Laing let the term stand, but noted its *impersonal* dimension. Laing understood that what Freud called defenses were mental devices we all employ to mitigate unwelcome experiences. Though I do so unknowingly, it is still *me* who performs the so-called operation, not some entity called "the unconscious." See Laing (1961/1969, pp. 25–26).
6 See Laing and Esterson's brilliant *Sanity, Madness and the Family* (1964) for a detailed study of deceptive practices in families of schizophrenics. See also Thompson (1996).

References

Cooper, D. (1967) *Psychiatry and anti-psychiatry*. London and New York: Tavistock Publications.

Evans, R. (1976) *R. D. Laing: The man and his ideas*. New York: E. P. Dutton and Co.

Foucault, M. (1965) *Madness and civilization: A history of insanity in the age of reason*. Translated by Richard Howard. London: Tavistock Publications.

Freud, S. (1953–1973) *The standard edition of the complete psychological works of Sigmund Freud*. 24 volumes. Edited and translated by J. Strachey. London: Hogarth Press. (Referred to in subsequent references as *Standard Edition*.)

Freud, S. (1916–1917) Introductory lectures on psycho-analysis. *Standard Edition*, 16:243–463. London: Hogarth Press, 1963.

Freud, S. (1937) Analysis terminable and interminable. *Standard Edition*, 23:209–253. London: Hogarth Press, 1964.

Laing, R. D. (1960[1969]) *The divided self*. New York and London: Penguin Books.

Laing, R. D. (1961[1969]) *Self and others* (Revised Edition). New York and London: Penguin Books.

Laing, R. D. (1967) *The politics of experience*. New York: Pantheon Books.

Laing, R. D. (1985) *Wisdom, madness and folly: The making of a psychiatrist*. New York: McGraw-Hill Book Company.

Laing, R. D. and Esterson, A. (1964[1970]) *Sanity, madness and the family*. New York and London: Penguin Books.

Meier, C. A. (1967) *Ancient incubation and modern psychotherapy*. Translated by Monica Curtis. Evanston, IL: Northwestern University Press.

Sartre, J.-P. (1943[1954]) *Being and nothingness*. Translated by Hazel Barnes. New York: Philosophical Library.

Szasz, T. (1961[1974]) *The myth of mental illness* (Revised Edition). New York: Harper and Row.

Thompson, M. Guy (1994) *The truth about Freud's technique: The encounter with the real*. New York and London: New York University Press.

Thompson, M. Guy (1996) Deception, mystification, trauma: Laing and Freud. *The Psychoanalytic Review*, Vol. 83, No. 6:827–847.

Thompson, M. Guy (1997) The fidelity to experience in R. D. Laing's treatment philosophy. *Contemporary Psychoanalysis*, Vol. 33, No. 4:595–614.

2

THAT DISCREET OBJECT
OF DESIRE

What does it mean to desire something, or someone, to be somewhere, some place, somebody? Is it merely a feeling that envelops and fixes me to its power? Or is it somehow more, or less, than emotion, something I purposefully *intend* with urgency, insistence, even despair? Whatever it is, do I always *know* that I am in a state of desiring, occupying the forefront of awareness? Or are my desires vaguely unbeknownst to me, hidden, lurking, fleeting, on the precipice of consciousness? Moreover, if desires are so important to psychoanalysts – and they claim it is the basis of their theory – then why is it not even a technical term in standard psychoanalytic nomenclature, disguised instead under locums like libido, wish, pleasure, eros? Freud initially cloaked desire inside the Latin *libido* (desire in English), then went on to talk about, not desires, *per se*, but "wishes," for this or that, conscious or unconscious, dreaming or awake, as though the two are synonymous. They are not.

To wish to have sex with someone, or to be handsome or beautiful, rich and famous, to live forever, to be someone I am not, is a *pleasing fantasy*, as when dreaming while asleep or daydreaming when awake. Freud was spellbound with wishes and the phenomenon of wishing, and for all the importance he assigned to interpreting the dreams that visualized them he was even more intrigued with the dreams we entertain when awake, if only relatively so. I believe it was Paul Valéry who said that the best way to make your dreams come true is to wake up! Yet waking up isn't so easy to accomplish. Freud probably had this in mind when he noted that all our waking hours are invested in such dreaming, that we often confuse our dreams with our inexact perceptions of what is happening in (for lack of a better word) reality. He had a gift for picking up on the implied fantasies that comprise our interpersonal relationships. He broke a social taboo when he invited his patients to share their fantasies with him, perhaps the first human being to initiate such a provocative undertaking. After years of listening to their confessions, Freud concluded that the daydreams we entertain typically revolve around three principal topics: the wish for sexual gratification, the wish for money, and the wish for power. Think about it. When you daydream, what are you wishing for? Freud's three categories are not exhaustive, but it is surprising how pervasively they dominate our waking life. I may also wish for love, good health, peace of mind, but only when I don't have them, not if I do. This is why the three that Freud suggested are perennial. No matter how much money, power, or sex we may have, we always want more. This tells us something about the human condition and its insatiable, unquenchable nature.

Desiring is more visceral than wishing, and unlike our fantasies that are inherently pleasing, desires occasion considerable anxiety. This is why we resist them. In one of his notebooks Kierkegaard suggested that:

> *Anxiety is a desire for what one fears*, a sympathetic antipathy . . . an alien power which grips the individual, and yet one cannot tear himself free from it and does not want to, for . . . *what he fears he desires*.
>
> *(cited by Marino, 2013, p. 221)*

Once we substitute a wish that something were so for the desire to *make* it real we are *intending* the thing we want and invest a stake in the outcome, whether, for example, we will succeed or fail. There are no partial victories when desiring, no negotiated settlements. We get what we want or we do not. We stay committed to our desire so long as it is viable, and let go when it is not. Having got it, we may discover that it's more difficult to hang on to than to obtain. The possibility of losing what we have acquired or accomplished occasions at least as much anxiety as not getting it, and suffering such losses is a ready source of unremitting desperation and heartache. Only in our most fraught moments do we ask ourselves, is it worth it? This is how we learn, at a tender age, that wishing costs us nothing, and wile away the time daydreaming when we could be *doing* something, we are admonished, more constructive. Freud believed that neurotics prefer to spend their time wishing for what they want instead of engaging in the task of getting it, or even having it. The two become so intertwined that we treat them synonymously. This is the source of the confusion and ambivalence that epitomize neurosis. It is both a problem and a virtue that wishing isn't as painful as desiring, or as complicated. Desiring comes at a cost that we neurotics are reluctant to pay. When we do decide to purchase such gifts, you had better believe that we want it for a bargain.

Desire has enjoyed a varied and much-checkered career throughout history and has occupied a central place in every culture. In Plato's *Phaedrus* he describes the soul as a chariot guided by two horses, a dark horse representing passion and a white horse that signifies reason. One is not better than the other as both are needed to make us complete. Passion is blind, so it needs to be guided by reason, which alone can discern if the passion that tempts me is a good one or bad. If passion gets the upper hand it may result in poor judgment and ruin. But if reason is sufficiently developed it may help us harness our passions in a more prudent direction. Plato mentions a similar division of the self's faculties in *The Republic*, where he divides it into desire, reason, and spirit. Both dialogues influenced Nietzsche in his development of the Dionysian and Apollonian aspects of our personality, as it did Freud's conception of the structural model, comprised of id (desire), ego (reason), and eventually superego (morality). In Aristotle's *De Anima* he arrives at a similar structure where passion and reason work together for an optimal balance in all our ambitions and endeavors.

In *A Treatise on Human Nature*, David Hume (2000), the British empiricist, argues that reason is always subject to our passions. Our actions are prompted by desires, passions, and inclinations so that desire in tandem with belief serve to motivate our actions. The British philosopher G. E. Moore (2004) develops this idea further by arguing that two theories of desire should be distinguished. He cites John Stuart Mill's view that pleasure is the sole object of desire, a thesis that was apparently inspired by yet another of Plato's dialogues, *The Protagoras* (1961). According to Mill my desire for an object is generated by the idea that I associate with the pleasure I expect to obtain from it (yet another source for Freud's theory of the Pleasure Principle). It is the *idea* we associate with pleasure that we repress, not the desire itself, which is indestructible. According to Mill, the anticipated pleasure serves as the motivating force of my desire, which is fulfilled once the pleasure is obtained. Moore isn't happy with separating the idea from the pleasure itself and argues that pleasure must already be present in my desire for something or I wouldn't be motivated to want it in the first place. These fine discriminations about how we should understand the respective roles of desire, pleasure, motivation, and the good are typical of how Western philosophers have attempted to get a handle on what desire is and its fundamental role in making us happier, or more miserable, human beings.

Whereas desire is highly valued in Hinduism, it has met a more complicated fate in Buddhism. There suffering is accepted as an inevitable aspect of living, that we shouldn't despise it but treat our anguish with respect. The cause of suffering is presumed to derive from our craving for or attachment to worldly pleasures that we cling to and covet. Suffering comes to an end when our craving subsides, and much of Buddhist practice is designed to overcome such craving. In the West this craving is often confused with desiring, but this isn't quite accurate. Buddhists have nothing against desiring, *per se*. It is only certain desires that are problematic, such as craving fame, lust, and the hedonistic pleasures we associate with gluttony, greed, or pride. The desire for liberation and excellence in living is, after all, virtuous, so it depends on the desire one is pursuing that may, in turn, interfere with the peace of mind, or Nirvana, that the Buddhist seeks. The goal of overcoming desires in Buddhism led Freud to coin the term Nirvana Complex for those neurotics who give themselves over to the death drive in order to erase the desires that occasion their frustration and disappointments. The Epicureans entertained a similar attitude about vanquishing any desire that is potentially frustrating, advocating instead an ascetic lifestyle rooted in minimalism.

So what does it actually mean to be neurotic, the prototype, according to Freud, of all psychopathology, and what of its relationship to desire? This isn't so easy to answer, because there is no universal, overarching theory of neurosis that everyone agrees with. Even the concept of desire has multiple shades of meaning and application. But since Freud more or less invented the concept and gave us its indelible structure, we should begin with his take on it and see where it leads. We are all familiar by now with his first hypothesis, that neurotic conflicts are the consequence of having suffered a trauma during the early years of childhood. This so-called trauma (or seduction) theory has various permutations, and Freud was initially convinced that the traumatic incidence was *real*, which is to say, the consequence of something that happened to the child. Because many of his patients insisted they had experienced a sexual romance with a parent, usually the father, Freud surmised that this memory of the event should be accepted at face value.[1] Freud then linked the alleged incidence of sexual congress to the neurotic symptom that had brought his patients into treatment, usually in the form of anxiety, sexual repression, or somatic symptoms consistent with hysteria.

After having first accepted the seduction theory as a fact, Freud eventually abandoned it after concluding that these so-called memories had been unconsciously fabricated and that his patients had not been molested as they had believed, but only imagined it. This insight hit Freud like a rock, because it deprived him of a simple theory that explained the etiology of mental illness, albeit a controversial one. His initial reaction to this disappointment was dismay, but it provided him with a breathtaking insight. In his *On the History of the Psychoanalytic Movement* (1914) Freud admits:

> The firm ground of reality was gone. If hysterical subjects trace back their symptoms to traumas that are fictitious, then the new fact which emerges is precisely that they create such scenes in *fantasy,* and this psychical reality requires to be taken into account alongside practical reality.
>
> *(pp. 17–18)*

Despite his disappointment, this discovery helped Freud become acutely aware of how prevalent our fantasy life is, and that we have considerable difficulty distinguishing between what we imagine to be the case from what is so (some would say that the difficulty in making this distinction is a symptom of psychosis, but Freud gave such difficulties a generous latitude). Freud has had his share of critics, some of whom claim he suppressed his original theory because it was too scandalous. Such critics tend to embrace the idea that all mental illness can be attributed to sexual molestation, so the subtlety with which Freud arrived at his conclusion is lost on them. Freud wasn't saying that children are never molested by their parents, siblings, or other adults who have proximity. Indeed, incest occurs with alarming frequency and such incidents are almost always traumatic to those children so victimized. As Freud predicted, such incidents typically lead the victims of sexual molestation to develop neurotic symptoms, or worse. All Freud surmised was that it defies credibility to suppose that virtually every neurotic on the face of this planet has been sexually molested, because if that were the case then *everyone* would have been so victimized, since each and every one of us, avers Freud, is to some degree or other neurotic.

Two important outcomes followed from Freud's startling discovery. He realized that our fantasy life is of crucial importance because it is prevalent and competes with our perception of what is actually occurring. Though Freud abandoned the seduction theory of neurosis, he never abandoned his thesis that our desires, at bottom, are always sexual in nature. Just because we are not sexually assaulted by someone in childhood doesn't take away from the fact – well, not a fact really, more a hypothesis – that children *imagine* they were lovers with a parent. Why? Because they secretly (and yes, unconsciously) *wish* this were the case. From this springs Freud's theory that most neuroses are indeed the consequence of a trauma, but now we have to redefine just what we understand by *trauma*. It no longer pertains to events that actually transpire (at least in most cases) but to things we imagine have occurred, or more typically, things that did *not* occur that we *wanted* to. The trauma Freud settled on was not that of molestation, or even the fantasy of having been molested. It derives rather from the heartbreaking discovery that the parent we love and imagine will one day be ours exclusively is not ours and will never be, at least not in the way that we covet. It doesn't really matter which parent I love the most, mother or father.[2] Whichever parent it happens to be belongs to someone else. Even if a parent is single and the child has no ostensible rival, it is still impossible for a child to assume the role of a *paramour* to that parent, which is what Freud surmised every child wants. He or she will always be that parent's child, for as long as he (or she) lives.[3]

Freud concluded that neurotic symptoms are, at bottom, the result of unrequited love, and that each of us suffers this "trauma" as a consequence of coming to know, usually by the age of five, that I am alone in the world and that my mother or father does not (and never will) belong to me exclusively, in the manner that I wish were the case. *This is the narcissistic injury that all of us, each in his or her private and uniquely personal way, suffers*, eliciting a wound that cannot be rationalized or wished away. This experience is so painful that our only recourse is to forget it as quickly as possible, by virtue of our most powerful weapon, repression, a self-imposed incidence of amnesia of the very same discovery that incited Oedipus to put out his eyes. Broadly speaking, the term repression as employed by Freud encompasses a variety of devices we employ to hide things from awareness, including denial, projection, dissociation, isolation, reaction formation, undoing, and so on. Whichever mechanism(s) we opt for, the problem with this undeniably magical solution is that it does not, indeed cannot remain, repressed (or hidden). It always re-emerges in another guise, but one that is far more acceptable to us because, well . . . anything is preferable to knowing that my heart has been broken by the person I love the most. One way around this harshest of truths is to pretend that my father or mother indeed loves and craves to be with me, but such fantasies are always entertained *unconsciously*. They transform into wishes that trigger the thoughts that may subsequently pop into consciousness in the form of "memories" of a certain nature, such as a sexual liaison. But just as often they do not take this course and find refuge in any and all manner of other neurotic symptoms. Harboring such wishes results in a double-edged sword. On the one hand I have got rid of a troubling, unacceptable discovery that I cannot accept, so I carry on as though nothing has happened. On the other hand my wish, despite its repression, hasn't been eliminated. It doesn't disappear but sits there, lying in wait, seeking alternate means of fulfillment. The harbored wish, as a consequence of denying it, generates a conflict that produces an intolerable quota of anxiety, but a special edition of anxiety that I'm unable to resolve because I'm not aware of it.

We struggle with everyday anxiety as a matter of course and, for the most part, don't give it a second thought. Anxiety is invaluable to us because it alerts us that something is the matter that we had better give our attention to. We may not like it, but we don't usually take this discovery personally. Our attention is not on the anxiety, itself, but on the matter that elicits the anxiety. Going out on a first date, being fired from a job, discovering the brakes in my car are inoperable, hearing the distant rumble of an earthquake, readying myself to give a speech, flying on an airplane, etc., have one thing in common: they all elicit anxiety. But the kind of anxiety that occasions a *neurotic* conflict is of a different order, because *we cannot see or experience it*.[4] The danger doesn't appear to be outside of me, but "inside." Neurotic anxiety manifests for one reason only: I am hiding something from myself that, paradoxically, I know, but fear that I will discover.[5] Yet I am fundamentally predisposed to *not* discovering it and keeping it hidden, as it were, in plain sight. The anxiety generated needs an outlet, something to hang its hat on, that diverts my attention from what I am anxious about. That something is my *symptom*, so-called because the symptom displaces an older, less manageable form of distress for a new one, but in effigy.

For example, I develop a rash, or sore throat, or some other somatic symptom that looks like a genuine illness and may go unnoticed until it becomes so chronic or acute that someone, myself or a companion, takes notice. Or I feel anxious and break out in hives or stomach pain. Or on my first day at school I'm so panic-stricken that I refuse to leave home. When finally I am obliged to attend school despite my reluctance, I become so timid I stay to myself, which only arouses the attention of my teachers and classmates. Or I develop an obsession with counting, avoid stepping on the cracks in the sidewalk, or become depressed and lose interest in playing, an activity children typically relish. This is only a sample of the kinds of symptoms we frequently observe in children, here or there, at one time or other, in the course of their childhood. What they share in common is that every one of them *gets our attention*, and that is what every child wants, because we associate attention with love, and for good reason. Our parents shower us with it from the moment we are born, and we relish it so deeply we cannot live without it. But lose it we must, sometimes gradually, sometimes suddenly. Our childhoods have no other purpose than to prepare us for the day we strike out on our own, by which time our relationships with our family will have changed dramatically. No one survives this transition without scars, resentment, hurt feelings, even ambivalence about finally becoming independent, and not really knowing what that means.

Now that I'm free I am ready to live my own life. What then? The frustrations I experienced as a child don't magically disappear. If anything, they increase. Ordinarily, when I am frustrated in getting, or keeping, what I want I have a choice in the matter, to either try even harder to get it or, failing that, let it go and turn my attention elsewhere, somewhere just as desirable and, with luck more accessible. I encounter frustrations all the time at school, work, with friends, sexual partners, anything I value. I meet frustration whenever I want something I cannot get as readily as I would like. Children struggle with this conundrum constantly, wanting what they want *now*, not later. Try telling a three-year-old that you have a lovely present for him that you will give him tomorrow. When children become frustrated we find it perfectly natural to tell them they cannot always have what they want the moment they want it, because this most fundamental fact of life is known to all of us. Just because a child wants something, and demands it, doesn't mean that child will or should get it, then and there, if at all. We have learned to delay gratification, and we in turn instruct our children to, by teaching them the power of the word no, and the pivotal place it occupies in our lives. We are laying the groundwork for that day in the not too distant future when our children will leave home and learn to fend for themselves. We call this act of delaying gratification, learning to bide our time, *self-discipline*, the capacity to delay gratification while *continuing* to want the thing we are obliged to wait for, without giving up on it. Some of us manage this more determinedly than others, but it is something we all share in common and the thing that binds us to the human world we live in.

Whenever success eludes me, as it will, and becomes more frustrating than I can bear, I can either stick with it and persevere, or conclude it is simply not worth the candle and give up. Sometimes I quit the job I hate or withdraw from the school I no longer value. Sometimes I am fired from the job I covet or expelled from the school I treasure. Whatever the source of frustration, whatever the circumstance, I always have a choice, implicitly or explicitly, which is mine and mine alone to render. Ideally, I pursue what I desire with more zeal, patience, and creativity, or move on to something or someone else that is more accessible and potentially rewarding. These transitions are never easy and take time to accommodate, but we are ostensibly capable of grappling with these consternations and learning from our failures, of which there are and will be many. This is the picture of the prototypical, perhaps mythical healthy person, who has managed to figure it out. In reality, sometimes I am that person and sometimes I am not. The neurotic in us, in Freud's observation, gets stuck and is incapable of exercising this choice, the choice to persist or let go. In a word, he succumbs to ambivalence, the cancer that lies at the base of each neurotic conflict. And what is ambivalence, if not a safe haven where the neurotic in us takes refuge in order to avoid the risk of committing ourselves this way or that? To choose this over that, I have to give that up, and that is the problem, letting go of one possibility for another. What if I regret the choice I made, what if it was the wrong choice and I can't get it back? Better to bide my time, keep both options in play, and give up neither. In effect, I tell myself I am keeping them both, but in reality I have neither. What I do have is a shelter from the storm that would have followed from the choice I avoided, because every choice we make puts us at risk, where the outcome of our desire is on the line, for better or worse. This is the reason it is so difficult to overcome ambivalence: it offers unblemished security from the dangers our desires expose us to.

When ambivalence takes hold in this way, the desire isn't crushed but merely repressed, Freud's term for when it goes into hiding. This is the same so-called mechanism I turn to whenever I suffer a disappointment, heartbreak, or trauma. By repressing the desire that was quelled, the pain I associate with it is mitigated. Freud's great insight was to realize that the denial of our deepest anguish becomes the catalyst for the varied forms of symptom formation that comprise our neuroses. I like to call this mechanism, in fact a stratagem we devise to re-make the world into something more to our liking, the "third choice scenario." It is a handy weapon to have, and we all have one, ready at the trigger, any moment we cannot bear to experience an anguishing incident. What happens whenever we aren't happy with the choice given us, when we opt instead to sit on the fence, and wait until a choice comes along that we prefer? We seek a third, albeit *magical* choice: our prized talisman, the neurotic symptom. This is a brilliant, even admirable feature of human ingenuity, a means we employ to distort reality and reshape it whenever and wherever it suits us. We encounter these circumstances all the time, over the course of our lives, and we never abandon this magic trick because it is so handy and ingrained. It is the *sine qua non* of our coping mechanisms, our way of coping *par excellence*. Our expertise in fashioning these magical choices begins early, long before we can remember having devised it. Children face such dilemmas as a matter of course. When I can't let go of the parent I covet but cannot have, I displace that anguish onto a symptom that mitigates that anguish by substituting in its place a more manageable mode of suffering. The only reason it is more manageable is because the symptom, unlike the anguish it replaces, is my creation. It isn't inflicted on me, I inflict it on myself, and therein lies the joy and illusion of control, to believe I have a handle on the situation because, after all, I made the anguish disappear. The new problem becomes the symptom I am stuck with, which I cling to for protection. This is why Freud believed it is so difficult to rid ourselves of our symptoms. At their kernel they are gratifying in two respects: first, they are strangely comforting in the way they numb us from pain; second, even after an interminable experience with therapy, we hold on to some of them because they continue to protect us from any memories and experiences we still find distasteful.

Whenever such memories and experiences are disclosed to us we are confronted with the same sense of loss and helplessness we had convinced ourselves was dead and buried. Freud's vision of therapy was rooted in the belief that it is usually – but not always – better to know where we stand than to live in denial, with its attendant confusion and anxiety. You could call this kind of therapeutic intervention an incidence of "tough love," because it confronts us with a truth that hurts. This is why therapy is necessarily painful, because its aim is to uncover truths we conceal from ourselves via the ambivalent compromises we settle for. Some people hate this about therapy and want nothing to do with it. That is their choice, and who can say that their choice is in error? Moreover, therapy cannot compel us to experience anything we are not predisposed to, so we are always free to protect those symptoms we believe are indispensable. This is why therapy isn't always successful. It depends on what we want to use it for.

Another implication of what I call the third choice scenario is that it implies a distinction between two fundamental kinds of mental suffering, though it isn't so easy to tell them apart. One is imposed on us by reality, which is to say, our relationships with other people. You might call it the slings and arrows of living, the inevitable and sometimes catastrophic disappointments with love relationships including friends, the stresses and strains from our work life. In a word, we're talking about the demands that are exacted on every aspect of those experiences we endure daily. There is nothing "pathological" about such suffering, it is the stuff of life, from which none of us can escape, and most of the time we handle it readily. The second kind of mental suffering is different because it doesn't originate from the world, *per se*. It originates from *me*, which is to say, self-inflicted. This self-imposed form of mental suffering is what Freud and every psychotherapist since who has adopted the medical nomenclature calls the "symptom." Not a symptom of mental *illness*, or psychopathology, or brain or nervous activity, or alleged chemical imbalances, but a metaphorical symptom that connotes a neurosis of my own making. But why in the world would I go to the trouble of inventing a symptom when I am already burdened with problems that, for the most part, are unremitting and insoluble? The answer is simple, if somewhat stunning. I use the second kind of suffering as a last resort, in order to distract my attention from the disappointment, trauma, what have you, that I find so intolerable. I resort to this second kind of mental suffering as a means of *manipulating these painful experiences* in order to cope with them better. Neurosis isn't a pathological condition, but a cleverly orchestrated strategy to mitigate intolerable pain.

What this suggests is that symptoms don't appear out of nowhere. Nor are they, strictly speaking, "caused" by traumatic injuries. In a sense I *choose* my symptoms, even if I do so without awareness or conscious volition. At the deepest recesses of my being all my thoughts, feelings, and reactions to my experiences derive from one place alone, my sense of *agency* that, in turn, says a lot about who I am. Even my so-called "unconscious," metaphorically speaking, is basically *me* and so an essential aspect of who I am. Because symptoms are my creation and not the machinations of my nervous system, such symptoms and the (so-called) pathological conditions they occasion are not incidences of a mental illness, but part and parcel of what Jay Haley (1963) termed *strategies* I employ to cope with the anxieties of living, as best I can.

Thus far we have been exploring the nature of desire, its relation to love and sexual being, and the attachment to our parents, an attachment that is more indelible than our common sense is able to appreciate. There is a reason why it was only recently (the beginning of the twentieth century) that our civilization was ready to entertain such a notion. When Freud came up with it, the public's reaction was one of outrage. We are talking about the idea, Freud's idea, that children fall in love with their parents and enjoy sexual relations with them, primarily the mother. Freud took the heat for his intellectual audacity, and his reputation never really recovered.

What was Freud really saying here? We have been using terms such as wish, desire, libido, pleasure, sexuality, fantasy. What do they mean? When Freud announced that all children possess sexual feelings and imagine having sexual relations with their parents, what was he trying to say? Freud was not a sex therapist. He wasn't even trying to improve our relationship with our sex lives.[6] He merely pointed out that at the bottom of every child's love for his or her parents is a passion so deep that for all intents and purposes the child is virtually *in love* with that parent, and wants to be the most important person in that parent's life, in the same way as the parent is the most important person in the child's. What Freud was trying to get at was the profound nature of *love*, not sex. So why didn't he just come out and say this in so many words?

Love is a difficult topic for psychoanalysts to talk about. In any discussion about the therapy relationship between therapist and patient, the topic of love is the elephant in the room, the elephant no one wants to acknowledge directly. I remember a conversation I was having with Charles Brenner, when the topic of Jonathan Lear's recent book on Freud came up. Brenner dismissively referred to it as Lear's "love book!"[7] The word love was nowhere in the title or subtitle of the text, but Brenner was referring to Lear's thesis that a great deal of Freud's theories concerned the nature of love and its relation to psychoanalysis. Brenner was not alone in his contempt for the notion that Freud was more concerned with love than sexuality, or even transference. Freud's motives for avoiding this word are obvious. He wanted psychoanalysis to be embraced as a new science and didn't want it confused with competing practices of therapy, some of which bordered on mysticism, including hypnotism. When you hear someone say therapy is about love you immediately suspect that the therapist is being seductive, perhaps inappropriate, or downright foolish or simplistic, that the therapist is going to treat you to his love for you because his love will make you better. This wasn't what Freud had in mind. He was rather explicit that the analyst's love does not, in and of itself, heal anything.

Yet Freud emphasized the role of love in various contexts. Two of his technical papers, "The Dynamics of Transference" (1912) and "Observations on Transference-Love" (1915), were not, strictly speaking, technical but meditations on the nature of love and how it manifests in the therapy relationship. He invokes the word constantly, but he also explains that love makes its appearance in the guise of what he terms *transference*, a catchy scientific-sounding term that comprises multiple meanings. We will explore Freud's concept of transference and the mystifying nature of its application later (in Chapter Six). Although we typically refer to transference as an unconscious *process* by which patients project aspects of their parents onto their analyst, the "thing" transferred is essentially love and its derivatives, including envy, jealousy, resentment, spite, idealization, even hatred.

It is misleading to suggest that it's not really the analyst who inspires these feelings to occur, but the patient's parents. Freud makes it perfectly clear in both of the transference papers cited that it is the *person* of the analyst that patients develop these feelings for, but in a fashion similarly felt for the parent. It is in this sense and this sense alone that transference is a repetition of the original parental object. But, as Freud points out, this is how we love *everybody*, not just the analyst. This is why Freud insists that one's analysis won't be much of an experience if the patient does not fall in love with the analyst. Not all patients do, and they very well may derive some benefit from the experience without it, but it will only be an echo of the kind of full-bore experience one is capable of experiencing by "falling" for the person that their analyst happens to be. Which is to say, by developing a strong attachment to the analyst, then gathering into that relationship all the hopes and aspirations we develop for any person with whom we feel this way. The therapist isn't special in this. Most therapists would hardly strike you as someone with whom you would readily fall in love. For this reason Freud was convinced that neurotics may fall in love with anyone they spend time with, any person who gives all his or her attention to them, while never judging or criticizing them, never admonishing or making demands on them, etc.[8] Who else treats you that way, *unless* he is in love you? You might argue that treating someone this way, the way that therapists are supposed to treat their patients, including the regimen of a fee-for-service relationship, is a loving thing to do. I'm not opposed to that way of putting it, but such a claim has to be couched carefully and explained fully so that we know precisely what we are saying.

I have been arguing that neurosis and every other form of "psychopathology" originates from the slings and arrows of childhood, a time when we were madly in love with our parents because they doted on us hand and foot and, after all, insured our survival. Somehow along the way during the course of every normal childhood we suffer an existential heartbreak from which we never fully recover. We nevertheless enjoy abundant opportunities over the course of our long apprenticeships as children to correct or compensate for these injuries, but sometimes not. We are most vulnerable when we are in love and dependent on a person we are devoted to. Laing agreed with Freud's premise that every person who shows up in therapy is suffering from a broken heart.[9] I like to think that most thoughtful therapists come to this conclusion. Freud even allowed that psychotherapy, in a measure we should approach with caution, is indeed a cure through love, both the love patients feel for their therapist, and the extraordinary sympathy therapists feel for their patients. Otherwise, their patients would drive therapists crazy.

Yet our penchant for hiding the injuries we have suffered, real or imagined, cripples our capacity to recover from such experiences by finally putting them behind us. Because of our extraordinary intelligence and the gift of language that facilitates abstract thinking, we humans are alone blessed with the capacity to disguise such truths from ourselves, by engaging in varieties of self-deception that dominate our waking and un-waking life. Why are we so reluctant to come to grips with our vulnerability and let ourselves suffer the anguish that is a vital part of our nature? *Because we can.* We have far too many resources, too much power for our own good, so we naturally take advantage of them. We become so accustomed to the attention we derive from others that, when we lose it, we wreak havoc on our bodies and sensibilities, for no other reason than to distract ourselves from the heartache inattention engenders. The picture Freud paints is a dark one, but he is not the first to make these observations about our frailty, and tenacity. Creatures of modern culture, we are obsessed with the theme of unrequited love in mythology, poetry, literature, opera, film, television, you name it, we cannot seem to get enough of it, *in absentia.* Pastimes serve both to distract us from our own, private situations, while affording proxies that bring home to us our follies, but at a distance, opportunities at the ready to relive our drama through *others*. Sometimes our dramas inspire us to better ourselves, but sometimes they provide a ready diet of escape, the distinction Graham Greene once made between art and entertainment.[10] It doesn't take a genius to recognize the extent to which fantasy occupies our attention, yet it required a genius to rub it in our faces and force us to look at it. For this we owe Freud our undying appreciation.

But how did our penchant for folly, self-deception, and denial become the stuff of mental illness, psychopathology, and the conviction that the genesis of our symptoms has nothing to do with our agency or intentionality? Though not a psychiatrist, Freud the neurologist approached the treatment of his patients as though they were suffering some form of pathology, or psychopathology. He was especially intrigued with hysteria, a prevalent condition among Viennese housewives that psychiatrists of the day were having little success treating. Though Freud was gaining insights into the personal situations that elicited their symptoms, he still treated his patients as though they were suffering from an illness that warranted medical "treatment." His initial efforts met with little success. He treated them first with hypnosis, and when that failed he proffered interpretations that explained why their hysterical symptoms had developed, a consequence of having repressed their desires (i.e., love). Freud initially believed that simply knowing the purpose symptoms served would remove them. This too did not work. Eventually it occurred to Freud that he needed to regard his patients as active and participating *agents* in this so-called treatment relationship. This was a considerable departure from how we typically define a treatment relationship. Usually, the doctor treats the patient who passively cooperates with the treatment, then lets the healing begin. Instead, Freud informed his patients that they were going to have to struggle with their symptoms and engage them with all their will. Meanwhile, he encouraged his patients to continue talking to him, spontaneously and unreservedly, without direction or purpose, about anything and everything that occurred to them. They were no longer communicating their pain to him; they were letting him into their world, by revealing it to him heart and soul.

This regimen didn't look like the kind of treatment psychiatry was familiar with because it no longer resembled anything that could be labeled a medical "treatment." What Freud was calling psychoanalysis morphed into an intimate kind of friendship in which the one party reveals everything of a personal nature to the other. In effect, the patient was doing all the work, not the doctor. What kind of treatment is that? But Freud didn't completely grasp the radical nature of how far he had strayed from established treatment protocols and continued to see himself as a doctor who treated psychopathology, albeit unconventionally. What this told Freud was that psychiatrists were fools who were too unsophisticated to grasp how complicated the mind and its machinations are. But by this stage Freud was no longer doing psychiatry. He was helping neurotics initiate an uncommonly intimate relationship with a stranger who treated them in a remarkable and loving fashion, allowing them to be who they were without guilt or judgment. In so doing, he let the relationship *itself*, over time, provide the healing, by reawakening the patient's desire and capacity for love. Once awakened, they were for all intents and purposes "cured" of their mental illness. At least sometimes. Naturally this stratagem had to be couched in the most scientific-sounding garb in order to be embraced by psychiatry as a *bona fide* treatment method, arrived at scientifically, to be sure.

So what were these mental illnesses that Freud was supposed to be treating, if they were not genuine illnesses in the way medical treatment is typically conceived? The science of psychological diagnosis was still in its infancy in the early part of the twentieth century, so Freud had a pretty blank canvas on which to work. As noted in Chapter One, the idea that madness should be construed as a specifically medical condition occurred more or less accidentally, and by default. By the beginning of the twentieth century little had happened by way of developing psychiatry into a systematic science of diagnosis and treatment of psychiatric conditions. Janet and Charcot made fledgling attempts to understand hysteria, but to little effect. It was Freud and the German psychiatrist and philosopher, Karl Jaspers, who wrote the book on diagnostic nomenclature and, for the most part, that is what we use today. Freud tried to simplify what was fast becoming an unwieldy plethora of nomenclature that had little consistency from one country to the next, or indeed from one psychiatrist to the other. Like Charcot, Freud was interested in developing a treatment method for hysterics and had little interest in treating psychotic disorders because they did not readily conform to the rigors of the psychoanalytic method as he then conceived it, which required considerable volition and facility with language by the patient. Whereas Charcot was credited with inventing neurology and coining the term neurosis, it was Freud who developed the concept into a more practical and exhaustive system that could be readily assimilated.

For practical reasons, Freud divided patients suffering from psychopathology into two groups, those who responded to psychotherapy and those who did not. Hysteria became the prototype for the kind of person Freud could work with and at first it appeared that all "neurotics" were hysterics, a convention initiated by Charcot. The term hysteria is an ancient one, going all the way back to the Greeks who believed that women suffering from somatic conditions were stricken by a "wandering womb." The term was appropriated by Charcot who subsequently became famous for treating hysterics with hypnosis. Freud distinguished hysterics from patients who suffered psychotic symptoms, such as delusions and hallucinations, and for the most part focused on the former. It was Freud who soon discovered a different kind of neurotic who did not fit the picture of the typical hysteric. Hysterics usually suffered from either somatic symptoms that were psychological in nature, which is to say, fabricated or exaggerated, or from anxiety that manifested phobias. In their personality structure hysterics could also be dramatic, emotional, and crisis-ridden. The other kind of neurotic that came to Freud's attention didn't exhibit such symptoms. Instead they seemed obsessed with guilt, and were often highly intellectual and detached from their emotions, even aloof. Moreover, whereas hysterics typically repressed their early experiences, this new kind of patient possessed excellent memory. Freud invented a novel nosological category for this type of neurosis, the obsessional. Now there were two types of neurotics, the hysteric and the obsessional. This served as Freud's most original contribution to the fledgling science of diagnosis.

Freud, however, was reluctant to demote hysteria to just another type of neurosis. After all, he had become famous for developing a novel treatment regimen that had a measure of success treating hysteria, a then-prevalent disorder. He concluded that the obsessional was not an entirely original form of neurosis after all, but rather a previously unrecognized edition of hysteria, so the two were ineluctably intertwined. Most patients, after all, exhibit characteristics of each, though one often dominates the other. Most hysterics were women, but Freud allowed that some men suffered from hysteria also, meaning the diagnosis was not gender specific, though Freud believed that male hysterics were relatively rare. We know today this is not the case. On the other hand, obsessionals were predominantly men and Freud's two famous obsessional case reports, the Rat Man and the Wolf Man, were both male, but many obsessional patients also happened to be women. Though many patients presented as depressed, Freud was reluctant to deem this yet a third type of neurosis. Instead he viewed depression as a "subtype" of the hysteric or obsessional (or even psychotic) who possessed underlying depressive features. What all neurotics shared in common was their ability to function in life more successfully, say, than psychotics were able to, depending on the extent to which their symptoms compromised their pursuit of happiness.[11] As Freud showed in his treatment of the Rat Man, even neurotics suffer psychotic symptoms, now and then.

What about those who possess no neurotic features whatsoever, neither hysterical nor obsessional? Freud's answer was simple. Those people simply don't exist! Freud cautiously admitted in *The Psychopathology of Everyday Life* (1901) that all human beings suffer from neurotic symptoms to varying degrees, some more than others, some less. Moreover, our mental states are not stable; we are buffeted by the stresses and strains of everyday life and respond with an arsenal of neurotic weapons, always at the ready, to rescue us from the impingement of any reality that is too onerous to bear. In the last year of his life, in his seminal penultimate paper, "Analysis Terminable and Interminable" (1937), Freud observed that psychoanalysis, however successful in a given case, cannot inoculate a person from succumbing to a future neurosis. It all depends on how things go in one's life. Sometimes issues that have never been satisfactorily resolved reappear in times of stress or panic. But even the healthiest person is susceptible to new neuroses in times of crisis. In other words, anyone, no matter how seemingly happy or together, may fall prey to neurotic defenses, employed to ward off the kinds of anxiety prompted by devastating loss or other calamity, such as divorce, a debilitating medical condition, or catastrophic business failure. For most of us, we have orchestrated an uneasy alliance between our aspirations for happiness and our intolerance of pain. Our psychical defenses are our primary means of facilitating an optimally satisfactory existence, for the most part underneath the surface of awareness.

We have to ask ourselves, how in the world can such sophisticated mental maneuvers be construed as anything remotely "medical" in nature? What we see here are not medical conditions, *per se*, but *existential situations* to which we are vulnerable and with which we are constantly grappling every moment of our lives. We do this so routinely we rarely give it notice, not unlike all the other creatures in the world that grapple with survival each moment of their existence. We can call these devices anything we like. So why not call them "mental illnesses" and say that fostering conversations with those who suffer from them comprise a method of "treating" their illness? We can do that and in fact we do, but it is also undeniable that this way of depicting this kind of human suffering is not literal, but metaphorical. The only thing that a medical pathology, such as cancer, and a psychopathology, such as hysteria, share in common is that each is concerned with the phenomenon of *suffering*, and that we often somaticize such suffering in order to mitigate it. My thesis is that suffering is a human, at bottom existential, phenomenon, not a, strictly speaking, medical one. It just so happens that among all the ways we are capable of suffering, some of them happen to be medical conditions located in the body.

What other forms of psychopathology did Freud recognize? He had a lot to say about the psychoses, though they have changed – in fact, never stop changing – in subsequent years. Paranoia, schizophrenia, and manic depressive psychosis were the principal forms of psychotic conditions typically encountered.[12] Freud found he couldn't work with these diagnoses because the agency of the people so diagnosed was too compromised to engage in such a demanding treatment regimen as psychoanalysis. As we have seen, other analysts, including Jung, Melanie Klein, Winnicott, Frieda Fromm-Reichmann, and of course Laing, and many others enjoyed considerable success with this population, so long as improvement is the goal and not the more elusive "cure." The fact that psychoanalysts and other psychotherapists no longer speak of curing their patients says something about just how medical this process is not. After all, even neurotics, by Freud's admission, are never entirely cured of their neuroses, so why should we expect psychotics to be cured of theirs? Their condition, indeed, their *situation*, as Laing and other psychoanalysts have discovered, is no less existential than the neurotic's. The situation they are in is simply more extreme and the hill they are obliged to climb is higher, so the summit is for the most part beyond reach. Everything else, however, remains more or less the same.

Freud also recognized a third category of psychopathology, the so-called *perversions*, a controversial pathology if there ever was one. He believed that perversion could not be construed as another edition of neurosis because, unlike the neurotic, the pervert doesn't repress his desire, indeed he is devoted to it. According to Freud, the distinguishing feature of perversion is an aversion to heterosexual genital intercourse, which is substituted with sexual foreplay. With a typical flourish, Freud argued that all of us are perverts – indeed, "polymorphously" so! The heterosexual couple readily enjoys perverse sexual activities, including fellatio, cunnilingus, exhibitionism, voyeurism, fetishes, sadomasochism, and more, in the service of conventional sexual intercourse at its culmination. The pervert, by Freud's definition, does not engage in, or if he or she does, does not enjoy, sexual intercourse because he or she can only be satisfied by activities we typically employ as means of arousal. There is a vast literature on this phenomenon, and we no longer recognize homosexuality as a perversion. Though Freud treated the pervert with psycho-analysis, he believed that it was the neurotic that responded best to his invention, talking therapy.

So what do all these modes of suffering have to do with *desire*? Freud believed we are all driven by a kind of energy that is sexual in nature. He refers to this energy as *Libido*. From the moment we are born we pursue release from this dammed-up energy that we usually associate with something prototypically pleasurable, the sexual orgasm. Freud also believed that men possess a lot more *Libido* than women. Though it was unknown in his day, testosterone, the steroid hormone that is found in all mammals, reptiles, birds, and other vertebrates, enjoys a striking resemblance to what Freud termed *Libido*. Like *Libido*, testosterone is more prevalent in men than in women and accounts for why men are on the whole physically stronger than women, and pursue sexual intercourse more aggressively. Naturally, there are variations. One of Freud's keenest insights was the discovery that men and women alike are capable of repressing their interest in sex despite the amount of *Libido* in their bodies. Though our urge to engage in sex is in some measure determined by our testosterone, sexual arousal is a predominantly psychological phenomenon that the body responds to. Freud believed that when we repress our interest in sex our *Libido* is channeled into other outlets, such as the production of neurotic symptoms which, alleged Freud, are unconsciously pleasurable, the principal reason we resist giving them up.

Testosterone doesn't work that way. The amount of testosterone in our bodies remains the same when we repress our interest in sex, so at this point the compari-son of *Libido* with testosterone breaks down. Freud's conception of *Libido* was key to his notion that symptom formation is simply another way of enjoying sexual pleasure (or relief from sexual unpleasure). Without it, there is no reason to assume the two are related. Desire in Freud's thinking is essentially sexual desire and the prototype for all the things in life we value. Even the desire to become a psycho-analyst, say, or to write books, to become successful or perhaps famous, are all ways of achieving a kind of sexual gratification. Freud had to invent a new kind of sexual outlet, sublimation, to explain why intellectual activity could also occasion sexual pleasure, but without affecting one's genital organ. I once had a girlfriend who said that having sex with an intellectual really turned her on, but I don't think this is what Freud had in mind! Ultimately, the argument that all that we aspire to in life is at bottom a quest for sexual gratification is unsustainable, and virtually all psy-choanalytic schools succeeding Freud's, even Lacan's, have rejected this. As noted earlier, Freud stretched the meaning of sexuality so broadly that it can mean just about anything, which effectively renders it meaningless. At bottom, love, which is not identical with sex but enjoys a special relationship with it, is what desire seizes as its ultimate object, not the sex act, *per se*. It is nevertheless astonishing how preva-lent our preoccupation with sex is in our daily affairs, and how severely neurotics typically repress theirs. It is ironic that this has become the taboo topic number one, now that psychoanalysts rarely talk about sex with their patients. I can't count the number of patients I have treated who had been in analysis with someone earlier for many years, and who told me the topic of their sex life never came up. The patients never brought it up because they thought it wasn't permissible to talk about it, and their analyst never brought it up either. Obviously, I brought it up or I would not be telling you this! I have to credit Freud with having taught me that our sex life is always, somehow or other, tied to our neurotic symptoms, even if his *Libido* theory doesn't explain as neatly as he would have liked how and why this is the case.

Another feature of desire in Freud's schema is that it is predominantly unconscious, which is to say, it has a history. We don't just decide to desire something, it is a part of us and, as such, not responsive to acts of will, as anyone suffering from impotence will tell you. Though we may demand this or that from others, what we desire most urgently is love, which cannot be obtained by demanding it. It is impossible to understand Freud's conception of desire (or the wish) without accounting for its relation to our pursuit of love. Though the two are related, we have never managed to figure out exactly how. Freud couldn't stand for something so basic to remain a mystery, so he forced the connection with his *Libido* theory. This theory implies that the reason I fall in love is to secure and perpetuate a sexual partner in order to ensure procreation and the survival of the species. If it were not for our biological need to reproduce, love would not exist, but then neither would the perpetuation of our life-form. We cannot really disprove this theory, any more than we are able to prove it, and in the absence of a way of disproving it Freud concluded that it was sound enough for his purposes. This isn't how science works, that something is so unless you can prove otherwise. Freud, shall we say, was a master of creative speculation, and it is a wonder to follow him in all his glory and penchant for the most amazing conjectures about our all too puzzling human condition. The sceptic in us is satisfied with not knowing all the answers, but the dogmatist in Freud could not let it rest.

No doubt our quest for love is somehow tied to our sexuality, but one does not "cause" the other. Erotic love is only one way of connecting with another person, and much of what we love in life goes beyond our relationships with other people. Yes, the friendships we love probably harbor unconscious sexual arousals that we never experience genitally, though we sometimes might, but we are also capable of loving animals, walking by the ocean, gazing at the stars, wearing fashionable clothes, driving over the speed limit, amusing our friends, accumulating wealth, smoking cigars, getting high, and on and on. It is difficult to think of these ways of loving as specifically sexual in nature, even unconsciously. To say these activities are substitutes for sex is too pat an argument to be taken seriously by anyone except the most diehard Freudian. On the other hand, the issue that brings most people into therapy is not the neurotic symptoms we have been talking about, but their relationships – or lack of – with other people. In other words, the lack of love in their lives. Before long we soon discover there is a connection between their quest for more intimacy, or love, in their lives and the neurotic symptoms their quest occasions. Alongside all these considerations is the question we began this chapter with: What does this say about the nature of our desire and our relationship with *it*? How does all this get back to the symptom, and the unconscious wish that arouses it?

First, I shall return to the question: What is the relation between wishing and desiring? Freud never explicitly talks about desires. He has a great deal to say about wishes. In his seminal work, the one that made Freud famous and became the prototype for everything he says subsequently, *The Interpretation of Dreams* (1900), Freud introduces a radical and admittedly disturbing theory of why we dream at night. All dreams, says Freud, have a singular motive, and a purpose. No matter what they are, on close inspection we discover that each tells a story, and that story reveals the fulfillment of a wish. The wonderful thing about interpreting dreams (and we shouldn't forget that Freud wasn't *explaining* dreams, just interpreting them) is that you can interpret them any way you like. There is no way of proving that a given interpretation is correct, and there is no way of proving it is not. Interpretations are nothing more than opinions, and in the context of dream interpretation, my interpretation of a dream reveals what that dream means to *me*. We aren't seeking correctness in our interpretations, but the satisfaction in understanding something about the dream, some kernel of truth that hadn't occurred to me before. Whether or not it has any relevance or credibility depends on my personal reaction to it, how it moves me, as in looking at a fine painting that says something to me that is at once wonderful and provocative. Interpretation is an art, and the analyst, like all artists, is trying to get at something truthful in his or her interpretations. The more effective the interpretation, the more satisfaction it affords the patient, the finer artist the analyst.

Freud's conception of dream interpretation is important to us, not because the interpretation of dreams occupies a prominent place in our clinical practices – for the most part, it does not – but because it is the prototype for how Freud went on to interpret the meaning of *symptoms*. The interpretation of symptoms is of enormous importance, because it is impossible to conduct a psychoanalytic or psychotherapeutic practice without pondering the meaning of the symptoms we are confronted with daily. Like the dream, says Freud, the symptom is the fulfillment of a wish. This means that the act of repression does not bury wishes, but makes them come true. This is why it is difficult to give them up: we adore them. Yes, we fuss about them, complain about them, curse them even, just like that old pair of shoes I cannot throw away, the automobile that is always breaking down, the lover who gives me nothing but grief. I love the symptom, in precisely the same way I love anyone or anything that has complete control over my interest. It means too much to get rid of, but it is also too obvious that it is slowly killing me. What am I supposed to do about it?

The wish, we noted earlier, is tethered to a fantasy. I wish I could rule the world, means that I have a fantasy, a daydream, of ruling the world, and what I would do with it if it were mine. In a way, this wish is operatic and mythic, but it is also, because I don't always think about it, unconscious. Like the dream, my fantasies may harbor unconscious elements that rarely occur to me. I have a fantasy of humiliating my girlfriend's former boyfriend who remains a colleague of hers, but it might turn out that the unconscious motive for this fantasy is the wish to expel my father from the household so that I can have my mother to myself. This means that the symptoms of anxiety, or depression, or sexual inhibition, for example, by their nature satisfy a hidden wish. The wish is not known to me, and Freud was convinced that uncovering this wish would be instrumental in relieving ourselves of our underlying neurotic conflicts. But if the symptoms I suffer don't merely allude to the wishes I entertain, but actually fulfill them, then why don't they make me happy? Why would I seek therapy to relieve me of the very fulfillment of a wish that I had been seeking in the first place? It is easy to understand why one would resist giving up such an achievement. But why would we want to?

Lacan tries to formulate this dilemma using a different language and conceptual vocabulary, but staying with Freud's intuition that the symptom serves to fulfill the wish, which is why it is hard to give up. For Lacan, the symptom not only fulfills a wish; it *satisfies* it. This poses the problem even more enigmatically because, after all, isn't satisfying our wishes what life is about? Don't we seek therapy because we have been unable to satisfy our wishes and want help doing so?

Lacan's explanation, following Hegel, is that the wish that gives rise to the symptom has first to be discovered, but then must be transformed into a *desire*, and only then will we see the truth of its hidden meaning. Desire, so conceived by Kojeve's interpretation of Hegel, can never be satisfied, for to do so, by bringing it to an end, would serve to kill it. Desire, by its nature, is never brought to a close but remains obstinately open, like a wound, which both defines and motivates me. The neurotic is not as interested in bringing his desire to life and finding objects for it, because he is keeping it on the level of a wish that never quite makes it to the status of a desire, strictly speaking. This places him in an untenable position because the purpose of a wish is to make it real, which is to say, transform it into a desire that can engage someone or some activity through which it can be *realized*. This sets up a tension that can only be "satisfied" by transforming it into a symptom.

But this so-called accomplishment is a hollow one because all it achieves is to hold my desire in abeyance, neither killing it off completely nor giving it a place to breathe. Once it finds refuge in a neurotic (or other form of pathological) symptom, the anxiety that is wedded to my desire increases and becomes impossible to tolerate. No matter how well I cope with this situation I will always be burdened with the sense that something in my life is missing or, alternately, that something in my life is encroaching on me. This is what my neurosis does for me: it hijacks my desire and holds it hostage, and like all hostage situations it can neither be ignored nor easily resolved, so in every manner of the word I am stuck in it. And there you have it, the purgatory of the neurotic condition.

How does this understanding of desire affect the goal of analysis? Rather than satisfying our desires, the goal becomes one of coming to the realization, no matter how long it takes, that in order to be happy, which is to say that place in my life where I no longer strive for what is obstinately elusive, I have to stop trying to satisfy my desires and learn to *serve* them instead, by first acknowledging, and then embracing them. In other words, learning to let them *be*. No one can be happy with his lot in life if he isn't doing what he wants with it, and living the life he genuinely desires to live. *Living the life we desire doesn't entail bringing our desires to any end, but keeping them open.*

Let us look at a couple of case vignettes to see how this works. Jack says that his recently acquired girlfriend, Jill, is wonderful, exciting, beautiful, smart, fun, that he is madly in love with her, and she with him. Yet they fight constantly. Jack says that his only complaint about their relationship is that Jill won't let him see her more often, which is to say as often as he wants. Though they live apart and each shares an apartment with others, they get together three, four, five times a week. When they are together, however, Jill's focus isn't always on Jack. They are both college students, but Jack resents that Jill's studies sometimes prevent her from being available to him, even when they are together. Another complaint is that they don't have sex as often as Jack would like. When they do have sex it is great, but sometimes Jill isn't in the mood and seems emotionally distant and aloof. This drives Jack crazy, because whenever Jill isn't attentive to him, whether they are separate or together, he feels rejected by her. Jill admits she can be moody, and sometimes needs time to herself, even when they are together, but she says this doesn't affect how she feels about Jack and how much she loves him. They get into fights because he presses the issue and wants her to change, to be more available to him than she is willing to be. The fighting is so prevalent that Jill wonders if it is possible for them to stay together.

Jack says he is acutely sensitive to rejection and that this has been a problem with previous girlfriends, that they have broken up with him due to his demands. He admits he is emotionally "needy" and this has also been a problem for him in previous relationships. We have learned in his analysis that this dynamic with his girlfriends is a recapitulation of his relationship with his mother, who was busy in her life as a professional woman and wasn't as attentive to Jack as he needed her to be. Jack says that his father was more nurturing than his mother, but that his work as a business executive meant that he too was seldom available, despite Jack being an only child. Jack says he was always angry with his mother and that he never felt that she understood him, or that she was responsive to his complaints. She seemed oblivious and out of touch. His mother told Jack she loved him very much and wanted him to be happy, but she wasn't there for him emotionally. When his parents subsequently divorced, Jack went to live with an uncle because he didn't feel close to his mother, and his father couldn't provide a home for him. Since his analysis began Jack has become increasingly aloof from his mother and avoids contact with her. He isn't sure why he is angry with her because he no longer counts on her for support. He seems surprised when he tells me his mother is grief-stricken because she has lost contact with him.

When I ask Jack why he can't accept Jill for who she is, he says he doesn't know. When he thinks about it he realizes he is being unreasonable and selfish, yet he can't help the way he feels and he cannot control the anger that gets aroused every time Jill disappoints him. He is beginning to wonder if this relationship is viable. He would like to accept Jill for who she is and doesn't want to lose her, yet he feels helpless when trying to curtail his demands on her, demands that he knows she cannot or will not satisfy. So what is the matter with Jack? When Jack is not in a relationship with a woman he is chronically lonely and unhappy. He needs a woman in his life in order to feel happy. He says he cannot do without love in his life the way other friends of his apparently can. Yet, it appears that what Jack is calling love is limited, and for the most part narcissistic. He loves being loved by Jill but doesn't cotton to the feeling of *loving her* as a person with a life, worries, and concerns independent of her relationship with *him*. Jack treats love like a drug that he can't get enough of. No matter how much he gets, he always wants more. But when it comes to thinking about Jill's needs, what it might take to make her happy, what he might give her that would demonstrate how much she means to him, Jack is lost. This is a language that is foreign to him, because it is a language that his mother was unfamiliar with, so she could not teach it to him nor show it in her love for his father.

Jack doesn't really love *Jill*, which is to say who Jill is, he only loves how she makes him feel when things are going his way. When things are not going so well he cannot stand how this makes him feel. He wishes she loved him more, and wishes they could be happy together. He demands that she give more, as though love can be poured from a faucet, sometimes more, sometimes less. On a deeper level Jack cannot permit himself to be with his desire for Jill and permit this desire to mature into the kind of love that is giving, generous, protective. To genuinely *be* with his desire is painful, and pain is offensive to him. This is what prompts Jack to attack Jill, and by attacking her he is also attacking his desire for her by transforming it into hate, which momentarily feels better. In effect, Jack is punishing Jill for not giving him what he wants, which drives her further away from him, until he finally gets what he is after: her attention. She will eventually break up with him and by doing him that favor will finally put his desire for her to rest. Jack isn't able to do this himself because he tells himself that he loves her and doesn't want to lose Jill. This is only partially true. The more basic dilemma is that Jack cannot bear being in a *state of desiring* and the sense of helplessness and vulnerability his desire puts him in. He is too busy carrying a torch for his mother to take on something so challenging as loving a woman and giving himself to her. Jill finally couldn't take it anymore and broke up with Jack. Now he is heartbroken. He is back in that place that brought him into therapy initially, forlorn and lonely, but strangely liberated and free. Jack feels happier now. At least for the moment.

Jack reminds me of another young man I saw in therapy years ago. Paul came into analysis complaining that he was unable to sustain relationships with women. For the past several years his dating ritual followed a familiar pattern. He would find himself attracted to a woman, take her out for a date, wine and dine her, go back to his place and have sex with her. In the morning after they said good-bye, he would promise to call, but that was a lie. Paul had no intention of ever doing that. By the time she left that morning he had lost all interest in her and never wanted to see her again. Paul said that he had never had sex with a woman on more than one occasion. He was puzzled by this because he told himself that all he wanted was to settle down with someone and make a life together. He wondered if he had simply not met the woman who would prove the exception, who would compel him to commit to her. Paul happened to work as a tech consultant and, because he wasn't steadily employed by the firms he worked for, they paid him an enormous sum of money on a contractual arrangement. His jobs typically lasted six months, a year at the most, and then he was off to another job in another part of the country. He had lived in about a dozen states over the past six or seven years.

I asked Paul how he could expect to commit to a relationship if he moved around so frequently. He acknowledged this was a problem, but that the money he was making was too lucrative to give up. During the six months that I saw Paul in analysis he dated thirty or forty women, each once, never to be seen again. Each time he hoped this would be the exception. It never was. So what was the deal with Paul? Paul suffered from what Otto Rank described as a Don Juan Complex (1975). Love-them-and-leave-them Paul. Paul's unconscious goal was to seduce a woman, then kill her, by "cutting off" their relationship with no warning or apology, never to be heard from again. In the immortal words of Tony Soprano from the TV show *The Sopranos*, she was dead to him. The goal was not to enjoy the sex, or even to seek love, but to serially kill one woman after the other, symbolically. By killing her off he also killed his desire for her, thereby ridding himself of it before it got control of him. Paul sought complete satisfaction in what he presumed "true love" would feel like. In fact, his satisfaction was perfect already. That was the problem. He was repeatedly committing the perfect crime. By it he killed his desire, but it was a murder no one could prosecute him for. Paul didn't know it, but he was succeeding brilliantly in the stratagem he had unconsciously orchestrated to slay women, the consummate lady-killer, and by these acts, keep his troublesome desire in check.

Paul told himself he sought the perfect love, but what he really wanted was the perfect death. One of the more interesting facets of Paul's mental state was the calm he affected in recounting his episodes to me, the complete lack of empathy or anxiety, or guilt. Anxiety was not what brought Paul into analysis, but boredom. Because his desire had never come alive, there was nothing in any of his conquests at stake, nothing to be anxious about, nothing to lose. He was a citizen of the walking dead, a zombie disguised as the handsome suitor he affected. This is what happens when nothing is on the line. We feel nothing. Even Paul's analysis was never at stake. Six months into his treatment Paul's contract ended and he took a new job in another state, never to be heard from again. He killed me too.

What both Jack and Paul share in common is the relationship with their respective desire, a desire that has been savaged by the pain and heartbreak each associates with it. Once we get to know the person we are treating, we eventually come to know something about why this is so. For reasons that are not always clear to us, their acute sensitivity to the disappointments and frustrations they suffer prompted them to put their desire in check. They resorted to treating it like an enemy instead of the foundation of who they are. Plato says somewhere that love is the wish to perpetuate one's desire. In other words, to truly love someone is to want to keep your desire for that person alive, in perpetuity. Without love as its goal, desires are fleeting, here today, gone tomorrow. What both Jack and Paul couldn't seem to accomplish was to let their desire have its way with them, to give themselves to it, to let it be. This would require embracing the pain that desiring occasions, and the vulnerability that goes with it. This is the price we pay for desire. We can't get it for nothing.

I have tried to show in this chapter something about the elusiveness of desire and its role in our so-called psychopathology. I know I have raised more questions than I answered, but I hope to address some of them in the chapters to follow, especially Chapter Seven, which addresses the relation between love and madness. I now want to turn our attention to the role of emotions in the context of sanity and madness, and the parameters of what we customarily designate "emotional distress."

Notes

1 Some might say that Freud was gullible to believe everything his patients told him, but taking people at their word was probably his most effective virtue and the quality that made his patients fall in love with him. Freud was an honest man and probably gave others more credit than they deserved, but where would psychoanalysis be if we didn't suspend such judgment with our patients?

2 This is a matter of equal indifference if my parents happen to be gay.

3 Freud suggested that in cases where the single parent effectively treats the child as though he or she replaced the departed father (or mother), that the child would suffer from the opposite complex, that of an Oedipal victor. This child would have circumvented the fateful and near universal trauma of Oedipal loser and would instead find it even more impossible to cope with rejection.

4 Neurotic phenomena, *per se*, are outside the realm of experience because they are always unconscious. In order to experience anything we must be cognizant, which means to be aware, of the issue in question.

5 Freud's most famous case of obsessional neurosis, the Rat Man, centered around the Rat Man's complaint that he was anxious that he would bring harm to his father – who had been dead for several years.

6 Freud believed that psychoanalysis may secondarily affect sexual repression, but the primary aim was to increase our capacity for love and work. In fact, psychoanalysis does very little to improve our sex lives, other than to think about it.

7 The title is simply, *Freud* (2015).

8 Freud also admonishes that the typical neurotic, given the ambivalence that lies at the heart of his symptoms, is actually incapable of loving another person in a manner that isn't for the most part dominated by guilt or narcissism, and that it will take time, only after the neurosis has receded, before that patient will be capable of genuinely loving the analyst, and others. Patients who remain in therapy for the requisite amount of time (which varies with each person) already exhibit a capacity for such love, otherwise they would abandon the treatment at the first sign of frustration, or simply dig in and resist the analysis for its own quota of perverse reward.

9 See my "Deception, Mystification, Trauma: Laing and Freud" (1996), for more on similarities and dissimilarities between Laing's and Freud's respective views on the relationship between love and psychopathology.

10 Greene labeled his serious works of fiction novels, while reserving the marque "entertainments" for the lighter fare that was intended, not for edification, but escape.

11 Inspired by Plato's dialogue, *The Protagoras*, Freud accepted that the fundamental goal of life is the pursuit of happiness, which served as the model of the Pleasure Principle. This remained the case even after he abandoned the Pleasure Principle for his dual instinct theory, comprised of *Eros* and *Thanatos*. For more on how this principle guided Freud's conception of neurosis, see my essay, "Happiness and Chance: A Reappraisal of the Psychoanalytic Conception of Suffering" (2004).

12 Freud initially referred to psychosis as "narcissistic neuroses" and depression as "melancholia." Earlier terms employed for schizophrenia include *dementia praecox* and *paraphrenia*.

References

Freud, S. (1953–1973) *The standard edition of the complete psychological works of Sigmund Freud.* 24 volumes. Edited and translated by J. Strachey. London: Hogarth Press. (Referred to in subsequent references as *Standard Edition.*)

Freud, S. (1900) *The interpretation of dreams* (two volumes). *Standard Edition*, 4:1–338, and 5:339–723. London: Hogarth Press, 1958.

Freud, S. (1901) *The psychopathology of everyday life. Standard Edition*, 6:1–279. London: Hogarth Press, 1960.

Freud, S. (1912) The dynamics of transference. *Standard Edition*, 12:97–108. London: Hogarth Press, 1958.

Freud, S. (1914) *On the history of the psychoanalytic movement. Standard Edition*, 14:3–66. London: Hogarth Press, 1957.

Freud, S. (1915) Observations on transference-love (Further recommendations on the technique of psycho-analysis III). *Standard Edition*, 12:157–171. London: Hogarth Press, 1958.

Freud, S. (1937) Analysis terminable and interminable. *Standard Edition*, 23:209–253. London: Hogarth Press, 1964.

Haley, J. (1963) *Strategies of psychotherapy.* Bethel, CT and Bancyfelin, Wales: Crown House Publishing.

Hume, D. (2000) *A treatise on human nature.* Oxford and New York: Oxford University Press.

Lear, J. (2015) *Freud.* (2nd ed.). London and New York: Routledge.

Marino, G. (2013) *The quotable Kierkegaard.* Princeton, NJ: Princeton University Press.

Moore, G. E. (2004) *Principia ethica (Principles of ethics).* New York: Dover Publications.

Plato. (1961) *Plato: The collected dialogues.* Translated by W. K. C. Guthrie and edited by E. Hamilton and H. Cairns. (Bollingen Series, 71, pp. 308–352). Princeton, NJ: Princeton University Press.

Rank, O. (1975) *The Don Juan legend.* Translated by David G. Winter. Princeton, NJ: Princeton University Press.

Thompson, M. Guy (1996) Deception, mystification, trauma: Laing and Freud. *The Psychoanalytic Review*, Vol. 83, No. 6:827–847.

Thompson, M. Guy (2004) Happiness and chance: A reappraisal of the psychoanalytic conception of suffering. *Psychoanalytic Psychology*, Vol. 21, No. 1:134–153.

3

RESSENTIMENT

Toward an existential paradigm
for symptom formation

What are emotions? It is perhaps both startling and amusing that after millennia of searching for an answer to this question, we really can't say. There is no shortage of theories that endeavor to tackle this problem, yet no consensus on a definition. For some, emotions are distinct from cognition and judgment, while for others our feelings are essential to our decision-making and determine our judgments. It cannot easily be refuted that emotions tell us things that our cognitions often miss. Moreover, emotions are often the driving force behind our motivations, whether of a positive or negative nature. Then there is the physiology of emotions, and their psychology. Is it one or the other, or both? And what about the relationship between emotion and desire? Are emotions derivative of desire, or are they determinant? Or both, or neither? Whatever they are, there is little dispute that we would be not be human without them.

The term emotion dates back to 1579 when it was adapted from the French *émouvoir*, meaning "to stir up." It was first introduced to academic circles to replace a similar term, passion. Though the two terms have often been used interchangeably, passion is typically employed when referring to sexual feelings. There is also the problem with their respective etymology. Passion derives from the Latin *pati*, meaning to suffer or endure. One can see why the term passion began to take on different connotations than when simply feeling this or that. The French *émouvoir* appeared to solve the problem. Like the term feeling, with which emotion is used synonymously, an emotion is of brief duration, whereas "moods" last longer. The more recent "affect," adopted by psychoanalysis, encompasses all three. (We will have more to say about passion in Chapter Eight.)

Psychoanalysis has come a long way in explaining how human behavior is not orchestrated by random events, because actions always have a motive, an intention, a specific end, even if we cannot determine what the end is. Psychoanalysts were the first to emphasize the *significance* of psychic phenomena, that this seemingly innocent thought or act or emotion usually stands for something else. The child who steals from his mother's purse is only trying to reclaim the mother's love. A girl who faints at the sight of parsley can't bring herself to face the memory of a painful childhood incident when she was forced to eat vegetables with her meal. Yet, as often as not, the psychoanalytic interpretation, if only surreptitiously, tends to privilege causal antecedents masquerading as interpretations in order to explain pathogenic behavior. History plays an important role in our lives, and this is just as true for persons suffering from emotional disturbance. This is why I can project onto all women the quality of withholding because my mother was too depressed to comfort my needs. I cannot bring myself to hate my mother, but I cannot rid myself of the hurt that eats away at my soul. Every time I am attracted to a woman, I find myself consumed with ambivalence, fear, consternation. The feelings I experience in these situations not only color my understanding of reality; to a significant degree, they determine *who I am*.

I can remember how, as a young boy living in Cuba, I used to escape home to see American movies at every opportunity. Though I grew up in Cuba, America was still home to me because, after all, I was an American. American movies took me to the world I came from, but that I did not live in, except when enjoying an American movie. I especially loved *film noir* and can vividly recall the first time I saw one of the films made from a Dashiell Hammett novel, *The Maltese Falcon*. I immediately identified with the protagonist, Sam Spade, the private eye who Hammett created in the 1930s to personify the incorrigible iconoclast caught between two corrupt forces on the mean streets of San Francisco, the cops and the robbers, neither of whom were worthy of the public trust. Sam Spade was the one person who could be trusted, and it was that trust you were purchasing if you hired him to work for you. It was only much later that I realized psychoanalysis served the same ambition.

Hammett also helped invent the concept of the *femme fatale*, the woman who was at the center of each story, a damsel in distress who was beautiful, alluring, sexy, and in desperate straits. Only a white knight like Spade possessed the requisite *gravitas* to save her. I don't think it's an exaggeration to suggest that Spade was something of a superman, both a reincarnation of Oedipus and a modern version of Nietzsche's *Übermensch,* who alone was capable of slaying the dragon that threatened the hapless dame. True to every *femme fatale* in the *film noir* canon, this woman lures you into her web, fetching and irresistible, suggesting eternal bliss if only you come to her rescue. Naturally, only a fool would trust her. Yet Spade was so incorruptible, yet vulnerable to her talents, that he was inexorably drawn to her web, little suspecting her principal motive was to subdue him.

This is the theme of many such *noirish* films of the post–World War Two era, when America was climbing back from the brink of what could have easily been the destruction of the world as it then existed. The *femme fatale* represents something that every heterosexual man can relate to, the woman of his dreams, there for the taking; all he need do is slay the dragon and claim the prize that is his. I don't have to tell you that the story never ends that way. Typically, the damsel, once the problem is solved, rids herself of the hero with a dismissive shrug of her shoulders, not unlike the termination of a successful analysis. What made Spade a superhero was how he was always one step ahead, the escape artist orchestrating his exit just before she springs her trap. Spade was the exception. In the real world there are no superheroes, just we mortals taking it one day at a time, always one step *behind* the action. I think I was fascinated with this mythic tale of seduction, conquest, and destruction because it symbolized for me the feelings that every young boy experiences in relation to his mother, the *femme fatale* who loves him completely until it is time to let go. This is the moment he discovers that the bliss he anticipates is an illusion. I don't know if this phenomenon is as universal as Freud envisioned; I can only say that it was true for me.

Freud's term for that traumatic moment every child is supposed to succumb to is the Oedipus complex. What makes this complex so compelling is the sense of treachery and betrayal that occasion it, feelings that every boy must eventually, somehow, come to terms with. This drama is never worked out directly with one's mother (or in the case of a girl, with the father), but with the other women he loves by proxy, who wield a power no boy can resist nor surmount. Anyone who has had his or her heart broken knows what I'm talking about. And who hasn't? I am alluding to the anguish of unrequited love, the incidence that Freud believed is the most grievous trauma any human being is capable of suffering. But why is this experience so traumatic, and why so irreparable? What is the secret of our capacity to give ourselves, heart and soul, to another, knowing in the back of our minds that the path to happiness may just as easily be the road to perdition? Moreover, why has it compromised our ability to love again, as openly and eagerly as, with the innocence of a child, we loved our mothers and fathers? What is this grip that our emotions have over us, and what role do they play in our quest for happiness, or ruin?

Emotions may be pleasing or painful. The pleasurable kind we don't question until they become self-destructive, but even then we rarely oppose them. The painful variety are more invasive and, so, problematic. Because they elicit distress, we can bear them for only so long until, like Jason clutching the Medusa, we divert our eyes, and blind our experience of them with magic, in the form of our most reliable weapon, the "defense mechanism." Our emotional life, always a mystery to us, inhabits a spectrum between desire and anxiety, each feeding the other. If we are creatures of desire, and anxiety is the price we must pay for them, then emotions must be entwined somewhere inside those desires in principle. Emotions are not just barometers that inform me when my desires are satisfied or thwarted. They also possess an intelligence that aims to make my life as agreeable as possible, whether I want them to or not. But that isn't all. My emotions shelter me from realities that are too harsh for me to stomach. Sartre suggested that emotions are our way of magically transforming a situation that we get stuck in, like a fly on a sticky-mat, that we can neither accommodate nor escape. In a manner reminiscent of Freud's "magical choice" scenario (and a precursor to symptom formation), the emotion provides a magical way of escaping situations that may otherwise drive me crazy:

> When the paths before us become too difficult, or when we cannot see our way, we can no longer put up with such an exacting and difficult world. All ways are

barred and nevertheless we must act. So then we try to change the world; that is, to live it as though the relation between things and their potentialities were not governed by deterministic processes, but by magic.

(1962, p. 63)

The woman who faints at the sight of her attacker does so, not because it reminds her of some previous event, but because it removes her, albeit magically, from the present situation. She no longer has to face the immediate danger she is in. But this isn't to say she willfully faints with self-aware deliberation. She is seized by the situation, a situation that makes demands on her and with which she is unable to cope. Or rather, her manner of coping is so ingenious that it is unrecognizable as such to the unwary observer. The unlikelihood of finding a solution to the problem she faces demands that she invent a solution instead. If she can't take flight in reality, she can do so emotionally, as if magically. Yet an emotional response isn't just a substitute for other kinds of action, other ways of coping, because, says Sartre, it isn't effectual. It doesn't act on the world but merely changes my perception of it. In other words, "emotional behavior seeks by itself, and without modifying the structure of the object, to confer another quality upon it, a lesser existence or a lesser presence" (p. 65).

Moreover, emotions aren't merely a magical way of fleeing from a dangerous situation. On a more basic level, the emotion is a structure of desire. It may be a way of enhancing a desire I enjoy, or a way of coping with a desire that is too risky. The person in danger wants to be somewhere else, so the fainting magically fulfills the wish to disappear. Similarly, if I want something I cannot have, my emotions can help remove the desire itself, conveniently removing what may have been a bitter disappointment. Sartre invokes the sour grapes analogy as a common rationalization for this strategy:

> I lift my hand to pluck a bunch of grapes. I cannot do so; they are beyond my reach; so I shrug my shoulders, muttering: "they are too green" and go on my way . . . . [T]his little comedy that I play under the grapes, thereby conferring this quality of being "too green" upon them, serves as a substitute for the action I cannot complete . . . I confer the required quality upon the grapes magically.
>
> *(1962, pp. 65–66)*

Sartre's purpose in this early phenomenological study, *Sketch for a Theory of the Emotions* (1962), was to show why behaviorism is incapable of explaining the phenomenon of emotions, because behaviorism is stuck in a cause-and-effect universe that explains mechanical engineering superbly, but cannot account for the *intentional structure* of human folly or sagacity. Psychoanalysis goes further because it is sensitive to human agency, but then ascribes our motivations to "unconscious" aims that, if we aren't careful, may be just as causal as behaviorism. At its best, what is often lacking in the psychoanalytic explanation is the personal dimension to motives, because unconscious motives are not, strictly speaking, personal, so we can't assume responsibility for them. There is no better example of an existential approach to our understanding of emotions than Nietzsche's conception of *ressentiment*, outlined in his twin works on ethics, *Beyond Good and Evil* (2002) and *On the Genealogy of Morality* (1994). No one can say why Nietzsche opted for the French term, *ressentiment*, when he wrote in German, but one of the problems he probably faced was the lack of a precise equivalent in German for the French *ressentiment* (or the English resentment). Nietzsche could have chosen the German *Groll*, meaning "rancor" instead, a close enough equivalent to serve his purpose. But like Kierkegaard before him, who also employed the French *ressentiment* instead of its Danish equivalent, he opted not to. A possible factor is that other nineteenth-century Germans (and apparently, the Danish) typically employed the French *ressentiment*, following the Enlightenment vogue for all things French. But Nietzsche chose to employ the word, not in its ordinary, everyday usage, but as a technical term that conveyed a particular, unconventional meaning, so the French variation probably served this purpose well. There's no denying it gets our attention. For my purposes in this chapter, however, I render the French *ressentiment* as simply resentment, whether in the everyday sense of the word or the more nuanced meaning to which Nietzsche, and later Scheler, ascribed it.

Before turning our attention to the role that *ressentiment*, or resentment, plays in neurotic and other symptom formation, I should say a brief word about the treatment of emotions in the psychoanalytic literature. For example, though Freud positioned anxiety as the catalyst for every defense mechanism, he conceived his notion of neurosis in juxtaposition to the experience of jealousy, which typically triggers anxious worry or rage. The so-called Oedipus complex is comprised of a triangle: mother, father, and child. The child falls in love with the parent of the opposite sex (*positive* Oedipus complex) or alternately with the parent of the same gender (*negative* Oedipus complex), and alternates between the two before settling on the most accommodating option. In either case, the consequence is the same. The child becomes jealous of the favored parent's relationship with the other parent, who then becomes the child's rival. Freud believed that children aren't capable of jealousy until three or four years of age, give or take, and its intensity increases until the age of five or so, when the child resorts to repressing his or her desire for the "libidinally cathected" parent. It is at this juncture that the Oedipus complex is formally inaugurated. In Freud's formulation, jealousy is a profoundly unbearable emotion, epitomizing the singular traumatic event that serves as the source for virtually all our pathology. Jealousy is so painful that children have no way of surmounting it, other than to repress any desire that reminds them of it. This in turn serves to remove the basis for their jealousy, so it goes into hiding. While this explanation is farfetched to some, the incidence of jealousy in our daily affairs can hardly be overestimated. It wields such power that the problem of jealousy is probably the reason marriage was invented in the first place. Yet, no matter how faithful we (or our partners) aspire to be, once we are wedded jealousy obstinately rears its head. Because it elicits anxiety, we contrive all sorts of ways to avoid it. But even when it isn't pronounced, jealousy haunts our waking and sleeping hours alike. It seems that the only decisive cure for jealousy or, even better, to avoid it outright is to love no one.

Melanie Klein (1928) disagreed with Freud's thesis and chose instead to situate the Oedipal drama earlier, beginning at the age of six months and culminating around end of the first year, at the culmination of the *depressive position*. Klein was more interested in the child's earlier, more primitive relationship with the mother than she was with the relatively mature development that Freud associated with the Oedipal drama, and she was more interested in psychosis than neurosis. This explains why she was so taken with the period from birth to six months, what Klein christened the *paranoid-schizoid position*, the phase of development during which the child, according to Klein, is psychotic. Because her focus favors the mother–child relation over the triangular Oedipal constellation, Klein focused most of her attention on the far more nascent emotion, envy. It is one of those anomalies that the distinction between envy and jealousy is confusing for most, which says something about how little thought we give these emotions. It is lost on many, for example, that jealousy always involves three people whereas envy comprises only two. With jealousy, I wish to possess the person I covet and claim that person for myself, to be one with them. When an interloper enters the scene I instinctively want to protect what is mine and vanquish the intruder. This is what so poignantly personifies the pain of jealousy: *I have something that is encroached upon by someone who threatens to steal it.* This is why Freud found this emotion so compelling. The experience of jealousy and my intolerance of it speaks volumes about my most basic insecurities, as well as the fragile nature of love relationships, whether between sexual or marital partners, or friends. It comes into play with anyone I love.

The reason envy is more primitive than jealousy is because it involves two people instead of three, which Klein situates at the earliest phase of development. I experience envy when another person has something I want for myself. I don't want something *similar to* the thing, persona, or quality the other person has: *I want to dispossess that person of what I covet and make it my own.* This is why envy may be far more destructive than jealousy, though jealousy is no walk in the park. After all, jealousy is the most common motive for murder and, according to Freud, may lead to psychosis due to its proximity to paranoia. Say a friend of mine has purchased a beautiful home in a desirable part of town. I fall in love with the home and wish it were mine to have. If I am a healthy person I will work harder to afford such a place and purchase a similar house for myself. Or, if this is not feasible because, realistically, I will never earn enough money to buy such a home, I can accept that such a domicile is beyond my means, so I make do with what I can afford, but without acrimony or rancor. If neither of these options is available to me and I continue to covet my friend's home, my wish to possess it becomes envious. For a moment, this solves the problem, because envy offers a way to possess it. But then I begin to resent my friend for having something that should belong to me *instead*. I silently blame my friend for his bounty and entertain malevolent thoughts about his person. He didn't earn what he enjoys, I say to myself, so he doesn't deserve it. His fortune came too easily, so I imagine, and a sense of injustice overwhelms my constellation of feelings, making my envy grow even stronger. Though he remains my friend and I love him, in the moment of envy I hate him and resent the injustice that he has something that should, by rights, be mine.

This is the picture of envy that all of us are familiar with. It is a part and parcel of our human condition and virtually everyone struggles with it, no matter how enlightened or morally advanced. Klein believed that even a young infant is consumed with such feelings, an infant that cannot even know what envy is because it has yet to acquire a language with which to conceptualize it. This is the one piece of Klein's theory that even her most ardent followers have a problem swallowing. Freud believed that infants are incapable of such complex feelings, the reason he situated the Oedipal drama at a later stage of development (following the acquisition of language). Klein sought an explanation for why infants express hostility to their mothers and why they become so embroiled in love and hate toward the same person or object (to be precise, part-object) that they may even reject the mother. We needn't go into Klein's theory of child development in order to appreciate what she understood by envy and why it became important to her, so I will turn our attention to the crux of the issue, instead. Klein is saying that every baby's feelings of envy are so strong that the infant turns away from the mother, because the child is overwhelmed by the mother's (or rather, the mother's breast's) *goodness*, which the baby feels that it itself lacks. The contrast between the two, the bounty of the mother's goodness against the impoverishment of the baby, elicits insurmountable anxiety.

But why would envy help the baby overcome the sense of disparity between itself and the mother? By invoking envy, in the same manner that we invoke defense mechanisms, the baby turns the tables and *makes the mother's goodness its own*. Now the baby, in its newfound omnipotence, no longer needs what the mother has, because the baby just robbed her of it and rendered the mother's goodness its own. As Sartre might have put it, the infant sets out to accomplish *magically* what it cannot marshal in reality. This short-lived solution, however, is hardly viable. Because the mother is left with no goodness to offer, the baby has no use for her, and pushes the mother away. This is exactly the same attitude, and the same ploy, argues Klein, that personifies the mind of the psychotic. One needn't be diagnosed psychotic, however, for this explanation to be pertinent. Because all of us are imbued with unconscious psychotic elements in our minds, anyone is capable of experiencing envy toward others, especially those with whom we fashion our most cherished relationships. In the context of therapy, for example, Klein believed that some patients may become so envious that they won't allow the therapist the satisfaction of having helped them. In order to deprive the therapist of feeling successful, such patients "rob" the goodness the therapist has to offer and takes that goodness for themselves, by not deriving any benefit from the therapist's best efforts. The patient consequently fails to improve and the treatment ends in failure. This is the kind of patient, Klein conjectured, that cannot be helped. It doesn't matter how effective or skillful or devoted the therapist may be. The envious patient, no matter how long the treatment persists, will never improve. The so-called victory of diminishing the therapist makes that patient feel better than any improvement in his own situation the patient could possibly obtain, so says Klein. This is how envy works: it is spiteful to the core.

Lacan (2006) wasn't especially interested in emotions and strangely ignored them, so there is very little he has to say about them that is relevant for this discussion. For Lacan, it is neither envy nor jealousy that is the issue, but paranoia, stripped of its emotional baggage. The type of paranoia Lacan is concerned with isn't the kind that emanates from pathological jealousy, as with Freud, or envy as with Klein. It is a paranoia that emanates from the split between the self that is reflected back to me via mirroring, and the self that exists prior to mirrored identifications. Lacan offers not a whiff of the emotional devastation that we often associate with paranoia. Instead, he reduces it to a desire for an abstract form of "recognition" that assumes a life all its own, unmindful of what the child happens to *feel* about it. For Lacan, what matters is the dynamic between *desire and anxiety*. Any emotions that derive from them are off the table.

I offer this prelude to my critique of *ressentiment* in order to show how closely related these three emotions are, and how jealousy and envy each relies on resentment to fuel their crippling power. I will also explore why neither jealousy nor envy explains the neurotic and psychotic conditions that Freud and Klein respectively describe. Now, what *is* resentment?

In order to appreciate how Nietzsche understood the nature of resentment and the power it holds over us, we will first review what he meant by slave morality, first introduced in *Beyond Good and Evil*. Nietzsche believed that there have been two types of morality throughout history, *master* morality and *slave* morality. Whereas master morality privileges strength, vitality, and nobility, slave morality privileges the opposite: sympathy, kindness, humility, and other sentiments of a ruthful nature. Master morality is autocratic whereas slave morality is democratic. Master morality assesses good and bad *consequences* whereas slave morality focuses on good or bad *intentions*. Nietzsche rejected the idea that the good should be equated with what is helpful and the bad equated with what is unhelpful, even harmful. Nietzsche goes on to argue that the very concept of morality is dubious. It goes without saying that Nietzsche was not a liberal. He does not regard the person as inviolable nor human life as sacrosanct. Nor does he believe that all human beings should be treated equally. Whereas liberalism privileges peaceful coexistence, Nietzsche emphasizes human greatness. Nietzsche's *Will to Power* is about realizing one's potentialities for self-actualization, to be the best person one can be. A lot of this sentiment goes back to Nietzsche's critique of Greek culture. He thought the Athenians, for example, were far too mesmerized with the role of rationality in our lives and favored the Spartans, who were devoted to accruing power through military conquest. It was the Spartans, Nietzsche reminds us, who won the Peloponnesian War against Athens, subsequently changing the course of Greek history.

In prehistory, Nietzsche suggests that actions were originally judged by how effective they were, not whether the motives for one's actions were good or bad. By today's standards there would have been no morality, as such, in the prehistoric era, though one may have engaged in moral interpretations of one's actions *after* the fact. The good were strong-willed whereas the bad were weak and cowardly, so the latter could not be counted on when things got tough and one's fate was on the line. This set the stage for subsequent civilizations, which based their initial societies on master morality. Other virtues that characterize this type of morality include courage, truthfulness, trust, and open-mindedness, so master morality wasn't based exclusively on brute strength but revolved around the ability to accomplish one's ambitions as decisively and impeccably as possible. Master morality is the recognition that the individual is the measure of all things, not God or public opinion. We may surmise how some of these sentiments from Nietzsche's philosophy inspired elements of the existential perspective, as well as his thoughts about spirituality.

Nietzsche argued that slave morality doesn't really invent new values but counters the values already in place, previously initiated by the master. In effect, the slave moralist *resents* the autocratic values of the master class and seeks compensation from them. This is where intentions become the favored measure of morality over the more consequential standard of the master. Master morality emanates from the strong whereas slave morality emanates from the not so strong. Because slave morality perceives the master as oppressing the less fortunate, it tends to villainize its oppressors. This is what leads Nietzsche to accuse slave morality of *inverting* values by identifying the strong as bad and the weak as good. The slave doesn't accomplish his or her mission directly through strength, power, or aggression, but indirectly by resorting to subversive activities that aim to enslave the master. The good becomes what is best for the community *as a whole*, not for the privileged master class, who are always a minority. Biblical principles of turning the other cheek and the like are the consequence of universalizing the plight of the slave and convincing the master class that slavery is inherently "bad."

Nietzsche blames the Judeo-Christian tradition for inaugurating slave morality, contending that ancient Greek and Roman cultures were grounded in master morality. Greek culture reached its zenith with the conquests of Alexander and Caesar, leaving behind legacies that changed the world. Notwithstanding his preference of Spartan over Athenian city-states, Nietzsche saw the Homeric hero that inaugurated Greek culture as embodying strong-willed men of extraordinary power, no better illustrated than in Homer's two classics, *The Iliad* and *The Odyssey*. In *The Iliad*, for example, Homer crystallized the idea that "men of nobility" were wise and courageous leaders ready to die for a cause that bound them together in common cause. Though Jewish religion introduced slave morality, it was the Christians, whom Nietzsche loathed, who defeated master morality when the Roman Empire was Christianized. Nietzsche concluded that the struggle within cultures has always been between the Roman and Judean sensibilities, between the strong and the weaker. In modern times, Nietzsche remarks that the hegemony of Christian morality gave way to contemporary notions of democracy, which propound that all humans are equal. It seemed patently obvious to Nietzsche that humans are not equal. The weak are envious of the strong and plot to displace them in society, inverting their respective stations in the ensuing power struggle. The result, says Nietzsche, is that democracy has made us all slaves, via the perpetual bidding war of political correctness that has emasculated those societies that have adopted democratic principles. Nietzsche was perhaps insufficiently prescient to foresee that even in democratic institutions the powerful usually prevail over the less powerful, the rich over the poor, as demonstrated in every boardroom in the world. The human spirit is even more corrupt than Nietzsche imagined, but his point is well taken. Power is often accrued through indirect means by those who utilize schemes that are more clever than the more powerful competition. But in pointing this out Nietzsche wasn't suggesting we should simply rid ourselves of slave morality and resurrect the morality of the master (as though history could ever be reversed). Akin to his complaint that the Apollonian trend in Greek culture's dominance over the Dionysian generated an imbalance, Nietzsche believed we now favor the slave mentality excessively. What we need is to correct the imbalance we have created between the slave and master classes and treat them equally. Due to this imbalance, the world order (and Western culture especially) is epitomized by a seething resentment toward others, thereby losing our dignity while suppressing our desire.[1]

What does this tell us about Nietzsche's conception of resentment when applied to a more personal idiom? How has it affected us in our day-to-day activities and interactions with others, and how has it impacted our psychology? Similar to envy, resentment is aimed outside oneself toward others. Unlike envy, resentment is exacerbated by an intense sense of injustice that has been perpetrated by someone more powerful or wealthy, or more beautiful than me, so I harbor a wish for revenge against the responsible culprit. The resentful person is always in an impotent position, and so lacks the power to achieve his or her aims. This doesn't mean that powerful people are incapable of resentment, but they are less likely to dwell on it to the same degree. The resentful person initially sees himself as a failure, but when this self-perception becomes intolerable he inverts his failure into a posture of moral superiority, seeing himself as better than the people who have what he covets. The key to the resentful attitude is not that it merely inverts conventional values, but that in so doing succeeds in *erasing the desire that prompted the resentment in the first place.* If I cannot have what I want, then the next best thing is to convince myself that I never wanted it in the first place. Sour grapes in its essence.

Because resentment is always associated with vulnerability, the possibility of exposure prevents the resentful person from fighting back openly. To do so would risk retaliation, rejection, humiliation, or worse. The self would not be simply diminished by this turn of events, but annihilated. So one's vengeance must be secretive and measured, subversive, invisible, in order to ensure that the enemy will never suspect one's actual motives. The resentful person would make a perfect spy. Because resentment is always associated with a thwarted desire, it is compounded by a lust for power that the resentful person either never had or lost, as in the Oedipal drama. Though similar to self-pity, resentment is not the same. What self-pity lacks is the sense of blame that fuels the seething insistence of resentment, a sense of outrage and injustice that is not merely a quest for revenge, but an all-encompassing and obsessive mission in life, no matter how long it may take to achieve it. We need to also distinguish resentment from spite, which typically lasts a briefer duration. Nietzsche believed that spite can sometimes be even more self-destructive than resentment because the resentful person will stop at nothing to get his way, patiently, strategically, ruthlessly, whereas the spiteful person is prepared to sacrifice *himself* if that is what it will take to punish his oppressor. Suicide is the spiteful person's weapon of last resort, but also the most powerful. This is what Hegel was getting at with the master–slave dialectic, wherein the slave has the real power over his master, brilliantly demonstrated in Joseph Losey's film, *The Servant.*

Nietzsche indicted Christianity as the most resentful of all religions, because despite its protestations of weakness and humility, it has become the most powerful religion on earth, and until recently, the wealthiest.[2] This is one of the reasons why Nietzsche believed those imbued with resentment eventually hold the real power in the ever-present dialectic between master and slave morality. Resentment is dangerous because the person so imbued slyly goes about getting his way while those less resentful are encouraged to bear the guilt of their success and even wonder if they genuinely deserve it. Nietzsche's argument that resentment insinuated its way into every fabric of modern society, including every religion, was a generalization that Max Scheler didn't share. An erstwhile Catholic, he made liberal use of Nietzsche's concept in his book, *Ressentiment* (1972), but didn't view Christianity as an inherently resentful religion. Nor did Scheler share Nietzsche's distaste for liberal politics and values. Despite their differences, Scheler was keenly interested in the deeper psychological aspects of resentment and its role in psychopathology.

Scheler's critique of resentment, though indebted to Nietzsche, was also indebted to Freud's Oedipus complex, which helped inform Scheler's perspective immensely. Scheler perceives resentment as a structure of behavior that is beyond one's ability to consciously grasp, yet difficult to resist. Scheler believes that resentment does not so much diminish desire as redirects it, arguing that the most common precursor to resentment is the hatred I feel toward any person I believe has deprived me of what I am after, the thing I most basically desire. Because hate is so pivotal to Scheler's conception of resentment, anger plays a crucial role in this thesis. If anger or hatred is overtly *expressed* and acknowledged, then resentment is less likely to develop. This is because feeling hatred toward the other is never sufficient for developing genuine resentment. Rather it is the act of *internalizing* one's hate toward the other, argues Scheler, that is responsible for planting the seeds of the resentful character, the moment when one is transformed into a *l'homme du ressentiment.* If I am free to express my hate and act on it, there would be no reason to feel resentful. For Scheler, every resentful person is secretly angry with someone, but dares not let that person know for fear of retribution. This results in a kind of lying in wait and subterfuge that epitomizes slave morality. On the surface one may be compliant, polite, self-effacing, coping with a well-developed false self. But inside, this person is locked in a cloistered turmoil that consumes every waking moment. Unlike ordinary anger, which passes with time, resentful hatred exists for its own sake, detached from the original injury that inspired it until it becomes a basic attitude toward life itself. Now imbued with a loathing toward everyone and everything that was once desirable, including love, pleasure, beauty, friendship, and success, resentment desires nothing because *its aim is to destroy everything desirable*, finally destroying desire itself. Its aim, in the end, is the death of desire.

This is why resentment is suicidal in a manner similar to Freud's conception of the *death drive*, which doesn't literally seek nonexistence but wishes instead to deaden any desire that elicits frustration. In its triumph, resentment accomplishes nothing, but then nothing is what resentment is after, so its victory is almost perfect. Whereas Nietzsche sees the resentful person as one who slyly turns the tables on the master to finally achieve victory for himself, Scheler perceives the resentful person as inept. This is because his victory over the master is a secretive one based on his contention that he is better, while unconsciously coveting what the master enjoys. This conflict, says Scheler, forms the basis of a specifically *pathological* edition of resentment, because we have no awareness of it.

Now we are in a position to understand the psychology of madness, embodied in the neurotic and psychotic. Because they are unable to obtain what they desire, they unconsciously rationalize their failure as evidence of their moral superiority, driven by the kind of guilt that Freud describes in his case studies of the Rat Man and Wolf Man, respectively.[3] According to Freud, guilt is the driving force of the neurotic's incapacity to live his or her desire, resulting in his moral superiority over those whose desires he deems less admirable, via reaction formation. His only consolation is the admiration he gives himself, via self-pity. Though Scheler acknowledges the importance of guilt, he is more interested in the role played by hate in the etiology of the resentful character. Coming from Scheler's more Christianized perspective, this makes some sense because hate is a sin in Christian theology, and guilt often serves as a vehicle for saving grace. Freud, an atheist, situates guilt at the fulcrum of the neurotic personality. This would be difficult to understand were it not for the resentment that lies underneath Freud's theory of neurotic symptom formation (which we reviewed in Chapter Two).

Briefly, Freud argues there that the child internalizes the moral prejudices of his parents, identifies with them, and then makes those prejudices his or her own. This internalized moral agency, the superego, becomes the basis of one's conscience, but it may also be the source of premonition that tells me it is wrong to have what I want, to be happy, to do as I please, so I suppress my basic instincts and strive instead to be a "good person," a well-developed false self. It isn't that difficult to recognize the similarity between Freud's superego and Nietzsche's slave morality, for either cannot help but breed the resentful conviction that others have what I am denied (Nietzsche) or deny myself (Freud). Specifically, it is my *internalized* parental prohibitions that deny me what I want, evolving into the source of the chronic ambivalence that epitomizes neurotic conflict. Freud couldn't seem to make up his mind as to whether anxiety or guilt plays the greater role in neurotic symptom formation. Either may result in a person who is too inhibited to fight for what he wants by opting instead to take the easy way out – though there is nothing easy about neurotic conflict. The problem with this easier way, whether we conceive it as anxiety-laden or guilt-ridden, is that it denies us what we most want from life. The "better" we are, morally speaking, the more we sacrifice our happiness for an abstract reward that never materializes. The respective steps that Freud and Scheler take in order to bring this picture into focus are not the same, but they complement each other. For Freud, either anxiety or self-punitive guilt may prompt me into repressing a desire that feels dangerous, resulting in neurotic symptoms that serve to displace the desired object. Resentment is only one of those symptoms. In Scheler, however, I repress not my desire but my *hate*, toward a parent, for example, in response to an injury. This injury, as with Freud, is likely the consequence of jealousy which, in turn, is transformed into a deep-seated, slow-burning resentment that inaugurates a resentful attitude toward life itself. Both theories lead to more or less the same destiny: a person whose relationship with his (or her) desire is so crippled he no longer knows what he desires, or even that he desires anything. In both explanations, the more alienated from desire I become, the more extreme the psychopathology.

The feeling of hatred that Scheler privileges is initially elicited by anger, but an anger that is more momentary and less seething than the hate it ultimately becomes. Moreover, anger isn't necessarily nor always a bad thing. There are times when it is perfectly appropriate to feel angry and act on it. The real issue is how prevalent the anger is, what we set out to do by it, and how impulsively we act on it. Perhaps the most complex of emotions, anger occupies a special place in our lives because it is probably the most commonly experienced emotion, and most potentially destructive. Suppressing this anger may be what Christianity had in mind. Whereas *expressed* anger doesn't usually prompt feelings of resentment, should it persist it invariably leads to hate, which, whether or not it is suppressed, will morph into the kind of resentment we have been reviewing. *For Scheler and Freud alike everything hinges on whether the desire or hatred is repressed or permitted expression.* But even consciously experienced anger may serve as both a source for and symptom of severe psychopathology. What happens after I become angry, and what prompts me to feel angry in the first place? Anger stems from frustration, when I cannot get what I want or if something I have is taken from me. As with resentment, anger is always a reaction to thwarted desire. For example, whenever Jane says no to Dick, Dick gets angry with her. Dick told me this happens frequently. As often as not, when Dick makes a sexual overture to Jane, Jane is not in the mood, doesn't feel well, or is simply too tense. She seems to suffer from some kind of virus or kindred ailment more often than not. I ask Dick why this makes him so angry. I can see why Jane's behavior may elicit frustration, but why get angry about it? Frustration doesn't necessarily lead to anger; it may lead to confusion, consternation, disappointment, humiliation, rejection, sadness, self-pity, even compassion, instead. Jane always has a good reason why she doesn't want to have sex, but she never says she just doesn't feel like it. She loves Dick and reassures him that her rejections have nothing to do with him. It's her. She has always had this problem, of not being in the mood for sex as often as her boyfriend would like, so the issue predates her relationship with Dick. It isn't Dick's fault; it isn't something he is or isn't doing.

Dick wonders if Jane is a hypochondriac, or some other kind of neurotic who represses her sexual interest by displacing it onto somatic symptoms. It isn't as though they never have sex. Dick says they have sex several times a week, but he would like to have sex more often than that, to basically have sex on demand. Is Dick, perhaps, oversexed, and using sex as a way of mitigating his anxiety, or a bad mood? And why doesn't Dick feel compassion for Jane when she is feeling too sick or stressed to enjoy sex? If he is correct in his assessment that she is neurotic, then she obviously can't help it, cannot make herself want to have sex when she clearly doesn't. Dick doesn't know why he lacks such compassion, why the frustration is immediately transformed into anger. After some time, Dick comes to the conclusion that Jane's rejection of his sexual advances reminds him of his mother, how she was never available to him emotionally. Throughout his childhood he was angry with her and felt closer to his father, who was more present. His mother was always somewhere else, preoccupied. Even when she was home she was absent, on an emotional, visceral level. He just couldn't seem to get the love from her that he needed, or wanted. No matter how much love or attention he got, it was never enough. Now Dick is with a girlfriend who is always busy, a medical intern, and no matter how much attention, and sex, she gives him, it is never enough. It makes Dick angry every time she rejects him. So who is Dick angry with? Jane or his mother? And why is he in a relationship with someone who isn't as available as he wants, or needs her to be? If she is that frustrating, that un-giving, that preoccupied, why doesn't Dick end his relationship with Jane and find a more compatible girlfriend? He says he doesn't want to do that because he loves Jane.

Dick's anger serves various functions. First, it mitigates his desire for Jane. Once he is angry with her he pulls away. He continues to demand sex, but he doesn't feel as helpless about it. He doesn't feel like a dick. All the same, he's behaving like one. Underneath the anger, Dick *resents* that Jane isn't more attentive, loving, and available on demand. But the resentment he feels isn't caused by his anger; *the anger is a consequence of his resentment.* This is what Scheler got backwards. Rather than feel impotent and unattractive, Dick likes the power his anger gives him. Despite his thwarted desire, he still feels in charge. Now he has Jane's attention. She stops what she is doing and feels obliged to deal with Dick's anger and talk him down. By virtue of his anger, Dick is also taking revenge on Jane. She hates it when he gets angry and feels persecuted by him, which is Dick's intention. Though Dick complains about these impasses with Jane that have become a pattern, he holds onto the anger and still wants what he cannot have: Jane whenever he wants her. Punishing her is the next best thing. It seems to me that Dick exemplifies a common situation that psychotherapists run into all the time with their patients: the incidence of anger, why it arises, how often, what prompts it, and the ways it leaks into the patient's transference with the therapist and even undermines the therapy.

Anger can be, and often is, a way of transforming a momentary feeling of impotence or helplessness into a moment of potency, power, and vengeance, from a posture of slave morality to one of master. If I can't get what I want by asking you, then I will force you to give it to me. I'm confident this isn't what Nietzsche had in mind with his concept of master morality. This is because anger, Dick's way of trying to get what he wants, is never a very effective way of getting what I want, because what I want is for the other person to *give* it to me, not merely relinquish it. I want the other person, as Dick wants Jane, to *want* to give me what I want, to identify my desire with her own, willingly, even eagerly. Forcing the other person to give me what I want never really works, not when love is the goal. This isn't a legal matter, a matter of righting the scales, but a personal one. My anger never gets me what I want when the thing that I want is affection, because anger has a way of destroying that, for both parties. This is why, in the moment of anger that wells up in me, all I want is to destroy the object of my desire and, by it, my desire for the object. It is basically a wish to annihilate the world.

But there is more to it. Anger is never content with mere destruction; its ultimate aim is to reconstitute the world, a world more acceptable to my whims. In the instant that anger manifests itself I am transformed from a loving person into a scary one. Everyone fears anger, no one likes to be the object of someone else's vitriol. And that's the idea. We want to scare the other person with our anger and intimidate him or her with its power. The eruption of anger means only one thing: that I have basically lost control of the situation and am prepared, verbally or with brute force, to overpower what stands in my way – even if in so doing I destroy the very thing I want so desperately to get. What are the alternatives? I could try instead to consciously suppress my anger, bite my tongue, count to ten, take a walk around the block, and bide my time until the moment passes and I come to my senses. Sometimes that takes too long. Instead of consciously suppressing my anger, I *unconsciously repress* the desire that elicited the anger instead. This heads off the anger as though it never happened. In this scenario, I didn't even realize that I became or was about to become angry, so I had "nothing" to consciously suppress. This is the model that Scheler favors as the source of resentment, the act of suppressing the anger (that has turned into hate) when I can't have what I want, which then culminates in resentment, instead of the opposite.

It's worth noting that the shorthand expression for anger in the English language is the word "mad." Mad can mean to be angry, and it can mean to become mad, to become crazy. Extreme anger is a form of madness, because by it I lose my senses, my judgment is severely compromised if not entirely AWOL, and I become a different person. I become a madman. In a manner of speech, I have become stark raving mad. That's all it takes for us to slide from a perfectly sane place to one that is psychotic. The difference between the angry person and the madman is that the angry person recovers, the madman does not: he becomes somebody else. Another item worth noting is that etymologically, the words anger, anguish, and anxiety share the same root, *Angst*. This makes sense because anxiety is the consequence of feeling frustrated, which turns into anguish, which often evolves into anger. There is no etymological link between anger and madness. This is a connection we have come to on our own, without the guidance of language. The word hate has numerous antecedents, including the Greek *kedos*, meaning affliction. It is also cognate with the Old Saxon word, *hatan*, to be hostile. So the anguish we experience when we feel angry may, if it persists, become an affliction which, in turn, makes us want to attack or take vengeance on the person who we feel caused us to become angry.

Borrowing from Freud, Scheler believes that the key to resentment is not just feeling hate toward someone, but the *suppression* of the hate generated. This is a common truism among psychotherapists. If you suppress your anger, the logic goes, you will only bottle it up and it will be transformed into just about every form of psychopathology you can imagine, including neurosis, psychosis, depression, addiction, you name it. This isn't actually Freud's position, who, we noted earlier, argued that the act of repressing *desire*, not the consequent anger or hate (as with Scheler), results in symptom formation. This, however, is not a popular view amongst the legions of therapists who currently run amok in our midst, who tend to reject anything smacking of sexuality, who prefer to pin all our problems on anger management, or rather the absence of such "management." Support groups are the gold standard for keeping such impulses in check. If only we could harness all that energy we might obtain a new source of fuel.

I am admittedly surprised that someone of Scheler's sophistication would go down that path, effectively pinning all the resentful person's problems on the suppression of hate instead of the obvious culprit, desire. What Scheler didn't realize is that hate is the consequence of resentment, not its cause. The impotence that resentment always occasions prompts me to hate those I perceive as superior, but oppressively so. Naturally, hate and anger are crucial factors in every incidence of "psychopathology" and always in play when our desires are thwarted. From my forty or so years of experience with both neurotic and psychotic patients, I incline toward the view that resentment, on its most basic level, is always a response to *thwarted desire*, not suppressed anger or hatred. Contra Nietzsche, I don't see the resentful person as someone who has cleverly found a way to get what he or she wants, by hook or by crook, however deviously but in the end successfully. The resentful person has only succeeded in subverting his desire and, by it, carrying on without it. The more profoundly this destruction is hammered home, the more he rationalizes his moral superiority over those who have what he covets: the simple happiness of living one's desire, win or lose. I don't believe Nietzsche got this. For the most part, Nietzsche got it right, including his observation that we humans are ruled by passions, not reason. Nietzsche also realized that our motives are at the mercy of our desires, and that thwarting our desires usually culminates in anger, resentment, and random acts of madness that we seldom recognize as such. For those insights we own Nietzsche a considerable debt.

To sum this up, the neurotic wants what he wants until the frustration is unbearable, and then he doesn't want it any more, or wishes he could rid himself of it. This he cannot entirely succeed in pulling off, so he does the next best thing. He gives himself an out by a feat of magic, the third choice scenario, rooted in the most basic attribute of neurotic symptom formation, ambivalence. He vacillates over his wants, one moment this, the next moment that, but nowhere can his desire gain a foothold. He entertains aspirations, but whatever he aspires to his eye is fixed on what he has *yet* to achieve: the glass is always half empty. He resents that too. The psychotic also wants what he wants but, unlike the neurotic, is more determined to get it, which is to say, less inclined and less able to give it up, even when surrender is the only sane option. It was this feature of psychosis that prompted Freud to label it "narcissistic neuroses" (as opposed to "psychoneuroses, or simply, "neuroses"), before settling on the term that we have stuck to ever since, *psychosis* – literally (and etymologically) a mind that is *animated*. In order to ease his frustration the neurotic *defuses* his desire, turning it into perpetual, ambivalent, narcissistic confusion, unable to decide whether he wants something or doesn't. Let's call this place of ambivalent impasse his *purgatory of desire*. On the other hand, the psychotic resents that he cannot get what he wants, so instead of repressing his desire he opts to *invert* the object of his desire instead, in order to convince himself that he wants what, in fact, he does not. What *was* good is good no longer. Now it is bad, and what was bad is good. For example, intimacy is bad and alienation is, if not good, the best alternative. Now that he has mutated into a *slave moralist* he becomes not a slave but a master of alienation. By inverting what he truly desires – the love of another – into indifference, he takes comfort in his self-imposed isolation from others, all of whom serve to remind him of his inferior station. Because desire always comes at a cost, this is no less true for the psychotic's desire. He is resigned to his resentment and seeks to convince himself that his carefully developed, negative take on the world is not only the right one, but the one he wanted all along. In the depths of his unconscious, he knows this isn't true, and because of this his life is in unremitting turmoil. He isn't living the life he wants to, but the one he *pretends* to. That is what's driving him crazy.

This switching (or inverting) of what was but is now no longer desirable accounts for the state of confusion commonly associated with profoundly disorganized forms of psychosis, epitomized by schizophrenia. So how do we distinguish between the relatively healthy person, for whom resentment occurs but soon passes, and the person who becomes so resentful that it prompts the loss of his senses, culminating in madness?

The healthy person possesses a naive and non-reflective awareness of his own value, which permits him to acknowledge the merits of others without needing to begrudge them. He even rejoices in their virtues because there is no better source of potential love objects than those very people who possess a healthy attitude toward life and, by extension, themselves. The *l'homme du ressentiment* constantly compares himself with others and consequently experiences his own value by pitting himself against the other, perceiving only those qualities that constitute potential differences. Whereas the healthy person seeks common ground with others and experiences his value without indulging in such comparisons, the resentful person determines his value *by means* of these comparisons. His capacity to identify with others, in order to minimize their differences, is compromised because he needs to diminish the value of those very persons he might otherwise identify with. This makes it impossible to ever rise to their level and form truly reciprocal relationships, the foundation for any friendship. This is why the strategy to diminish others only exacerbates his inadequacy and the anxiety associated with it. In order to obtain some relief from this impasse, the resentful person has no choice but to devalue even further the other's virtues by blinding himself to those qualities. He now has to falsify the other's virtues, because by leaving them intact they will remind him of his inferior status.

This results in the drive to subvert his desire by negating the value of every potentially desirable object.[4] Desire, as a principle guidepost to living, gradually vanishes and is substituted for a more general negative attitude, a seemingly unsystematic rejection of all things, people, and situations whose loose connection with the earlier injuries that precipitated his resentment are long forgotten. According to Scheler, "The *ressentiment* experience is always characterized by this 'transparent' presence of the true objective values behind the illusory ones – by that obscure awareness that one lives in a *sham world* which one is unable to penetrate" (1972, p. 60).

By telling himself that all objects (or objectives) of value are unworthy of his attention, the *l'homme du ressentiment* finally weakens his capacity to judge reality. By undermining the basis of his own desiring, he promotes a sense of newfound power, but on an illusory foundation. He tells himself, "I don't need anyone," when in fact he is saying, "I don't want to acknowledge how useless and impotent I feel." Those who, like himself, suffer miserably are now more "authentic" in his eyes than those who are genuinely (and overtly) happy. The effect is a falsification of his experience and with it his world view. He turns away from those things that represent positive (desirable) values and adopts negative (undesirable) ones instead, while telling himself they are positive. He now develops an uncanny ability to scold and belittle everything he sees. This person would make an excellent film, art, or food critic, except that the film he critiques, the art he dismisses, or the food he rejects is the *world* he is resigned to. He takes pleasure in slandering the world, often with pinpoint accuracy, in order to justify his failure to have found a place in it. If he cannot appropriate the "good life," or even approximate it, at least he can appropriate a bad one, but disguised as good. He makes this life good by simply calling it so. The street person whose only possession is a grocery cart treasures his collection of discarded stuff as covetously as you would your new BMW, or your home in the hills, your vacation in Hawaii. He no longer even needs a home of his own because he is finally "free" to come and go as he pleases and where he pleases, bereft of possessions or responsibilities. What could be freer than that? So he thinks.

Though everyone struggles with resentment from time to time, especially in periods of frustration or loss, what concerns us here are the ways that resentment may breed the most profound pathological strategies, eventually resulting in the most crippling forms of madness. Freud's conception of neurosis and Laing's depiction of the schizoid condition that lies at the core of psychosis are the models I will now employ to show how the resentful attitude is situated at the heart of each.

Neither Freud nor Laing arrived at a convincing etiology of how neurosis or psychosis (both of which I generalize, in contrast to sanity, as editions of madness) develop. Though many etiological theories have been offered, no one has arrived at an irrefutable explanation that is embraced as incontrovertibly true. No one really knows why this person becomes mad and that person remains sane. Because our environment has such a profound impact on our experience and is the locus of where our outlook on life develops, it is where we are most likely to focus our attention. Freud situated the development of neurosis in the trauma of unrequited love. The reason this explanation is so compelling is that everyone has suffered such experiences, so it stands to reason that the younger we are when we suffer rejection the greater impact it will have on our outlook. But no two people are the same, so to suggest that the environment is crucial, even decisive, isn't to suggest we are blank slates upon whom sensory impressions make their indelible mark. There is a joker in the deck, because each of us brings into the world a *sensibility* that is our own and belongs to no one but me. It is this sensibility – what Freud dubbed the constitutional factor[5] – that *encounters* the environment that envelops us. No two people encounter the same environment, even one they share, in precisely the same way. No two siblings, even identical twins, experience their environment identically, because the way each of us encounters our environment *changes* that environment and consequently our experience of it. I prefer to characterize this not a constitutional factor, *per* Freud, but an *existential* one, because it is utterly unpredictable and unique in the way each person experiences his or her environment.

If, as Freud suggests, no one survives childhood without a broken heart, we cannot predict how each of us will *respond* to having our hearts broken and what we subsequently learn from that experience. What is most basic about our childhoods is not *what* "happens" to us, but *the sense we make of what happens* to us, and how our interpretation of what happens shapes us. Every time one's heart is broken it is perfectly natural to feel, not merely rejected, but rejected *unfairly* so. Our reaction is immediate and instinctive, which is to say we don't have to think about it in order to experience the rejection. However, once we have a chance to recover we may appraise the situation on reflection and realize that the rejection we suffered, when considered from the other person's point of view, makes sense. We may even forgive the person who, as we say, broke our heart. Some people, even when arriving at this judgment, feel rancor toward that person but continue to love them. Insight doesn't always resolve the pain we experience and the yearning to hold someone other than ourselves accountable. As long as we blame the person we feel rejected by we will continue to resent that person for it, because the resentment harbored is what (magically) *holds* that person accountable. *Resentment is always born from a wish to hold someone other than myself responsible for my misfortunes.* This is the poison that fuels the raw power of resentment, that inverts values by transforming someone I love into someone I despise, in turn making me the victim, but one with whom I *sympathize*. The need to blame others for my suffering may be the only way I have left to love myself, if only relatively so, by wallowing in that inverted form of compassion we call self-pity. As Freud reminds us, neurosis is not, strictly speaking, narcissistic, but a *failure of narcissism*, which is to say, a failure to genuinely love oneself, warts and all. (We will explore this point further in Chapter Seven.)

A child who struggles to understand his jealousy toward the mother's relationship with the father isn't capable of reflecting on the anguish suffered. Even the resentment that the child's jealousy engenders is too scary to comprehend. So what do we, at this tender age, do to cope with it? We try to forget it, put it out of our minds, pretend it didn't happen, even if what "happened" was not, strictly speaking, a rejection, *per se*, yet was *interpreted as such by us*. What is actually the case is not nor can it be noted in the heat of battle. What does register is whatever sense I am able to make of my experience, imbued with the fantasies of a vivid imagination. This is why it is rarely "reality" that serves as the basis of what I experience as traumatic, but the *interpretation* I give myself at the time, and even subsequently, the interpretation that I am stuck with. The jealousy thus suffered becomes frozen in time, coloring the world in broad strokes with a mistrustful attitude that suspects anyone's motives who arouses my desire for them.

Neurotics aren't the only people who suffer unrequited love. Laing believed it is just as prevalent among those who get labeled psychotic, schizoid, manic, and schizophrenic. The difference for the psychotic, or schizoid, personality is that the damage is even greater, but also confusing. Neurotics don't typically give up on love; they continue to seek it while trying to insulate themselves against the feared traumatic rejection, a contradiction in aims. They are still capable of love in principle and do relatively well in the kind of intimate settings that both love and work relations occasion. Freud believed that successful therapeutic experiences result in increased capacity for love and work. This is because love and work are what personal relationships are about. On the most basic level, loving and working are the avenues through which we typically seek and, when lucky, find happiness. Without them one's existence is on life-support.

As noted in Chapter One, love and work are problematic for the person who suffers from psychotic states of consciousness. Because one of the principal features of schizoid phenomena is to insulate oneself from intimate relations, one's task becomes one of engaging in love or work relations *without getting too close*. What constitutes being "too close" varies from one person to the next. The schizoid person has the same reasons to feel resentful that the neurotic does, but because more is at stake – one's safety, keeping the ground from collapsing, preserving body and soul – the resentment is stronger, and more determined. The neurotic doesn't withdraw from the world; he just doesn't feel that it's giving him a fair shake. The schizoid person is more likely to be convinced that the world is a hostile, unforgiving arena where he has been condemned, and from which he must, but cannot find a way, to escape. How best to make oneself at home in a prison bent on one's inevitable destruction? If I cannot escape from my prison in *fact*, then maybe I can do so in *fantasy*, by keeping my aspirations private.

There is an obvious problem with this strategy. The more psychotic a person becomes, the less able one is to fend for oneself and achieve a degree of autonomy. One remains, by any measure, *at the mercy of others*, the same people who cannot be trusted nor depended on. One of the things that has always amazed me about working with people diagnosed schizophrenic and other kinds of psychosis is how dependent they are on their families. They almost always remain financially and emotionally dependent on them, or a substitute, whether they live with their families or not. When they go to a mental hospital or residential therapy setting it becomes a sanctuary for them, the setting and the people in it become a surrogate family that, to all intents and purposes, is caring for and about them, the same way a family does, or ought to. This has always struck me as paradoxical, that the schizo-phrenic avoids intimacy with others, yet is totally dependent on them. Naturally, this makes conducting therapy with them tricky, due to the resentment they harbor toward anyone who offers to help.

These are the people who Klein believed don't want you to succeed with them because they are too envious of your "goodness." I don't buy this explanation, though I admit it may characterize those individuals who are simply not suited for therapy for lack of trust, who are too resentful to admit they want anything from anybody. What is more typical, in my experience, is that they probably resent being in the situation they are in, needing to count on a stranger to help them when others have failed. They are used to not fitting in, accustomed to the absence of someone with whom to connect, someone who takes them seriously, and patiently. They resent those who are less crazy as they because they've given up on finding sanity for themselves. It is simply too painful and scary to try. Their only recourse is to contort themselves into the inverted posture that Nietzsche depicted so well. Now *you* are the crazy person and *they* are the sane ones. It is your fault they can't connect with you, not theirs. You profess to know what it's like to be them, to empathize, but you are not one of them, so how could you know their pain? The challenge in working with a person that crazy and resentful is to convince him (or her) that his strategies for survival aren't working, because those very strategies are illogical. In order to get someone to see this you must first succeed in *de-inverting the inversion of values that his resentment has methodically arranged, over the entirety of his lifespan, to now*. If you can manage to do that, you're now ready to get down to work. In a manner of speaking, your work is more or less finished by then. Becom-ing less resentful and assuming more responsibility for one's actions is essentially how therapy works. The rest is fine-tuning. Naturally, positing that as a goal is a lot easier than pulling it off.

The reason this is so problematic is a consequence of the insidious nature of resentment and the way it permeates each nook and cranny of our lives. All of us are resentful, to some degree or other, now and then, some more, some less. That is why the extent to which we can free ourselves of resentment will determine how happy, how content with the life we are living, we can be. Our resentful nature probably explains why it is so hard to recover from unrequited love, why every time we lose someone precious, we blame him or her for making us miserable. We even blame those who have died for abandoning us. It is so common to blame others that most therapies today take it as an article of faith that this indeed explains why we are so damaged, because we have been victimized by others. Yet, this is not an altogether sane way of perceiving the world. Moreover, it is profoundly self-defeating. Yet, because this conviction is so common, we are all collectively crazy for seeing it this way, and implicated in it. Slave morality, as Nietzsche predicted, has taken over the world, and we pay a heavy price for thinking any differently and stepping outside the boundaries of what is currently "politically correct."

Freud was insightful for tracing the source of this socially sanctioned bitterness to childhood. The problem is in determining how to understand what our childhoods were about, and what lessons to learn from them. Do we tell our patients what they want to hear, or do we challenge them to look at things afresh, even if it means abandoning our most cherished beliefs? We sometimes come away from childhood convinced we have put the pain of it behind us, but more likely we have not. To some degree, it is always there, in some form or other, conscious and unconscious alike. Our pain is never really healed or behind us. Like a virus, it stays dormant until something or someone insults our narcissism, breathing new life into our intransigent pain yet again. And again it has its way with us, always at the ready to right the scales of each injustice we are convinced someone or other has perpetrated against us.

In the final analysis, as Nietzsche suggested, the neurotic resents life when it isn't fair, when others have more than he, when he can't get everything he wants, that he cannot live forever, that no one loves him, because he suffers from this or that, because the glass is always half empty, no matter how hard he tries to fill it with anything that is handy. After all, "someone" must be accountable, responsible, to blame for his shortcomings, and when that doesn't get anywhere he blames life, maybe God, or the devil, but ultimately himself. That, too, brings no mercy. You can't go through life blaming someone, anyone, for your misfortune and expect to find any measure of happiness or contentment. Life is a game of chance that no one controls, so no one is to blame for what it is. Each of us enjoys a measure of luck as well as misfortune, and the task each of us faces is to play this game the best we can, win or lose. In life, as with the turning of the world and the rotation of the planets, another morning is always on the horizon. Therein lies the hope for us. It is never too late to take a good look at the choices we have made, the folly that occasioned them, and the choices that lie ahead. It is never too late to decide how best to play this game and to enjoy the playing of it.[6]

In this chapter I reviewed the basic parameters of sanity and madness in the context of resentment and its role in symptom formation. Due to the breadth of its application I was obliged to invoke some of the basic nosological categories employed by mental health professions, including schizophrenia, mania, schizoid phenomena, bipolar disorder, neurosis, hysteria, obsessional neurosis, and so on. My aim is to dispense with such categories, as they so easily interfere with our effort to get to the bottom of what our psychological suffering, sanity, and madness are about. Still, this is the language with which we are familiar, and it isn't going away any time soon. If we are to dispense with such language, then to what do these terms ultimately refer, if not "psychopathology?" It is now time to turn our attention to this nomenclature and translate its connotations into a more personal, existential, less medicalized context.

Notes

1 Freud's *Civilization and Its Discontents* (1930) might seem like an homage to Nietzsche, for it comes to the same conclusion: modern culture does everything in its power to suppress our desires via guilt, turning us into a race of neurotics. See my "Happiness and Chance: A Reappraisal of the Psychoanalytic Conception of Suffering" (2004) for an extensive synopsis of Freud's thesis.
2 Ironically, the wealthiest religion today is Scientology, not Christianity. Ironic because Scientology is not rooted in slave morality but master morality. Its goal could even be described as Nietzschean, the self-actualization of the individual in pursuit of self-mastery.
3 See my *The Truth About Freud's Technique* (1994) for a summary of Freud's conception of obsessional neurosis and the role of guilt in its incidence.
4 Read: other people, or objectives.
5 The term "constitutional" is confusing and open to misunderstanding. When contrasting environmental (traumatic) versus constitutional factors in the etiology of a person's neurosis, it is typically assumed that what Freud meant by the term constitutional was synonymous with genetics, that one's predilections toward the environment are inborn, which implies they are coded in our DNA, the so-called biological factor. This is not what Freud intended. The constitutional factor is simply that aspect of the personality that is impervious to environmental considerations. The notion, for example, that people diagnosed schizophrenic are more sensitive to their environments and more susceptible to traumatic experiences doesn't necessarily suggest that such sensitivity is a biological predisposition or genetic flaw. We have no way of determining whether sensitivity is a genetically inherited trait, or predisposition. If such children don't develop schizophrenia they may just as well mature into exceptional artists or musicians, even psychoanalysts. Sensitivity, by its nature, is a double-edged sword. This is why I prefer to call this factor *existential*, a term that retains the x-factor but free of biological prejudice. See Thompson (1994, pp. 250–252) for more on Freud's conception of the constitutional factor.
6 For those wishing to explore how the basic elements of life may be construed as "playing a game," see *Homo Ludens*, by Johan Huizinga (1949), the Dutch historian. For more on the concept of "playing," see also D. W. Winnicott (1971).

References

Freud, S. (1953–1973) *The standard edition of the complete psychological works of Sigmund Freud.* 24 volumes. Edited and translated by J. Strachey. London: Hogarth Press. (Referred to in subsequent references as *Standard Edition.*)

Freud, S. (1930) Civilization and its discontents. *Standard Edition*, 21:59–145. London: Hogarth Press, 1961.

Huizinga, J. (1949) *Homo Ludens: A study of the play-element in culture.* Translated by R. F. C. Hull. London: Routledge and Kegan Paul, Ltd.

Klein, M. (1928) Early stages of the Oedipus conflict. In *Love, guilt and reparation and other works 1921–1945* (pp. 186–198). London: Hogarth Press and the Institute of Psycho-Analysis, 1981.

Lacan, J. (2006) The mirror stage as formative of the "I" function as revealed in psychoanalytic experience. In *Ècrits: The first complete edition in English* (pp. 75–81). Translated by B. Fink. New York and London: W. W. Norton and Company, 2006.

Nietzsche, F. (1968) *The Will to Power.* Translated by W. Kaufmann and R.J. Hollingdale. New York: Vintage Press.

Nietzsche, F. (1994) *On the genealogy of morality.* Translated by C. Diethe. Cambridge: Cambridge University Press.

Nietzsche, F. (2002) *Beyond good and evil.* Translated by J. Norman. Cambridge: Cambridge University Press.

Sartre, J.-P. (1962) *Sketch for a theory of the emotions.* Translated by P. Mairet. London: Methuen and Co.

Scheler, M. (1972) *Ressentiment.* Translated by W. Holdheim. New York: Schocken Books.

Thompson, M. Guy (1994) *The truth about Freud's technique: The encounter with the real.* New York and London: New York University Press.

Thompson, M. Guy (2004) Happiness and chance: A reappraisal of the psychoanalytic conception of suffering. *Psychoanalytic Psychology,* Vol. 21:134–153.

Winnicott, D. W. (1971) *Playing and reality.* London: Tavistock Publications.

4

DECIPHERING "PSYCHOPATHOLOGY"

The first question we should address before inquiring into the kind of suffering psychopathology occasions is, how do we distinguish pathological suffering from all the other kinds of suffering we ordinarily encounter, the kind of suffering we think of as normal? Or is there such a distinction? After all, if we are all mad, to relative degrees, then madness is an everyday occurrence that, if not always desirable, is perfectly common. So why call it *pathological*? The word, pathology, from the Greek *pathos*, can mean any number of things. It may mean to *suffer* or to *experience* an emotion, such as pain, fear, desire, pleasure, or to *feel* compassion for or passionate about something or someone, which may elicit in turn empathy, sympathy, pity, or sorrow. Apathy, antipathy, and pathetic are also derived from the word *pathos*. The word *patient* derives from the same root. A patient is a person who expects to *receive* something *from* someone, such as sympathy, understanding, attention, treatment. A patient is also someone who suffers, who happens to be in a state of suffering. The term pathology was adopted by medicine to connote a condition, the result of illness or injury, that may or may not warrant treatment. From this angle, pathological symptoms manifest in a variety of ways. The most common way that we are alerted to a pathological condition is when something painful or unpleasant occurs in or on the surface of the body. The common cold, for example, is caused by an invasion of a virus, resulting in an ensemble of uncomfortable symptoms that we associate with illness. There is no treatment for a cold, so if such is diagnosed we are told to simply give it time, rest, and drink liquids. You might also take an aspirin to relieve headache or inflammation that often occasions a cold, then let time do the rest. The body's immune system will fight the virus and eventually neutralize it. Some colds, however, may sit in one's chest and, if chronic, result in bacterial infection, a secondary illness elicited by the first. The body will endeavor to fight the infection in the same way it does the virus, but if the infection persists medication may be indicated, in this case an antibiotic, that will help the immune system do its job of killing the bacteria. Unlike the cold, bacterial infections are treatable with medical intervention.

Once psychiatry was instituted as a branch of medicine, it too became involved with treating medically based, pathological conditions that occasioned their own set of symptoms and diagnosis of illness. Because psychiatry is explicitly concerned with mental pathology, the term psycho-pathology was adopted to connote illnesses associated with mental functioning. The term *psyche* is another term of etymological interest. Also of Greek origin, psyche has several meanings, including breath, soul, spirit, or mind. When you connect the word *psyche* with the word *iatros* (from the Greek meaning healer or physician) you get psych-iatry. Psychopathology, psychiatrist, and psychologist all share the same root (*psyche*) and have been taken to denote suffering of the mind, a mind healer, and one who studies the mind, respectively. The signification that psychiatry has given the Greek variations for the many possible meanings of a term such as psycho-pathology is specific. In its wider application, psychopathology may simply mean an occasion of spiritual suffering, mental anguish, soul murder, or the death of desire. From the perspective of psychiatry the term is employed in the narrow, psychiatric context that connotes an unambiguously medical condition. This means that the word psychopathology has been appropriated by the medical community and is employed as a medical term to denote a condition that can be diagnosed and perhaps treated, if the pathology in question is deemed treatable. Anyone who practices psychotherapy or psychoanalysis is supposed to be engaged in this endeavor. But are they?

What, if anything, distinguishes common suffering from pathological suffering? Does such a distinction make sense once we strip the term of its medical connotation? I believe that it may, but not necessarily in the way that psychiatry intends. Just because we suffer in myriad ways, some of which include mental or emotional suffering, doesn't necessarily imply that mental anguish is a specifically *medical* event. If I need an accountant to help me sort out my taxes, that doesn't mean that I suffer from a form of tax "illness" that warrants fiscal "treatment." We seek help with all kinds of things, and most of the things we seek help for are not medical in nature. They concern how we live and the problems that arise from efforts to obtain maximum happiness and well being, or when we get into trouble. Helping and being helped is what human beings do. It couldn't be more ordinary.

Though psychiatry was inaugurated as a medical specialty in the middle of the nineteenth century, it wasn't until the beginning of the twentieth century that the psychiatric perspective with which we have become familiar was developed. Two of the pivotal figures in its development were the German existential philosopher and psychiatrist Karl Jaspers and the Viennese neurologist and psychoanalyst Sigmund Freud. Jaspers (1997) can be credited with devising the practice of writing a personal history of the psychiatric patient, in order to review the biographical context in which the patient began to suffer his or her symptoms. This is the standard by which the contemporary psychiatric interview is conducted and, by it, identifies the human element of pathological symptoms and diagnoses. The other pivotal figure, Sigmund Freud, was not a psychiatrist, but his theories about psychopathology and treatment revolutionized the twentieth-century handling of psychiatric patients.[1] Freud argued that pathological symptoms are not caused by organic or genetic factors, but that they convey a meaning, so there are *reasons* associated with the symptoms neurotic patients suffer, not, strictly speaking, *causes*. Though he lacked a theory of intentionality, Freud surmised that hysteria, for example, was a symptom that served an unconscious purpose unbeknownst to the patient. If the physician treating this patient could divine what purpose the symptom served, Freud believed that sharing such insights with the patient may render the unconscious purpose that was driving the neurotic conflict moot, thus relieving and in some cases eradicating the symptom.

Though Freud was wedded to the medical model of symptom, diagnosis, and treatment, he was dubious of how psychiatrists typically treated their patients and was critical of psychiatry as a discipline. One of the reasons Freud pursued a career in neurology instead of psychiatry was because the profession of psychiatry was then (as it is now) of ill repute and was openly ridiculed by the medical profession at large as not really medicine, and not really science either. One of the more unkind accusations was that it served as a dumping ground for medical students of feeble intelligence or ability. As noted earlier, Freud was probably the first anti-psychiatrist. Freud thought he could do what psychiatrists were supposed to be doing much better, so in accordance with the way medical treatment typically proceeded, his conception of psychoanalysis encompassed two basic goals: first, provide an *explanation* for how and why psychopathological symptoms occur, and second, develop a form of *treatment* that will succeed in relieving those symptoms. I lack the space to review the entire history of Freud's conception of psychoanalysis, so I will limit my inquiry to those aspects that explain why psychoanalysis (and other forms of psychotherapy) should not be mistaken for *bona fide* medical treatment schemes.

Unlike the psychiatrists of his day, Freud talked to his patients and, more importantly, listened to them. I don't believe I am exaggerating when I suggest that the treatment model he developed was more or less comprised of just listening, by getting his patients to talk in such depth that it was hard to find the time to listen to everything they wanted to tell him. After listening in the uniquely attentive manner he developed, Freud concluded that the kind of suffering his patients complained about was more complicated than he first realized. All patients, whether medical, psychiatric, or analytic, talk to their doctors about their suffering. This is nothing new. But the kind of suffering Freud heard his patients describe was not typical of what physicians ordinarily heard, or wanted to hear. These patients were describing virtually everything that concerned them, not about their "illness," but about their lives. This went far beyond the scope of the psychiatric history that Jaspers developed. This is why the kind of suffering Freud's patients wanted to talk about was not medical, strictly speaking, but *existential*. It was this inherently existential component of their suffering that led Freud to conclude that his patients' symptoms weren't merely the effect of some agent that caused them, but that they revealed strikingly personal meanings of the most intimate nature instead. By learning what their lives meant to them, Freud was able to fathom how their symptoms were connected to the anguish they suffered, and why. This isn't medicine, properly speaking, but philosophy. Some would suggest it is witchcraft.

By now (circa 1915) Freud had abandoned the notion that he was treating medical conditions, and no longer referred to the psychoanalysts he was training as "doctors," and began calling them *analysts* instead.[2] Freud also realized that the kind of suffering that brought his patients into treatment needed to be differentiated from common, everyday suffering. Ordinarily, the emotional suffering we encounter in life is a consequence of our relationships, whether of a personal, intimate, or collegial nature, with others. This isn't to suggest that others want us to suffer, though sometimes they do, but we need to appreciate how dependent we are on our relationships and the kind of vulnerability our dependency on them engenders, and how they affect us emotionally. As we saw in Chapter Three, for example, when I want something from someone else, perhaps love, friendship, or their attention, that person has the power to grant me that wish or not. If he rejects me I may feel disappointed, and disappointments are necessarily painful, frustrating, or unpleasant, to varying degrees. As noted in Chapter Two, my desires often make me vulnerable to others. This is because the frustration of not having my desires gratified is the most common source of anguish. Sometimes I recover and move on, sometimes I do not. This is what makes all of us the same. Every human being is vulnerable to the situation their desires put them in, and no one can have everything he wants. Failure and disappointment are as common as the air we breathe. Coping with frustration is something all of us contend with from the moment we are born until the day we die. This is part and parcel of being human. Our capacity to love and suffer the anguish of heartbreak is universal.

Though we all share this predicament, some people are more able to handle their disappointments than others. One of the reasons our childhoods last as long as they do is to give us time to develop tolerance of the disappointments we suffer growing up. This is why we are taught to bear our frustrations with composure and a minimum of resentment. Yet each of us has a breaking point, that moment when we are no longer able to bear our frustrations nor cope with the pain we experience. What then? How do we cope with acute levels of anguish without completely checking out, or going stark raving mad? This question led Freud to have an epiphany. It dawned on him that there are *two* kinds of suffering that we typically experience, not one. I'm not referring to the distinction between medical kinds of suffering (that pertain to injury or illness) and ordinary suffering, the distinction, say, between an infected toe and tired feet. I'm referring to the distinction between the kind of suffering that is a consequence of *life* and that I encounter every day, and an explicitly (let us call it) *pathological* kind of suffering that is caused, not by life, precisely, but by *me*. The latter is a kind of suffering that is orchestrated by myself, but without awareness, and is only secondarily related to the slings and arrows of everyday misfortune. This second kind of suffering, the kind that gets labeled neurotic, psychotic, or any number of other pathological categories at our disposal, has an intelligence all its own. For lack of a better word, Freud called it the "unconscious" (more about that later). This is a kind of suffering that is paradoxical, because it is nothing more than *my response to the suffering that life occasions* and my effort to mitigate that suffering by replacing it with a *second* kind of suffering that I believe is preferable to the first. Psychopathology, properly speaking, is not a medical occasion, but a semantic one. Neuroses and the like are *self-inflicted* forms of suffering that I employ to help me cope with the everyday suffering life occasions, but which I find inconvenient, even intolerable. This coping[3] mechanism doesn't really solve my problems, instead it merely helps me ignore them. This is why this manner of coping isn't all that effective, because it is rooted in magic, the kind of magic that children are expert in devising, because children live in a magical world.

I referred to this magical way of coping earlier when reviewing my conception of the "third choice scenario" (Chapter Two). Whenever we meet frustration while pursuing something we want, we are invariably faced with a choice. We either decide to hang in there and commit ourselves to what we desire, or we decide to abandon the desire and opt for something or someone else, a desirable object that is more accessible, or at any rate, realistic. Neurotic symptoms result when I can choose neither, and I resort to a third, magical choice instead. This so-called "choice" results in the ambivalence that we recognize in every neurotic conflict. Because it isn't a genuine choice, it takes us to a kind of "Neverland" where we enjoy a time-out from the anguish that is too much to bear. Like the Cargo Cults[4] of the South Pacific, we go to this special place to wait it out and, like the ostrich, hope it will eventually go away, or will magically resolve itself.

In the short-term, the formation of a neurotic conflict may momentarily mitigate the anguish via any number of defense mechanisms (repression, denial, dissociation, projection, etc.), but it only creates a new problem in its place. The problem is that any neurosis I choose (we will explore psychotic strategies shortly) renders me helpless by making me passive or heedless, thus incapable of surmounting the problem I am defending myself against. I withdraw into ambivalence and the comfort my symptoms afford me, by effectively deadening my pain, and with it the desire it occasioned. I hunker down, resentfully insisting I will never forget the insult I have repressed, and hold on. We have to ask ourselves, what is even remotely "medical" about such a constellation of mental and emotional activities? In a word, nothing, because tactics of this nature are not medical *conditions*, but existential *stratagems*. Though I do so unconsciously, it is still me who performs the strategy, not some underlying condition or gremlin that does it to me. Nothing invaded my organism to cause havoc and no one took control of my psyche. Though I'm not responsible for the pain others sometimes subject me to, I am responsible for the stratagems I devise to ward it off, the same stratagems that occasion my so-called diagnosable psychopathology.

Freud's conception of neurosis effectively removed psychoanalysis from medicine and psychiatry and transformed it into a new discipline that had not previously existed. Though madness (i.e., psychopathology) has existed throughout human history, it has always been consigned to medical, religious, shamanistic, or philosophical disciplines. We continue to borrow from those disciplines today. Freud created a new paradigm that, because it evolved out of a medical context, borrowed some of the language we associate with medical practices. "Psycho-therapy," though it combines the term *psych* with *therapy*, is neither medical nor, strictly speaking, even psychological.[5] It is nothing more than two people joined in a peculiar form of friendship attending to a specific kind of suffering one of them is experiencing, with a view to understanding that suffering better, perhaps relieving it by the simple act of sharing it with someone. From this angle, Laing allowed we can still retain the word, *therapy*, in a non-medicalized context so long as we are cognizant of what we intend by it. We can still speak of "pathological" suffering, as distinguished from ordinary suffering, so long as we appreciate how the former is generated in order to mitigate the latter.[6]

This is the only honest, non-medicalized way we have at our disposal of grasping the subtle, yet maddening nature of what we term psychopathology.

Now that we know what it means, how do we disentangle the myriad terms we employ in order to "diagnose" the kinds of psychopathology, or mental illness, that we assign to this or that set of symptoms? Freud's other contribution to the science of psychopathology is embodied in the context in which he addressed this phenomenon. Freud was able to appreciate, and so tolerate, the enormous ambiguity that any effort to understand the mind poses. When the object of our study is *the very instrument employed to study it* we are necessarily limited in our ability to comprehend the subject matter, because the matter studied isn't out there, it is *me*. This is probably why Freud painted psychopathology with such broad strokes, dividing virtually the entire scope of our self-imposed modes of suffering into two basic categories, neuroses and psychoses. As noted in Chapter Two, the third pathological category that Freud entertained, the so-called perversions, are not, strictly speaking, pathological since their aim is to increase pleasure rather than compromising it, so I will not include this category in our present discussion.[7] What, then, are neuroses and psychoses? Which ones are treatable, which is to say, which ones respond to psychotherapy, and how is that determined?

People suffer all the time. It is so common that Buddhists observe life *is* suffering. This doesn't necessarily mean that every time a person suffers that person needs someone's help. Even when our scope narrows to pathological suffering, most of the time I suffer quietly and deal with it. So what determines that juncture when I decide that my suffering is no longer supportable, that I can no longer go it alone and need help, when I want someone to talk to because the people I may already be talking to about it, friends, lovers, family, and the like, are unable to help? Suffering always occasions anxiety, which I may or may not be aware of *as* anxiety. All of the painful emotions we talked about in Chapter Three are the consequence of anxiety, and they either mitigate our anxiety or exacerbate it. We often hide behind this or that emotion, such as anger, resentment, envy, jealousy, or spite, as a way of avoiding anxiety. Even sexual arousal may be a buttress against anxiety and, sometimes, even enhance our sexual performance. More commonly, anxiety destroys sexual arousal and renders us incapable of enjoying it. Whether I consciously experience my anxiety, *per se*, or another emotion in its place, such as depression, that serves to dwarf my anxiety, I cross a threshold experience when my anxiety is not merely a stressful inconvenience, but *distressing*. To feel distressed is, by definition, to feel that I can no longer handle what I am experiencing and need someone to help me.

People seek therapy only when they are in a state of distress. This is a highly subjective state and some of us reach the point of distress sooner or more readily than others. It is one of those truisms that men are more reluctant to seek therapy, to seek help, than women. Granted, this is a generalization. Many men are eager to ask for help and many women are reluctant to. It is impossible to help someone who does not want to be helped. This is why therapy is of no use to someone who is dragged there by a family member or spouse, or coerced into doing so. People don't go into therapy because they should, but because they must, because they want to. Without the sense of desperation that occasions my experience of distress, therapy will be of little consequence. Children and schizophrenics are typically taken to therapists or psychiatrists for treatment by a family member. They seldom do so on their own. Does this mean they cannot be helped? It depends.

The psychoanalytic community is divided as to whether it is possible to conduct psychoanalysis with either a child or a person diagnosed schizophrenic. Why? Because those groups rarely seek therapy on their own volition. Children, by definition, are not responsible, so they go to therapy because their parents tell them to. Children aren't expected to talk to their therapists about their problems because children typically lack the self-reflective awareness and verbal agility to engage in the kind of therapeutic discourse that psychotherapy entails. Instead, children engage in play, because that is where they live, so play activity, whatever it entails, is the vehicle of the child's relationship to the therapist. There is no play therapy available for someone suffering from psychotic disintegration. Psychotics also lack the verbal skill that we expect from the high functioning neurotic, and if their psychosis is predominantly manic the heightened speech they engage in is not of a reflective nature. What is lacking in both cases is the sense of *agency* that a person in distress calls upon when taking responsibility for his situation and doing something about it, by reaching out to someone. No matter how crazy or psychotic a person may be, he is always *in principle* (though not necessarily) capable of recognizing he needs help, but that doesn't mean that he will. He may simply be too frightened to trust anyone, and fear can be a terrible thing. The same may be said of someone suffering from neurotic symptoms. I don't have the statistics to back this up, but I believe a very small minority of persons suffering from neurotic conflicts, even those suffering distress, are willing to consult a psychotherapist for it. More often, they take matters into their own hands and seek alternate means to mitigate the anxiety they suffer, e.g., by ingesting food, alcohol, pot, cocaine, heroin, speed, tobacco. When that fails they may seek the drugs marketed by the pharmaceutical industry (as we discussed in Chapter One). And what about all the other forms of compulsive behavior that some turn to, such as gambling, sex, shopping, hoarding, and the like? All are ways of mitigating anxiety when it has become insupportable, which is to say, when we can no longer cope.

One of the appealing features of psychopharmacology is that, when taking a drug, you don't have to bare yourself to another person. Yes, you still have to reach out and ask for help,[8] but what kind of help are you asking for? If you just want to be shed of the anxiety or depression that are often catalysts for reaching out, then you may ask a doctor, whether a family practitioner or a psychiatrist, to just "give you something" to make you feel better. Ironically, the simple act of reaching out to someone and talking to them is often all it takes to feel better, whether the person you consult is a psychiatrist who gives you drugs or a therapist who offers a relationship. Freud attributed this phenomenon to the transference, a little-understood concept that is often used to explain everything we don't understand about human relationships. A person feels better, it's the transference. A person feels worse, it's the transference. There is no discernable change, it's the transference. And so on. Just the act of beginning therapy, of making a commitment to take it on and place oneself at the mercy of another human being, is all it takes to make most people feel better. I prefer to call this the "placebo effect." In the same way that taking a placebo that you believe is an anti-depressant can make you feel less depressed, just talking to another person can, in and of itself, make you feel better, whether that person is a therapist, a bartender, or a friend. The mind is an amazing thing, and we understand very little about it. Just *believing* that something or someone is going to help you may trick you into believing you already feel better. Or does it?

The fact is, we don't really know what makes people get over their neurotic or other psychopathological issues. Every school of therapy claims to have an answer, yet all of them cannot be correct, which means we are unable to determine which ones are. If there actually were a type of therapy that is guaranteed to work, everyone would go to that therapy and the others would become obsolete. None of them actually "works" because no one is really suffering from a mental illness, so there isn't literally any *thing* to treat. Drugs can manipulate the chemistry in our nervous systems, but so can going out on a date, getting laid, enjoying a meal or a round of golf. The measure for what works and doesn't in terms of psychotherapy is highly subjective. There are no objective measures with which to determine the alleged "outcomes" that the media and members of the mental health professions are currently infatuated with. The truth is, it is difficult to determine whether and to what extent any experience of psychotherapy has helped, even when we believe it has. If you leave therapy feeling better about yourself and your life than when you began, how do you know it was your therapist, or the therapy, that was responsible? Just because one thing follows another doesn't necessarily mean that the one *caused* the other to happen. Maybe all those brilliant insights that your therapist shared with you, though "meaningful" and occasionally breathtaking, were irrelevant? Maybe it was all the work that *you*, the patient, accomplished that accounted for the change you experienced. Or maybe it was just a matter of time, that no matter what you were doing all those years, you would have come to the same place where you are now. How can you be sure *what* it was that accounted for your successful experience? You have your opinion, and your therapist has hers. You may agree about it or disagree. How do you determine who is correct? You can't. No one can.

Same problem if you had a bad experience, which is to say, you feel nothing changed. Why did you receive no benefit from this experience, despite all the time and expense you put into it? Was it your fault or your therapist's? Again, there is no way of determining the answer to this important question. You may go to a new therapist and try again, and this time you have a better experience and feel more satisfied. Was that because you found a better therapist, or because all the work you performed with your previous therapist finally paid off, after enough time had passed to have its effect? Or none of the above? We just don't know, and there is no way of knowing. You may decide it was the therapist you liked that really helped you, and the one you didn't like was of no help. But for all you know it was the one you didn't like, because he made you face some harsh truths about yourself, but you resent having to learn them, which was the real catalyst for the help you now feel blessed with, but that you attribute to someone you thought was simply nicer to you. As I mentioned in Chapter One, this is a matter of judgment, and where judgment is concerned, no one is in authority. It is a matter of opinion.

Let's not get ahead of ourselves. Our topic of concern is psychopathology, not psychotherapy, but it is impossible to ignore the therapeutic process entirely and gain the understanding we are aiming for about what madness entails and how we come to encounter it in people other than ourselves. Though I have my madness to contend with, and that of everyone I happen to know, my work as a psychoanalyst has afforded me the opportunity to enjoy the kind of relationships with seekers of truth that have taught me the most of what little I have learned about it. I have learned far more from people who sought someone to help them when the chips were down than I have from those who would not be caught dead in the company of a psychotherapist. This needs to be acknowledged, because it is the sample from the population that comes my way as a psychoanalyst that I have had the most access to. I personally believe that therapy can, and often does, help people who invest the time and effort in the process. That is my opinion. The placebo effect, whatever it is, is not a fantasy, it is real, it just isn't what we expected, that taking another person into our confidence can make all the difference in the world. (I will say more about this process later, when I review the role of authenticity toward the end of this book.)

Freud was principally interested in neurosis, so let's turn out attention to how he conceived of it before moving on to the more psychotic aspects of madness. Freud's conception of neurosis is both elegant and simple, which is no doubt why it has lost popularity. Yet, we wouldn't be able to make much sense of madness without it. Freud was initially drawn to treating hysterics. What is a hysteric? The term, of Greek origin, means literally "wandering womb" because it was believed to be a condition exclusive to women following childbirth. In the nineteenth century, Charcot, with whom Freud studied, surmised that hysteria was a hereditary illness that produced symptoms of an illness of apparent physical origin that was in fact nonexistent. There was then a great demand for treatments of hysteria as none of the ones then existing seemed to work. Freud decided to devote his efforts to finding a cure for this obstinate condition. Freud was initially convinced that hysterical symptoms, whether of a somatic or emotional nature, were the consequence of repressed sexuality. There was apparently considerable evidence that many of the women he treated lacked satisfying sexual relations with their husbands, and because they happened to exhibit hysterical symptoms, Freud linked them together.

The symptoms fell into two broad categories. The first were those of a somatic nature, such as a skin rash, coughing, paralysis, or other symptoms that had no discernable medical foundation. This means that *any* physical complaints that resisted a readily recognizable medical diagnosis were assumed to be signs of hysteria. Physicians assumed these patients were deliberately fabricating their "illness" and had little sympathy for them. The second type was associated with irrational fears, such as agoraphobia and claustrophobia that had no basis in reality. Underpinning both was anxiety, which Freud recognized as the catalyst for hysteria and neuroses generally. Freud struggled with understanding what anxiety was and what caused it, and never really settled on a conclusive answer. This is one of the endearing things about Freud: he was determined to find an answer to everything, but no sooner had he found it than he concluded it contained flaws that obliged him to keep searching. Though dogmatic, Freud could also be sceptical, the secret to his success. He initially attributed anxiety to the dammed-up libido that was consciously experienced as anxiety, but he soon replaced that theory with castration anxiety (for men) and penis envy (for women).

This theory was just as dubious as the first, even though it was embraced by Freud's most devoted followers, and still is. But even in the absence of a compelling explanation for what *neurotic* anxiety is so anxious about – in other words, what is the difference between ordinary and neurotic anxiety – simply attributing pathological symptoms to anxiety was a monumental step in the evolution of psychoanalysis. Anxiety has always been a compelling topic for existentialists beginning with Kierkegaard, but it was Heidegger who situated it as a fear of nonexistence. This explanation is not that easy to wrap our minds around, because it is impossible to conceptualize our *nonexistence*. How can you conceive of something that does not exist? We fear it all the same. Freud was correct in assuming that sex is of exceptional concern to us and we have long since linked the moment of sexual orgasm, which is to say its *satisfaction*, with death. Freud's hysterical patients were probably repressing their sexuality due to their fear of death. This fear was in turn linked to the relationships with their husbands who they worried did not love them and may, perhaps, abandon them. This is likely why the attention Freud gave them made his patients feel special in his eyes, and the sympathy expressed must have felt like love to them, which Freud noticed. Though Freud believed it was his understanding of the patients' neuroses that cured them, it was probably the sympathetic attention he gave them that ultimately did the trick, a conclusion that he came to later.

Freud initially approached hysterical symptoms as any psychiatrist might. What is the illness the symptoms indicate and what must be done to eradicate those symptoms in order to cure the patient of his or her illness? This strategy, however, didn't work. Symptoms that went into remission would reappear later in another form, so getting rid of them wasn't enough. Today, somatic neurotic symptoms are a truism. We now know that one of our favorite ways of coping with anxiety is to displace it onto a physical symptom, such as rashes, colds, body aches such as back pain, headaches, or general feelings of malaise and fatigue. There is no cure for these symptoms, though they can be abated. If they happen to arise in therapy, it is relatively easy to trace these aches and pains to psychological distress that the patient is already aware of, or becomes aware of when brought to their attention. Either way, simply knowing that we displace anxiety onto our bodies doesn't make the symptoms go away. Only if the source of the anxiety is addressed do we no longer have a motive for somaticizing our distress. That is probably why hysterics suffering from somatic symptoms no longer consult psychoanalysts or psychotherapists about them. After having no luck with their medical practitioners, they are more likely to try acupuncture, massage therapy, Chinese herbal remedies, crystals, psychic readings, and any number of other "alternative" medicines for relief, however momentary the relief turns out to be. Not to be outdone, the medical profession has even invented a new "illness," *fibromyalgia*, a phantom illness if there ever was one, that supposedly explains chronic pain, for which, to be sure, medications are readily, if not cheaply, available. I digress, but I thought I should mention why the diagnosis of hysteria has nearly disappeared among contemporary analysts, though we know it is alive and well in every one of us!

To make matters even more complicated, Freud recognized that underneath the symptoms his patients were distressed about were other, secondary symptoms that Freud happened to observe, but which his patients did not complain about or even notice. These were the characterological symptoms that were features of the patient's personality, what Freud termed ego-syntonic symptoms (as opposed to ego-dystonic) because they were *not* distressing, though neurotic just the same. These symptoms included excessive attention-seeking, inappropriately seductive behavior, and excessive need for approval. Unlike the picture we often have of the shut-down, repressed neurotic, these patients sometimes exaggerated their emotions, engaged in sexually provocative behavior, were overtly dramatic, lively, vivacious, even flirtatious. They often behaved like children, and like children could be egocentric, self-indulgent, easily influenced by others, impressionable, longing for approval, and could engage in starkly manipulative behavior to get what they wanted. Though men could also fit this diagnosis, the majority of such hysterics happened to be women.

Now we have the picture of a hysteric who demonstrates distressing symptoms about which she complains, but with an underlying character pathology about which she does not object. Moreover, these patients feel so identified with these traits that bringing them to their attention may prove counterproductive, often eliciting denial and early termination. Freud concluded that neurotic symptoms had to be separated into two distinct categories, those that were ego-syntonic and others that were ego-dystonic. Because the ego-dystonic kind occasion distress, only these can be effectively, shall we say, treated. The others are ingrained features of the personality and remain so, no matter how much analysis is commissioned. This confirmed Freud's suspicion that therapy could only be effective with those who are highly motivated and whose distress is sufficiently acute that they are committed to remaining in treatment, even when they begin to feel worse, but especially when they begin to feel better.

Up to now, hysteria presented the basic picture of neurosis and the two terms were used interchangeably. But then Freud began to notice a second type of patient whose symptoms diverged from that of the typical hysteric. These patients, like the hysteric, were also anxious, but they were more concerned about obsessive thoughts they entertained, chronic worries, an unremitting sense of uneasiness and guilt, and they often displayed compulsive behavior of a ritualistic nature. These patients also exhibited underlying obsessive character traits that complemented the overt symptoms that were of a more distressing nature. Whereas the hysteric was often flamboyant, manipulative, and emotional, obsessive patients were more likely to be perfectionistic, meticulous, intelligent, risk-averse, studied, deliberate, studious, and cut off from their feelings. They were also typically moralistic and professed to hold the highest ethical principles, somewhat *too* high for Freud's taste. Though both men and women suffered these symptoms, the majority were typically men.

Now we have two kinds of neurosis, each seeming to be the polar opposite of the other. Freud decided, however, that obsessional neurosis – a category of psychopathology that he was the first to recognize and label – was merely an edition of hysteria, so the prototypical picture of neuroses as hysterical in nature was slyly retained. This meant that all neurotics, whatever their surface appearance, were hysterics who suffered from excessive anxiety, whatever the cause of that anxiety may be. Freud now saw hysteria everywhere he looked, and he came to the conclusion that *everyone, no matter how well-adjusted or happy they may be, possessed neurotic character traits and symptoms.* In other words, we are all stark raving mad, to varying degrees, we just don't know it and, for the most part, it doesn't seem to bother us. It is part of the human condition to which we belong, and our lives are a delicate balancing act whereby we manage our anxieties the best we can while pursuing the goals we deem worthy. However, Freud couldn't resist entertaining a theory that might explain why some people become hysterical and others obsessional. He proposed that the former were fixated at the oral stage of their development and were thus slightly more primitive in nature, whereas the latter were fixated at the anal stage, so their symptoms exhibited features associated with bowel control, following Freud's psychosexual stages of development. This distinction has become a bit moot, since it is rare to encounter a "pure" hysteric or obsessional neurotic that fits this picture. If neuroses are a part of the human condition, then each of us shares in both types of neurosis and are a blend of the two, to varying degrees. In effect, we are polymorphously neurotic, through and through.

This is Freud's singular contribution to the science of psychopathology, the most detailed and creative portrait of neurosis that has ever been conceived. Indeed, it is difficult to meet any human being who does not show elements of this portrait, because Freud wasn't really talking about the features of mental illness, but of the *human condition*. By characterizing these personality features as "pathological" Freud persuaded the psychiatric community that he had discovered a key to unlocking the mystery of mental illness. In fact, he discovered an important key to the nature of anxiety and how it rules our lives, oftentimes resulting in the most extreme feats of mental ingenuity to avoid those very emotions that are displeasing to us. By saying that we are all, to relative degrees, neurotic, Freud was also saying that there is no such thing as mental illness. Humans suffer, sometimes in ways they are loath to acknowledge and come to terms with, and this is a very real and vexing problem we all share. Freud's genius was in recognizing that this is indeed part of the human condition, and then developing a novel activity – psychotherapy – that has proved useful in relieving this very dilemma, though in no way eradicating it.[9]

Freud was just as disinterested in psychosis as he was fascinated with neurosis, so there isn't a whole lot he has to tell us about the more severe forms of madness. He did, however, make an important distinction between the two in a couple of seminal papers published in 1924,[10] shortly after devising his second theory of the unconscious. With his new structural model of the unconscious in hand, Freud assigned the passionate side of our nature to the id, the rational side to the ego; the superego represents our conscience, which is derived from the authority of our parents.[11] What both neurosis and psychosis share in common is their etiology: in each case the individual suffers a frustration due to non-fulfillment of a wish or desire. The frustration always originates from the outside, which is to say, from other people. Their difference lies in the respective strategies that each develops to relieve the frustration. The neurotic remains faithful to his dependence on the outside world and so silences the id by repressing his desire, whereas the psychotic allows his id free play by tearing himself away from the objecting reality. But in order to pull this off the psychotic is obliged to invent an *alternate reality* to replace the one rejected. This accounts for the distorted picture the psychotic has of reality and the problems he encounters with it. The devil, they say, is in the details, and the details of how the psychotic is supposed to go about inventing a different reality to live in is the weakest part of Freud's explanation. Though it contains an intuitive truth, Freud's lack of experience treating psychotic patients compromised his ability to dive into those details and paint a more compelling picture. For that we will now return our attention to R. D. Laing, who many believe did the same thing for the schizophrenic that Freud did for the neurotic: he understood them.

What about the word *psychosis* itself? The term was first introduced to the psychiatric literature in 1841 by Karl Friedrich Canstatt. He used it as a shorthand for "psychic neurosis." In those days neurosis was understood as a disease of the nervous system, in effect a brain disease. It was employed as an alternative to the terms *insanity* and *mania*. Like so many other terms we have been looking at, the term stems from Ancient Greek, *psyche*, giving soul or life to, animating, breath. The suffix -*osis* alludes to an abnormal condition, so psychosis was an abnormal condition of the soul or mind. Subsequently the word was used to distinguish a specific disorder of the *mind* from a neurosis, a disorder of the *nervous system*. The division of psychosis, or psychoses, into manic depressive illness (now bipolar disorder) and *dementia praecox* (now schizophrenia) was initiated by Kraepelin, who used the term "manic depressive insanity" to describe a wider sense of mood disorders than is employed today. It remains the preferred term that we use when referring to someone who has ostensibly lost his or her mind.

Though we may never be able to determine the etiology of any form of psychopathology, whether neurotic or psychotic, it is impossible to think about what these
entities are without some notion of their origin, however inexact or provisional. All
psychoanalysts and, for the most part, psychotherapists are joined in the common
conviction that the kinds of issues their patients bring to them are environmental in
nature. Though we have wildly competing notions of what we mean by "environmental," the basic notion is that we have *learned* to become neurotic or psychotic.
This includes the idea that something traumatic occurred that led us to snap or
become profoundly defensive. Whether that something is an environmental failure
that is specific to my unique family milieu, or because I simply find the demands
of living and loving inherently precarious, is the principal issue we are investigat-
ing when engaging in psychotherapy. Though lip-service is paid to the possibility
that our biology also plays a role in our symptoms (e.g., post-partum depression,
menopause, etc.), the issues that a therapist is most likely to have any influence about
are those that have culminated from things that we *experienced*. As noted earlier, the
concept of trauma has always been a central tenet in psychoanalytic theories, though
what it is that may be deemed traumatic is open to dispute. Freud, for example,
abandoned the idea that all neurotics were sexually molested by their parents, his
original "trauma theory," and replaced it with the notion that we are often traumatized, not *necessarily* by molestation, but by unrequited love. This alters our picture
of trauma from something that has been done *to* us, to something that was *not* done.
Not being loved in the way that I want to be, or having lost the love I once enjoyed
at that moment of Oedipal awakening may, Freud conjectured, result in my repressing all evidence of having loved so deeply. This turns the concept of trauma on its
head and, in so doing, renders it vaguely unrecognizable.

This notion of trauma was perhaps too subtle for some of the British object
relations theorists who, following Winnicott's lead, retained the more traditional
conception of trauma as something that literally *happened* at a pivotal moment in
time. Literally meaning wound, the concept of psychic trauma was adapted from
medicine and the procedure used to treat injuries. When you think of something
traumatic, the words violation, shock, and violence readily come to mind. Whereas
Freud surmised that the simple experience of disappointment is sufficient for a
trauma, the British Middle Group gravitated to the notion that the mother was the
key figure, and that she had failed the child at a key moment, resulting in developmental failure. According to this theory, the child doesn't receive the nurturing and
safety it requires and, due to neglect, is beset with untoward anxiety. In Winnicott's
theory of a "good-enough" mother, he too utilizes the notion of trauma as something that did *not* happen, in this case establishing a psychic wavelength with the
baby that the mother failed to effect. Both theories, Freud's and that of the object
relationalists, are environmental, and both speak to the child's acute vulnerability
and dependency, but the precise nature of the trauma and the "environment" in
question differ. For Freud, *life* is traumatic, and our lust for love is guaranteed to
subject us to traumatic experiences no matter how nurturing the environment. But
for Winnicott, the former pediatrician, it isn't life, *per se*, but the relationship *with*

the mother that is paramount. It follows that the environment generated between infant and mother may be so neglected as to result in catastrophic anxiety, perhaps resulting in psychosis. Variations on this thesis are dominant in the contemporary psychoanalytic community, resulting in the accusation from the parents of the world that analysts "blame the mother" for their child's predicament. Someone failed to mention that this theory was a terrible marketing ploy.

The idea that psychotics are more loyal to their desire than neurotics led Freud to conjecture that they are also more narcissistic in the way they withdraw from the world. Freud's thesis for this withdrawal was that the disturbing reality is replaced with one that is preferable to the psychotic. Yet, the fantasy life of the psychotic is often *distressing*, and fueled with incredible anxiety. The fantasies the psychotic withdraws into are not always gratifying but frequently tormenting and delusional. So why does the psychotic withdraw into something so hellish? As usual, Freud was ready with an explanation. He compared this phenomenon to dreams which, when they are pleasing, are a means of taking a break from reality by fulfilling wishes that reality is reluctant to accommodate. But what about dreams that are anguishing and don't conform to this picture? Freud conjectured that nightmares are a means of punishing ourselves for having entertained fantasies that are forbidden to us in waking life, which is to say, the superego punishes the ego for the dreams orchestrated by the id. Similarly, the psychotics' withdrawal from reality is equally untenable. A portion of the reality they seek to escape seeps in and, in life as in dreams, punishes them for their flight. An elegant explanation, but not altogether persuasive.

Laing, who was supervised by Winnicott when he trained as a psychoanalyst, was partial to the environmental thesis offered by the Middle Group, but he also brought an existential sensibility to bear in his thinking that the British analysts lacked and were predisposed against.[12] Laing also appreciated the subtlety of Freud's conception of trauma and his thesis of unrequited love. Moreover, Laing was impressed with the existential elements of Freud's take on the human condition, that life entails suffering, for example. Laing agreed that psychosis was not the result of organic predispositions, nor was he taken with Klein's thesis that psychosis emanates from the internal operations of our defenses during the first year of life, an argument that was contrary to the environmental considerations championed by the Middle Group. What Laing did appreciate about Klein's thesis was the assumption that we are all crazy, but he rejected the notion that we are born that way. Moreover, Laing believed it was not paranoia, as per Klein, that lay at the core of the psychotic experience, but *confusion*. Something happened in the environment, but it wasn't deprivation or lack of safety that gets to the core of the problem.

Laing agreed with Freud that unrequited love is probably the most painful experience that anyone is capable of suffering, and that this probably explains why neurotics, as Freud proposed, repress their desires in the face of unavoidable heartache. But does it account for losing one's mind? Can the hurt one feels when rejected drive someone crazy, which is to say, elicit a psychotic reaction? Laing wasn't sure that brokenheartedness was enough, though it is likely part of the equation. Though the term schizophrenia is typically taken to mean a "broken mind" (from the Greek *schizo* = broken, *phrene* = mind), the Greek *phrene* can also be taken to mean "heart." Laing concluded that, in addition to mental anguish, the schizophrenic suffers from a *broken heart*, or brokenheartedness. Some of this can be traced back to Nietzsche's conception of *ressentiment*. When someone breaks my heart, for example, a bit of it is torn away and sits there. I consequently find myself in an untenable position: I can neither tear myself away, nor can I bring myself to trust the person who inflicted the injury. The resentment I feel at having been narcissistically rejected is all it takes to prevent me from healing the wound I carry with me. This is reminiscent of the schizoid person whom Laing describes in *The Divided Self*. The schizoid person also finds himself in an untenable position: he can neither allow himself to get close to others, nor can he manage being alone. Though Laing never made this connection, it is obvious that the schizoid individual, and by extension the person who gets labeled schizophrenic, are trapped in their own resentful mindset, which they can neither escape nor accommodate. Like the neurotic, they are trapped in the bitterness they feel at having felt violated when vulnerable, yet helpless to protect themselves, even from their desire to be loved and, in turn, to love again. But unlike the neurotic, their anguish has driven them mad. However, we still don't know what accounts for the difference, why some people keep their wits about them and others do not.

Laing believed there must be an extra element, a factor-x, that accounts for why we become psychotic instead of merely neurotic, though both are probably consequences of brokenheartedness. Rejection is hurtful and readily elicits anger, self-pity, and resentment. But what transpires between a young child and the persons in the environment that could account for the loss of one's sanity? A possible answer came to Laing early in his professional development, even before he trained as a psychoanalyst (in the 1950s). His conclusion: *deception*, a common theme in the existential literature.[13]

Sartre had a profound influence on Laing in his youth. Though he had studied virtually every existentialist philosopher by the time he completed his university education, Sartre stood out as the philosopher, after Nietzsche, with whom Laing most identified. It was Nietzsche and Sartre (and to a considerable degree, Kierkegaard) who wrote the template from which many of Laing's ideas about psychopathology were born. What they held in common was their unforgiving assessment of the human condition, and the enormous power that anyone we love has over us. Moreover, they assumed that human beings are incapable of honesty and are committed to deceiving those with whom they share their most intimate relations, beginning with the relationship they establish with themselves. Nietzsche saw human beings as inherently resentful creatures who envied anyone who was more successful than themselves. Sartre, though influenced by Nietzsche, was more interested in how we lie to one another, why we are incapable of genuine love, and how bad faith becomes the doctrine by which we aspire to gain power over others. Winnicott came to a similar conclusion with his notion of a compliant false self. But whereas Winnicott believed we develop a false self by concealing who we are from our mothers (at a critical stage of development), Laing rejected the idea that such strategies could be enacted at such a tender, uncomprehending age. He also doubted that these sentiments were always directed at the mother. Instead, he surmised that the *entire breadth* of our childhoods offer a protracted training ground during which we learn how to be false with others, in order to elicit love. Our need for love inaugurates our career as deceivers, beginning with the need to deceive those closest to us. Sartre's conception of intimacy, epitomized in his play, *No Exit*, suggests there is no escaping the heartbreak that relationships subject us to. There is no exit from the hell of relationship. This is obviously no blueprint for happiness.

But if this is the *normal* human condition to which each of us is doomed, it still doesn't account for why some of us become more or less permanently and pervasively psychotic whereas most of us do not. For that Laing had to journey beyond even Sartre's gloomy picture of the family.[14] He turned to Karl Marx, the self-proclaimed expert in the unique form of *alienation* that Marx believed epitomizes modern, European culture. Marx, following Hegel, believed that power was the currency that guided all relationships. He was especially intrigued with how despots were able to maintain their hold over the populations whom they subjugated for their venal ends. Why did the vast majority of the population of nations such as, say, Iraq (or Iran or North Korea or Cuba) not rise up against such an obvious oppressor as Saddam Hussein? Why not rebel and replace him with a leader more benevolent and fair? After all, the many outnumber the few. Marx believed that fear is not sufficient for such control, because the populace will eventually tire of it and engage in open rebellion. Marx's conclusion: he holds onto power because the despot has managed to pull the wool over the populace's eyes. Though Hegel's conception of the master–slave dialectic played a role, Marx believed it took more than the inherent power imbalance in every relationship to explain how the despot maintains power over a nation. Despots tend to have a certain charisma about them and are experts at seduction, so they know how to convince the populace that *everything they do, no matter how despicable, is in the people's interest.* No matter how bad things are in their daily lives, especially economically, so long as the populace *believes* that their leader has their interests at heart they will put up with just about anything. In a word, dictators are able to manipulate the populace's minds via *mystification*, a subtle form of hypnosis. By it, the leader fools them, but without their ever being the wiser. How is this accomplished? By getting them to see things the dictator's way. The dictator is expert at convincing the population that the reason they suffer economic hardship, or are deprived of basic rights, is due to factors that have nothing to do with their being *exploited*. The blame always lies somewhere else, usually another nation. Their leader wants only to help them, so they should be grateful and, of course, loyal. Everything their leader does and says is evidence of the dictator's love and benevolence. How can they blame him when all he cares about is their welfare? The key lies in what he is able to persuade the populace to *believe*.

Laing was keenly impressed with Marx's assessment of how the powerful few are able to reign over the many, and could see the parallels between the power imbalance in nations and nuclear families (Laing, 1965, 1971). In the early 1960s Laing and a colleague, Aaron Esterson, conducted a study of families of schizophrenics that was subsequently published as *Sanity, Madness and the Family* (1964), one of the most impressive phenomenological studies into families ever undertaken. The study, conducted at the Tavistock Institute for Human Relations, entailed extensive interviews with the families of eleven women who were hospitalized for schizophrenia. Laing and Esterson deftly demonstrated how, in every family they studied, massive forms of trickery, deception, and mystification were systematically employed against each of the schizophrenic family members, by their parents. One of the patients, whom Laing calls Maya, is typical of the families studied. Her parents, who come across as pretty crazy themselves, believed that their daughter possessed special powers that enabled her to read their minds. The father spoke openly – whenever his daughter was not present – of having systematically conducted "tests" on his daughter to prove that Maya could tell what her parents were thinking. Maya, in turn, suspected that something of this sort was being done to her, but when she confronted her parents with her suspicions in one their family sessions, they coyly winked at Laing and denied it, as they had done all her life.

In case after case Laing and Esterson unearthed casual and often chilling arrays of deceptive maneuvers of this kind, all employed by the parents against their children. In effect, they were systematically distorting the truth about their efforts to manipulate their children and, by that distortion, twisted their children's hold on reality by confusing them, in much the same way that Marx believed despots were able to confuse their populace. Does this mean that mystification "causes" schizophrenia? That was a claim that Laing and Esterson were unwilling to make. Phenomenological studies do not seek to determine causes the same way that empirical studies aspire to. Instead, they search for *meanings* in order to gain insight into the complexity of the situation and to understand it better. Laing did not specifically explore what might motivate the parents of schizophrenics they studied to manipulate their children in this fashion, nor did he and Esterson argue that mystification is unique to such families. In a follow-up study that was never published (Laing, 1974), Laing and Esterson conducted a similar series of interviews with normal families, which is to say, families in which no one had been diagnosed as suffering from any type of psychotic disturbance. What they learned was dismaying. They found that normal families engaged in similar acts of mystification with their children as well.

The only difference they were able to determine between the two types of families was that the children in the normal families engaged in similar acts of deception themselves, whereas in the families of schizophrenics the daughters so diagnosed did not appear to engage in such practices. They were always one step behind the stratagems employed by their parents. Moreover, the daughters diagnosed as schizophrenic tended to be uncommonly naïve and gullible, and as Winnicott might have observed, extremely *compliant*, whereas the sons or daughters in the normal families engaged in open conflict with their parents that frequently culminated in impasse or rebellion (Laing, 1986). What all the families studied shared in common, both the normal ones as well as the schizophrenic, was that duplicity was a common occurrence and taken, more or less, for granted. Laing, following Sartre, attributed this discovery, not to disturbed families, *per se*, but to society at large, and the human condition. People are naturally devious with each other and, always with justification, betray one another as a matter of course. Schizophrenia is only one of the many possible consequences of this state of affairs, but duplicity is not necessarily the *cause* of what prompts a person to go mad. Again, the very concept of cause is probably irrelevant where interpersonal relationships are concerned.[15] Laing nonetheless believed that deception plays an important role in the kinds of internal conflicts that bring most people to therapy, and was the principal reason Freud insisted that honesty is essential to a successful outcome. It stands to reason that if deception is a common occurrence in relationships, then the conflicts that individuals have with themselves are in some measure a consequence of being deceived by others.

It was the *state of confusion* that the schizophrenic person typically struggles with that led Laing to observe that their most desperate preoccupation is that of their personal identity, as existential a theme as there is. Among all the people I have seen in therapy over the past forty years who fit the diagnostic picture of schizophrenia, the most agonizing symptom they exhibited and complained about was that they were not at all certain *who they were.* This is the one feature of the "broken mind" metaphor of madness (the other being brokenheartedness) that embodies Laing's thesis of mystification. The relatively intact neurotic sometimes wonders who he really is, even who he wants to be, but he is not as dismayed about this question as he is anxious about and intrigued by it. For the schizophrenic, this question is so basic to his (or her) state of mind that it dominates his experience of psychotherapy. Indeed, it is the principal reason he pursues therapy.

Schizophrenia was always an abiding interest of Laing's, perhaps because it is the most extreme example of how crazed and crazy a person is capable of becoming, and because it is the one "mental illness" that is not only the most debilitating, but the most challenging to ameliorate. The fact that his mother was also quite crazy was no doubt a factor for his interest in this topic.[16] The official position of psychiatry is that schizophrenia is, by definition, incurable. This has become such a truism in the psychiatric community that if a person so diagnosed enjoys a complete recovery, the consensus is that the lucky patient was obviously *misdiagnosed.* It is one of those ironies that cure continues to be the rallying cry of a discipline as misguided as that of psychiatry, when we all know that no one is cured of anything we label a mental illness, whether the illness in question is neurosis, depression, mania, or any number of psychotic symptoms. Yet schizophrenia, of all the psychopathologies, continues to be the most feared of all possible diagnoses. The *DSM* categorizes schizophrenia into a cluster of subtypes including paranoid, disorganized, catatonic, undifferentiated, and residual. In fact, all of these features are present in nearly every person who receives a diagnosis of schizophrenia. Because some tend to be more prominent than others in a given person, it is assumed that such distinctions help differentiate the severity of a given case. Paranoia and auditory hallucinations are among the most blatant symptoms, but disorganization – or confusion – is by far the most prevalent. Schizophreniform and schizoaffective disorders have been added as additional psychotic, but not strictly schizophrenic, symptoms in order to account for telltale signs of a schizophrenic-like condition that does not meet the criteria of chronic duration normally associated with schizophrenia. A person who appears to be schizophrenic but exhibits significant depression would most likely be diagnosed schizoaffective. And so it goes.

One can see why Laing threw his hands up trying to differentiate among these crazy-making distinctions, as though enumerating subtype after subtype lends to this exercise the alleged proof of its scientific validity. Basically, all we are witnessing in this plethora of never-ending minutiae is psychiatry's efforts to match diagnostic criteria to the drugs that are brought to bear for sedating the symptoms. The hundreds of disorders listed in the *DSM* have virtually nothing to do with how a psychoanalyst or psychotherapist treats persons so diagnosed, except for the complication that many therapists, perhaps most, are simply not willing to work with someone who suffers psychotic symptoms, including paranoia, confusion, hallucinations, mania, or severe depression. By now we have completely lost sight of the human equation, of the *person* being treated, if such a person has access to psychotherapy, or even wants or can afford it. Each of us suffers from delusions, hallucinations, confusion, depression, mania, anxiety, and the like, so all we are talking about is a question of *degrees*, not whether this person or that is crazy or sane. The schizoid person whom Laing discusses in *The Divided Self* is simply less crazy than the schizophrenic, but perhaps more than the neurotic. This degree of ambiguity does not sit well with the scientifically trained practitioner who wants to know precisely what it is he is dealing with. Perhaps this is a diagnostic category all its own, the psychiatrist or psychotherapist who is *ambiguity-averse*, for which we should endeavor to find a suitable label and treatment, perhaps LSD. Indeed, it would appear that we already have a treatment for this condition. It is called the *DSM*!

That being said, psychopathology is relatively easy to recognize in the typical schizoid and schizophrenic personality structures we reviewed in Chapter One. But what about other forms of madness, like the manic personality or the high functioning paranoiac who seems perfectly at home in the world, and manages to get by with little notice? Laing doesn't address this type of psychotic process because it doesn't conform to the kind of patients who typically sought him for treatment, neither in hospital nor in private practice. This is one of the problems in determining the broad range that psychosis – essentially, any loss of contact with reality, however brief or long-lasting – may entail. Unlike the neurotic who seeks therapy due to insupportable distress, those suffering from psychosis, including schizophrenia and its myriad subtypes, bipolar disorder (but basically mania), and paranoia (e.g., prevalence of delusions), rarely seek treatment due to lack of insight that there is anything the matter with them. This is not surprising as lack of insight is a prominent feature of psychosis. This means that the popular psychiatric criteria for diagnosing mental disorders, including psychoses, derive more or less exclusively from those who show up for treatment. This happens either voluntarily (the person so labeled seeks treatment himself) or involuntarily (the person is brought to treatment by a concerned family member, friend, or police officer). Neurotics invariably seek treatment themselves, whereas psychotics almost always bring attention upon themselves due to erratic or threatening behavior. That hardly covers everyone who suffers from psychosis. If my thesis is correct, that virtually everyone experiences psychotic symptoms now and then, then most people so afflicted do not show up in the *DSM*'s statistical criteria.

For the most part, it is psychotherapists who wonder about such things and are equipped to notice, among those they encounter in their everyday lives (as distinct from their professional practice), who happen to show signs of psychosis in their conduct with others. Yet, only those specifically seeking treatment are likely to show up on our radar. Those we encounter outside this context rarely afford us the opportunity to know them intimately. The exceptions are everyone we encounter in our social network, including friends, spouses, colleagues, and the like. Given the peculiar nature of psychotherapy, a relationship based on the patient's willingness to disclose in considerable detail how he experiences the world, this has to remain the optimal opportunity afforded to study such people. Friends and spouses, for example, keep a great deal to themselves, so our only access to their madness is what we observe through their behavior, not what they self-reflectively disclose. This tells us a lot, but at the same time, not very much.

For example, a friend of mine whom I got to know through a work situation impressed me with her acumen and professional skill, which was superb. She was attractive, charming, affectionate, worldly, accomplished, and my then-wife, and I enjoyed her company and saw her on social occasions. I began to notice, however, that each year she inexplicably disappeared. She fell off the map and we didn't have a clue where she had gone. We left messages that went unanswered, so we concluded she was just busy or traveling. Then one day out of the blue she reappeared, exuberant as always, and when we asked where she had been she made an excuse about being busy or out of town. This pattern continued for some years until one day, while enjoying dinner at her home, she confided that she felt extremely happy, that her life had never been better, but that her adult children were concerned she may be *too* happy. She said they were worried that she was having a manic episode, and she asked me what I thought. After some prompting she said she had never seen a therapist in her life and had never had any reason to. Sometimes she felt down, and when this occurred she withdrew from her social activities to "recharge her batteries." This explained the periods when she disappeared from view.

I suggested it wouldn't do any harm to consult a psychoanalyst, and offered to refer her to a colleague who would be willing to meet with her and explore what was going on. She laughed this off and said she couldn't see what purpose that would serve because she felt perfectly wonderful. That appeared to be that. Then, a few months later, she confided that she had met this attractive woman on the street, and that she was head-over-heels taken with her. She made this woman her lover and in due course decided to hire her for a position at her law firm. The mystery woman had no credentials to practice law, yet my friend brought her on board at a high salary to help run the firm. Naturally, this got my attention and I asked her if everything was alright. She explained she had never felt better and that her new friend was helping her redesign the firm. They would soon be making some personnel changes. A few weeks later my friend told me that the partners in her firm had confronted her and decided to terminate her partnership with them, and to fire her friend. She was devastated and worried about what she was going to do for a living. Her relationship with the woman abruptly ended.

Now that her life was in shambles she was open to consulting the analyst I had offered earlier, and she began a several times a week analysis with him. I subsequently learned that her partners had implored her to seek treatment, to no avail, so they took matters into their hands and fired her. She continued in therapy for some years, and for a brief time medication, but she was never the same. This episode had ruined her professionally and she now found it difficult to earn a living. She fit the criterion for what gets diagnosed as bipolar disorder, but this wasn't at all obvious to me until she took me into her confidence that day and asked me what I thought. I don't believe this kind of thing is uncommon. Lord knows how many friends and acquaintances of mine suffer from mania, but I suspect a great many. If her condition were severe she would have decompensated and been taken to a mental hospital, but she avoided that humiliation by seeking treatment voluntarily. Mania is like that. It can fool you, and if you don't know someone intimately, like my friend's children for example, you may not think twice about this fetching and vivacious mystery woman.

What, then, is mania? The term derives from the Greek meaning mad, rage, or fury. So the term lies at the basis of what we have historically understood madness to mean. I use the term madness more generally, to connote any phenomenon that we typically label as a form of psychopathology, including neuroses, psychoses, melancholia (depression), paranoia, schizoid, schizophrenia – as I said, *everything* we usually label as psychopathological. By this definition, we are all mad, but to varying degrees. So the manic person is a special category of madness that shows up in a variety of contexts. The person who is diagnosed bipolar (previously manic depressive) is the poster child for our culture's contemporary obsession with those in our midst who challenge psychiatry's efforts to make them normal. Depression we all know about because there isn't a person in the world who does not feel depressed now and then, some more than others. The manic side of this equation is more mysterious, and perhaps less prevalent, but no one really knows, nor can they.

According to the *DSM*, mania varies in intensity, from mild mania (hypomania), to the full-bore variety that occasions extreme energy, racing thoughts, forced speech. This covers a fairly broad range of phenomena. So-called hypomania, for example, is probably just as common as obsessive-compulsive disorder, a neurosis that is so prevalent it has been called the "normal neurosis." Some people present themselves characterologically as excitable by nature. Do they possess manic personalities? Technically, yes. We sometimes call such people hysterical, because they are behaving excitedly, perhaps too excitedly, as though in a crisis, or in love. One of the features of the hysterical personality type is a person who is prone to crises. Freud believed this was a compensation for having repressed their sexuality, so the excited, anxious behavior they exhibit is a displacement of the sexual energy that was repressed. How do we tell them apart, the hysteric from the hypomanic? No one can say. The reason such people aren't ordinarily "pathologized" is because we often like being around them. They don't act as though they are distressed, but behave as though they are happy. We enjoy their energy vicariously, and feed on it. The more manic and less hysterical side of this phenomenon is a person whose sexuality is not repressed but the opposite. They may be extremely sexual and if we chance to be their sexual partners we will usually find their energy infectious and irresistible. Other manifestations of this kind of energy are evidenced in artistic work, which may lead to extraordinary accomplishments such as in the work of Jackson Pollok, Salvador Dalí, Franz Kafka, or Nietzsche. We like to say that artists are a bit crazy, and we grant them considerable latitude in how crazy we are willing to allow, *because* they are artists. It is impossible to generalize about the psychopathology of the gifted artist, even the mad artist. They may be happy or miserable, but mad all the same. There is no necessary correlation between mania and misery. Some are miserable and some aren't. It is a mystery.

On the other end of the spectrum, manic episodes are not always happy or productive occasions. Thomas Szasz told me a story of a woman who brought her husband to see him when he began suffering from a manic episode. The husband began to withdraw all of their savings in order to purchase expensive automobiles and prostitutes. The wife was understandably alarmed as she witnessed her husband behaving in a way that was foreign to his nature. Plus he was spending all their money and would not listen to reason. What could be done? Szasz offered that this man was not suffering from a mental illness, because there is no such thing as mental illness. Therefore, what this woman had on her hands was a husband whose spending she could not control, pure and simple. Szasz suggested she divorce him before he had a chance to run through all their funds. This she was unable to accomplish in time and when they eventually divorced she was destitute. Szasz thought she should have acted sooner.

In fact, there isn't much one can do in such a case, because the person suffering from this condition cannot be reasoned with, by definition. The standard treatment for such mania today is, you guessed it, medication, usually Lithium. If a person so diagnosed can be persuaded to take medication she may return to a modicum of normality, which is to say, her excitable state will likely diminish, so long as she remains sedated. There are other forms of mania that are not associated with bipolar disorder because they exhibit a predominance of paranoid or other psychotic symptoms as well (e.g., schizoaffective disorder). In the early days that I worked with Laing in London we occasionally encountered a person whose family brought him to Portland Road for safe haven. They did not want their family member medicated but couldn't handle his behavior at home. This was an example of a psychotic person who had embarked on the famous Laingian journey through madness or "transcendental voyage" of psychotic breakdown, with a potential for breakthrough and resolution. Laing's thesis was that if such a person were permitted to complete this journey uninterrupted (and un-medicated), he would come through this ordeal with his senses, and sanity, more or less intact. The reason families are ill-equipped to contain such episodes is that once it begins, the "maniac" stops sleeping and is going at it twenty-four hours a day, for a period of two weeks or more, before it finally abates. It takes a crew of people working in teams to keep up with it. Medication dispenses with such requirements, and is far cheaper and more convenient.

This was exactly what happened with this person. Two weeks or so after it commenced, the crazy journey that occasioned all manner of delusions and hallucinations abated, and he appeared to be perfectly normal once more, just as Laing predicted. At any rate, he returned to his senses. Naturally, the question arose, what had prompted this episode in the first place? Initially Laing confused such psychotic journeys with schizophrenia, but it eventually became obvious this was not the case and that we were dealing with an entirely different kind of madness than the one we anticipated. Now that he had come to his senses, this young man was invited to embark on another, more relaxed journey of ongoing, twice-weekly psychotherapy, to get to the bottom of what had elicited his psychotic episode in the first place. He rejected our suggestion, insisting he was perfectly fine, thanked us for the help we had given him, and went his merry way. We wondered how long his "recovery" would last. Could it be that easy? Sure enough, less than a year later he returned, suffering another manic episode, and we accommodated a second journey through madness. After the successful culmination of the reprised episode we insisted with more gravitas that he pursue some therapy before returning home. His answer was the same. He was just as incapable of insight on this occasion as he was a year earlier, and nothing we said would convince him that, though his symptoms had gone into remission, he had been cured of nothing. Did he want to spend the rest of his life repeating these episodes, annually? Apparently, this was acceptable to him. It was his choice to make.

The maddening thing about trying to help someone who is experiencing manic episodes in general, however severe or slight, is that the person who is under its spell is impervious to reflective awareness. This makes the prospect of psychotherapy understandably dubious. Whether they feel good or bad, they are so caught up in the experience that they have little capacity for doubt, a prerequisite for self-inquiry. Unlike many of the people I have seen in therapy who get labeled schizophrenic, the manic person categorically *lacks insight*, a feature of the euphoria that occasions this condition. The schizophrenic, because he is usually in a state of distress and considerable confusion, is often capable of at least some insight and, so, can benefit from psychotherapy. This is a paradox. No one is more psychotic than the schizophrenic, yet this person is often more capable of pursuing psychotherapy than the typical maniac, who is usually less disturbed. Perhaps this says something about the relative aversion to psychotherapy in our culture, a culture so obsessed with becoming happy that there is little room to even question what it entails.

Many people coast through life in what may be characterized as a simmering manic condition. Unlike the schizoid personality that is intolerant of either intimacy or isolation, this person is extremely engaging with others. In fact, they need to be with others as much as possible, but not too much with any one person. They feed on attention and engagement, usually of an optimistic nature, but they are always going somewhere, always on the run. If married, they want their partner to be with them constantly, yet they need to replace their partner with others, perhaps business partners, or jobs that requires frequent travel, always going here and there, never in any one place for too long. Though most people like them, what is most striking is their inability to become truly intimate with others. They need to control when they appear and when they leave. Like the sex addict that needs a constant supply of new partners because the beginning of a relationship is the most intense, this form of mania thrives on the greeting that occasions coming and going. They are never really alone, but never really *with* anyone either, though this may go unnoticed. Beneath all the excitement is an anxious fear of depression and the underlying despair that is lurking, and always fended away. Though ostensibly polar opposites from the typical schizoid, the manic person simply has a different cover and a striking abundance of energy. Beneath the surface appearance both conditions are more or less the same, with the same excess of anxiety. They simply have different ways of coping.

Do people who are prey to manic episodes also suffer from resentment, or is the etiology of their condition of a different trajectory? Though mania is usually devoid of the kind of distress, guilt and self-doubt so typical of schizophrenia-related symptoms, I suspect resentment is always in play. Contrary to how it appears, mania isn't driven by *desire*, as it seems to be, but by anxiety. It is not always so easy to distinguish between the two. With milder forms of hypomania anxiety and desire are present in equal measure, and more liable to occasion a feasible balance. But with full-blown mania the person appears to be saying, "I don't abide by the strictures of normal society because I am not like you, but better. Let me show you how." The resentment is hidden beneath the bravura, but it is there all the same. The friend I mentioned earlier, once the bottom had fallen out of her life and she was forced to live within her means, in due course came into contact with the pain she had been avoiding, and this did her some good. Yes, the amazing heights she had achieved were now destroyed, and she would never realize such elation again. But she took the opportunity to know herself better, and to acknowledge the bitter hatred she felt toward her mother. Whenever we live a double life, what Kierkegaard calls "double-mindedness" (1956), the internal conflict so engendered is always fueled by resentment, the wish to punish others and, oftentimes, ourselves.

Before leaving our exploration of psychopathology, I want to say something about the phenomenon of depression, the only major category we have not touched on. What we call psychopathology may be conceived as the seasons of our human condition, including the states of mind, emotions, and moods to which we fall prey daily. We might think of neuroses as days of the week, one day hysterical, the next obsessive, though both are present on a continuous basis below awareness. At night we fall prey to the darker forces within us, our propensity for psychotic withdrawal from reality, to greater or lesser degrees. In the summer we are blessed with a manic sense of bliss, and in the winter we succumb to the dark night of the soul, melancholia. Again, summer and winter are seasonal, and we sometimes favor one over the other, or access both simultaneously. All of us suffer from mania, and for the most part we enjoy it. It is an essential ingredient of our happiness and without it we would be miserable. Our most common experience of it is when we fall in love (we will turn to the relation between love and mania in Chapter Seven). Moreover, all of us are equally depressed, which occasionally elicits a calming effect, not the least bit distressing. We could not sleep at night without it. I may be, for example, a hysteric, but with obsessive features that keep my life organized and fuel my quest for perfection, which I enjoy. Complementing this picture, I may also be a depressive, but with a propensity for hypomania that drives my lust for life and a sense of adventure. Any extremes of these aspects of how my desire is organized for optimal reward would compromise my capacity to render sensible judgments and to enjoy what life has to offer. And anxiety? Where would you situate that in the seasons of your life? As with desire, it is a constant presence, with me at all times on every occasion. My desire is what makes me *feel* alive, and my anxiety is what *keeps* me alive, alert and aware of who I am, and what in the world I am doing here.

Depression has a bad rap because we don't always like how it feels, but more importantly some of us, if sufficiently depressed, decide that life is no longer worth living, so we end it, or threaten to. To lose someone we love that way is traumatic in a double sense. We lose someone who is dear to us, and our existence, to varying degrees, is diminished. But suicide also confronts us with our own mortality and fear of nonexistence. Moreover, it reminds us that, there but for the grace of God, go I. This is another paradox. I fear death and, for the most part, deny it. But I also fear how tempting it may be to take my life and end it. Living with the ambiguity of when and how I will die is an ever-present source of anxiety, and for some it is too much to bear. This is because the *anticipation* of death is its single-most feature that exacerbates my anxiety, compelling me to imagine any number of scenarios that suggest I am immortal. We all know, in the depths of our being, we will never die. That is the lie we live with daily. If it were not for depression and its cousin, suicide, the medical profession may well have never invented mental illness and taken it upon itself to "save" the depressed person's life. The possibility of death is what makes our unmitigated suffering a medical affair. We all want a cure for our suffering. We all want a cure for death.

Freud made a distinction between the person who is melancholic (the term for depression in his day) and the person in a state of mourning. He surmised that when suffering a loss we are given a choice, an existential choice to be sure. We either accept the loss, suffer it, and succumb to our grief, or we deny the loss, fight it, and try our best to keep it alive. The second course of action results in that peculiar phenomenon we call depression. The person who mourns a loss feels sad, and the sadness envelops him, takes over his life, and rules it for as long as it sees fit. Traditionally, all cultures recognize the need to mourn a loved one's death for a circumscribed period of time, anywhere from six months to a year. For the duration, one wears black, does not participate in festive activities, and lives with the absence that the loss elicits, until finally it lifts. Everyone in the community rallies around, offering comfort to ease the pain, not to distract but to console. Some cultures recommend getting drunk, though such measures are risky, though no less effective for many. We who live in developed cultures seldom engage in such rituals. Instead, we go to our doctors and obtain prescriptions for Prozac or whatever mood stabilizer that is recommended to help us "cope" with our grief, which is to say not coping at all, but a licensed form of institutional denial. Our culture appears to be, not only risk-averse (the typical neurotic), but grief-averse as well. We are haunted by those we have lost and are convinced that ghosts are real, because we cannot let go of the dead. We seem strangely intolerant of *sadness*, which is sad because, as you no doubt know, to feel sad can also be exquisite, for it reminds us of the people we have loved, and still do. It is also a helpless feeling, and maybe that is the crux of the problem. We just don't want to suffer any more than we have to. I sometimes wonder if our intolerance of mourning, sadness, and other modes of everyday suffering have contributed to the escalating incidence of mental illness, now of near-epidemic proportions.[17]

Whether Freud's thesis is correct I do not know. If this applies to people who have been depressed all their lives, then the loss they deny is a very early one. Perhaps, like schizophrenia, it is constitutional? If all of us are subject to deception, mystification, and manipulation as a matter of course, then it may be that those among us who are more vulnerable than the next are more liable to take these matters on the chin, and are more susceptible to, say, schizophrenia, mania, or depression than the next person, given the right environmental triggers. Laing was depressed all his life, and nothing he tried, including psychoanalysis, meditation, and LSD made the slightest difference. All the understanding and self-awareness in the world did not help him. He had to suck it up and cope with it the best he could. He preferred alcohol to anything he could obtain with a prescription. Because many who kill themselves initially threaten to in a very public way, it is inevitable that we, as a society, will intervene and try to save them. That seems like a good thing. And because we put them under watch and administer drugs to relieve the depression, medical doctors are invariably called upon to administer such drugs and provide protective scrutiny. That seems to me not such a good thing, that we have turned that service over to doctors and, through them, deem these incidents as signs of "illness" that must be "treated." Does that really get to the bottom of the anguish that drove that person to attempt suicide in the first place? I doubt it.

Notes

1 See Thompson (1994), for a review of Freud's evolution as a theorist of psychopathology from an existential perspective.

2 Though Freud and most of his early followers were doctors, other non-medical converts to his cause began to train with him as well, so-called "lay analysts." He even wrote a book, *The Question of Lay Analysis* (1926), where he argued that medicine is a poor preparation for training as an analyst and that the study of literature, history, and the humanities would prepare the would-be analyst far better.

3 I employ the term "coping" in the Heideggerian sense, which is to say we are coping as a matter of course in every activity we engage in. Driving a car, riding a bike, making love, writing a book, doing my job, taking a walk, eating a meal, relaxing by the beach, etc., are all activities in which I bring to bear my intentions and abilities, heart and soul, to accomplish the task at hand, or to maximize a source of pleasure that may be no more active

than reading a book or gazing at the heavens. The way I handle my anxiety, frustrations, disappointments, and heartaches also brings to bear the ways I cope and deal with them. This is a far broader usage than the psychoanalytic conception of a "coping mechanism" because it pertains to everything I do, including the way I manage my emotions and the stratagems I develop to cope with them, whether consciously or unconsciously. Some of these stratagems are naturally more effective than others.

4 Cargo Cults occurred periodically in various islands of the South Pacific when the local natives first encountered technologically advanced civilizations for the first time. Typically, ships would land on the island, whether merchant or military vessels, and the natives would be exposed to goods and foods with which they were unfamiliar. Visitors gave them some of their "cargo" and then they left. The locals assumed these visitors were gods or brought by the gods to deliver the gifts "from the heavens" to them, and assumed they would return with more gifts. As they waited they concocted elaborate myths about the people who brought the goods and their motives for doing so, developing prayers and other practices to bring the cargo back.

5 Psychology, as a discipline, is no better equipped to formulate coherent theories about the nature of madness than psychiatry is. The kind of pathology, or suffering, we are talking about is no more located in the mind or our behavior than it is in the body, because the kind of suffering we are concerned with is not mental, but existential: it inhabits our *being*. As such, it concerns the manner in which we live our lives and the intelligence we bring to bear when trying our best to manage painful experiences. It is *where we live* that we develop these stratagems, not, strictly speaking, in our thoughts or feelings.

6 See Thompson (1994, pp. 1–50), for a more thorough discussion of the two kinds of suffering that psychopathology implies.

7 As indicated in Chapter Two, perversions may be healthy and normal, or pathological. The ones we deem problematic because they are pathological contain elements of neurotic or psychotic stratagems.

8 Unless, of course, you are being forcefully treated against your will, which often happens if someone is taken to a mental hospital because they are so crazy they are deemed a danger to themselves or others.

9 Like the Buddhists, Freud developed a form of meditation that focused on speaking to and listening *to another person* rather than meditating silently and alone, which managed to help some people become more accepting of who they are. If this process cures us of anything, it is the myth of mental illness.

10 "Neurosis and Psychosis" (1924a), and "The Loss of Reality in Neurosis and Psychosis (1924b)."

11 Freud actually derived the structural model of the unconscious from Plato, a principal source of Freud's picture of the human condition. Just as he lifted his theory of *Eros* and *Thanatos* from Plato's dialogue, *The Symposium*, he lifted his idea about id, ego, and superego from Plato's dialogue, *The Republic*. His views about the Pleasure Principle came from yet another of Plato's dialogues, *The Protagoras*. Many of Freud's views about psychopathology and the workings of the mind are derived from Plato and Aristotle, as well as other Classical thinkers.

12 Laing tried to interest Winnicott in existential philosophy while in supervision with him, but to no avail. Winnicott admired the MS for Laing's first book, *The Divided Self*, but couldn't understand why Laing chose to contaminate such brilliant clinical work with "speculative philosophy" (Laing, 1985).

13 Especially in Sartre, who influenced Laing profoundly. Sartre's masterwork, *Being and Nothingness* (1954/1943), is replete with examples of interpersonal deception as a common, everyday occurrence.

14 Laing's conception of family dynamics, outlined in his *The Politics of the Family* (1971), is essentially a Sartrean schema.

15 See Heidegger's *Zollikon Seminars* (2001) for an exhaustive explanation as to why the concept of causation is useless in comprehending the human condition.

16 See Laing's autobiography, *Wisdom, Madness and Folly: The Making of a Psychiatrist* (1985), for a description of his own family.
17 See Robert Whitaker's *Anatomy of an Epidemic: Magic Bullets, Psychiatric Drugs, and the Astonishing Rise of Mental Illness in America* (2011), for a detailed study of the rise of psychopathology in America in the last thirty years, since the first edition of this book was published.

References

Freud, S. (1953–1973) *The standard edition of the complete psychological works of Sigmund Freud*. 24 volumes. Edited and translated by J. Strachey. London: Hogarth Press. (Referred to in subsequent references as *Standard Edition*.)

Freud, S. (1924a) Neurosis and psychosis. *Standard Edition*, 19:148–53. London: The Hogarth Press, 1961.

Freud, S. (1924b) The loss of reality in neurosis and psychosis. *Standard Edition*, Vol. 19: 182–187. London: The Hogarth Press, 1961.

Freud, S. (1926) *The question of lay analysis. Standard Edition*, 20:179–258. London: Hogarth Press, 1959.

Heidegger, M. (2001) *Zollikon seminars: Protocols – Conversations – Letters*. Edited by M. Boss and translated by F. Mayr and R. Askay. Evanston, IL: Northwestern University Press.

Jaspers, K. (1997) *General psychopathology – Volume 1*. Translated by J. Hoenig and Marian W. Hamilton. Baltimore: Johns Hopkins University Press.

Kierkegaard, S. (1956) *Purity of heart is to will one thing*. Translated by D. Steere. New York: Harper Torchbooks.

Laing, R. D. (1965) Mystification, confusion, and conflict. In *Intensive family therapy: Theoretical and practical aspects* (Eds., I. Boszormenyi-Nagy and J. Framo) (pp. 343–364). New York and London: Harper and Row, 1965.

Laing, R. D. (1971) *The politics of the family*. London: Tavistock.

Laing, R. D. (1974) Personal communication.

Laing, R. D. (1985) *Wisdom, madness and folly: The making of a psychiatrist*. New York: McGraw-Hill Book Company.

Laing, R. D. (1986) Personal communication.

Laing, R. D. and Esterson, A. (1964) *Sanity, madness and the family*. London: Tavistock.

Sartre, J.-P. (1954/1943) *Being and nothingness*. Translated by H. Barnes. New York: Philosophical Library.

Thompson, M. Guy (1994) *The truth about Freud's technique: The encounter with the real*. New York and London: New York University Press.

Whitaker, R. (2011) *Anatomy of an epidemic: Magic bullets, psychiatric drugs, and the astonishing rise of mental illness in America*. New York: Broadway Books.

5

WHAT TO MAKE OF AN INCIDENCE OF INCOMPREHENSIBLE MADNESS (OR A CLINICAL CASE NOT SO EASY TO DIAGNOSE)

If you are a therapist who is seeing someone in psychotherapy suffering from a neurotic conflict, then it shouldn't be a stretch for you to do so without rendering a diagnosis, which is to say without having to treat that person like someone suffering a "mental illness," a diagnosable disorder with such and such a set of symptoms that obliges you to wear the hat of a "mental health practitioner." But how does that work when the person you are seeing is stark raving mad, who meets the diagnostic features of someone suffering from acute schizophrenia, or a manic episode, who is so out of it that he (or she) cannot be on his own, whose only option is to be taken to a mental hospital because there is nowhere else such a person can go to that won't alarm the people around him? Suddenly, you have no way of continuing to see that person in therapy, because the most immediate problem confronting this person is: *Where is he going to live?* That question has to be settled before anything else. Where is he going to go? In order to continue seeing him you will have to wait until after he has been discharged from the hospital, medicated so that he is no longer a "danger," and returned to his domicile. From there he can make an appointment to resume seeing you, weeks, days, or months later, in your office, now that he is no longer at risk. But what if there was a place where this person *could* go to that was not a mental hospital, and what if the place he went to didn't require him to be medicated, if he did not want to be, but would let him live there *as is*, symptoms and all, so that it would be possible to continue seeing him, and to be with him, either in your office or at the house where he is now residing? What if such a place existed? Then it wouldn't matter if he were neurotic or psychotic, because he wouldn't be perceived as being any different than anyone else. Wouldn't it be amazing if such a place existed?

If you were like me back in the early 1970s, you probably haven't given this question much thought, unless you or someone dear to you flipped out and found himself in the situation described above. I never had the slightest interest in working with people suffering from psychotic symptoms until that summer day in 1970, strolling on Muir Beach just north of San Francisco, when I happened upon a friendly hippie with hair down to his shoulders and a glint of delectation in his eyes. We began to chat and when he asked me what I was up to I told him I was in graduate school studying to become a psychologist. One thing led to another and before long I confessed that my true passion was philosophy, and that I was currently reading *Being and Nothingness* by Jean-Paul Sartre, my intellectual hero at the time. He asked if I had ever heard of R. D. Laing and I had to admit that I hadn't. Then, like a magician pulling something soft and furry out of a hat, he withdrew a worn paperback book from his knapsack and handed it to me. He said, "Here, I think you're going to like this." It was a copy of Laing's *The Divided Self.* Upon reading the back cover I saw that Laing was a psychiatrist (one strike against him), that he was an existentialist (better), and that he was famous for his radical perspective on the nature of schizophrenia (bummer). Not wanting to sound ungrateful, I reluctantly explained that I wasn't really all that interested in schizophrenia, that I was more attracted to working with relatively healthy, which is to say neurotic, individuals who were searching for some meaning in their lives, who, like most people in the 1970s, were seeking personal transformation, perhaps living more authentically. The gentleman with the long hair replied, "Like I said, I think you're going to like this!" He then proceeded to pick up his knapsack, gave me a friendly wave, and trundled off down the beach, never to be seen again.

I have often wondered about that day, about the amazing way that fate sometimes plays such tricks on us, when something happens out of the blue that changes the course of your life. I happen to believe in luck, good fortune, happenstance. The word happy derives from the Old English "hap," meaning chance. That would suggest that happiness is the consequence of having been blessed with a stroke of luck, or good fortune. Something amazing comes your way that will change your life forever, so long as you seize the moment. If that is true, then the day when this perfect stranger walked up to me and gave me his gift, even insisting that I take it when I expressed reluctance, was one of the luckiest days of my life. Upon reading that book my life did change, and opened me up, not only to the world of R. D. Laing, but to a world filled with wonder, significance, and adventure. Moreover, though I didn't suspect it at the time, this was a world that would virtually save my life. Upon reading that little book I realized that sanity and madness are not separated by a distinctive, impermeable line, but that they interpenetrate each other. This was unknown to me at the time. Like many of my fellow psychology students, I was smug in the illusion that I was perfectly sane, that it was those less fortunate than me who were crazy. I couldn't have been more self-deluded.

Two years later, in the autumn of 1972, Laing visited Berkeley on a lecture tour and I got to meet him. Six months later I was on a plane to London to join him. On a wing and a prayer I decided to drop out of graduate school and join Laing and his cohorts in their effort to create an alternative to psychiatric treatment for schizophrenia. As I was to learn, that only scratched the surface of what they were up to. I had just seen a documentary movie about Laing's work, *Asylum,* directed by the Canadian filmmaker, Peter Robinson, and read everything I could get my hands on about Kingsley Hall, the residential "experiment in living" that Laing had established in 1965 as an alternative to mental hospitals. From the film it was apparent that the people lived there as equals, with no paid staff to run things; some of the "residents" (no *patients!*) were crazy as hell, while others looked pretty depressed, and others still appeared to be perfectly normal. No one was ostensibly "in charge." This was the era of LSD, marijuana, communal living, the Beat generation, Acid-rock *a la* Jefferson Airplane, The Doors, and The Grateful Dead. Ken Kesey's *One Flew Over the Cuckoo's Nest*, then showing on Broadway (not the one in New York), was the longest-running play in San Francisco history. Change was in the air. It was an era of heady transformation, and Kingsley Hall epitomized the most out-there trip imaginable . . . you didn't even have to take a drug to get off on it. That, at any rate, was my expectation.

Kingsley Hall was the first of Laing's household communities that served as a place where you could live through your madness until, eventually, you were able to get it together to live independently. It was conceived as an *asylum* – not a Lunatic Asylum mind you, but an asylum *from* forms of treatment, psychiatric or otherwise, that many were convinced were not helpful, and even complicated their difficulties further. Laing and his colleagues, including David Cooper and Aaron Esterson, leased the building from a London charity and occupied it from 1965 to 1970. The house was of historic significance, having been the residence of Mahatma Gandhi when he was negotiating India's independence from British rule. Muriel Lester, the principal trustee of Kingsley Hall, agreed that Laing's proposal for its use was faithful to its long-established humanitarian purpose. Kingsley Hall was leased to his organization, the Philadelphia Association (PA), for the sum of one British Pound per annum.

In 1970 the lease expired and Laing moved his, by now famous, operations to a series of buildings that were acquired by various means. Esterson and Cooper and the other original members had departed and a new cadre of colleagues and students who shared Laing's unorthodox views about the "non-treatment" of schizophrenia joined him. They included Leon Redler, an American psychiatrist who had briefly lived at Kingsley Hall; Hugh Crawford, a fellow Scotsman and psychoanalyst; John Heaton, a psychotherapist and phenomenologist; and Francis Huxley, an anthropologist (who happened to be the nephew of Aldous Huxley, a hero of Laing's). Numerous post-Kingsley Hall houses steadily appeared, each adhering to the basic hands-off philosophy that had been employed at Kingsley Hall. Each place, however, was unique, reflecting the personalities of the people living there, as well as the therapist or therapists who were responsible for each house.[1]

By the time I arrived in London in August 1973 there were four or five such places, primarily under the stewardship of Leon Redler and Hugh Crawford.[2] I opted to join Crawford's house at 74 Portland Road, located in swanky Holland Park, a tony neighborhood noted for its huge Georgian mansions and manicured lawns. On the eve of marrying Diana, Prince Charles held his bachelor's party across the street at Julie's Bar, a favorite hang-out for the London intelligentsia (and a place that some of the crazy people I lived with, and I, frequented). Though the house was essentially like the others in the PA, I was drawn to Crawford's mischievous personality and the unusual degree of involvement he enjoyed with the people living there. Though most of the houses went to extraordinary lengths to adopt a hands-off approach among the members of each household, Crawford employed a more engaged, in-your-face intimacy that I found inviting. I had initially thought about going into analysis with Laing, but when I saw him after arriving in London he looked so haggard and morose that I decided to work with someone who was, shall we say, more upbeat. I opted to work with Crawford, who struck me as the healthiest person in Laing's group. Laing and Crawford were chums, and as both hailed from Glasgow they shared a street-smart intimacy that none of Laing's other cohorts in London could approximate. They both loved and respected each other in a brotherly way and Laing sometimes used Crawford as his informal therapist and occasional couples counselor when Laing was married to his second wife, Jutta. Most of the people living at Portland Road were also in therapy with Crawford, an arrangement that was unorthodox, even in Laing's group, though this practice had its advantages. The pluses were that I was effectively in analysis with Crawford seven days a week, twenty-four hours a day. Looking back on it, I can't think of any minuses. The concept of "boundaries" was more or less unheard of, although sleeping with one's patients was a definite no-no. Getting into Portland Road wasn't easy. Since there was no one officially "in charge," not even Crawford, there was no one from whom to seek formal admittance. And because I didn't happen to be psychotic, I lacked the most compelling rationale for wanting to live there. Some of the students I had met in the seminars and study groups I attended told me how they had visited Portland Road and, while sipping tea, offered to "help out." "What's in it for you?" they were asked. When they replied that, being students, they wanted to learn more about psychosis and what it was like to be mad, they were summarily rejected. Having failed the test, they were permanently shunned.

It occurred to me it would take some time, as with any relationship you take seriously, to gain sufficient trust to be welcome. I attended Crawford's seminars on Heidegger and Merleau-Ponty, frequented the occasional Open House that welcomed strangers, and slowly made my presence felt. Eventually I was invited to participate in a "vigil," a collection of around-the-clock, two-person teams organized to accompany a person who had succumbed to a psychotic, usually manic, episode. These affairs typically lasted a couple of weeks, more or less, and then abated. It was treated as a crisis situation, and only the most trusted members of the community were invited to help.

In my first such experience, a man in his twenties was in the throes of a manic episode, in Laingian terms, a psychotic "voyage" of self-discovery, a commonplace in the PA community houses at that time. When a person lost it, someone had to be with that person around the clock to ensure they didn't hurt themselves, and to offer succor. I had helped many friends in San Francisco who were trying LSD for the first time by serving as their guide on their journey, ensuring they were safe and could handle it. This experience served me well. Given the need for constant, around the clock attention, these periodic crises were simply too much for the other house residents to deal with, especially between midnight and breakfast, when they needed some sleep. Though the person experiencing the breakdown didn't need nor want to sleep, the others living in the house did, if they expected to be fresh and alert during the very long day. Having volunteered, I was joined by another helper in order to stay up with the person who was going through this experience. I will call him Jason. At first blush, Jason reminded me of someone – you guessed it – on an acid trip. He rambled incoherently about cherubim and seraphim, celestial creatures inviting and taunting him, a look of ecstasy and occasional panic in his eyes. He strolled into the kitchen and removed a carving knife from the drawer and began dancing around the living room to the beat of a distant melody that no one could hear but him. When I cautiously removed the knife from his grip he just smiled, then continued dancing and singing his merry way. It continued like this for seven or eight hours, by which time it was morning and the house, now awake, took over. I returned the following night for another session, and then the following day, and then the next. Some two weeks into his journey, it was over. Jason returned to his senses and a few days later he decided to return home, apparently recovered.

Having managed to stay cool and not panic, I suppose I proved I could be counted on to be sensitive to the vulnerability of everyone there, not just the ones in crisis or regressed. My year in Vietnam made me fearless in times of danger and, as with my previous experiences on acid, this proved helpful when being with someone like Jason. After six months or so of regular visits and befriending each person living there, I was invited to live at Portland Road. Crazier people fared better. Like Laing, I had struggled with depression since childhood. My mother committed suicide when I was fourteen, and I was still struggling with the guilt I felt at not being able to give her a reason to live. But depression was not usually a rationale for living at Portland Road or the other PA houses. In Britain, I discovered that just about everyone was depressed due to the wet, gloomy weather, so depression was more or less cultured in. Typically, a person who was interested in living there would call and explain he was going through a crisis, or had simply reached the end of his tether, and he would be invited to visit. On arrival, everyone who lived there, a dozen people or so, would meet with the visitor as a group. The visitor, in turn, would have the evening to himself in order to make his case heard. What were people at Portland Road looking for? By the same token, what criteria do psychotherapists use in evaluating a prospective patient's suitability for undergoing therapy, or analysis? At Portland Road this was especially problematical because many of the applicants were not interested in therapy and, if they were, had been frustrated finding a therapist who was willing to work with them if they were not willing to take medication. Still, there were similarities between the two frames of reference.

Freud, for example, had looked for patients who, irrespective of how neurotic they were, were nevertheless prepared to be honest with him. The fundamental rule of analysis assumes a capacity for candor.[3] Without it, therapy becomes a game of catch me if you can, wherein everyone loses. Similarly, at Portland Road people were expected to be candid with the people to whom they offered their case, no matter how crazy or regressed they happened to be. The residents who conducted the interview were looking for a sincerity of purpose and a hint of good will beneath all the symptoms the person they were interviewing was saddled with, seeking, no matter how crazed or crazy, to contact that part of their personality that was still sane. Applicants who came off as hostile or belligerent were not invited to move in.

To complicate matters further, every applicant had to be admitted unanimously. One negative vote and you were rejected. Yet, once in, the new member could count on the unadulterated support of everyone living there, because *everyone* there had signed off on his or her moving in. The other PA houses used a simple majority, but Crawford concluded that the ostensible democratic approach generated problems he wanted to avoid. The sense of community and fellow-feeling engendered after learning that everyone had voted you to become a member of their community was extraordinary. So was the frankness with which everyone exercised their "candid" opinions about everyone else. The effect could be startling, as one was slowly stripped of the ego that had been so carefully crafted for society's approval. I soon realized why candor is something most of us prefer to avoid (and why society takes such pains to instill "appropriate" behavior), however much we complain about its absence. The similarity to the psychotherapy experience was unmistakable. But now, instead of having to contend with merely one therapist for one hour a day or a week, at Portland Road you were confronted with an entire cadre of relationships, all of whom engendered transference reactions, all of which you had to manage and work through, twenty-four hours a day, seven days a week.

One of the most shocking things my friends react to when I describe what it was like to live at Portland Road is that there were no staff, hence no patients. Everyone was the same. How on earth could this work? That depends on the house, the people living there, and the therapist who takes it on to make this his or her mission. At its peak there were eight such houses in the PA network, each with a distinctive personality all its own. Laing's model at Kingsley Hall and the one that succeeded it at the Archway Community employed a hands-off approach. Everyone was promised a room of their own to which they could retreat whenever they liked. Living there was seen as a haven from "treatment," so the premium was on the political, the freedom to be who you were and to come and go as you wish. No one made demands on you. The only rules were that you paid your rent on time and you didn't assault anyone. Portland Road was different because Hugh Crawford was a very different man from "Ronnie" Laing (as everyone in the network called him). Laing was moody, unpredictable, and on occasion confrontational. This would have proved ominous had it not been for the extraordinary vulnerability you also sensed about him, and his undeniable charisma. Everyone was at the PA because of Laing, because they had read his books and enlisted in his cause even before meeting him in the flesh. Laing had a license to be as rude and unpredictable as he liked. Laing never assumed the role of the leader, but he was the star of the show. Allowances were made.

Both Kingsley Hall and Portland Road were informed by Laing's depiction of the schizoid personality (described in Chapter One) as the prototypical form of alienation that the houses were most suited for. Recall that Laing believed the schiz-oid person is alienated in a double sense. Because he is ontologically insecure, he is anxious about getting too close to others, for fear they will "engulf" him, or lay claim on his freedom and "petrify" him, thus compromising his autonomy. On the other hand, this person is also anxious about being alone in the world, isolated and profoundly alienated from others. He navigates a narrow corridor between engulfment and isolation that has shrunk his world to the edge of a precipice from which he dare not budge, so he is alienated from both himself and others. Laing believed that Kingsley Hall could provide a refuge or sanctuary where you were surrounded by other people, but you could also have your own room to hide in if you wished. Crawford agreed with Laing's depiction of the pre-schizophrenic, schizoid personality type, as well as those who fit the picture of schizophrenia, but saw their amelioration differently. For him, relief from their chronic isolation was the more pressing issue, so no one was guaranteed a room of one's own. Like Bud-dhist monasteries, privacy was neither a premium nor a virtue. Togetherness was. Besides, Crawford believed such people were already experts at their self-imposed isolation, whether in the company of others or alone, so why encourage them with more of the same? The trick was to generate an ambience of conviviality and safety that would not feel so threatening to them. If they typically found relationships frightening, then an effort should be made to render relationships more inviting. Two very different interpretations of how to address the problem from two very different personalities. Common wisdom in the PA was that Laing had the head, but that Crawford had the heart.

Hugh Crawford, though a Glaswegian like Laing, was not an isolate. He was always up, engaged and engaging, mischievous yet endearing, Ferenczi to Laing's Freud. Crawford was like a teddy bear, but there was also something of Yoda about him, not always easy to fathom. Medium height, like Laing, but more hefty. His grey beard was disarming, as was his manner. He was inviting. His vision of Port-land Road was not so much an asylum as a secular monastery or retreat. We were all in it together. There were six or seven bedrooms in the house and everyone was expected to share a bedroom (at one point I was sharing my room with two others). At its maximum, fourteen people lived there. Monday, Wednesday, and Friday eve-nings Crawford came to Portland Road for dinner and spent the rest of the evening with us, usually late into the night. Before dinner we participated in Hatha Yoga (Iyengar) together. Dinner was prepared by those of us who took it upon themselves to buy the groceries and prepare a meal that evening, the only communal meal of the day. The food was healthy, usually brown rice and vegetables, occasionally meat, followed by a fruit crumble. Coffee and tea were plentiful, and strong. No alco-hol. Pot was abundant, but never consumed at meetings. Crawford was especially careful to ensure the right balance of personalities living in the house. One of the things that struck me about Archway, which was modeled on Kingsley Hall, was how gloomy it was. It seemed that everyone living there was profoundly depressed. This is the irony of "schizophrenia." At the first meeting the applicant may come across as a lunatic, avoiding eye contact, muttering incoherently, looking the part of a crazy person as depicted in a Hollywood movie. After a week or two in the house, the craziness fell away and was replaced with a person who was surprisingly lucid, articulate, but depressed. Crawford concluded there needed to be a variety of people living there to balance the depression, so not everyone there fit the diagnosis of a schizophrenic. Many were considerably more manic, and some, like myself, were not at all psychotic, but neurotic, hysterical or obsessional. I was among the high functioning neurotics, but we all had our reasons for being there. I was looking for a way out of my depressive episodes, but I also wanted to experience, the adventure, this mind-blowing history-making phenomenon Laing had created. Because I came to the PA to train as a psychoanalyst, I attended seminars two or three evenings a week. I was also the PA administrator, so for much of the day I hung out in the basement of Portland Road, where the PA office and seminar room were located. There were others like me living at Portland Road, a school teacher, a philosopher, another student, and so on. A bored *prima donna* from Italy seeking enlightenment, a street-smart poet looking for her soul, a psychologist who saw living there as a spiritual haven, a couple from the United States with their young son, seeking a radical version of family therapy, assorted misfits and wayward strangers, looking for something they had never managed to find despite all their searching: *themselves.* They were a mixture of types, abilities, inclinations, and most of them were in therapy with Crawford, their common denominator. Those of us who had the presence of mind to care what the place looked like and how clean the house should be took it upon themselves to see that there was food on the table and that dishes got done. Being a typical sheltered Southerner, the only thing I had ever learned how to cook in my youth was breakfast and pie, so I became the house specialist for making peach cobbler or apple and plum crumble after dinners. Everyone had something to contribute, except for the person who happened to be the craziest individual in the house. That person got a pass for a period of time, until it was someone else's turn. Allowances were made for those most vulnerable and needy.

I lived at Portland Road for four years. I went into analysis with Hugh Crawford the same month I moved in, which was also the same time I was offered the PA administrator job. I attended seminars on the integration between phenomenology and psychoanalysis and threw myself into every form of activity available, including meditation practices, Tai Chi, Aikido, and so on. Though living in hell, I was also in heaven. I began reading William Blake's *The Marriage of Heaven and Hell*, and realized that I knew exactly what he meant! I had expected living at Portland Road to approximate an ongoing, 24/7 acid trip, and I wasn't wrong. It was terrifying and exhilarating, at the same time. It would take an entire book to do justice to what those four years were like, in order to describe the many exploits and adventures I experienced there, but all I can really give you in this brief chapter is a taste, an appetizer. Laing liked to say that because there were no rules, no patients or therapists (Crawford, like other house therapists, didn't live there), no pecking order, the effective rule was live and let live: "You take your chances, I'll take mine." Despite the care taken to ensure that those who were invited to live at Portland Road were not dangerous, the system wasn't perfect. Sometimes, unbeknownst to us at the time, someone slipped beneath the radar who proved to be deadly. In the four years I lived there, I was nearly killed on three different occasions by three different residents. Two were men, one was a woman.

On one occasion we were contacted by a Buddhist community in Scotland, *Samye Ling*, the first Tibetan Buddhist Center to have been established in the West, in 1967. A woman who had joined their center for a meditation retreat was experiencing a psychotic break and, because they weren't equipped to handle it, they asked if she could come to Portland Road. A number of people in the PA had connections with *Samye Ling*, so we said yes. Perhaps it was this connection and the assumptions we made about the kind of person who practices meditation that helped this woman slip through the net. I will call her Mary. On arrival Mary was given a cursory interview and moved into the house immediately. She was disoriented, delusional, and anxious. We learned from *Samye Ling* that she was American, from California, and that her brother was a California State Trooper. Mary was in her thirties, a large-framed woman who could carry her weight, but she was not obese. Far from it. She didn't say much but stayed close to the center of action, which was the large kitchen that included the only source of heat for the house, a large coal-burning furnace where the fireplace had once been. Everyone typically gathered around a large dining room table big enough to accommodate about a dozen people. This was where we gathered for dinner in the evenings and hung out with Crawford for conversation.

Mary had a peculiar habit of hurling the coffee mug she had just finished at someone's head without comment or warning. Sometimes it hit the mark and sometimes it missed. If it hit, it drew blood. We weren't accustomed to this kind of violence, but we were also puzzled and even intrigued by her inexplicable behavior. My mother used to tell me that, when a young baby and finished nursing from my bottle, I would unexpectedly hurl the bottle across the room without warning. As baby bottles were made of glass in those days (late 1940s) my mother or father would race to catch the bottle before smashing against the wall into pieces. This was interpreted by my family as a game I liked to play: catch it if you can. I often wondered why I had done this and concluded I was likely pissed off that I wasn't nursing from my mother's breast, but this, apparently, never occurred to my parents! I was reminded of this story when Mary hurled her coffee mug at someone, and wondered if, in a moment of regression, she was reliving a similar memory. No one, however, was amused by her behavior (at least I had aimed for the wall, not someone's head), and we told her so. We also wondered if someone had said or done something that may have offended Mary before she flung her mug at them. Sometimes, being inured to violence is not a good thing. For whatever reason, this action of Mary's didn't alarm us as much as it should have. In hindsight, we erred in being too understanding.

Unabated, Mary's violence escalated. One evening after dinner, on a night that Crawford was not scheduled to visit the house, I was in the living room adjoining the kitchen in front of the fireplace, minding my own business and waiting for some of my other housemates to join me. Suddenly without warning Mary raced into the room, grabbed ahold of me, and threw me down onto the floor (Mary was considerably larger than me, by maybe forty pounds). She then grabbed a tire tool from the fireplace, the kind with the pointy end, drew it back over her shoulder in order to bring it down onto my head, when just as suddenly someone came up behind her and grabbed it from her hands, before she could strike me. All of this must have happened in the space of three or four seconds, but it felt like one of those slow-motion films where it stretches out over half a minute. In all the commotion I had hit my head on the floor, but that was the only damage. The room filled with people who immediately confronted Mary, telling her she had crossed a line and we weren't going to put up with this any longer. Mary's only explanation for her behavior was that she didn't like the way I was gazing at the fireplace. We phoned Crawford and he came over. We spent the rest of the evening trying to understand what was going on with Mary and whether she should leave Portland Road. Ejecting a person from the house was rare. I believe this may have been the first time. A few weeks into her stay with us Mary had showed no signs of delusional or psychotic thought processes, but she had persisted in her silent violence with us and we decided it was time for her to go. Mary said she didn't follow our reasoning and that she wanted to stay, but despite her protests we kept to our decision. Because we felt there was no effective communication between us and her, we no longer felt safe with her in the house.

That evening, sometime after midnight when everyone else had gone to sleep, Mary stole into the room of Ginger, a small and shy woman living in a small room at the very top of the house in what used to be the attic. Mary brandished a kitchen knife and a broken milk bottle and savagely attacked Ginger while she was sleeping. We were awoken by the commotion and ran into the bedroom, by which time Mary had thrown her weapons onto the floor and sat there, immobile, acting as though nothing had happened despite the blood that was everywhere. Crawford was called, and when he returned we called the police. Ginger was still alive and was rushed to the nearest hospital (after some time she made a complete recovery). The police removed Mary to jail and after a more detailed inquiry the next morning we cleaned up the blood. We were shaken that Ginger, the woman whom Mary had attacked, was nearly killed and that we had let such a dangerous woman into our midst. This was a craziness the likes of which we had never encountered before, and we were in shock. Crawford made it clear to the police that Mary was not welcome to return to Portland and that she should be incarcerated in the nearest mental hospital for the criminally insane.

A couple of days later there was an unexpected knock on the door. It was Mary! She had been released and said she was ready to "return home," meaning us. Crawford called the police again, as well as the mental hospital Mary had been taken to, and demanded an explanation. He was told that Mary had been examined the morning after her arrival and that because she was exhibiting no signs of mental illness they saw no reason to detain her. An ironic conversation followed about the concept of diagnosis and why the psychiatric staff were unable to determine that Mary was quite mad, and dangerously so. Crawford replied that Mary met all the criteria of a sociopath, but the hospital administrator, eager to oblige, explained that Britain no longer recognized sociopathy as a *bona fide* diagnosis, so there was no way they could legally hold Mary. After some energetic words passed between Crawford, the hospital, and the police, it was agreed that the hospital would allow Crawford to perform the diagnosis on Mary so that she could be incarcerated, at least until the Home Office was able to deport her back to the United States. Two weeks later Mary was on her way home, to California. Case closed.

Mary was probably the most atypical resident who ever lived at Portland Road, and we learned something about those forms of craziness that slip beneath the radar. Unless you show signs and symptoms of delusional or agitated conduct, you are not deemed crazy, no matter how crazy you may ostensibly be. No one who ever lived at Portland Road had been subjected to a formal diagnosis. It is doubly ironic that the only diagnosis ever performed on a person was not performed in order for her to be admitted, but in order to keep her out!

I haven't the space to describe the other two incidents when I was assaulted by someone living at Portland Road. Besides, I don't want to give you the impression this was a frequent occurrence. In four years, this happened to me three times. That's not a bad track record, considering. Ginger was lucky to escape with her life. For the most part, life at Portland Road was very ordinary, even boring. People stayed for various lengths of time, anywhere from a year to several, nearly all leaving better off than when they arrived. For the most part, there was little drama, except when someone succumbed to crisis, which typically abated in due course. There is, however, another person I would like to tell you about, a young man who generated his own drama by the most un-dramatic means. Unlike Mary, I still have no idea how he might be diagnosed.

Jerome was a twenty-something young man who had been referred to Laing by a psychiatrist at a local mental hospital. He was a rather slight, dark-haired, and extremely shy person who, in a quiet and tentative manner, told us the following on his first visit to Portland Road. Over the past two or three years Jerome had developed a history of withdrawing from his family – mother, father, and a younger sister – by retiring to his bedroom and locking himself inside. His parents would try to cajole him to come out of his room, and when that didn't work they would threaten to punish him if he did not open his door. Jerome refused to budge. Eventually, his parents contacted the local mental hospital for help. Jerome was then forcibly taken from his room by the hospital orderlies and removed to hospital via ambulance and restraints. Once there, he persisted in his behavior, saying nary a word. All the while, he wouldn't say why he was behaving this way or what he hoped to gain by it. He simply insisted that he must.

He was soon diagnosed as suffering from catatonic schizophrenia with depressive features. A series of electro-convulsive therapy sessions were administered and before long Jerome was returned to his ordinary, cooperative self. Six months or so later he repeated the same scenario: withdrawal, removal to hospital, ECT, recovery. Never any idea as to why Jerome persisted in this behavior was ever determined. But each time he repeated this ritual, a lengthier course of treatment was required to bring him back "to his senses." He and his family endured this routine on several different occasions over a period of two years.

The psychiatrist who contacted Laing confessed that his colleagues at the hospital had become exasperated with Jerome and thrown in the towel, vowing that if he were admitted to the hospital again they would simply "throw away the key" (hospitals were able to do just that in the 1970s). They were clearly fed up with what they interpreted as his "antics." Jerome had played all of his get-out-of-jail cards and he had no place to go. On this occasion, when his parents implored Jerome to come out of his room, he replied that he would on one condition: that Laing would see him. Jerome had read *The Divided Self* and concluded that Laing was the only psychiatrist he could trust not to "treat" him for what he believed he needed to go through. Laing contacted Crawford and asked if Portland Road would consider meeting with Jerome. Crawford asked the house residents if they would consent to such a meeting and it was agreed that he could visit.

When Jerome visited Portland Road, he recounted the history I outlined above and what he hoped to do there. He wanted a room of his own, where he could stay until he was ready to come out. We were asked to honor his request and, with some trepidation, we agreed to his terms. I single Jerome out, of all the other people I came to know at Portland Road, because he presented us with the most serious challenge we had ever faced, excepting the disaster that Mary had subjected us to. Due to the nature of his terms, Jerome effectively deprived Portland Road of its most telling virtue: the communion shared by the people living there. Jerome's plan effectively undermined the philosophy that Hugh Crawford had formulated, a sensibility of fellow-feeling that honored a fidelity to interpersonal give and take, no matter how crazy or alarming a person's participation in that process might be. We felt that Jerome was entitled to pursue the strategy he felt called upon to follow, even if the outward behavior was problematic. Though a person's experience is a private affair, the behavior with which one engages others is not. Because the two are invariably related, the philosophy at Portland Road was to tolerate unconventional behavior to an unprecedented degree in order to facilitate the inherently private struggle that person was engaged in.

The conventional psychoanalytic setting, for example, places enormous constraints on a person's behavior, including the use of a couch to facilitate candor. At Portland Road, you were obliged to *live* with the behavior that everyone else exhibited, so the course of a given person's behavior was unpredictable, and sometimes, as noted earlier, violent. In other words, there was an element of risk at living in such conditions because no one knew what anyone else was capable of and what lengths some people may go to in order to be "true" to what they believed they were authentically about.

True to his word, Jerome took to his room and stayed there. He had his own room, which no one saw him come in or out of. Though it wasn't uncommon to forgo the occasional meal, the way Jerome removed himself from the household was not something we were accustomed to. No one ever even saw him sneak downstairs for food in the middle of the night, or to use the bathroom. Our sense of concern gradually turned into foreboding. Jerome apparently wasn't eating anything and it became increasingly apparent that he was also incontinent. We tried talking to him. Out of frustration we said, "This wasn't part of our agreement, to turn us into a wet-nurse and have to take care of you." "Yes it is!" Jerome insisted, in one of the rare moments he actually said a word. Still, Jerome wasn't in any ostensible pain. He didn't seem especially depressed, or anxious, or delusional, or confused, or even catatonic. He was just being stubborn, basically, as we soon realized why the mental hospital had become so exasperated with him! He insisted on doing things his way, even if he could not or would not explain to us why.

We reminded Jerome that we had put ourselves out on a limb for him, discreetly keeping his parents in the dark while he was jeopardizing his health. Where was the gratitude, a gesture of good will, in return? Jerome refused to discuss his behavior or explore his underlying motives. Nor would he acknowledge his withdrawal as a symptom that was generating a crisis for the household. He simply submitted to, and was inordinately protective of, his private wishes, the details of which he refused to share with us. Jerome eventually agreed to eat some food in order to ward off starvation, as long as we brought it to him. The stench of his incontinence became onerous, though Jerome was apparently oblivious to it. Not surprisingly, he soon became the topic of conversation each evening around the dinner table.

"What are we going to do about him," we wondered? Ironically, he had transformed Portland Road into a mental hospital. We were constantly concerned about his physical health, his diet, and the increasing potential for bed sores, which he eventually developed. He continued to lose weight due to the meager amount of food he was eating, one bowl of muesli a day. We could either tell him he had to leave or we would be obliged to capitulate to the onerous conditions he had created. As news of our dilemma leaked out, Laing became increasingly uneasy. Once Jerome developed bed sores he was in danger of being taken to a hospital for medical treatment, and his stay at Portland Road would be over. Compounding everything else, Jerome couldn't keep down most of the nourishment he was eating. Whether this was self-generated or involuntary we did not know. None of us possessed the expertise or inclination to serve as a hospital staff. Who was going to clean him, bathe him, and all the other things that were essential to his survival? Some of us eventually consented to be his nursemaid in order to stabilize his condition. At least he was alive and more or less coping. But how much longer would we have to wait before Jerome finally came out of it and abort his isolation?

Four more long months dragged by. By now Jerome's family insisted they visit and threatened legal action if we wouldn't let them. We weren't, however, about to let that happen. Crawford implored us to remain patient and let things to continue their course. Laing, however, became increasingly annoyed and asked to visit and talk it over with us. Once he saw our determination to see Jerome's trial through, Laing agreed to continue his support and keep Jerome's family, who had complained bitterly to him, at bay. Meanwhile, Jerome continued to lose weight and became ill. Now, six months into his time with us, we faced a new crisis. Jerome developed bed sores, but he continued to resist talking to us or relent. On the contrary, he bitterly protested our efforts to bathe him and even to prevent his starvation.

We finally decided that a change of some kind had to happen if we hoped to see this through to an acceptable conclusion. We decided that Jerome needed to be in closer proximity to the people in the house, whether or not he consented. The threat to his physical health and the lack of contact, in the most basic human terms, was untenable. If he could not, or would not, join us, perhaps we could join him. This occurred during one of those rare occasions that I had left Portland Road to visit my family in America. While I was gone it was decided to move Jerome into my bedroom, the largest bedroom in the house and in which I had been sleeping alone. When I returned from my vacation, much to my horror I discovered Jerome was living in my room! I had a choice: move to another, smaller and less desirable room, or share my room with Jerome. I opted to stay in my room. In deference to the sacrifice of my heretofore privacy, others agreed to bathe Jerome and feed him on a regular schedule, change his bed sheets, spend time with him, and endeavor to talk to him, even if he refused to participate. We gave him therapeutic massages to relieve the loss of muscle tone and to provide some human contact. We gradually resigned ourselves to the fact that we had, whether we liked it or not, become, for all intents and purposes, a "hospital." We felt confident, however, that Jerome's condition would eventually improve, given this new regimen of attention.

In fact, his condition did begin to stabilize, but that was about all. I grew accustomed to the stench, the silence, the close quarters. But it didn't exactly help my depression, sharing a room with a ghost who haunted the space but was unable or unwilling to occupy it. I needed something to relieve the deadness that now permeated our shared space, including the disturbing dreams that invaded me at night (my analyst concluded that I was dreaming Jerome's dreams!). I decided to invite the most floridly psychotic person in Portland Road, a young man in his twenties who believed he was Mick Jagger, to move into our room, and make it three of us living together. Our new roommate, whom I will call Elvis, serenaded Jerome morning and night with his guitar – which he had no idea how to play – which probably made Jerome even crazier. But at least it was a livelier, if more insane, living environment, and with all the commotion and Jerome's complaining I soon recovered from my depression. I had never felt better! Whether Jerome liked it or not, our "rock star" guest was there to stay, and I admit the guilty pleasure I felt in the comfort that Jerome was not in complete control of what was happening around him, nor of me.

Before long a whole year had passed, but still no discernible change in Jerome's condition. In the meantime, a number of crises had occurred between Jerome's family and Laing, Laing's growing impatience with us, our impatience with Jerome, and finally, between ourselves and Hugh Crawford for not supporting our numerous efforts to remove Jerome from the house. We were ready – eager! – to admit defeat and resign ourselves to an unmitigated failure. Jerome's condition, like Freud's treatment of the Wolf Man, was apparently interminable. His "asylum" with us had become for him simply a way of life. It seemed obvious to us now that this was all he had wanted from us, to live in the squalor he had generated around himself and to be left be. It was our custom each August for the entire household at Portland Road to vacate the premises and spend the month in Wales at a farm that Hugh

Crawford owned, to get out of London and get even closer to each other since there would be no distractions. But what to do about Jerome? We had no choice but to bring him along! Once there, his regimen continued as before, and when the month was over we regrouped to Portland Road and resumed our routine. Jerome's behavior had become a commonplace, and his odd way of being no longer received as much of our attention.

The time, in the immortal words of Raymond Chandler, staggered by and the urgency of Jerome's condition became humdrum, somehow less urgent to resolve or molest. Meanwhile, life continued at Portland Road independent of Jerome's situation. Others had their problems too, which were addressed in the communal way that was our custom. Crises came and passed, new residents arrived, others left. Jerome remained where he was. Another month slipped by, then another, until I finally lost track of the time and stopped counting. Jerome had long ceased being the nightly topic of conversation and his presence (or absence) had become a fixture, like the furniture in the house. Nobody even noticed when the year and a half anniversary since Jerome had moved into Portland Road arrived. Perhaps that was a good thing. We had become so habituated to his odd conception of cohabitation, the baths, the linen changes, the serenades, that we hardly noticed that evening by the fire engaged in a rare moment of lazy conversation when, unannounced, Jerome nonchalantly sauntered downstairs to use the bathroom. When he was finished Jerome flushed the toilet, peeked his head into the kitchen to say hello, then quietly returned upstairs. We were shocked, to put it mildly, and were pinching ourselves to make sure this wasn't a dream.

An hour later, Jerome returned, summarily announcing he was famished, and effectively terminated the fast that had reduced him to ninety pounds of weight. This was a Jerome we had never even met: talkative, cordial, suddenly social and at ease. We couldn't believe our eyes and ears. How long, I immediately wondered, would this last, before returning to our room and seclusion?

As it happened, that day proved to be momentous. Jerome had taken a new turn, and it stuck. Just as suddenly as it began, he was finally, if inexplicably, finished with whatever he had been doing, engaged in God-knows what manner of bizarre meditation. Naturally, we all wanted to *know*. The next day Jerome joined us for breakfast and acted as though nothing out of the ordinary had happened over the past year and a half, as though he had been behaving normally the entire time. He was cheerful, engaged, not manic but content, even happy. So I asked, "What on earth were you up to, Jerome, all that time by yourself? What do you believe you were getting out of your system?"

I don't think any of us expected an answer. We didn't think that Jerome had one, or had a clue himself what that time had been about. But it turned out that he did. He told us that the reason he had isolated himself all that time, for a year and a half, distancing himself from the life of the house, was because he was on a mission: *to count to a million, and then back to zero, uninterrupted, in order to finally achieve his freedom.* That was all he had ever wanted to do, over the past four years, since his first compulsion to withdraw into his bedroom at home. But no one had let him.

But why, we asked, did it take that long? A year and a half! Did it really require that much time? We had given him his way, hadn't we? Hadn't we accommodated what he asked of us? According to Jerome, yes and no. After all, we didn't just let him be. We intruded and interfered, interrupted his train of thought, talked to him, played music, gave him massages and generally distracted him from the task at hand, the *counting*. He said that every time he got to a few thousand, even a few hundred thousand, someone broke his concentration with a song, a massage, or whatever, and he was obliged to start counting all over, from the beginning. The worst, he said, was when we added the guitar player! "But why didn't you just *tell* us," I asked, "what you were up to? We would have eagerly obliged, if only we knew what you were doing." "That wouldn't have *counted*," he replied. "It was necessary that you let me have my way, but *without my having to explain why*." He added, "All my life I've had to explain my behavior to everyone, and I decided that it was time to take a stand, to be who I was without having to justify it."

Apparently, it was only when our collective anxiety over Jerome's behavior subsided, after the anniversary when we finally gave up and backed off, that he was able to complete the task he had set himself to accomplish. We had eventually, without appreciating its significance, submitted to his conditions, and let him get on with, and submit to, his own self-imposed mission of whatever mad inspiration had compelled him to count to a million and back again, uninterrupted, without excuse or justification.

The unorthodox nature of the experience that Jerome traversed at Portland Road is impossible to compare with conventional treatment modalities because, as Laing and Crawford were fond of saying, no *treatment* was ever administered, not even group therapy, as that would have been yet one more technique for treating someone for mental illness. Jerome was simply living there, albeit in an unorthodox way, but it was nonetheless *his* way, and he wasn't alone in it. We were in it with him. The question I am invariably asked: Did it "work?" And if so, how? Some forty years later, Jerome has never experienced another psychotic episode again. He left Portland Road soon after that fateful conversation we shared on completion of his regimen, he resumed his life (or rather, began it), and proved to be an unremarkable person, ordinary in the extreme. He moved to another city north of London, got married, had children, and to this day he is living a happy, fulfilling, uneventful life. Naturally, we wondered why Jerome had felt the need to withdraw in the first place. What were the dynamics, the unconscious motivation that prompted such a radical solution to his problems? These were questions that Jerome couldn't answer. It is telling, and doubly ironic, that Jerome didn't need those questions to be answered *in order* to repair what he, in his shattered condition, could not himself comprehend.

Jerome was never formally diagnosed by us, but if he were, what type of diagnosis would one give him? The most popular forms of psychoses diagnosed today are schizophrenia and bipolar disorder, or mania. You can be sure that champions of either would make a case for a bipolar Jerome, or a schizophrenic Jerome. But truth to tell, he fits neither. Jerome was never depressed, and his year and a half in bed could hardly be characterized a manic episode. Nor did he fit the typical picture of schizophrenia, in any of its forms. He never exhibited delusions nor hallucinations. The rare moments when he did speak he was lucid and persuasive. Many people who are diagnosed schizophrenic lack delusions or hallucinations, but they exhibit profound disorganization and confusion, or flat affect, or a profound inability to form intimate relationships, and their capacity for work is equally compromised due to their lack of organization and focus. None of these features fit Jerome, who after leaving Portland Road lived a rewarding, productive life. He didn't appear to have a trace of a typical schizoid personality profile, nor schizoaffective, nor schizotypal. Nor did he ever exhibit signs of paranoia. The regimen of counting he engaged in required a lucidity that isn't consistent with any form of schizophrenia I am acquainted with. So was he even psychotic? Perhaps he was just a stubborn neurotic, trapped in an adolescent impasse with his parents in a grudge match that went too far? After all, his counting could be construed as an extreme form of obsessive-compulsive acting out, couldn't it? I don't think so. Spending a year and a half in bed, nearly starving to death and incontinent while silently counting to a million and back is a crazy thing to do, despite the method in his madness. During that period Jerome was undeniably mad, but his madness had a purpose, as all of them do, with its own internally organized logic that contains a motive and a reason. Though we were unable to comprehend what he was doing, Jerome's peculiar form of madness served to give him a means of liberating himself and finding himself in a journey that he plotted for himself and himself alone. It proved to be a brilliant piece of workmanship, though hardly a blueprint for others to follow.

This story won't make much sense to anybody who attempts to glean from it an identifiable treatment philosophy, unless they take into account the central importance that Crawford gave to the problem of freedom as a prototypical feature of living together. This was a concern that had also preoccupied Freud in the development of his clinical technique, just as it did existentialist philosophers, such as Kierkegaard, Nietzsche, Heidegger, Sartre. How does one "help" those who are in some measure of personal jeopardy without impinging on that person's inherently private, though socially intelligible, right to privacy, to live in his own skin and experience his own thoughts, as he will? The O.E.D. defines privacy as "the state of being apart from other people or concealed from their view; solitude; seclusion." This aptly defines what Jerome wanted from us, what he had never before experienced but desperately needed to taste, and to have all his own.

Freud's solution to this problem was analytic neutrality, the cornerstone of his clinical technique. It followed the ancient dictum: "do no harm," what both Laing and Crawford recognized as a form of benign neglect, what Keats called negative capability. In many ways, Jerome's experience at Portland Road was a perfect example of benign neglect, or negative capability, in practice. The respect we tried to pay this young man was all that any of us felt qualified to offer. We didn't understand what was the matter with him, nor did we pretend to. We weren't sure what would help nor what might make matters worse, so we did as little as possible. Following the principle of neutrality, we employed benign neglect as unobtrusively as we could. Neither Laing nor Crawford directed the treatment, because there was no "treatment" to direct. Treatment was what Jerome came to Portland Road to get away from.

There is a reason that Laing and Crawford refused to characterize houses like Portland Road *treatment* centers. Psychoanalysis, properly conceived, is not a form of treatment like other treatment modalities, because it isn't treating mental illnesses. It is a form of conversation that elicits intimacy, an experience of intimacy that the "patient" desperately needs in order to find him- or herself, and to be himself. The treatment paradigm in that context is nothing more than a metaphor, because psychoanalysis does not treat illnesses: it is a cure through love. However, once you remove the context of therapy from a private office in which you meet occasionally in private, to a residential facility where you are expected to eat, sleep, and live, everything changes. Psychoanalytic hospitals such as Chestnut Lodge, Austen Riggs, and the Menninger Clinic were staffed by enlightened psychoanalysts who knew perfectly well that they were not treating illnesses, but simply helping people who had become lost find their way home. Some, like Chestnut Lodge, were locked facilities and others, like Austen Riggs, were open, so the types of psychosis they addressed varied. But the places themselves were *hospitals*. The hours patients spent with their analysts in psychotherapy were the times they were free to be themselves. The rest of the time they were patients in a hospital, with rules to follow, regimens of behavior to adhere to from morning till night. Yet a lot of good things happened there, despite what must have been a very confusing situation for most of the psychotic patients committed there, some against their will.

Laing wanted to dispense with that. In a way, he wanted to create a *genuinely* psychoanalytic hospital, but a "hospital" in the original sense of the term: a place of hospitality and sanctuary. This was why Kingsley Hall was structured (or unstructured) the way it was, why there were no paid staff, no nurses, no one in charge of anything or anyone, no pecking order, no power structure. It was a way of taking the consulting room into a residence where everyone was free to live as they pleased and to be who they were. They were places of hospitality, in the original sense, and *accommodation*, from the original meaning of the term, which was "to afford help." In order not to confuse things, formal therapy sessions, if desired, occurred elsewhere, off the premises. These were places to *live*, not therapize, and it was the living together that was the rule of thumb. It was the way people "treated" each other, that was "therapeutic." (The word "treat" derives from the Latin *tractus*, or "tract," meaning to draw. This gives rise to treatise, treaty, and treat, meaning "a negotiated agreement." In other words, when you treat someone you are engaging in a service that is *agreeable*.)

This rule was brought home to us one day when a local newspaper reporter visited Portland Road to learn what was going on there. Everyone in the neighborhood knew this was a house where crazy people lived, that it was associated with R. D. Laing, a local celebrity. Allowances were made by the neighbors, and for the most part they accommodated what we were doing, or *not* doing. The reporter was intrigued and wanted to write a positive article about the wonderful work we were engaged in. I mentioned that people who came to live there, like Jerome, were probably enjoying their last chance to get things straight for themselves, or spend the rest of their lives in a loony bin. The article appeared in the paper a few days later, headlined *Last Chance Clinic Helps Those In Need*. Yes, he missed the point entirely when naming it a "clinic," but there was no way the reporter could wrap his mind around the subtlety of the philosophy practiced there. The next thing we knew Portland Road was served a summons to appear in court to explain why we were running a mental health clinic, without the requisite license. Naturally we weren't registered as a clinic because there was no treatment being administered there. If anything, we were an "anti-clinic." Registering it as a clinic would have transformed it into a hospital, with health inspections, fire codes, you name it, to comply with. We could have never obtained such a license anyway because the neighborhood wasn't zoned for it. Some of the neighbors, after reading the article and worried that their property values would be affected, bolted into action.

When we appeared in court, we explained to the judge that we were not running a clinic. Yes, some people with psychiatric histories were living there, but that was all they were doing, living there, nothing else. No one was receiving treatment. The judge appeared to be swayed by our argument until the solicitor who brought the action showed him a brochure that the PA had commissioned back when Kingsley Hall was first opened, some ten years earlier. The brochure was an appeal for donations, and the articles of association of the PA, which was a registered UK charity, noted that among the purposes of the organization was "to relieve mental illness of all description, including schizophrenia." The brochure went on to explain that Laing and the PA were hoping to change the paradigm of how mental distress was typically conceived and treated, that they sought to change the existing *model*. But nothing could erase the impression left by that one damning comment that stared us in the face, that we were *relieving mental illness*. The judge replied that if it walks like a duck, talks like a duck, and swims like a duck, chances are that it is a duck. It seemed to him that we, in fact, were "treating" people for mental illness, and that we were doing so without a clinical license. Obtaining a license was not an option, as the action was initiated to close us down, as quickly as possible.

The judge ordered us to cease treating any of the residents living at Portland Road for mental illness within two weeks. We replied that we would be more than happy to comply with the judge's decision. Which we were. Because we weren't treating anyone, there was no action that we needed to take, or to cease. This satisfied the judge, but I'm sure it caused nothing but consternation among the neighbors who brought the action. They had hoped we would be forced to vacate the house and to sell it. Instead, we were simply told to stop the behavior we were allegedly committing. Nothing changed. We continued to operate the house as before, because we weren't *doing* what the neighbors, in their flash of paranoia, feared that we were. We dodged a bullet, but this story only goes to show how complicated this kind of "residence" is and how precarious its existence can be. I am convinced to this day that the judge knew perfectly well what we were doing, and that he had no intention of causing us any grief. He was protecting *us* from our neighbors.

Unlike Laing's conception of Kingsley Hall, which was rooted in the concept of asylum, Crawford based his conception of Portland Road on Heidegger's notion of "dwelling." This is a subtle philosophical concept that goes considerably beyond the common definition of dwelling, as nothing more than an abode where one lives. Not all buildings, such as factories, bridges, or office structures, are suitable for dwelling. A dwelling is a building where one lives, a domicile one inhabits. But what does it mean to live in a place, in a genuine, authentic manner? This is the question Heidegger was asking in his famous essay, "Building, Dwelling, Thinking" (1971), which served as the model for Crawford's vision of what it should be like to live at Portland Road. Dwelling has a double connotation. It is not only a *place* to live; it is also a state of mind. We speak of dwelling as when losing ourselves in thought, when thinking something over, when being thoughtful. To dwell is a verb and is an expression we sometimes use to denote thinking about something, but not in the academic sense. I'm not dwelling, for example, when I am taking an exam, or solving a mathematical problem, or conducting a scientific experiment. Dwelling is a kind of pondering, giving my attention to something or someone with whom I am engaged, perhaps in conversation, when losing myself in their company. For Crawford, both senses of dwelling depicted what living at Portland Road should feel like, a place where you can dwell with others, while dwelling on the issues that are uppermost on your mind. The two senses are intertwined, to the benefit of each.

Dwelling together is living together, for no other purpose than to become intimate. In such a context, your connection with others affords opportunities for friendship, tied to each other without strings within a structure of concern for your welfare, and theirs. Heidegger's concept of dwelling is also tied to his notion of homelessness. All of us are homeless, in the existential sense, but in a more practical sense we all seek a place where we can genuinely feel at home, where we can be ourselves without fear of consequences. Marriages and friendships share in common a venue where we find a kind of intimacy that furthers a sense of belonging, where we feel at home, but without sacrificing our most precious possession: the person we are. Marriages and friendships alike rupture when one or both participants feel they can no longer be themselves in the relationship. This happens when they no longer feel at home with each other and are estranged. Jerome was looking for a place where he could dwell, where he could be part of a community without sacrificing the person he was, where he could find friends who had his best interests at heart, where he could feel at home, maybe for the first time. This is something all of us need, and long for. Laing and Crawford were especially interested in those people who had *no* friends, who were homeless in both senses of the word. This is a typical plight among people diagnosed schizophrenic.

As the popular adage goes, a house is not necessarily a home. Those who came to Portland Road were, by definition, homeless. They had no place to go that would accept them for who they were. This can happen to anyone. Jerome became homeless when his family could no longer accommodate his way of being with them. The hospitals he was taken to were not homes, nor were they intended to be. Neither were they places of hospitality, what they *were* supposed to be.[4] They were treatment facilities designed to administer treatment, but Jerome wasn't looking for treatment and didn't seek it. What he did want and desperately needed was a home, a place where he could be for a while, where, in time, he may find himself.

At first we treated Jerome as an intrusion, a person who had subjected *us* to a regimen we resented. He invaded our home and turned it upside down, so it no longer felt like home to us. We wanted him to stop what he was doing and conform to our way of being together, which we thought was more enlightened, more authentic than his. But Jerome taught us something we hadn't realized, something we needed to learn. Even in the extremities of his weird way of inhabiting Portland Road, all he wanted was to be a part of our community. Once we finally gave up trying to "cure" him of his incontinence so he could join us at the dinner table, on our terms, we accepted him for who he was and abandoned our agenda, however well intentioned it was. I think it was the sojourn to Wales that changed everything for us. For whatever reason, when we returned from that month-long vacation during which we spent virtually every moment together, we finally relaxed and felt at home ourselves. It was the only occasion when Jerome was in close quarters with everyone, all fourteen of us! It was after that when Portland Road became a genuine place of dwelling for Jerome, when he was able to go through that amazing metamorphosis that resulted in his emancipation, when we finally found a way to dwell together.

The way we struggled with and responded to Jerome's impasse as it unfolded will no doubt be regarded as reckless, indulgent, dangerous, even bizarre, by the psychiatric staff of virtually every mental hospital in the world. His behavior – intransigent, stubborn, resistant – would no doubt be met with an even greater force of will, determination, and power than his own. Who do you suppose, given the forces at play, would ultimately win such a contest? Naturally, the use of medicating drugs would be brought to bear, and electric shock, as well as whatever form of incarceration deemed necessary.

Few, if any, psychoanalysts believe it is possible to treat such an impasse with "analysis." Yet, our treatment of Jerome was arguably a quintessential form of analysis, stretched to the limit. Because Jerome refused to talk, we were obliged to let his behavior do the talking for him. D. W. Winnicott, Harry Stack Sullivan, Frieda Fromm-Reichmann, Clara Thompson, Otto Allen Will, Jr., are only some of the prominent psychoanalysts in their day who helped people in this kind of crisis. Some have recounted the many hours they spent with patients who were silent, letting time run its course until something broke through their impasse. Who would deny that Jerome resisted treatment? But what manner of treatment can a person wholeheartedly submit to when it coerces its way in, without invitation or sympathy? And, let's be frank about this, without love. It seems to me, on reflection, that it was our love for Jerome that finally had its way, when we backed off from our efforts to "help" him, when we were able to let him be, as he had asked us to, and allow him to join our community on his terms, not ours.

One of the features of dwelling together is the chance to become friends. What is a friend? Friends are people who love each other. It wouldn't be much of a friendship without that, would it? Dwelling and friendship go hand-in-hand, and love is the medium that allows it to flourish. Love is a hard thing to pin down, because there are many types of it, and not all of them are applicable to a therapeutic process (we will visit the role of love in therapy in Chapter Seven). How do you explain to someone that you want him or her to love you? Love isn't something you can ask for; it has to be offered, spontaneously.

Laing saw his role as one of helping the people who came to him "untie" the knots they had inadvertently tied themselves in. He believed those knots were the consequence of brokenheartedness, or the complete absence of love in relationships where love may have one day thrived. He believed such knots untie themselves when we take care not to repeat the same types of subterfuge and coercion that had got us into those knots in the first place. Jerome had tied himself in a knot, and had come up with his own solution, how he designed to untie them. His way was to count his way there, and to do it silently. On reflection, the fact we were able to get out of his way and allow his untying to unfold was nothing short of miraculous.

This degree of non-intrusion in the context of conventional psychotherapy is a rarity. Those therapists who believe it is incumbent on them to run a "tight ship," who maintain their authority over their patients at all costs, who reduce the therapy experience to a set of techniques that can be learned by rote, aren't likely to embrace a method of transformation that is as modest in its claims as it is cautious with its interventions. Jerome taught me that techniques are of no use when all a person is asking is to be accepted for who he is, unconditionally. In such instances, it isn't what you *do* that counts, but the way you *are* with people, and with yourself. It's about how you make yourself at home.

Notes

1 The word "responsible" is used loosely here. It is perhaps more accurate to say that the so-called "house therapist" was the person who found a house to use for this purpose, so in that sense the therapist became the landlord of the house and served as the connection between the house and Laing's organization, while it was employed as an asylum. The house was then under the "auspices" of the Philadelphia Association, but not directly controlled by it. Apart from that, the only real involvement that the therapist had with the house was to visit regularly, with a view to instilling a live-and-let-live philosophy toward each other in the conduct of their affairs, and to mediate problems as they arose. The therapist's role was more of a facilitator or negotiator than a "group therapist." Residents, in turn, may choose to go into therapy or not, either with the house therapist or someone else, which was the only context where therapy formally occurred.

2 The only documentary feature film ever made about the post-Kingsley Hall houses was *Asylum*, made by the Canadian filmmaker, Peter Robinson, in 1972. Robinson and a small crew lived in one of the houses under the stewardship of Leon Redler in the Archway hamlet of north London while making the film. It is currently available on DVD.

3 For more on the fundamental rule of analysis, see my *The Ethic of Honesty: The Fundamental Rule of Psychoanalysis* (2004).

4 The words hospital and hospitality come from the same root, as does hospice. The original "hospitals" were places of hospitality run by monks to provide shelter to strangers who were traveling. It is only more recently that the term was appropriated by the medical community for places to care for sick people. Mental hospitals, in particular, are no longer places of hospitality, but rather places of involuntary treatment and confinement. See Foucault (2006), for a history of the incarceration for the mentally ill.

References

Foucault, M. (2006) *History of madness.* Translated by Jonathan Murphy and Jean Khalfa. London and New York: Routledge.

Heidegger, M. (1971) Building, dwelling, thinking. In *Poetry, language, thought* (pp. 143–161). Translated by Albert Hofstadter. New York and London: Harper and Row.

Thompson, M. Guy (2004) *The ethic of honesty: The fundamental rule of psychoanalysis.* Amsterdam and New York: Rodopi.

6

THE UNOBJECTIONABLE TRANSFERENCE

The relationship between the person who undergoes psychotherapy and the transference that develops between patient and practitioner is an enigmatic one. In any psychotherapy relationship, including those that are psychoanalytic, the person of the titular patient and the person of the therapist or analyst engage in a relationship together of an intrinsically personal nature. Yet the personal nature of that relationship is seldom addressed in psychoanalytic publications. Moreover, the words "person" and "personal" are not technical terms in standard psychoanalytic nomenclature. Though these terms are frequently alluded to they are never explicitly defined, as far as I know. Some analysts are not convinced that there is such a thing as a "person," let alone a personal dimension to the analytic relationship. Such terms are invoked, if at all, in a strictly offhand way when referring to non-transferential and non-technical behavior or experience in the context of the psychoanalytic treatment relationship (for those analysts who believe that there is such a distinction). But even then, what constitutes the personal aspects of this relationship is seldom explored. For the majority of analysts, so-called personal aspects of the treatment situation have little if any role to play in the psychoanalytic process as it is typically conceived. For many, it is the very absence of personal engagement with patients that distinguishes psychoanalysis from its user-friendly cousin, psychotherapy, as though the person, if he or she exists, may be subject to contagion.

There was a time when only those practitioners who refer to themselves as psychoanalysts were even remotely concerned with the concept of transference. Other, non-psychodynamic practitioners rarely employed the concept in their work and regarded the notion as one that was strictly limited to psychodynamic treatments. This is no longer the case. The concept of transference has entered the general psychotherapy marketplace and has even been incorporated into psychology licensing exams as a universal phenomenon that all practitioners, no matter which theoretical paradigm they adhere to, are expected to recognize when it manifests in their clinical work. More and more, it has become commonplace for virtually all therapists, whether cognitive behavioral, Rogerian, existential, or whatever, to incorporate the concept of transference into their work accordingly, if only to protect the patient from potential abuse by the practitioner. We now live in a transferential landscape, whether we like it or not. But what does the term actually mean?

It has become increasingly commonplace for psychoanalysts of virtually all schools to reduce the psychoanalytic process to the analysis of transference. This has resulted in the general assumption that all of a patient's reactions to the person of the analyst should be treated as transference manifestations. Similarly, most if not all significant interventions by the analyst in response to transference phenomena are informed by whichever technical principles a given analyst elects to follow. This is a view typically held, for example, by Kleinian, classical Freudian (i.e., American ego psychology), and most contemporary relational analysts, all of whom tend to deconstruct the very notion of a person-to-person engagement out of the psychoanalytic process.[1] Such analysts often concede that interactions of a personal nature invariably occur during every analytic encounter, but such occurrences are usually deemed irrelevant and even serve as impediments to the analytic process, so they are scrupulously avoided or, when unavoidable, systematically analyzed, *ad nauseam*.

As a topical example of just how far this attitude has evolved, you might look at an article in *Psychoanalytic Psychology* (Maroda, 2007), which was subsequently discussed in *The New York Times*, that questions the efficacy of analysts treating patients in their home office. The author of the article, Karen Maroda, offered that such arrangements may serve as "keyholes" into the analyst's personal life and consequently "over-stimulate and overwhelm" the patient. She argues that any contact with the analyst's personal life will inevitably result in an unsettling, even harmful experience (if indeed knowledge of a personal nature about one's analyst is inherently traumatic).

Even a cursory survey of the psychoanalytic literature over the course of its long history shows how surprisingly recent the trend to depersonalize the psychoanalytic relationship is. An extraordinary number of seminal contributors to matters of technique – including Freud, Ferenczi, Reik, Fairbairn, Lomas, Erikson, Loewald, Stone, Fromm, Leavy, Lipton, among many others – believe on the contrary that the personal relationship between patient and analyst should be acknowledged in order to accommodate the unpredictable nature of the *total* psychoanalytic encounter. These analysts argue that a wide assortment of object relations, in addition to transference phenomena, occur over the course of every psychoanalytic treatment, and that the astute handling of such non-transference and non-technical interactions are an indispensable component of the proverbial analytic process. On the other hand Ferenczi, an important advocate of informal technique, may inadvertently serve as a confusing model for a more personally engaged way of conducting psychoanalytic treatments. For example, Ferenczi was noted for his gregarious and affectionate personality in the way he typically behaved with patients. Ferenczi also engaged in a series of technical experiments that were designed to make the psychoanalytic process more democratic and less authoritarian. Ferenczi is often cited by contemporary relational analysts (Davies and Frawley, 1991; Ogden, 1994; Mitchell and Black, 1995) as the first advocate of a two-person psychology, yet his inherently outgoing personality traits are typically confused with his more deliberate technical innovations, so that both are erroneously conceived as aspects of *technique*, in the strict sense of the term. Consequently, the specifically spontaneous, unpredictable attributes of a given psychoanalyst's personality have been incorporated into deliberate, circumscribed technical recommendations that effectively compromise the uniquely personal component of the analyst's participation in the process.

Another example of this development can be found among relational analysts who take umbrage with the more classical characterization of transference phenomena as distortions of the patient's real or realistic perception of the analyst's behavior, about which the analyst may be unaware. Yet, in so doing, these same relational analysts tend to treat such ostensibly accurate perceptions as aspects of the patient's *transference*, not the personal aspect of their relationship. Consequently, such perceptions are not conceived as components of the ongoing personal relationship, but as an "expanded" notion of how classical analysts typically conceive the transference situation. For instance, whereas Hoffman (1983) advocates more spontaneity and truthfulness in the analytic relationship, his principal concern is a technical matter, that analysts should encourage their patients to reflect upon and verbalize how they are experiencing their relationship with their analyst. Hoffman points out that analysts have traditionally not been taught to perform such interventions. Moreover, he believes that many of the analysts (e.g., Stone, Loewald, Strachey, Greenson, Langs, Kohut) who have emphasized the importance of the real or personal relationship existing alongside the transferential do not encourage their patients to verbalize their experiences about the personal relationship. He also chides these analysts for adhering to the traditional depiction of transference phenomena as "distortions" of what is really occurring in the analyst–analysand dynamic, thereby setting themselves up as authorities on what is real and what is not. Analysts who encourage more personal or human engagement with their patients fall prey to what Hoffman sees as a stubborn adherence to the analyst as authority figure and the patient as supplicant; these analysts may be compassionate, but they call the shots as to what is actually going on. This characterization of the so-called classical or orthodox analyst has been roundly criticized by Haynal (1997) for oversimplifying the complexity of the historical evolution of psychoanalytic theory and technique over the past century, especially in Europe.

I admit to being puzzled by Hoffman's criticisms. It would seem to me that a relational perspective that is firmly rooted in the interpersonal tradition (initiated by Sullivan and subsequently developed by Fromm, Fromm-Reichmann, C. Thompson, O. Will, and numerous others) would privilege spontaneity *and* personal engagement by both analyst and analysand, a manner of engagement that cannot be reduced to technical interventions, however enlightened or perceptive such interventions may seem. Hoffman complains that there is no way of distinguishing between personal and transferential aspects of the analytic dyad and says even Freud, with his conception of the unobjectionable transference,[2] observed that transference is ubiquitous in virtually all human relationships. Hoffman chastises Stone, for example, for claiming that the transferential and real relationships are distinct but intertwined when Stone says that "the transference will, under [certain] circumstances, include realistic perceptions of the analyst" (quoted in Hoffman, 1983, p. 49). Hoffman argues that Stone cannot have it both ways, to say that one can distinguish between the two and yet insist they can commingle.

It seems to me that Hoffman is genuinely confused about the distinction between the personal and technical aspects of the analytic experience and, so, reduces it to unrelenting tech-ridden interventions that pervade the treatment situation. This problem probably originates with how Freud envisioned matters of technique and the subtle differences between real and transferential love, outlined in Freud's seminal (and most exhaustive) paper on the nature of love, "Observations on Transference-Love" (1915). Because Freud saw transference phenomena as contemporary editions of the patient's Oedipally charged, unrequited love, he recognized that so-called transference experiences occur in all human encounters, including outside the analytic situation. We only call this phenomenon transference (instead of what it really is, love) in the context of analysis because no one can fall in love with their analyst as innocently as they might otherwise in the normal course of events. This is because the comportment of the analyst with whom the patient forms a positive transference is essentially a *contrivance*. The analyst does not show concern, curiosity, and compassion for the patient because of the compelling character traits or charisma the analysand happens to possess, which outside the analytic situation may serve as a catalyst for falling in love. He does so because that is what he is paid to do; it is his job. That doesn't, however, mean that the feelings of concern and compassion he displays toward his patients are not genuine. They are, or at any rate should be. They are two human beings who spend a lot of time together and the analyst feels these things because that is what makes him human. He may also harbor his own personal reasons for wanting to help people. Perhaps he took care of his mother when he was a child and developed a tolerance and ease with such uncommonly intimate and intense relationships that he has opted to turn this talent into a vocation. The patient is effectively thrown into an intense relationship not unlike one she or he might have with, say, a married colleague. Proximity breeds intimacy and the situation that brings people together may elicit emotional reactions they would otherwise never experience with that person.

Another way of putting it is that transference is ubiquitous because our capacity for love is universal and always operative. If we were not capable of such feelings we would not be effective practitioners. Indeed, it is a prerequisite for and the foundation of every intimate relationship we have. The personal and the transferential do blend, but they can be distinguished, with effort and attention, so long as we are clear what that distinction is. A patient may come to trust me because I remind him of his grandfather, whom he loved and admired, but also because I treat him in such a way that invites his trust. The technique of non-judgmental neutrality is not just a technique, strictly speaking. It speaks to my capacity to suspend judgment and keep an open mind, a personal attribute. When this furthers my patient's analytic attitude and his ability to free associate and reflect on my interpretations, I don't necessarily have to bring to my patient's attention that "this is only transference, you know," even if it is. On the other hand, it is a judgment call as to when and how often I feel the need to offer transference interpretations, be they of the genetic or here-and-now variety. But the technique of rendering such interventions occurs in the context of a *personal relationship* that is guided by our respective character traits, including our respective capacities for intimacy, candor, and affiliation. Hoffman seems so intent on bringing our attention to a favored technique of his that he ends up throwing out the baby of personal engagement with the bathwater of classical technique.

Hoffman advocates a less dogmatic and more sceptical manner of sharing interpretations with his patients, and I applaud him for that. Behaving more compassionately and sensitively with one's patients is a no-brainer. But in my view, the inherently personal aspects of the analyst–patient relationship should not necessarily be subject to analysis, nor should they always fall under the rubric of technique. That which is personal is, by its nature, generally taken for granted and permitted to pass as that dimension of the analytic relationship that is both genuine and authentic. *It is from this foundation of the ongoing personal relationship that transference phenomena derive.* The significance of this distinction will become more apparent later.

What accounts for this glaring dichotomy in our conception of the personal relationship, and why is there such reluctance to recognize and, in turn, systematically explore the vital role this relationship plays in every analytic and therapeutic process? Why does the word personal arouse so much concern that it has been more or less banished from our characterization of the process, and relegated to psychoanalytic "psychotherapy"? Finally, what role does the psychoanalytic conception of the unconscious play in these considerations, and how did our conception of the transference as a strictly unconscious phenomenon become incompatible with the notion of a personal dimension to the analytic relationship?

It is a common assumption that the concept of the unconscious is the pivot around which psychoanalytic theory and practice orbit, and which distinguishes psychoanalysis from other kinds of psychotherapy, such as cognitive behavioral therapy (CBT), family therapy, or humanistic, existential, and psychodynamic therapies. It necessarily follows that one of the cardinal questions raised by the psychoanalytic conception of the unconscious is the role of the person who is engaged in this therapeutic endeavor. Freud's earlier topographical model addressed this question in a somewhat ambiguous manner when he coined the term, *Gegenwille* ("counter-will" in English) in order to locate the role of unconscious motivation and how intentions can be operative, yet unknown, to the person (Leavy, 1988). The term "will" has been historically marginalized by psychoanalysts for a variety of reasons. Being a verb as well as a noun, the term always implies a subject or person who is an agent behind acts of will. When I do something that I claim I didn't mean or intend to, it does no good to plead that blind, impersonal forces "did" the act. Those so-called unconscious forces, no matter how you choose to conceptualize them, are *me*.

Counter-will served as an early marker for how Freud conceived the unconscious as a subject who *performs acts* of which the actor is to varying degrees unaware. Though this term endured for some twenty years, after 1912 it began to disappear as the generalization collapsed into concepts like resistance, repression, unconscious conflict, and drive. Freud's subsequent structural model cemented this process even further, when he explicitly depersonalized unconscious agency in the language of id, superego, and defense mechanisms. But the gain in specificity was accompanied by the loss of a *personal*, thus responsible, will. As Freud pursued his project of establishing the (alleged) empirical causes of symptoms, his earlier notion of the unconscious as a secret agent or anonymous ego – i.e., counter-will – receded into the background.

The tendency to depersonalize the unconscious has been more or less adopted by virtually all subsequent schools of psychoanalysis and adapted to their myriad conceptions of the unconscious. Though these conceptions differ from Freud's in significant ways, what they all hold in common is the explicit *depersonalization* of the unconscious. Its unambiguously impersonal status has persisted while accompanied by technical interventions that emphasize impersonal dimensions to the transference, motivation, and resistance to such a degree that the "person" engaged in the process has effectively ceased to exist. Increasingly abstract and ever more arid conceptions of the unconscious have led to more and more impersonal and disassociated conceptions of the transference and the accompanying treatment relationship. Yet Freud's conception of the transference has not been universally embraced. It has even been criticized by some analysts as offering an all-too convenient defense for practitioners who are uncomfortable with the unavoidable personal engagement with patients that the intimate psychoanalytic situation is supposed to foster. For example, Chertok and de Saussure (1979) argue that Freud's conception of transference often serves, "a defensive measure – a kind of prophylaxis that depersonalizes the relationship and interposes a 'third person' between the patient and the doctor, like the duenna-nurse who peers over the gynecologist's shoulder during examination" (p. 13). Thomas Szasz (1963), back in the days when he was still a psychoanalyst, also alluded to the role of transference as a mode of defense when he observed that "the concept of transference serves two separate analytic purposes: it is a crucial part of the patient's therapeutic experience, and a successful defensive measure to protect the analyst from too intense affective and real-life involvement with the patient" (p. 437). Szasz avers, "the idea of transference implies denial and repudiation of the patient's *experience qua experience*; in its place is substituted the more manageable construct of a *transference experience*" (p. 437). These authors suggest that the analysis of transference is frequently employed to help analysts who are uncomfortable with the personal intimacy aroused between themselves and their patients by attributing such feelings to something they decide to call transference, instead of acknowledging the emotions they genuinely feel for each other, and simply letting them be, *sans* interpretation.

I suspect that a significant part of the problem derives from our conception of the unconscious psychoanalytic *process* and its role in our subsequent repression (and suppression) of the personal dimension to the therapy relationship. The term person, or *persona*, was first invoked in Roman law to refer to citizens who possessed the right to vote in a democratic political process. To vote implied an agent who possessed sufficient autonomy to assume responsibility for the decision-making process in which he participated. Because a slave lacked such autonomy he was not deemed a "person" and was accordingly denied the right to vote, as only persons (i.e., non-slaves) were granted these rights. Similarly, Freud, who saw the ego as a slave or servant to unconscious processes, decided over time that the unconscious is not personal but impersonal, meaning analytic patients could not be held responsible for acts, thoughts, or intentions they are unconscious of harboring or committing *at the time* they commit them. Unconscious ideation becomes impersonal precisely when and because it lacks agency. In principle, such thoughts can nevertheless become personal again (or for the first time) once they become conscious and the person in question accepts responsibility for them. Yet the trend in contemporary[3] psychoanalysis is to maintain the impersonal conception of the transference throughout the treatment experience, no matter what insights patients may have about the feelings they harbor toward their analyst.

The psychoanalytic conception of transference phenomena characterizes the patient's experience of and attributions about the person of the analyst as an inherently *unconscious* process. Efforts by relational analysts to render this dynamic more democratic have subjected the analyst to the same kind of scrutiny that is typically reserved for the patient, but the notion of an explicitly personal engagement of the kind I am describing, and that falls outside the purview of *technical interventions*, is typically overlooked or rejected outright. The contemporary relational psychoanalytic literature has consequently opted to focus on transference-countertransference phenomena, their specifically unconscious function, and the ways that analysts are affected by their patients' projections. This has led to a consensus that analysts should focus their attention on analyzing such projections while avoiding interactions of a personal nature which, by implication, are defined as *non-interpretative* communications because they do not allude to unconscious processes. To return to the slave metaphor, for relational analysts both analysands and analysts are *equally* enslaved by their respective unconsciouses, in an endless to-and-fro of intersubjective operations and infinite regress. Now the analyst is just as depersonalized as the patient, in equal measure. While this strategy may be more equal or democratic, it is not necessarily more therapeutic.

Consequently, all vestiges of the personal relationship shared with patients have been transformed into aspects of the patient's transference with the analyst and the analyst's countertransference with the patient, both of which are systematically interpreted and analyzed. From a classical perspective, transference is conceived as a rarefied, trance-like state of childlike hypnotic regression that places the patient in a one-down position from which she cannot extricate herself, because she is always "in" the transference, which she cannot, by definition, escape. This has the chilling consequence of perceiving the analysand as never really being the author of his or her experience or a proper adult in an I–Thou relationship, but the "effect" of unconscious forces that only the analyst is privy to. The more recent relational and contemporary effort to extend this process to a similar analysis of the *analyst's* conscious and unconscious process only duplicates the problem. Though it claims to be more democratic, it has unwittingly become just as depersonalized as the classical perspective which it claims to reject.

Ironically, these relatively recent developments fly in the face of a long history of analysts, going all the way back to Freud and Ferenczi, who embrace the concept of a personal or realistic component to the analytic relationship. Greenson, as Hoffman observed, focuses on what he calls the "real" relationship as distinct from the transference, which pertains to perceptions by the patient that are deemed realistic rather than fantastic and the consequence of unconscious projections. In Greenson's depiction of the real relationship, however, he tends to focus on the patient's experience of the analyst, neglecting the analyst's relationship with the patient. Because the relationship between analyst and analysand is not symmetrical, the correlation between their respective positions is not identical. Whereas the patient's experience of the analyst is couched in terms of varying degrees of transference phenomena, the analyst's experience of and behavior toward the analysand is typically couched in terms of technique, a circumscribed set of behaviors epitomized by interpretative strategies. The concept of countertransference also falls under the purview of technique, whether it is conceived as unconscious impediments to the analyst's optimal functioning in the analytic dyad, or as aspects of the analyst's conscious experience that conform to technical scrutiny. Increasingly, countertransference phenomena are defined simply as the totality of the analyst's experience, including what used to be deemed "personal" reactions, but subsumed under technical oversight, effectively compromising if not entirely eliminating a genuinely personal component to the relationship.

In other words, most of what the analyst says nowadays is monitored by *technical* considerations, whereas anything of a personal nature – which is to say, anything that is uttered spontaneously and without calculated regard for its intended effect on the patient's transference – is virtually eliminated. Greenson and other analysts who are concerned with distinguishing between transferential and real components of the patient's experience of the process do not specifically address its correlate: *the technical and non-technical components of the analyst's behavior.* It is this aspect of the analyst–patient dyad that I am specifically concerned with.

Even those relational analysts who object to the classical characterization of the patient's transference as nothing more than distortions of reality tend to conceive all of the analyst's behavior as aspects of technique. For example, though Renik (1999) advocates acts of self-disclosure by the analyst, he characterizes such revelations as conforming to a technical strategy whose purpose is to exercise a desirable effect on the patient's transference, reminiscent of Alexander's advocacy of manipulating the transference in order to facilitate a corrective emotional experience. In such a scheme, the analyst's acts of self-disclosure are not, strictly speaking, personal but rather calculated to have a specific effect. In order for such interventions to be personal they would have to emanate part and parcel from *who* the analyst is, not *what* the analyst does or intends. Renik does not advocate self-disclosure simply because that is who he is and sees no harm in being himself. Instead, he specifically contrasts what he calls self-disclosure with the idiosyncratic foibles of a given analyst's personality traits, characterizing his own self-disclosures as technical interventions. Renik argues that such self-disclosures should be adopted by all analysts, *as a new standard of technique.*

Yet, like Hoffman, Renik seems genuinely confused about the difference between the technical and personal domains of the analytic relationship. For instance, Renik says:

> My own style as a person, and therefore as an analyst, is toward the active, exhibitionistic rather than the reserved end of the spectrum. All things being equal, I usually prefer to mix it up with a patient and field the consequences rather than risk missing out on an opportunity for productive interchange. By suggesting that the analyst play his or her cards face up, however, I am not rationalizing my personal style or elevating it into a technical principal. *Willingness to self-disclose, as a policy, can and should apply across the individual styles of various analysts.*
>
> *(1999, p. 531; italics added)*

Despite Renik's claim that he is not elevating his personal style to a technique, as soon as he advocates this way of working for *all* analysts he is not suggesting that they be like him, but that they adopt a manner of working – by definition, a technique – that he believes will bear greater analytic success. If Renik put his observations down to an attribute of his personality, that it is simply who he is and that he adapts his technique to fit the idiosyncratic nature of his character structure, then he would be explaining how conducting analysis suited *him*, period (which, by the way, is precisely what Freud recommended). But as soon as he advocates his interventions for others to follow he is advocating a technical intervention. Self-disclosure is no longer the personal application of a character trait but Renik's bringing his mind and comportment to bear in the service of a desirable effect, in other words, an incidence of technique.

What would behavior of a specifically personal nature look like in contrast to a prescribed set of techniques? And how would such behavior be beneficial to the patient's therapy experience? Am I merely splitting hairs by attempting to distinguish between analytic behavior of a personal rather than technical nature? I don't think so. The recognition and elaboration of the personal relationship should obviously *enhance* the therapeutic process, not compromise it. Acting from the analyst's person simply for the sake of it would not make much sense if it had a deleterious effect on the therapeutic relationship. On the other hand, if its aim is to benefit the analytic process, then why wouldn't such personal engagement – on a par with Renik's definition of self-disclosure – entail a *technical* intervention, by definition?

The problem with conceptualizing the personal engagement that all analysts experience with their patients as a component of technique is that in order to come across as a genuine person analysts need to be true to their given personality traits and behavioral characteristics, whatever they happen to be. In order to be genuine, the analyst's way of conducting him- or herself should be natural, spontaneous, and without guile. The most common complaint patients typically make about analysts who conform to classical technique is the *lack of genuineness* concerning the way they conduct themselves.[4] Yet, one of the principal goals of analytic treatment is to increase the patients' capacity for genuineness in their manner of relating to others, as well as themselves. On the other hand, those analysts who object to a classical or austere way of behaving with patients and advocate doing the opposite, e.g., affecting a more conversational and emotional engagement with their patients, invariably argue that *all* analysts would be advised to behave that way, even if such a way of behaving feels out of character or unnatural to other analysts. It is my impression that most analysts are not naturally talkative nor do they wear their hearts on their sleeves. For them, being "themselves" might well entail remaining silent throughout most of their analytic sessions, not because their technique tells them to, but because that is what they are comfortable doing, with more or less everyone. To become talkative and responsive would not only feel unnatural to them; it would also be experienced by their patients as contrived and artificial, perhaps weird. Winnicott is a perfect example of an analyst who learned over many years the value of saying little, yet was regarded by all who saw him in treatment as uncommonly considerate and genuine. In my analysis with Otto Will, he too said very little, but his warmth was palpable. Analysts typically connect with their patients in ways they are not entirely aware of because, in so doing, they are just being themselves, whatever that entails. By extension, an analyst cannot be him- or herself and conceive doing so as a *standard of technique*. Being oneself is, by definition, personal. As such, it is an act of creativity that is *uniquely one's own*.

So what are the criteria for being oneself that most analysts find so objectionable that it has been factored out of the psychoanalytic treatment perspective? Unlike the techniques that analysts adopt, *there cannot be universal standards* for how a given analyst uses his or her personality in the treatment of each patient. Freud wasn't even comfortable with mandating strict standards for his technical principles, let alone the personal ones! As a rule of thumb, what is deemed personal is basically commonsensical, if not immediately predictable or obvious. It is both outside technique and subject to individual variation. It cannot be codified because, just as analysts differ from person to person, each analyst's conception of the personal relationship will vary accordingly. Moreover, analysts are liable to form different conceptions of what the personal relationship entails at different stages of their careers and with different patients, when they succumb to this or that mood, the time of day, how long they have been working with a given patient, and so on.

For the personal relationship to be spontaneous, unpredictable, and authentic, it has to be free of contrivance and subterfuge, a manner of being that, for lack of a better word, comes from the heart. This is why the most common incidence of the personal relationship is often manifested in the form of *spontaneous conversations* that evolve between analyst and patient. Such conversations may include self-disclosures by the analyst, but not necessarily. The basic idea is that not everything the analyst says is limited to offering interpretations, eliciting data, or other technical considerations. Classical analysts tend to reject conversation out of hand because they believe "conversing" has no discernable role in the analytic process, whereas relational analysts tend to reduce such otherwise spontaneous conversations to a technique that can come across just as contrived and manipulative as the so-called classical interventions they condemn. Conversations are obviously gratifying for patient and analyst alike and are necessarily restrained by the use of abstinence,[5] but to abandon them entirely becomes artificial for those analysts who, like Freud and Ferenczi, are naturally conversational. For example, there are times when patients may want to muse about ideas, whether philosophical, literary, or spiritual, when reflecting on the human condition and their place in the scheme of things, and ask their analysts to reciprocate. Analysts may in turn participate in such conversations without the need to reduce such musings to manifestations of transference and analyze them accordingly. Some analysts may even initiate such conversations when the spirit moves them to, for reasons that are not necessarily apparent to them at the time. It is my sense that such spontaneous, inherently extra-analytic exchanges have a profound impact on the analytic relationship and, hence, the outcome of treatment, but in ways that we may be incapable of determining on a case-by-case basis, let alone moment-to-moment.

Permitting one's personality to become part of the constellation of elements that therapists utilize serves as an invaluable source for authentic relating with patients. *It is my thesis that these incidents of feeling genuinely connected to one's analyst are critical, if unconventional, even controversial, components of every successful treatment experience, and a hallmark of the existential perspective.* Because each analyst's (or therapist's) personality is unique, each practitioner's manner of being personally engaged with his or her patients will vary. Feeling free to converse spontaneously is only one personality trait among many that cannot be reduced to technical edicts. For example, a given analyst's capacity for affection, disaffection, concern, kindness, courage, consideration, compassion, curiosity, and wisdom are all personal characteristics that will fundamentally differ from one practitioner to another. Moreover, such characteristics cannot be taught in clinical internships or psychoanalytic institutes, nor can they be learned in supervision. You might say they are so personal that each analyst has to struggle in her own analysis to discover which ones epitomize the peculiarities of her own personality, and determine those that are strengths and weaknesses by developing her clinical style accordingly. They are not only traits of personality, but part and parcel aspects of the practitioner's *way of living* and operative in all aspects of it, including the relationships that are fashioned with one's patients.

The personal relationship that all patients share with their therapists is not merely the background for the more decisive, "transferential" component. It is also the vehicle that helps the patient undergoing therapy to change. As such, it is the *transformational* component of the so-called transference relationship. What *is* this relationship and how can it be expected to serve as a catalyst for change? There are any number of terms that have been offered in an effort to characterize the peculiar nature of this relationship, including the unobjectionable transference (Freud, 1915), the working alliance (Zetzel, 1958), the real relationship (Gill, 1982, pp. 85–106), the personal relationship (Lipton, 1977), and so on. These terms, however, beg the question since whatever this relationship entails must in turn be modeled upon a form of relation that is in principle available to all of us, and one with which we are at least vaguely familiar, perhaps intimately so. After all, Freud reminded us that transference is ubiquitous and exists in all relationships of an intimate nature. The analytic relationship is essentially concerned with our capacity to *share confidences*, so that the analyst becomes that person in whom the patient endeavors to take into his or her confidence. In effect, the patient treats the analyst like a confidante or a friend, a person in whom she is able and, more importantly, willing to confide.

In other words, the personal aspect of the psychoanalytic relationship is a form of *friendship*. But what manner of friendship is it, and what, specifically, does this form of friendship entail? Moreover, how does one's notion of friendship inform the context in which Freud's conception of transference arose? Friendships are as old as human beings, but their nature has changed over time, as have cultural mores. In a paper titled "The Catalytic Role of Crucial Friendship in the Epistemology of Self-Experience,"[6] Masud Khan (1970) explored the pivotal role that friendship plays in the development of self-experience, contrasting post-sixteenth-century accounts of friendship in European culture with earlier attitudes.

According to Khan, the beginning of the modern era, which was inaugurated in the sixteenth century, occasioned the decline of religion in European cultures, culminating in Nietzsche's declaration in 1885 that "God is dead." Khan observed that the erosion of God's presence in the culture at large coincided with increasing interest in science, replacing a theistic interpretation of our place in the cosmos with a secular model. Whereas previously humans had been conceived in the image of God, now people served as a model for man-made machines. Khan, however, notes that "the human individual, from time immemorial, has always needed someone other than himself to relate to and to know himself with" (p. 99). In other words, it is the mediating influence of other people through whom the person finds the measure of himself and never, strictly speaking, "by himself" in isolation.

Khan believed that before the relative demise of God in European culture, human beings didn't depend on each other emotionally in the way they do today. As religious faith weakened people experienced greater isolation and felt the absence of someone in their lives to whom they could turn, not merely for companionship but for baring their souls for the purpose of plumbing the depths of their existence. More than ever before, people were searching for meaning in their lives through their connections with other people. Michel de Montaigne was probably the first example in literature of a person who relied on a friend in order to engage in a form of disciplined self-inquiry, almost spiritual in its scope and purpose. His deep relationship with his close friend, Etienne de La Boétie, is a case in point. They became profoundly intimate, but just as suddenly as their friendship began La Boétie died, leaving Montaigne feeling isolated and depressed. This culminated in Montaigne's decision to retire to his castle where he begin writing his voluminous *essais*, one of which was devoted to the loss of this friend. Montaigne's *Essais* enjoy a remarkable similarity to Augustine's *Confessions*, both highly personal accounts of a spiritual crisis that they were subsequently compelled to write down. Yet, it hadn't been necessary for St. Augustine, centuries earlier, to rely on friendship in order to pen his *Confessions* because Augustine, unlike Montaigne, had turned to God for his inspiration.[7] This difference is what makes Montaigne the primogenitor of the Modern Man (or woman), the quintessential loner who, having rejected his reliance on God to heal his soul, turned to friendship to serve the same function.

A self-confessed student of the Classics, Montaigne was especially indebted to Aristotle's views on friendship, outlined in his *Nicomachean Ethics* (1915, pp. 1155a–1163b). There Aristotle distinguished amongst three forms of friendship, each corresponding to the types of relationships in life that we most love: a) those who offer us pleasure; b) those with whom we engage in commerce, for prosperity; and c) those people whom we love simply for who they are. According to Aristotle, this last form of friendship is the only one of the three that can endure. Unlike the first two that are subject to the whims of narcissistic reward, the last is the only one whose purpose is to confide in another person, a person who will not render judgments but will embrace us for who we are in our being, warts and all. Only the last of these three forms of friendship are capable of genuine intimacy.

Montaigne (1925, vol. I, pp. 243–260) argued that the third category of friendship, characterized as true or genuine, was superior to the others for several reasons. Friends who we seek for pleasure may vanish as cavalierly as they enter our lives. Because they don't really want to know about our troubles, we conceal things from them that we suppose will sour the relationship and spoil the enjoyment we share together. Similarly, friends whom we accrue for financial or political benefit are sometimes people we don't necessarily like, but because we rely on them for reward they are crucial to our ambitions as well as our livelihood, so we exercise caution in not offending them for fear they turn against us. The old adage, "a former friend is one's most dangerous enemy," is particularly apt in this example. Montaigne emphasized that nothing can be done to preserve such friendships because we grow weary of them just as easily as they tire of us. Besides, such people are not essential to our happiness and, even if we remain fond of them or they continue to be useful, there remains an unbridgeable distance between us. The true friend relieves us of such complications and enjoys a treasured status in the kind of relationships we are capable of fostering.

Unlike Aristotle, who entertained a fairly broad opinion about the kinds of relationship friendships entail (including family members), Montaigne separated friendships from other intimate relationships with which they are sometimes confused, such as the relation between a child and parent, or husband and wife, or mentor and student, benefactor and supplicant. The child's relationship with the father, for example, is rooted in respect, whereas friendship, like the transference relation in psychoanalysis, is rooted in the *exchange of confidences*. Montaigne argues that a child can never wholeheartedly take his father (or mother) into his or her confidence because their relationship is complicated by the kind of obligations and expectations that interfere with our capacity for candor, a point Freud noted three centuries later. Similarly, tensions arise between most siblings despite (or, perhaps, because of) the blood ties that define them. And while some siblings grow uncommonly close to each other, others grow to hate and even fear the other, so the relationships among siblings don't necessarily guarantee a bond of intimacy. (Freud would have suggested that Oedipal rivalry renders genuine intimacy between siblings a fiction.)

A more ambiguous category of relationship involves sex, the nature of which renders friendship problematical because lovers are usually too possessive of each other to tolerate the self-sacrifice that friendships aspire to. When we endeavor to form friendships with those we feel attracted to – or with former lovers – we are always in doubt that one of us is not feigning friendship for ulterior motives, perhaps as a means of seduction, or revenge. Even the hint of sexual attraction may foster suspicion that renders the potential for genuine candor dubious. Due to their complexity and mutual obligation, the same can be said for marital relations, epitomized by contractual obligations that engender expectations, which inevitably manifest the occasional crisis. Admittedly, in Montaigne's time marriages were arranged by one's family and furthered practical or political alliances that compromised the likelihood of developing genuine intimacy. But even today when we typically marry for love, the marriage is nonetheless occasioned by obligations that inspire secrecy and deception, if only to safeguard the union. The marital relation, especially when children are concerned, is so complicated it invariably gives rise to tensions, frustrations and, when successful, compromise. The form of intimacy created is unique in the depth of love it is capable of fostering, but it also exacts an unavoidable burden that is the consequence of sharing a destiny together, with all its attendant sorrows and misfortunes. The marital contract is such that it *aims* at survival, so one's fear of betrayal or failure is in proportion to the fidelity with which the married partners undertake their vows. This explains why the sexual dimension of marriage offers the most frequent source of tension, sometimes leading to dissolution.

Such considerations inspired Montaigne to conclude that *the absence of sexual desire is the key to the unique form of freedom that genuine friendship aspires to.* Whereas sex joins people together in passionate if unpredictable ways, friends usually forgo this source of pleasure in favor of a relationship that is rooted in alternative, aim-inhibited rewards. This feature of friendship may explain why self-disclosure is both easier and more readily anticipated in friendship and why a similar dynamic is repeated in the analytic relationship. Because the *raison d'être* of friendship is epitomized by the confidences shared, all that matters is the ease with which friends are able to offer and, in turn, elicit confidences from each other. Such confidences aren't offered by the pressure of obligation or expectation but as a *gift*, in effect, a gift of love that serves as the fulcrum of their union.

Montaigne concluded that friendship is characterized by two essential criteria: First, by an uncommon degree of *forgiveness*, elements of which Freud included in his conception of neutrality.[8] This is because friends typically overlook the faults and idiosyncrasies that drive others to distraction. Whereas acquaintances are eager to condemn each other for alleged misdemeanors, a friend will instinctively reject condemnation and offer a friend the benefit of the doubt. This is the same attitude that analysts are expected to adopt toward their patients, the effects of which facilitate the capacity for rapport. Second, friendship is characterized by an unusual degree of *generosity*. Patients make uncommon demands on their analysts, seldom realizing the frustration such behavior engenders in the person who, after all, is only trying to help them. A good friend, as with a dedicated analyst, never complains about this uneasy arrangement, even when appreciation for the sacrifices endured is unacknowledged. A friend is giving to his or her friend in a manner that no one else is able or willing to, because their relationship is explicitly predicated on this implicit expectation.

The endeavor to help people with their most intimate concerns implies a capacity for friendship on *both* sides of the equation: for the analyst who must gain the trust of the patient who seeks his counsel, and for the patient the ability to accept such counsel (e.g., interpretations) without suspicion or resentment. However, this form of "friendship," whether systematized in the guise of a treatment relationship or spontaneous in the case of a confidante, is incapable of flourishing in the absence of intermittent breaks in the time the two participants spend together. Friends do not typically live together, and when they do, such proximity may damage and even destroy the friendship. The boundaries provided by regular absences (duplicated in the therapy relationship schedule) allow time for each to regroup and recover from the stings and frustrations that invariably accumulate when together. Even in the present era when marriage is often characterized as a friendship with sex, excessive time together can undermine the intimacy shared and dilute sexual attraction. This probably accounts for why sexual activity between spouses wanes over time. Though Aristotle believed that friendship requires frequent contact in order to endure, *excessive* contact may prove equally deleterious.

Masud Khan characterized Montaigne's relationship with La Boétie as an example of what he terms "crucial friendship," an intense form of friendship in which the confidences shared are so personal they occasion a transformation in the personality by one of the participants. This new, *transformational* form of friendship is not noted by either Aristotle or Montaigne, yet many of the elements of what they depict as genuine (or candid) friendship are contained in it, but goes even further. Khan suggests that this type of friendship also characterizes Freud's equally intense relationship with his friend, Fliess. In the same way that La Boétie served as someone to whom Montaigne could bare his soul, Freud's lengthy and unusually intimate correspondence with Fliess served a similar function. Whereas Montaigne's friendship with La Boétie culminated in the latter's death, Freud's friendship with Fleiss culminated in a falling out which Khan believes may be unavoidable in friendships that occasion a transformation in one's self-experience. The termination of the transference relationship at the end of analysis suffers a similar fate, for analogous reasons.

Freud was thirty-two years old when he met Fleiss and on the threshold of his most important discoveries. In their correspondence Freud shared virtually everything with him, his doubts, anxieties, his innermost feelings, as well as progress and setbacks with his patients. The time period of this correspondence, from 1887 to 1902, was a time in which Freud's most important discoveries were made, discoveries he first shared with Fliess. It was during this period that Freud was also immersed in his self-analysis. Because self-analysis by itself is not a genuine treatment experience, which requires two participants, it was probably Freud's bond with Fleiss that provided both the interplay and *gravitas* which, in combination, rendered his self-discoveries palpable. Freud even acknowledged in a letter to Fleiss (dated November 14, 1897) that self-analysis was not all that he had hoped due to the absence of an "other" in whom he could confide: "My self-analysis remains interrupted. I have realized why I can analyse myself only with the help of knowledge obtained objectively (like an outsider). True self-analysis is impossible; otherwise there would be no (neurotic) illness" (Masson, 1985, p. 281).[9]

Khan suggests that Fleiss, though Freud failed to realize it at the time, served as this "actual other" without which the gravity of the analytic experience would prove negligible, because there would be no one *to whom* Freud was able to reveal himself. According to Khan:

> With the hindsight available to us through Freud's researches and analytic method, it is not difficult to ascertain how much of Freud's relation to Fliess has all the patent characteristics of a transference-relationship: his lurid over-idealization of Fliess, his over-estimation of Fliess's intellect, his impassioned dependence on Fliess's judgment and approval, and its transience. It lasted twelve years, had its climax, and then it sundered.
>
> *(1970, p. 108)*

Freud's and Montaigne's respective uses of friendship nevertheless diverged in significant ways. Whereas Montaigne idealized his friendship with La Boétie even after his death, Freud's feelings about Fliess changed dramatically, prompting him to adopt a more subdued attitude about the limits of friendship and the dimensions of its power. Contrary to Montaigne, Freud derived a more complicated assessment about the forces that determine its significance and the undercurrents that may lead to its termination. Freud experienced a change in his self-development due to the candid nature of the rapport he shared with Fliess over a period of some twelve years, whereas Montaigne experienced similar changes in his personality due to the mourning he endured *following* La Boétie's death.[10] It wasn't the intensity of their friendship that transformed Montaigne's personality but the subsequent trials of self-disclosure, manifested through the composition of his essays, culminating in the cure of Montaigne's depression.

Because of Freud's painful and decisive falling out with Fliess, he must have realized the potential power that self-disclosure is capable of harnessing, and how quickly a friendship is transformed when a previously serviceable dependence on it expires. Though Freud never explicitly equated the transference with friendship, his views about friendship obviously informed his conception of the transference, especially its personal aspects. Freud was able to make use of the most ordinary and spontaneous experience with which all of us are in some measure familiar, and contrived a therapeutic technique that helps instigate our longing for love in the therapy relationship. Freud would have probably never made this discovery had he not appreciated the ubiquitous nature of love and the way it invariably insinuates its way into every relationship, but especially friendship. For example, in *Group Psychology and the Analysis of the Ego* (1921), Freud categorized friendship as one of those "aim-inhibited" forms of affection that has at its base the same longing for love that is manifested in sexual relationships, but that:

> [I]n relations between the sexes these impulses force their way towards sexual union, but in other circumstances they are diverted from this aim or are prevented from reaching it, though always preserving enough of their original nature to keep their identity recognizable (as in such features as the longing for proximity, and self-sacrifice).
>
> *(pp. 90–91)*

In Freud's view, the strength of friendships – their longevity, duration, devotion, and self-sacrifice – are only possible because the "satisfaction" we seek from them is unobtainable. This is why the obsessive and devotional quality of crucial friendship is a compensation for non-gratification as well as a respite from the emotional upheavals that sexual relations thrive on. This also explains why friendships – and by extension, the patient's transference to the analyst – are invariably frustrating, because the gratification we seek in all our relationships is necessarily thwarted in friendship. The experience of feeling thwarted and our acceptance of this unspoken condition is the test upon which the success of every friendship is finally measured.

In effect, the transference is a form of friendship, manifested by the trials of aim-inhibited love. The inexorable course of the therapy and sacrifices suffered finally bring home to the patient the measure of love that genuine friendship entails. For Freud, the "higher" our capacity for love, which is to say, the more self-sacrificing, the more suffering we are inclined to endure for the sake of displacing our repressed libido onto other outlets. In other words, *our capacity for enduring frustration is the measure of our capacity for friendship*, as well as a successful therapeutic experience.

In the transference, this is occasioned by a steady diet of frustration and disillusion. In Freud's relationship with Fliess, he discovered that the depth of their friendship and his inordinate dependence on it finally exacted a costly but necessary price: the friendship itself. Freud had changed so much during the course of it that he finally outgrew the relationship and, like a treatment that has finally served its purpose, no longer needed it. Once the therapy is terminated, most patients find it impossible to continue a relationship with their therapist after the conditions for their intimacy expire. Even if the therapist is agreeable, or they become colleagues, the erstwhile patient usually feels the former therapist knows too much to feel comfortable in his presence. Ideally, according to Khan:

> One could argue that what is unique about the clinical situation is that the analyst survives both the loving and the hating of the patient as a person, and the patient as a person at the resolution of the relationship survives it, too, and is the richer for it.
>
> *(1970, p. 111)*

Of all the psychotherapeutic perspectives that have emphasized the role of the personal relationship, the interpersonal and existential perspectives are the most explicit in addressing this aspect of the analyst–analysand (or therapist–patient) relationship. This is not to suggest that other perspectives have neglected this issue. On the contrary, there is a rich psychoanalytic literature that both addresses and advocates the role of the personal relationship in the analytic process, as noted earlier.[11] The existential tradition has even questioned the efficacy of making clear-cut distinctions between the personal and transference relationships.[12] Existentialists have historically tended to avoid terms like technique and focus instead on those phenomena that the patient is aware of and those that the patient is not aware of, that which is accessible to awareness and that which is inaccessible.[13] The fact that analysts occupy a necessarily professional role in their work doesn't necessarily imply that the relationships fashioned with their patients isn't personal. Yes, there are professional relationships that don't occasion a personal dimension. For example, x-ray technicians in a hospital setting may have little if any opportunity to engage in personal conversation with their subjects because they can carry out their role with minimal, if any, personal contact. Psychoanalytic relationships, however, like other psychotherapeutic collaborations, cannot avoid such contact because the personal medium of engaging in conversation is the *essence* of their professional activities. The boundaries between the personal and professional are constantly evolving in ways we are not necessarily aware of, despite all the attention the relational analysts pay to this phenomenon.

It should be apparent by now that the character, or person, of a given practitioner is of critical importance to how that therapist's patients will experience and benefit from their relationship. Whereas technical principles are indispensable to every analytic or psychotherapeutic endeavor, the question I am addressing is the often neglected but equally important issue of the analyst's unique personality and attendant character traits. For some analyst's, and I would include myself among them, the role of the analyst's character is of far greater importance than the technique a given analyst opts to employ. There is no way of empirically substantiating this claim but I adhere to it, nonetheless. If I am wrong, then I take responsibility for it, but it is difficult for me to see how it could be proved to be right or wrong, as though there is a test that may provide the answer. Such questions are not a matter of science, but of personal discrimination. You believe me or you don't, which is your choice.

That being said, the psychoanalytic conception of *character* has been historically pathologized and construed as an embedded structure of personality that compromises the person's ability to obtain maximum reward from or adaptation to life. Freud employed the word character in two distinct ways. In his earlier writings, but also sporadically in later papers, he referred to character in the sense of a virtuous, upstanding individual. But the majority of his publications allude to the second sense, as a form of psychopathology embedded in the patient's personality. The first character type to catch Freud's attention was the obsessional type, soon followed by a host of others and subsequently expanded on by new generations of analysts. Because they are so deeply embedded, each person is profoundly adapted to a given constellation of character types, e.g., histrionic, obsessive, schizoid, narcissistic, paranoid, and so on. The notion that character may refer to features of one's personality structure that are inherently *virtuous* is not a typical preoccupation in contemporary psychoanalytic literature or nomenclature, or the psychotherapy literature generally. We speak in an offhand way of a person possessing good character or strong character to signify an individual of exemplary moral fiber, who epitomizes excellent values, such as the ones I listed above, e.g., kindness, generosity, courage, integrity, honesty, resolve, and the like. But these examples of character are usually invoked only when employing non-technical terminology about a patient, outside the therapist–patient dynamic.

Though Freud referred to his first use of character only fleetingly (see, for example, Freud, 1905), he never abandoned his belief that virtuous character traits are an indelible ingredient of every successful therapy experience. He perceived the British, for example, as a culture he admired for possessing "excellent character" (an opinion he did not share about Americans). Moreover, he believed that candidates for analytic treatment should possess a quota of good character, but the character traits they should exhibit are left for us to ponder. Since Freud, analysts have tended to remain silent about such considerations. As the treatment of severe psychopathologies (e.g., schizoid, narcissistic, and borderline character structure) has increasingly dominated the psychoanalytic and therapy literature, the question of analyzability has receded into the background. Freud questioned whether schizoid and narcissistic patients could be analyzed because he believed they were too self-absorbed; yet this assessment was based on their pathology, not their character, specifically. Freud's focus, as we know, was on neurotics, yet many of them he deemed "good for nothing" and unsuitable for the kind of perseverance, honesty, and will that he expected analytic patients to embody. These character traits were, in his way of thinking, independent of the pathology (whether neurotic or psychotic) a given patient happens to experience.

Similarly, Freud (1913) expected analysts to possess an even higher degree of virtue than the patients they treat, most prominent among them honesty.[14] Freud didn't say a lot about honesty because it is not a matter of technique but concerns the analyst's personality. He or she has got it or hasn't, but it cannot be turned on or off like a switch or learned from a course of study. Moreover, analysts who don't possess a high degree of character will find the trials and demands of clinical work not to their liking. They may very well succeed in becoming analysts or therapists, but it was Freud's opinion they will not be good at it because they serve as poor role models for their patients. Until recently analytic institutes typically assessed for character in screening prospective applicants for training, but increasingly this question is omitted from consideration because character is so difficult to measure and depends more or less on the subjective opinion of the analysts conducting the interviews. Ironically, in order to make the admissions process less subjective and more democratic, the relevance of and preoccupation about the relation between the practitioner's character and techniques employed has receded into the background.

Even if personal virtue cannot be taught, the concept can and should be included in the curriculum of psychoanalytic institutes and other psychotherapy training schemes, including the existential. Though we cannot "learn" to be virtuous, we can raise our awareness to those aspects of our personalities that disclose our attitudes about our work and the frustrations suffered. This may help us to become more cognizant about the role character plays in our notions about theory and technique, the outcomes we aspire to, the kinds of patients we like to work with and the ones we do not. Given the vast amount of literature on character pathology, it would also be instructive to distinguish between the two types of character I have been outlining, including their relationship to personality (now employed more or less interchangeably with character) and what I depict as the personal relationship.

In conclusion, the capacity to acknowledge the existence of a personal relationship with our patients, and the wherewithal to freely engage it in a manner that complements the specific needs of each treatment situation, lends a dimension of genuineness and authenticity to the relationship that has profound implications for the way the therapy is experienced, and even how technical principles are applied. Fortunately, most practitioners know this intuitively, if not deliberately, and conduct themselves accordingly.

Notes

1 Though relational analysts often characterize their perspective as more personal than classical analysts, I will show that this is not always the case.
2 This term is rarely invoked nowadays, having been replaced here and there with terms like the personal or real relationship, or the working or therapeutic alliance.
3 I mean contemporary in the "present day" sense, not in the sense of relational psychoanalysis specifically.
4 For an illuminating example of such complaints, see Daphne Merkin (2010) in a recent article in *The New York Times Magazine*, August 8, 2010, pp. 28–47.
5 I employ the term abstinence to connote the curtailment of overly friendly or affectionate behavior by the therapist that may interfere with the patient's ability to focus on the work that therapy entails. Though friendly banter, as I employ it, has a crucial role in the service of the personal dimension to the therapist–patient relationship, its incidence should not be excessive. How much is optimal is a matter of judgment and discrimination, the patient

being analyzed, and the context. See Freud (1915), for a thorough discussion about the relationship between abstinence and affection. See also Thompson (2004, pp. 61–77).

6 Subsequently published as "Montaigne, Rousseau and Freud" in *The Privacy of the Self*, (1974, pp. 99–111).

7 I'm not suggesting that Montaigne was an atheist, he wasn't. The point I want to make in this comparison is that Augustine *explicitly* turned to God for the purpose of finally understanding himself, whereas Montaigne used his friend to serve the same function.

8 Freud's conception of neutrality rests on the analyst's capacity to remain non-judgmental about the character, symptoms, and behavior of his or her patients. There is no other relationship as forgiving and open-minded as the one between analyst and patient. See Thompson (2004, pp. 39–60) for a detailed treatment of this technical principle.

9 Which is to say, because neuroses always imply a relationship with an "other," the resolution of neuroses also assumes such a relationship.

10 Montaigne's intimate reflections in the form of his *essais* eventually cured him of the melancholy he suffered over his friend's death.

11 For example, see Bouvet (1958), Nacht (1958), Reich (1958), Gitelson (1962, 1952), Ticho (1982), Ticho and Richards (1982), and Gill (1988).

12 See Laing (1967), Buber (1970), and Tillich (2000), for informed discussions concerning the personal nature of every therapeutic encounter.

13 See Askey and Farquhar (2006), for an illuminating review of existentialist and phenomenological critiques of the unconscious.

14 See Thompson (2004), for more on Freud's views about honesty.

References

Aristotle (1915) *The works of Aristotle, Volume IX: Ethica Nicomachea.* Translated by W. D. Ross. London and New York: Oxford University Press.

Askey, R. and Farquhar, J. (2006) *Apprehending the inaccessible: Freudian psychoanalysis and existential phenomenology.* Evanston, IL: Northwestern University Press.

Bouvet, M. (1958) Technical variation and the concept of distance. *International Journal of Psychoanalysis,* Vol. 39:211–221.

Buber, M. (1970) *I and thou.* Translated by Walter Kaufman. New York: Free Press.

Chertok, L. and de Saussure, R. (1979) *The therapeutic revolution: From Mesmer to Freud.* Cited in Malcolm, J. *Psychoanalysis: The impossible profession,* p. 13. New York: Alfred A. Knopf, 1981.

Davies, J. and Frawley, M. (1991) Dissociative processes and transference-countertransference paradigms in psychoanalytically oriented treatment of adult survivors of childhood sexual abuse. In *Relational psychoanalysis: The emergence of a tradition* (pp. 269–299) (Eds., S. Mitchell and L. Aron). Hillsdale, NJ: The Analytic Press, 1999.

Freud, S. (1953–1973) *The standard edition of the complete psychological works of Sigmund Freud.* 24 volumes. Edited and translated by J. Strachey. London: Hogarth Press. (Referred to in subsequent references as *Standard Edition.*)

Freud, S. (1905) On psychotherapy. *Standard Edition,* 7:257–268. London: Hogarth Press, 1953.

Freud, S. (1913) On beginning the treatment (Further recommendations on the technique of psycho-analysis I). *Standard Edition,* 12:121–144. London: Hogarth Press, 1958.

Freud, S. (1915) Observations on transference-love (Further recommendations on the technique of psycho-analysis III). *Standard Edition,* 12:157–171. London: Hogarth Press, 1958.

Freud, S. (1921) *Group psychology and the analysis of the ego. Standard Edition,* 18:67–143. London: Hogarth Press, 1955.

Gill, M. (1982) *Analysis of transference, Volume 1: Theory and technique.* New York: International Universities Press.

Gill, M. (1988) Converting psychotherapy into psychoanalysis. *Contemporary Psychoanalysis,* Vol. 24, No. 2:262–274.

Gitelson, M. (1952) The emotional position of the analyst in the psycho-analytic situation. *International Journal of Psychoanalysis,* Vol. 33:1–10.

Gitelson, M. (1962) The curative factors in psycho-analysis. *International Journal of Psychoanalysis,* Vol. 43:194–205.

Haynal, A. (1997) A European view: *A meeting of minds: Mutuality in psychoanalysis* by Lewis Aron (Hillsdale, NJ: The Analytic Press, 1996). *Psychoanalytic Dialogues,* Vol. 7:881–884.

Hoffman, I. (1983) The patient as interpreter of the analyst's experience. In *Relational psychoanalysis: The emergence of a tradition* (pp. 39–75) (Eds., S. Mitchell and L. Aron). Hillsdale, NJ: The Analytic Press, 1999.

Khan, M. (1970) Montaigne, Rousseau and Freud. In *The privacy of the self* (pp. 99–111). London: The Hogarth Press and the Institute of Psycho-analysis, 1974.

Laing, R. D. (1967) *The politics of experience.* New York: Pantheon Books.

Leavy, S. (1988) *In the image of God: A psychoanalyst's view.* New Haven and London: Yale University Press.

Lipton, S. (1977) The advantages of Freud's technique as shown in his analysis of the rat man. *International Journal of Psycho-Analysis,* Vol. 58:255–273.

Maroda, K. J. (2007) Ethical considerations of the home office. *Psychoanalytic Psychology,* Vol. 24:173–179.

Masson, J. M. [Ed.] (1985) *The complete letters of Sigmund Freud to Wilhelm Fliess: 1887–1904.* Translated by J. M. Masson. Cambridge, MA and London: The Belknap Press.

Merkin, D. (2010) My life in therapy: What 40 years of talking to analysts has taught me. *The New York Times Magazine,* August 8, 2010, pp. 28–47.

Mitchell, S. and Black, M. (1995) *Freud and beyond: A history of modern psychoanalytic thought.* New York: Basic Books.

Montaigne (1925) *The essays of Montaigne, Volume 1.* Translated by George Ives. Cambridge, MA: Harvard University Press.

Nacht, S. (1958) Variations in technique. *International Journal of Psychoanalysis,* Vol. 39:235–237.

Ogden, T. (1994) The analytic third: Working with intersubjective clinical facts. In *Relational psychoanalysis: The emergence of a tradition* (pp. 459–492) (Eds., S. Mitchell and L. Aron). Hillsdale, NJ: The Analytic Press, 1999.

Reich, A. (1958) A special variation of technique. *International Journal of Psychoanalysis,* Vol. 39:230–234.

Renik, O. (1999) Playing one's cards face up in analysis: An approach to the problem of self-disclosure. *The Psychoanalytic Quarterly,* Vol. 68:521–539.

Szasz, T. (1963) The concept of transference. *The International Journal of Psychoanalysis,* Vol. 44:432–443.

Thompson, M. Guy (2004) *The ethic of honesty: The fundamental rule of psychoanalysis.* Amsterdam and New York: Rodopi.

Ticho, E. (1982) The alternate schools of the self. *Journal of the American Psychoanalytic Association,* Vol. 30:840–862.

Ticho, E. and Richards, A. (1982) Psychoanalytic theories of the self. *Journal of the American Psychoanalytic Association,* Vol. 30:717–733.

Tillich, P. (2000) *The courage to be.* New Haven and London: Yale University Press.

Zetzel, E. (1958) The therapeutic alliance. In *The capacity for emotional growth* (Ed., M. Khan) (pp. 182–196). New York: International Universities Press, 1970.

7

LOVE AND MADNESS

Of all the words that we use as a matter of course in our day-to-day affairs, love is probably the most difficult to define or comprehend. I have yet to meet anyone, no matter how wise or worldly, who claims to know precisely what love is. Yet even if no one understands it, there is little doubt that love in fact exists, for virtually everyone, no matter how rich or poor, crazy or sane, handsome or ugly, has experienced it, both passively and actively. We have no paucity of opinion as to its effects and, like happiness, we employ all manner of cunning and device to procure it, despite our failure to ever finally possess it, ensure it, or exhaust it. Like a visitor we wish would stay but has other places to go, we reconcile ourselves to its presence on terms we can neither dictate nor control. It is a matter of common wisdom that we are never more vulnerable – and foolish – than when we are in love with another person. Our only protection from its artifice is to defend ourselves against it, to tell ourselves we don't need or want it, or to set our standards so high that no one can meet them. Such strategies are employed by the neurotic most effectively, though not without substantial cost. For what value does life have without it? No matter how vociferously we deny it, all of us share a common bond that makes us the human creatures we are: we cannot live without love in one form or other. No matter how loath we are to admit it, our singular goal in life is to procure love and possess it, however successful or ineffective we may be in this mission. Even when we have ostensibly given up on finding it, our longing persists in the deepest recesses of our being.

My aim in this chapter is not to offer yet another theory of love or an amalgam of those that have come before, but to focus on the relation between love and its kissing cousin, madness. In speaking of their relation I will have no choice but to allude to what love and madness are, if only tangentially. But I hope that by exploring their relationship we will arrive at a preliminary understanding about the nature of love and what it means to be crazy, and to be madly in love.

I will begin by explicating the gist of the two most influential thinkers on the matter, Plato and Sigmund Freud. Though they are separated by more than two thousand years, a good measure of Freud's thinking about love derives from Plato. Yet there is much in Freud's conception of love that is original and which exercised a profound impact on contemporary Western culture. Like every good analyst I will proceed regressively, beginning with Freud and working back to Plato.

So what did Freud have to say about love? That isn't so easy to determine, because first we have to bore through the bedrock of misconceptions about what he in fact said, not what he was alleged to. The most common misconception is that Freud believed love is another word for sex, or that love derives exclusively from our sexual nature. He never actually said that. According to Bergmann (1987, p. 157), "What he did [say] is to follow Schopenhauer and look upon love, a human emotion, from the point of view of the sexual drive." Lust for sex may lead some people to marry, but we know that marriage (or any other type of intimate relationship) cannot survive on sex alone. Relationships built upon sex rarely endure, and when they do they are often transformed into hate. On the other hand, relationships built upon love may, and often do, prevail with or without the sexual component. I don't think I have to convince you of this. Obviously erotic love is a fine thing and the pleasure we derive from it is unparalleled. When it is complemented by what Freud calls aim-inhibited love, what we ordinarily designate as affection, we cling to it at any cost. The relation between sex and love is further complicated by the paucity of our understanding of love, what it is, how to procure it and, once procured, sustain it.

One of Freud's most original contributions to our understanding about love is contained in a statement he made in his seminal *Three Essays on Sexuality* (1905), the first book of Freud that I ever read: "The finding of an object [of love] is in fact a refinding of it" (p. 222). This statement is perhaps Freud's most profound contribution to our understanding of love, and just about everyone is familiar with it. The child's first experience of love is at the mother's breast, which represents the most blissful and fulfilling experience that any person can possibly enjoy. It is also the prototype for all our subsequent experiences of love and the model against which each is subsequently compared. That we have no memory of this originary experience matters not the slightest, because it is ingrained in each of us. Moreover, this experience is so powerful that our quest for happiness feeds on the hope that we will one day discover a Shangri-La that approximates what it felt like to suckle at our mother's breast. This is why Freud characterizes any new experience of love a "refinding" of it, a facsimile of the original. It is also why Freud was convinced that the feeling we associate with happiness is rooted in this early suckling experience.

The connection between love and sex is also illuminated by this model, because suckling at the breast is not only a source of nourishment but a highly charged sexual experience as well, in fact our very first. It never ceases to amaze me how many of my students are not only shocked by this thesis, but sometimes offended by it. I am not surprised that men find this notion farfetched (though most of them do not), or women who have never born children. What does amaze me are those mothers who have breastfed their own children yet insist there is nothing remotely sexual about it. Being a father, it was perfectly clear to me when witnessing my sons feeding on their mother's breast that the experience was of a sexual nature, for the mother as well as the child. All I can say about those mothers who deny this is that the powers of sexual repression are alive and well in our brave new twenty-first-century world.

Though our love for the mother and the sex we enjoyed with her are joined in infancy, they are split off during latency and the sexual aspect is then repressed, though its affectionate edition survives and remains conscious. In adolescence our sexual desires break loose from their original (incestuous) moorings and are directed at new, non-incestuous love objects. However, in order for this to happen the new love must in some respects resemble the old, though we typically don't notice the similitude. Moreover, a second condition has to be satisfied in order for this to happen. Our feelings for this new person mustn't arouse the guilt that is associated with the original Oedipal object. Otherwise our guilt will serve as an efficient source of repression. According to Freud, "What is left over from the sexual relation to the first object helps to prepare for the choice of [a new] object and thus to restore the happiness that has been lost" (1905, p. 222). Though the infant, whether a boy or a girl, is effectively (if not reflectively) "in love" with the mother when breast feeding, it is only later when the child enters the Oedipal period (from roughly three to five years of age) that the child consciously falls in love with one or both of the parents, and is cognizant of it. Freud believed we are born bisexual so that during the Oedipal phase we alternate between both parents, loving each in turn while experiencing the other as rival, eventually settling on one. At this point our sexual orientation, whether gay or straight, is fixed, though we may not know it at the time. This is usually the mother for the boy and the father for the girl, but it might just as well be the opposite, and often is. Whichever the case may be, this is the prototype for the relationship we seek to "refind" in another person when we reach sexual maturity. Whereas the earlier suckling experience is the prototype for the epitome of sexual *pleasure*, or bliss, it is only later that the Oedipal love object becomes the prototype for the *person* with whom we fall in love, but with whom we associate our earlier experience of bliss. The two are inevitably comingled, which is why oral sex, whether kissing, fellatio, or cunnilingus, are ways we typically recapitulate the bliss from the oral stage of development. That some people don't enjoy kissing says something about their early nurturing experience, or lack thereof.

Naturally, there is much in this model that may go wrong, otherwise there would be no neuroses. So what does this constellation tell us about neurotic love, and how do we distinguish it from normal, happy love? *Basically love is the restoration of a happiness that was lost.* This may explain why people who fall in love often have the feeling that they have known their new love object forever. However, if the attachment to the parental object is too strong (a result of the child's anxiety) it will inhibit the choice of a new love object. On the other hand, if the attachment is more subdued, resulting in greater psychic freedom, the adolescent will be able to find and successfully affix him- or herself to a new love object. Happy love is free from the ambivalence or inhibition that we associate with neurotic conflict, a conflict between desire and guilt. Neurotic love is epitomized by the inhibition that prevents us from loving fully. Remember that while breast feeding, sex and love converge onto the same object, the mother; in latency, they split off. In adolescence, they typically converge once again. According to Freud, "Should these currents fail to converge, the focusing of all desire upon a single object will be unattainable" (1905, p. 200). In other words, if we fail to fall in love in adolescence, chances are we never will. That doesn't mean we cease longing for it.

One of the most common neurotic symptoms that therapists encounter is the inability to both love and feel sexually attracted to the same person. Freud explains that, "Where they love they do not desire, and where they desire they cannot love" (1912, p. 183). This often results in debasing the sexual partner while idealizing the person with whom sex is of no interest. In order to get as far away from the original incestuous love object as possible, some can only experience sexual pleasure with partners of other nationalities or race. Others love once, are rejected, and spend the rest of their lives avoiding intimacy ever again. In order for happy, healthy love to flourish we have to be capable of loving and desiring the same person, and not fear the possible rejection and heartbreak if the love doesn't last, as usually happens.

The other great discovery of Freud's is his theory of narcissism. Freud observed that the darling prince or princess baby is omnipotent, knows nothing of death, and lives in a state of narcissistic self-sufficiency. This state will eventually be shattered. And if this is not enough, more tragedies will visit upon the baby as well, whether the arrival of other siblings or the death of a parent – either of which will wound the child and elicit anxiety or depression – or both. These transitions are inevitable and no human being manages to avoid them. It is worth noting that Freud didn't coin the term narcissism, which was introduced by Havelock Ellis. But Freud embellished it with such genius that he made it his own. (Due to its Greek origin, Freud subsequently renamed his Father complex the Oedipus complex.)

We actually begin life with two love objects, not one: the mother as well as oneself. In order to free ourselves to love others we have to free ourselves from *both*, the incestuous as well as the narcissistic. Freud's theory of narcissism also gives us a clue as to how he understood megalomania and other forms of *mania*, the Greek word for madness. Freud believed that homosexuality is a variant of normal development. In his essay on narcissism (1914), Freud noted that identification plays a pivotal role when falling in love. He believed that the future homosexual baby first forms an intense fixation to the mother (or some other woman) and that after leaving her behind identifies with that woman and takes *himself* as a sexual object. From this basis he then looks for a young man who resembles himself and whom he then loves as his mother loved him. The gay man who falls in love, in effect, becomes his mother, and his lover becomes his former self. This kind of secondary narcissism Freud distinguishes from primary narcissism, which is when we fall in love with ourselves. (Freud also believed that it was through identifying with this or that personality trait of each parent that we are able to extricate ourselves from our attachment to them, by effectively "becoming" them. This notion was never fully articulated, and it remains one of the perplexities of psychoanalytic theory.)

In the Schreber case, the only one where Freud explores the nature of psychosis, he observes that in megalomania the libido is focused on the self, when in love we are focused on the love object. When in love one overvalues the other person, but in megalomania one sexually overvalues one's self. Let us explore the two types of love further, the narcissistic and the incestuous (or attachment) type. With the narcissistic type a man may love himself, what he once was, or what he would like to be. With the attachment type a man may love the woman who feeds him or the man who protects him. Homosexual men usually choose their love object based on the narcissistic model whereas heterosexual men typically choose their love object based on the attachment, or incestuous model. However, it is also possible for heterosexual men to adopt the narcissistic model and homosexual men to adopt the attachment type, though this is more likely among those who remain bisexual. The same process is repeated with homosexual women, but in reverse.

Freud's discovery of narcissistic love (which escaped the attention of Havelock Ellis) ranks among his greatest discoveries. One of its most important features concerns the nature of the ego ideal. In the first stage of narcissistic development we fall in love with ourselves. In the second stage this love is transferred onto the ego ideal, the person we aspire to be. Traditionally, we contrast self-love (receiving love) with loving another person, but Freud introduces a third option, narcissistic love. With this alternative I fall in love with a person *modeled on my love for myself.* There is an inevitable tension between the love I seek from others, which is narcissistic, and the love I give them, which is sacrificial. Freud believed if I love the other person too much I deplete my narcissism, which is not a good thing. Those with poor self-esteem will be devastated if the love relation were to end, whereas the more self-confidant person will survive to love another day. Says Bergmann (1987), "The highest form of development of which object libido is capable is in the state of being in love. Then the subject is ready to sacrifice his own personality in favor of a love object" (p. 171). This would explain why some people appear to become someone else when falling in love. Ironically, the neurotic is not sufficiently narcissistic. He impoverishes his self-love by overvaluing the love object who embodies what the neurotic lacks. Falling in love can impoverish the self to such an extent that the self is decimated. In some cases the lover's self-esteem is restored by having his love reciprocated, but in other cases the love object consumes his self, to the self's detriment.

Ordinarily, there is a tension between the ego, or the self, and the ego ideal. We are always trying to bridge the chasm between them, because the closer together they are the happier we become, and the further apart the more miserable. If they are too far apart it may result in psychosis, when we appear to be two different people. The tension between them can be beneficial or detrimental. When beneficial the ego ideal prompts the self toward greater achievement and is the source of ambition. If excessive it may become the totality of one's existence, as with workaholics, or a life devoted exclusively to work, religion, or a political cause.[1] If the self can't keep up with such demands this may result in a sense of personal failure and despair. In such cases psychoanalysis may be helpful in reassessing the value of enslaving oneself to one's ego ideal, and learning to reduce it to a more realistic, achievable standard.

When we fall in love the ego ideal is projected onto the other person, in the same way the child idealized the parent prior to the ego ideal's formation. This means that the lover regresses back to that period in childhood when his or her idealization of the parent was most intense. When the ego ideal is projected onto the love object the tension between the self and the ego ideal is eliminated, the same process that ensues in a manic state. When love is reciprocated there is no finer experience. This is what it feels like to be madly in love, head over heels, at the complete mercy of the other, along with our capacity for judgment, which is severely compromised. It is as though the self is now loved by the ego ideal, though this piece of the experience remains unconscious. Only the blissful feeling achieves consciousness, and this is about as happy as any human being can be and, for most, the prototype for how we conceive happiness.[2]

We can begin to understand why it isn't so easy to distinguish between what it feels like to fall in love and when we succumb to a manic episode. In both cases the ego and ego ideal merge in an explosion of incredible proportions. Judgment is abandoned, and the sudden transformation may serve as either the beginning of a viable relationship or initiation into a psychotic episode. Phenomenologically, it is impossible to tell which is which, though anyone who knows the person going through such an experience can usually tease them apart. Anyone who has fallen in love and completely given him- or herself to another person has lost his or her senses. There is nothing rational about this experience, which is also the most remarkable thing about falling in love: the respite it gives us from the obsessive worry and relentless strategizing that the dangers of our day-to-day existence impose on us. If, sometime later – months, years, even decades – I fall out of love and the relationship ends badly, I may wonder what came over me and how I managed to fall in love with this person in the first place! If I was crazy to do so, it was a craziness that is unavoidable and, let's be honest, irresistible. That being in love is costly we take for granted, for nothing in this world makes us more vulnerable than falling in love.

A life without love and its attendant irrationality would be a sad life indeed, with nothing unexpected or amazing ever happening. Only the most depressed people are incapable of being in love, the principal occasion of their unremitting despair, to be alone with no one but oneself to turn to, but a self with meager narcissistic rewards to rely upon. With mania, the loss of judgment is even more extreme, and the consequences may be far worse than when falling in love. The key difference is that the person who succumbs to mania is able to access this form of madness *whether a love object is part of the picture or not.* If the former, the ego ideal is projected onto the love object so that the other becomes a reflection of oneself. When the latter, the aggrandized self remains aggrandized and megalomania compensates for the absence of an interpersonal relationship. Yet, at bottom, every state of mania is reflected back to the self and is a glorification of the self, whether or not another person is involved.

For all this, Freud was never able to account for how the drive for sex is transformed into love, or where else love may originate from this union, only that it does. Nor was he able to explain how love turns into hate, whether hate is an edition of love or something altogether independent of it, perhaps just as basic. He revisited the problem again and again, finally entertaining the dual instinct theory of *Eros* and *Thanatos*, one drive for love (or life) and the other for death (and hate), but virtually none of Freud's followers followed him in this, save for Melanie Klein and Jacques Lacan.[3] In his *Instincts and Their Vicissitudes* (1915), Freud determined that love and hate, however they are related, are never simple manifestations of the instincts. Rather, they are *emotions*, and as such they are regulated by the ego, not the id. This is an important distinction and renders the process of falling in love far more complicated and selective than if our passions were truly blind. Freud also recognized that any person toward whom an emotion is felt, whether love or hate, is not as interchangeable as in the case with sexual objects. Yet as early (circa 1885) as in a famous letter to his then-fiancé Martha, Freud ruminated about the complexities of love, why we resist it and why the neurotic is so hesitant about succumbing to it: "Why don't we fall in love over again every month? Because with every parting something of our heart is torn away. . . . Thus our striving is more concerned with avoiding pain than with creating enjoyment" (cited in Thompson, 2004a, p. 17). Why does love have such a hold over us, the source of such wonder and happiness, but violence and turmoil as well? Freud was never in doubt that our lives are completely controlled by its quest and is the source of our so-called psychopathology, but also our greatest achievements. For answers we must turn to the most important expositor on love in Western history, Freud's teacher, Plato.

Freud took from Plato his conception of love and its powerful sexual current. He also borrowed his notion of sublimated love, that "higher" calling (*sans* its erotic component) in the service of intellectual and artistic compositions. Plato devoted two dialogues to love, the *Symposium* and the *Phaedrus*, which together have influenced our understanding of love like no other author since. These are highly detailed and complex treatments of love that deserve the many books that have been written about them, but for my limited purpose I want only to glean the essential contribution of each for the topic of this chapter, the relation between love and madness. The *Symposium* is a gathering of several of Socrates' friends who decide to spend the evening together sharing their respective conceptions of love, for the purpose of honoring *Eros* and his many gifts. Together, the participants exhaust just about every conception of love imaginable. The one I want to focus on is the last, presented by Socrates himself. Because Socrates was famous as an interrogator who professed to know nothing except that he knew nothing, he slyly avoids presenting his own views on the matter. Instead he chooses to report what he learned from the Sophist, Diotima, one of the few female philosophers in Athens.

Diotima doesn't exactly convey a theory of love, but instead shares a fable about its birth, which is to say the birth of *Eros*, instead. One of the things that the dialogue establishes before Socrates begins is that *Eros* is not a god, but a *daemon* spirit, something between a god and a mortal.[4] If you sought love in your life you made a sacrifice to Aphrodite, the goddess of love and *Eros'* master. If she was pleased, Aphrodite would dispatch *Eros* to find you a partner (on the other hand, if you displeased her she may instruct *Eros* to take the love you already have away). Diotima, says Socrates, was his personal muse and the woman through whom he was able to grasp what little he had learned about love. The essence of what she taught him was conveyed in the following myth:

> On the day of Aphrodite's birth the gods were making merry, and among them was Resource [*Poros*], the son of Craft. And when they had supped, Need came begging at the door because there was good cheer inside. Now, it happened that Resource, having drunk deeply of the heavenly nectar – for this was before the days of wine – wandered out into the garden of Zeus and sank into a heavy sleep, and Need [*Penia*], thinking that to get a child by Resource would mitigate her penury, lay down beside him and in time was brought to bed of Love [*Eros*]. So Love became the follower and servant of Aphrodite because he was begotten on the same day that she was born, and further, he was born to love the beautiful since Aphrodite is beautiful herself.
>
> *(Hamilton and Cairns, 1961, p. 555)*

Diotima explains to Socrates how love, or *Eros*, comes into being and, especially, its nature. Because his parents are Resource and Need, says Diotima, it is "his fate to be needy; nor is he delicate and lovely as most of us believe, but harsh and arid, barefoot and homeless, sleeping on the naked earth, in doorways . . . always partaking of his mother's poverty" (Hamilton and Cairns, 1961, pp. 555–556). Not a pretty picture, but it explains the "driven" nature of love, especially the insatiable insistence of its aims, and its hunger. In the service of those aims, *Eros'* best qualities emerge, born of Resource, his father.

> But, secondly, he brings his father's resourcefulness to his designs upon the beautiful and the good, for he is gallant, impetuous, and energetic, a mighty hunter, and a master of device and artifice – at once desirous and full of wisdom, a lifelong seeker after truth, an adept in sorcery, enchantment, and seduction.
>
> *(Hamilton and Cairns, 1961, p. 556)*

Despite Love's lifelong searching, he never rests. He has his ups and downs, at times full of life and happy, but oftentimes lonely and bereft. According to Diotima, "Love is never altogether in or out of need, and stands, moreover, midway between ignorance and wisdom" (Hamilton and Cairns, 1961, p. 556). Love is born of our acknowledgement that we have these needs to begin with, that we are always in a state of wanting, coupled with the resourceful determination to persist till we have it, but always in its service, never it in ours.

Some of us, like the Greek gods on Olympus, try to rise above our plight. We pretend we don't need love and live in denial. If we apply Diotima's example to Freud's thesis, the narcissist comes to mind, one for whom love is less an object of devotion than a pacifier for unquenchable craving. He cannot recognize the beauty in others because he is so enamored with himself. She also describes those who lack the intelligence, resource, or character to pursue love. They don't even know it exists, "and do not long for the virtues they have never missed" (p. 556). In Freud's adaptation, this depicts the person who is so repressed he doesn't realize that something is dreadfully missing in his (or her) life. In order to be a candidate for love and capture *Eros'* attention, we have to acknowledge our state of wanting and bring all our resources to bear, by devoting ourselves to love's call.

Another problem with Freud's observations about love is his conviction that all love is essentially erotic, even the aim-inhibited variety, as well as that which is sublimated. I believe Freud has a point in suggesting that beneath the aim-inhibited editions of love characterized by friendship and familial relations lies repressed eroticism, to varying degrees, depending on the relationship in question. In the case of sublimation, however, Freud suggests that the erotic component of one's passion for work or artistic production is not repressed but displaced onto this or that endeavor. While it is true that neurotics substitute work for pleasure, it doesn't follow that the energy expended in such endeavors is of a sexual nature, despite Freud's concept of displacement which can explain just about anything. This, I believe, is a rare mistake that Freud committed in his musings on the nature of love due to his neglect of the other types of love the Greeks cherished, and about which he was aware, especially *agapé*. The Greeks had not one, but four words for love, each with a distinctive role and function in our lives, depending on the object of love and its aim. There is some disagreement, however, as to how they should be differentiated and how to further distinguish the Greek usage of *agapé* from its appropriation by Christianity. The four words are in turn: *Eros*, sexual love; *storge*, familial love; *philia*, brotherly or friendly love; and *agapé*, selfless or soulful love. Plato uses only two of these terms, *Eros* and *philia*. Virtually everyone agrees that *Eros* represents sexual or passionate love, but we noted already that *Eros* is more complicated than that, because the word passion, as noted in Chapter Three, has such varied meanings (see below).

According to Santas (1988), both Plato and Aristotle employed *philia* to signify two kinds of love: familial love, including parents and siblings, and the love of friendship. Unlike *Eros*, *philia* generally lacks sexual desire. Like *philia*, *Eros* always connotes love between persons, whether of the same or different gender. *Eros* is usually more intense and passionate than *philia* and with greater motivating power. *Philia*, however, tends to be more steady and lasting. There is an ambiguity in *philia* because our feelings about family members and friends, though usually lacking in (conscious) sexual attraction, are determined by blood ties whereas friends are deliberately chosen. What *Eros* and friends have in common is that, unlike family relations, each is selected. Freud turned these distinctions on their head by arguing that all of our familial relations are of a sexual, incestuous nature, though such feelings are usually repressed. That doesn't mean they disappear. Today friendships often morph into sexual liaisons of a momentary or lasting nature, and increasingly we look upon marriage as a friendship that includes sex and procreation. Freud's argument that sexual desire may rear its head in virtually any context would appear to have some merit.

C. S. Lewis, in *The Four Loves* (1971), removes some of the ambiguity from *philia* by introducing a third Greek term for love, *storge*. According to him, *storge* refers to familial love, whereas *philia* refers strictly to friendship. This term is rarely used, however, and we never see it mentioned in either Plato or Aristotle. Similarly, the fourth Greek term for love, *agapé*, is never used by Plato or Aristotle. The term was appropriated by Christianity to connote love of a higher, predominantly divine nature, though it may occur between humans. It is also used interchangeably with *caritas*, a Latin term meaning charity. Both signify love of God, or the love that God feels for humans. It may also mean selfless love, but a spiritually advanced edition of it that requires spiritual development in order to access. A God-fearing person may, for example, feel *agapé* for humanity as a whole, not just for this or that deserving person. When Jesus admonishes us to love thy neighbor as thyself he is referring to *agapé*. The reason we don't run into it all that often is because in the King James translation of the Bible the Greek *agapé* is translated as "charity." For the present I will restrict my focus on *Eros* and *philia*, as these are the two terms that were familiar to Plato and the ones most useful in examining the relation between love and madness. As we will see, even though Plato doesn't employ *agapé* in his dialogues, both *Eros* and *philia* occasion interesting implications for "divine love" as well. I will turn my attention to *agapé* and *caritas* later, when we look at the nature of sympathy and our capacity to love.

We now turn our attention to the *Phaedrus* and examine what it tells us about the relationship between love and divine madness. "Our greatest blessings," says Socrates in the *Phaedrus*, "come to us by way of madness, provided the madness is given us by divine gift" (cited in Dodds, 1951, p. 64). This passage is in stark contrast to the nature of *Eros*, or love, in the *Symposium*, where there is no mention of the passionate irrationalities of love, much less the conflicts it generates. It's as though in the *Phaedrus*, which was written after the *Symposium*, Plato decided he had to correct this oversight. And correct it he does. The impression one comes away with after reading the *Symposium* is that the highest love is what Freud terms "aim-inhibited," a high-minded love stripped of its baser, lustful proclivities, what we today typically (though mistakenly) designate "Platonic love." Yet long before Socrates introduced us to *Eros'* finer qualities, Greek literature predating the *Symposium* acknowledges his dark side, a *daemon* who is capable of savagery, injustice, drunkenness, even madness. After all, one of *Eros'* principal features is his ability to possess and bewitch those mortals he would destroy, those who got on the wrong side of Aphrodite. There is not one of us who has not experienced the sting of his poison-tipped arrows, at her behest. The purpose of the *Symposium* was not to recount these baser qualities but to praise *Eros* instead, so the speakers take turns celebrating his nobler attributes.[5] In her critique of the *Phaedrus*, Nussbaum (1986) acknowledges this new perspective that recognizes a type of goodness that only madness can foster:

> Certain sorts of madness are not only not incompatible with insight and
> stability, they are actually necessary for the highest sort of insight and the

best kind of stability. Erotic relationships of long duration between particular individuals (who see each other as such) are argued to be fundamental to psychological development and an important component of the best human life.

(p. 201)

On the other hand, one of the first speeches in the *Phaedrus*, says Santas (1988), "maintains that the lovers' passion is a kind of madness or sickness, transient and unreliable, and that one would be better off having as a lover someone free of such a malady" (p. 59). The *Phaedrus* introduces us to not one, but two terms that characterize those aspects of *Eros* that are innately crazy: *mania* and *hubris*. As noted earlier, Plato argues there are two kinds of madness, divine and human, in other words, healthy or not so healthy. Some forms of madness are good and consistent with happiness, whereas others are destructive. In order to appreciate how Plato distinguishes between the two we turn to a characteristic of madness noted earlier in Chapter One, lack of judgment. For Plato, desire may be rational or irrational. If a pleasure we pursue is deemed good in our judgment, it is rational, but if we should pursue a pleasure that is not good, if by it we lose all sense of proportion and discretion, then our judgment has abandoned us and the pleasure we pursue is destructive, hence irrational. This is how Socrates articulates his thesis:

> We must observe that in each one of us there are two ruling and leading principles, which we follow whithersoever they lead; one is the innate desire for pleasures, the other the acquired opinion which strives for the best [i.e., the good]. These two sometimes agree within us and are sometimes in strife; and sometimes one and sometimes the other has the greater power. Now when opinion leads through reason toward the best and is more powerful, its power is called self-restraint, but when desire irrationally drags us towards pleasures and rules within us, its rule is called excess (*hubris*).
>
> *(cited in Santas, 1988, p. 61)*

Plato isn't saying that pleasure is inherently irrational. It is irrational only when our pursuit of it conflicts with our ability to judge the best action. *Hubris* is when we lose this capacity, when we strive for something for the sake of how good it feels, heedless of the consequences. In this instance we're not talking about divine madness, but a madness that is all too human and short-sighted. In the next speech, Socrates addresses the relation between madness and *mania*.

> If *Eros* is, as indeed he is, a god or something divine, he can do nothing evil; but the [speakers] just said that he was evil. So they erred about *Eros*. . . . If it were a simple fact that madness (*mania*) is an evil, [what the speaker said] would be true; but in reality the greatest of goods come to us through madness, when it is sent as a gift from the gods. . . . Therefore let us not be afraid on that point, and let no one disturb and frighten us by saying that the reasonable friend should be preferred to him who is in a frenzy [*mania*]. . . .

> We on our part must prove that such madness is given by the gods for our
> greatest happiness.
>
> *(cited in Santas, 1988, pp. 62–63)*

Let me be clear, not all madness is evil or problematic. *Eros* is a spirit of divinely
given madness. Falling in love is an act of madness, but it may be divinely sanctioned or not. If the latter it may lead us to ruin. This says something about love,
yes, but it also tells us something about madness. Throughout history we have been
ambivalent about madness. In virtually all cultures the mad person was said to be
possessed by some kind of spirit or other, demonic or divine. Plato's explanation
isn't ambivalent but ambiguous. It may be one or the other, a good kind of madness
or a bad one. Either is possible, so it may enrich our lives or destroy us. It may even
contain elements of each, leaving it to us to make what sense we are able to make
of it, lick our wounds, recover, and move on, perhaps to a higher plane than before.
We see elements of this duality in Nietzsche's distinction between the Dionysian
and Apollonian aspects of our nature, and we see in it Freud's demarcation between
id and the ego.

This was also a distinction that Laing entertained at Kingsley Hall and Hugh
Crawford at Portland Road, which we discussed in Chapter Five. Jerome's madness
was deemed demonic by the psychiatrists who administered electric shocks and
anything else they could lay their hands on in order to arrest what was happening
in him. But at Portland Road there was no evidence of a demonic presence, no sign
of violence, hatred, or aggression. Just a lost youth who needed someone to help
and to love him, leaving him be (the etymological root of love is "leave," cognate
with "believe") in his tortured mission to traverse the demons inside him and come
through it transformed, a new man. It doesn't always turn out that way, but then
again, sometimes it does.

Plato never actually explains what *mania* is. That is left for us to ponder. The
closest he comes to an explanation is his characterization of *Eros* as possessed by
hubris, a condition of excess, lack of self-control, loss of judgment. *Hubris* may also
be an overpowering lust for food, drink, or sex, when our appetites have lost all
sense of proportion. Plato comes to the surprising conclusion that not all madness
is irrational, only the kind touched by *hubris*. Other forms of madness are perfectly
acceptable, whether in a sexual, mundane, or religious context. Throughout history mystics, shamans, and other spiritual personages have advocated spiritual quests
that occasion or culminate in experiences of madness. Even Christians have been
known to cherish it. I remember going to a Sunday church service in a Southern
Baptist town with a girlfriend in Tennessee. I was shocked to witness members of the
congregation spontaneously roll about the floor, shouting incoherently, muttering
incomprehensible words in a language not of this world, while the rest of the congregation chanted "Amen!" in harmony. It was stunning, frightening, and exhilarating
at the same time. I had never witnessed anything like this in the church services my
Methodist parents took me to as a child, correct in the extreme. The passion in that
Baptist service was palpable, strangely beautiful and moving. And yes, sexy.

We are left with the question, and for our purposes the decisive one, why is it that falling in love is sometimes the path to happiness, and sometimes a path to ruin? Why is it that in some contexts it is healthy and the epitome of our psychological development, and in other contexts an agent of *hubris* that compels us to lose our senses? In order to wrestle with this question, I want to look at the relation between desire and happiness, and then between desire and love, and see if this brings us any closer to an answer.

We saw in the *Symposium* that happiness was the aim of desire, and that happiness consists of being in possession of good things. In other words, the lover of good things wants the good things to be his, to *possess* them. You might say this model of happiness is egocentric. The lover wants these things *for himself*, and it is crucial that he possess them in order to attain happiness. This possessive quality of love is instrumental and characteristic of how we typically view the person with whom we fall in love. We distinguish, for example, between a casual fling and an affair of the heart we take seriously. The more seriously we take it, which is to say, the more profound our feeling of love is, the more we want to have it for ourselves. We also want it to last. When desire is transformed into love we temporalize it – we hope it will never end, and in the throes of irrationality we convince ourselves that it won't. This is how Plato distinguishes between merely desiring an object and loving that object: *love is the desire to possess the love object forever and always.*

This, it seems to me, is why we get married. Marriage is the vow to maintain one's love forever, until death. It is the final confirmation that one's love is genuine and sincere, that it isn't a momentary thing. We are united as one. The impulse to marry is not about procreation, in the existential sense, but the wish to possess the object of our affection. This is why gays feel it is imperative to marry, just as heterosexual couples do, not to legitimate having children (which they may or may not want), but to prove to the love partner how much the other means to him or her. The issue of possession is not only crucial for love, but for madness too. Desire makes us crazy because, by its nature, it is only a heartbeat away from mania. This is why Buddhists believe we should harness desire by tethering it to a short leash. This, however, isn't a Western attitude toward desire. We see the virtue in unbridled desire, even when it floods its banks. Perhaps we are more forgiving of transgression and accept madness as, perhaps, the unavoidable price for happiness. If the apex of the love relationship is the need to possess its object, then perhaps we should make peace with it by embracing it as part of our nature.

As noted earlier, throughout history all cultures have viewed madness in terms of *being possessed* by something that no one can see, a god or demon, or some other kind of presence that has taken control of the mad person, who has lost all reason. I am seeing a young man in analysis I call Peter, who has been diagnosed schizophrenic because he hears a voice inside him that not only tells him what he may or may not do, but who makes it plain that he wants Peter for himself. The voice's only mission, says Peter, is to have total and utter control over him. Peter is unable to work or to have relationships with women or friends because his voice won't allow it. Peter lives at home with his parents because without them he would be destitute.

He wants desperately to be shed of this voice and to have his life back again, find a job, procure friends, get married, raise a family. But the voice wants Peter to himself and, according to Peter, isn't willing to share him with anyone. It would seem that this voice is madly in love with Peter, and that Peter needs someone in his life to be madly in love with him. In the absence of a (real) love partner, who Peter is too fearful to pursue, he has his voice. That this love is of a predominantly tormenting nature doesn't make it all that different from many of the marriages I have witnessed. It is undeniable that the voice loves Peter passionately, and that Peter feels passion for the voice, in turn. Etymologically, the word passion derives from the Latin *pati*, which means to suffer or endure. This is why the word passion is also a verb, so that "to passion" means to suffer. The passion of Christ, for example, alludes to his suffering on the cross. The Latin *pati* is cognate with the Greek *pema*, which also means to suffer and gives us the Greek word *poros*, which Plato's translators, as we saw in the myth of *Eros*, rendered as need or penury, but may also be translated as unhappy or unfortunate. Coming full circle, this is why the person in love, one who feels passionately for another (as with Peter and his voice), suffers love in equal measure to relishing it, or may not relish it at all.

We no longer believe that people who are mad or psychotic are possessed by spirits or unseen forces, but they do often *behave* as though they are possessed by some entity or other. Similarly, when a person falls in love that person also may act as though he (or she) has taken leave of his senses, as though he was bewitched by the person with whom he is smitten and under that person's spell. Loss of control and the appearance of having been possessed by something or someone is basic to both madness and falling in love. The only way we have of distinguishing between the person who falls in love in the healthy, happy sense of the word and the person who falls in love in the unhealthy, self-destructive sense is how erratic and out of the ordinary the latter person's behavior becomes. Ordinarily, when a person falls in love the rest of their life goes on, more or less unchanged, but happier. The only thing that changes is the new relationship in that person's life, but the consequences may be seismic. Over time changes occur, but they are usually gradual. Lovers who decide to marry ordinarily become engaged and give their family and friends time to get used to the change in their status, often six months to a year. But when a friend who just met someone a few weeks earlier runs off to Las Vegas to get married we may wonder, what came over him? The suddenness of the decision to make such a significant change in his life is enough to suspect he may have taken leave of his senses.

In such cases we may conclude that the friend acted impulsively, perhaps rashly, but there is nothing necessarily insane about that. As we have seen, irrational behavior is not necessarily psychotic. But what if this friend tells us he has decided he no longer wants to be an accountant, because of the new love in his life and the influence she has over him he realizes his true calling is to become a spirit guide, or a fortune teller, or psychic healer, or beach bum? What if he had been happily married and, now that he has met his one and true love, he decides to leave his family, his wife and children, his friends, and embarks on a fundamentally new life he had never imagined wanting before falling in love with this person? Would we wonder at this point if he had indeed taken leave of his senses? Would we suspect that because he had experienced such a fundamental personality change, so suddenly and without warning, that he must have lost his mind? Would we suspect he was in the throes of a manic episode, or would we wonder if he had embarked on a new spiritual plane that we are incapable of understanding, or distinguishing from a psychotic episode?

The first thing that comes to mind when trying to assess whether a friend has simply fallen in love or is experiencing a psychotic episode is: *How do we assess his judgment?* Do the changes he has effected in his life make sense to us? The second thing we consider is: How *sudden* did this change occur? If this friend is indeed experiencing a manic, or psychotic, episode, the two things that alert us to this conclusion is how rational (or irrational) this friend is behaving and whether this change happened so suddenly that he has become another person, a person we hardly recognize. Neither of these criteria are necessarily easy to assess. If this person is not a friend but a perfect stranger whom you don't know from Adam, you may think he is perfectly normal, perhaps flamboyant, but who appears nonetheless sane. But if this person is a friend whom you know intimately, or your spouse, then you are acutely aware of how significant the change is, and how much your friend's personality has changed. Yet your friend doesn't feel he has lost his senses and insists he never felt happier. So what right do we have to question his sanity if, after all, he doesn't think there is anything the matter with him?

This is a political question, not a psychological one, and we may have absolutely no right to do any more than raise our eyebrows at our friend's sudden transformation. Perhaps he will take a fall when he comes down from his high, or maintain this new constellation of manic character traits he has "become" for an indefinite, extended period of time. Our question is not concerned with whether such a person should or should not be in treatment, or should want to be. We are merely trying to make a distinction between sane, or happy, love and mad, crazy love, and take into account the potential consequences. I believe this kind of episode, including its ambiguous nature, happens all the time, sometimes dramatically and sometimes in so understated a manner that we hardly notice – unless one happens to be that person's therapist. Freud might have said that the love object in this case has been substituted for his ego ideal, and that his ego was in turn transformed into the personage of that ideal, as if magically. But such changes don't occur simply because you meet someone who is irresistible. True, when we fall in love we invariably fall prey to our lover's influence. That is inevitable because that's what love is, a merging of two people into one. If my friends don't happen to like this new person in my life, and if she in fact turns out to be a gold-digger who is preying on me, my friends may have genuine cause for alarm. But that doesn't mean I am necessarily crazy for loving her or that I lost my senses, in the psychotic sense. These lines can be difficult to draw and you would have to know me intimately and be knowledgeable about what it means to be psychotic in order to render a tentative a judgment on the matter. And who says that your judgment on the matter is any better than mine? This is the crux of the problem.

Perhaps easier to determine is the case for megalomania. In this instance the person in question may or may not fall in love with another person. That is probably beside the point because the person he falls in love with is essentially *himself*. But it isn't so easy to determine if the alleged megalomaniac is crazy or an eccentric genius. L. Ron Hubbard, the founder of Scientology, comes to mind. Hubbard was a prolific author of science fiction in the earlier part of his life. He holds the Guinness Book of Records for having written more novels than any other person in history, over a thousand, in a relatively short period of time. Was he manic when he wrote all those novels, or just remarkably prolific? One day he had a vision and decided he was more than an author, but a spiritual leader, blessed with extraordinary wisdom and insight into the human condition. He founded a new religion, unlike any other, that was based on hypnotic techniques he used to help people overcome their fears and inhibitions. He collected followers, his religion spread, and the rest is history. Today Scientology is the richest religion in the world.

As far as I know Hubbard was never hospitalized for psychiatric treatment and never diagnosed with a mental illness. That doesn't mean he wasn't insane. Were he schizophrenic his organizational abilities would have collapsed (the principal difference between schizophrenia and mania) and may have ended up a street person, or in treatment. Manic episodes don't work that way. Organizational abilities are often enhanced and creativity may be energized beyond belief. Many of the world's greatest artists were prone to manic episodes (think of Nietzsche!), but they also suffered miserably. Most were never treated for it, and that is probably a good thing. Unlike those who suffer from a schizoid condition or are diagnosed schizophrenic, the manic person can usually manage his or her affairs or enlist followers (or a staff) to attend to business, while he or she is being creative. Hubbard was not only a megalomaniac who mistook himself for a prophet; he also suffered from paranoia and created a following that robbed people of their money and punished those who crossed him. Most of his followers were probably gullible, but many were highly intelligent and accomplished individuals whose judgment was likely intact. They were simply attracted to a very charismatic person who possessed powers that helped them. Hubbard was no Jim Jones, whose madness deteriorated into a schizophrenic collapse that culminated in ending his life and that of his followers. To this day a controversy surrounds Hubbard and his creation, Scientology. In Hubbard's case, despite the pathology and irrational nature of his behavior, some good came from his efforts. Hubbard comes to mind because he was someone who happened to be in the public light, but was also a megalomaniac, a form of madness that may contain both good and bad qualities. With some it borders on the demonic, as with Jones.

What about those who fall in love and subsequently suffer a mental breakdown? Some have a penchant for falling in love with the wrong person. They fall in love to escape their misery but it only makes matters worse. Theodore Reik (1975) believed that the unhappier a person is, the more vulnerable to falling in love. Love and happiness are ineluctably intertwined. In *The Symposium*, Plato portrayed love as one of the principal means for obtaining happiness.[6] Freud believed that falling in love is the most common path to happiness, but also an unreliable one due to its unpredictable nature. Some who are chronically miserable but capable to getting their lives together, though unhappy, have a penchant for falling in love in order to obtain a level of well being they are otherwise incapable of accessing. Drugs provide some respite, but not enough to make that much difference. So they fall in love, as Freud would say, by projecting their ego ideal onto the love object, and if that love is returned they are for a time happy. Their problem is that they have a pattern of falling in love with people even more dysfunctional than themselves, so the relationship is doomed. When it crashes and their ego ideal is demolished, their sanity is shattered with it. They become obsessive, possessive, paranoid, vindictive, suicidal. They turn to drugs for solace and may or may not eventually try rehab, once they hit bottom. But no sooner does such a person begin to put his or her life back together than the pattern repeats itself, with the same love object or a new one. This person is incapable of learning from his mistakes because his life is bereft of meaning, save for those occasions when in love. In this case love, the original prototype for the optimal drug experience, becomes a drug and, due to its obsessive nature, a new kind of addiction is born, but one that is predominately mental, not physiological. The ecstasy elicited by succumbing to a love of this nature is short-lived, but probably worth it for the person so subjected. Both the state of being in love and the consequent collapse are incidents of madness, each joined to and feeding the other. Because love is the most exquisite experience possible, it is also the most common catalyst for personal ruin. Freud's theory of psychopathology is based on this simple observation.

Freud focused on two aspects of love that may be understood as typical of how love can make us mad, but in a manner so common we rarely recognize it as pathological. The first we discussed in the context of the Oedipal phase and how the triangular nature of this complex introduces the child to the experience of jealousy for the first time. Jealousy is universal, and everyone wrestles with it in his or her fashion. It may be mild and the source of amusement, or extreme and lead to destruction in the form of physical violence, murder, or suicide. Desire may excite, but just as easily incite one to violence. I read somewhere that the most common motive for murder in the United States is jealousy. Most murders are committed by someone who knows the victim intimately. The need to possess is so powerful that the prospect of sharing the love or losing it altogether is intolerable. In every broken heart there is the feeling that a part of oneself has been torn away and destroyed. This can be so painful that suicide is a welcome solution.

This form of madness is closely related to the most common neurosis, obsession. In every love relationship one is obsessed with the love object, thinks about that person all the time, and cannot get him or her out of one's head. This is especially poignant when losing a love object. The most common symptom of a person who is rejected is the resulting obsession with the lost love. Why become obsessed with something so painful? Why not forget it instead? Because keeping the lost love in mind is a *magical* way of maintaining the relationship and keeping it alive, if only in fantasy. It's as though by preserving the lost object in one's head one is able to keep possession of it. This is distressing, to be sure, but due to its hopeful nature somehow preferable to the thought of never thinking of that person again (Santayana's adage, he who lives in hope dies in despair, seems apt). It is a way of keeping that person alive, but in a fashion that is self-abusive and tormenting. Freud surmised that the obsessional, seized by all that thinking, is engaged in a kind of work, and that over time the obsession may burn itself out, at which point one is finally set free. Perhaps this is why analyses take so long! Once love holds us captive, it is no easy matter to escape its clutches. So goes the dark side of *Eros*, that aspect of love that is most maddening.

But loss isn't the only way that love incites madness. The act of love itself may also occasion madness, but of a positive sort. After all, what is sexual arousal, if not a form of madness? How aroused one gets, and how aroused one is capable of getting, determines just how ecstatically mad one can become during the journey to, and culmination of, sexual release. When turned on one becomes, not only vulnerable, but *another person*, someone you may not otherwise be acquainted with. Think of all the uncommon, bizarre rituals and artifice employed to arouse oneself and pre-pare oneself for love's beacon. The transformation one experiences throughout the stages of coitus, and the madness this occasions, is not, however, equally accessible to everyone. The frigid woman who is incapable of arousal, or can be aroused but not brought to orgasm, or the man who is impotent (and what man has not suffered this injustice?) or explodes too quickly once the flame has been ignited, are unable to access the madness that, once touched by it, will set them free.

So far we have focused on madness in relation to love, *Eros*. Dodds notes that the Greeks spoke of four kinds of madness, erotic madness being only one. The others were prophetic madness, ritual madness, and poetic madness. Perhaps Hubbard is also an example of prophetic madness, since megalomania may be a mixture of both erotic and prophetic forms of *mania*, in some cases. The Greeks believed that all four were divine gifts, each emanating from a province of a given god or goddess. The patron god of prophetic madness was Apollo, the god of wisdom and prophecy; Dionysus, the god of winemaking and religious ecstasy, was the patron of ritual madness; Aphrodite, the goddess of love, was the patron of erotic madness; and the Muses were said to be the catalyst for poetic madness. Dodds notes (1951, p. 68) that the line between common insanity and prophetic madness is not easy to draw, which we noticed in the case of Hubbard. Because the prophet hears voices that no one else notices it may be impossible to determine whether he is mad or a visionary, or both. Moses and Jesus must have seemed mad to those who didn't believe either was communing with God. Given the wisdom they handed to us, it is unlikely they were psychotic, but then again they may have been, on this or that occasion. Shamans also belong to this category, with their special powers to heal and diagnose conditions they are implored to treat. Treatments sometimes include rituals to be followed while ingesting drugs to aid in the healing, including Ayahuasca, the hallucinogenic ingested by shamans and their adepts in South America. Some shamans are just as mad as their charges, and yet it works for them.

Dionysus, the patron god of ritual madness, was also the god of dance, which plays a central role in ritual exercises whose function is cathartic. According to Dobbs:

> It purged the individual of those infectious irrational impulses which, when dammed up, had given rise . . . to outbreaks of dancing mania and similar manifestations of collective hysteria; it relieved them by providing them with a ritual outlet.
>
> *(1951, p. 76)*

Whereas Apollo promised security to his followers, Dionysus offered freedom. He was basically a god of joy. Sexual pleasure no doubt also plays a role in the kind of release such rituals occasion.

The final form of divine madness we haven't touched on is the one where the person is possessed by the Muses, goddesses who were loyal to Apollo. Muses were thought to be the source of knowledge that was contained in poetry and myth. The word music comes from Muse, as do the words amusement, and museum. The history between madness and artists is a long one, and many people have suggested that the madness in the mad artist may be the catalyst of the art generated. Extreme examples may include artists such as Van Gogh, Sylvia Plath, Ezra Pound, Salvador Dalí, and Edgar Allan Poe, but if this is so then nearly everyone possesses latent artistic abilities since each and every one of us, in some measure or other, is mad to varying degrees. Yet there is no obvious correlation between madness and artistic ability and there very well may be no direct relation between them. Not everyone has a Muse, and among those who have one, as with Laing, some often lose her. Perhaps the Muse is merely an agent of artistic production that is not at all crazy in the way we normally think about madness, but refers instead to a mysterious something or other that motivates our artistic expression, which we are incapable of understanding?

For example, as I write this I notice that the words coming out of me don't follow a premeditated design, such as, for example, is the case when composing a legal document, or doctoral dissertation. There are times when I am more "into " this process than others, when my Muse is with me and helps me along, but other times she is absent and everything I write comes to drivel. Laing's Muse abandoned him after his sojourn to India in 1971, following an incredibly productive decade during which he wrote eight books, most of them amazing works of intellectual and artistic expression, including his experiments with poetry, *Knots* (1970), *Do You Love Me?* (1976), and *Sonnets* (1979). He continued to write after that decade but none of the works produced impressed the critics or his fans and did not sell well. Laing knew something was missing, as his ability to write became increasingly difficult until it all but left him. This was a source of unremitting anguish, because Laing felt his primary identity was that of a *writer*. The Greeks might have said his Muse abandoned him because he was punished by Apollo, the god of wisdom. He certainly felt that his wisdom had deserted him, but whatever crime he was being punished for was unknown to him, for he had committed many. The most common sin in Greek mythology is *hubris*, a kissing cousin of *mania*, and Laing was no doubt prone to this sin, evidenced in his eager quest for fame and money. His collapse into whisky did not help matters, but it made him, if only momentarily, a happier person, if not altogether a contented one.

Laing's dilemma harkens back to the belief that artistic inspiration is not chosen, but "given," reflecting Hesiod's observation that some men are poets by the grace of the Muses, just as some men are kings by the grace of Zeus. That it is given to us implies a divine blessing, but it might just as well be the unconscious that is our benefactor. In D. H. Lawrence's little book on the unconscious (2004), he put forward the notion, contrary to Freud, that the unconscious is our Muse and the source of creativity. Freud didn't believe the unconscious is creative[7] in the sense that Lawrence was proposing, but I prefer Lawrence's take on the matter. It is fairly obvious that our creative abilities are "given" to us by a power outside our conscious control. Heidegger's conception of language also hints at this. Heidegger rejects Freud's conception of an unconscious "portion" of the mind and instead conceives of language, as he puts it, as the "house of being," the wellspring from which our thoughts and creativity derive, independent of conscious awareness or volition.[8] Just about everything is outside our conscious control, says Heidegger, but especially language. If words are one of the gifts that the Muses give us, we cannot say precisely where those words come from, nor how they occur to us. It is one of those mysteries that, try as we may, we will never entirely comprehend. Heidegger loved language and believed that of all the arts poetry was the highest, or as Plato might have said, the most divine. Heidegger is often accused by other philosophers of not being a philosopher, but merely a poet!

What the four types of divine madness share in common is their reference to a kind of madness that is not only harmless but helpful, even essential to our nature and our happiness. Though we cannot control our madness nor bend it to our will, it is possible to induce it. Both ritual and prophetic madness occasion elements of induction. While most prophetic experiences are spontaneous, prophets or shamans may employ techniques in order to "call" a divine visitation. Of all the four paths to divine madness, ritual madness relies on induction the most, whether the agent for accessing these experiences is dance or drugs. During the counterculture explosion of the 1960s and 1970s, LSD, mescaline, and psilocybin were frequently employed to open regions of the mind not otherwise accessible. The way hallucinogens enabled their practitioners to approximate madness, or psychosis, was not lost on Laing,[9] who used to employ Sandoz acid in his therapy sessions with some of his patients, when it was legal to do so. Laing also believed that experimenting with acid himself could be helpful in accessing the psychotic portion of his mind, and this may have helped him relate more intuitively with those living at Kingsley Hall, among those who had previously been diagnosed schizophrenic. For a period of time Laing and Hugh Crawford entertained the notion that, under certain conditions, falling prey to a psychotic regression may be an opportunity to take a step forward in one's spiritual development, and come out of it more enlightened than before. I had many such acid trips during this time and I am convinced it was decisive in my decision to embark on a clinical career. I believe it also helped me become more empathic with my psychotic patients. Though these drugs are currently banned and not legally accessible, the South American drug Ayahuasca has similar properties and is consumed by increasing numbers of new adepts with similar motives, even some psychoanalysts I know!

Drugs have been used to commune with spiritual entities or as a means of personal transformation for as long as history has been recorded, and probably longer. Alcohol, pot, coffee, tea, opiates, coca, and other native plants that induce sleep, relaxation, or energized ecstatic states, have always been used as aphrodisiacs or as a means of feeling less anxious, more engaged in the company of others, or euphoric. Whether they are divine or simply natural, there is no question that drugs are capable of inducing a form of madness that can be exhilarating but also terrifying, whether for recreation or self-improvement. As aphrodisiacs, drugs are also an undeniable aid for eliciting sexual arousal, but also for putting us in a mood for love that relieves us, if only momentarily of our worries, by refocusing our attention. Because they are so readily available we run the risk of using drugs for short-cuts to experiences that we may be perfectly capable of accessing without them. They are also used to escape forms of suffering we may be better advised to put up with and divining what our suffering is telling us. Psychotherapy and especially psychoanalysis are singular tools for getting to know oneself better and facing the darkness inside, soberly. It seems to me that the new generation of so-called psychotropic "medication" dispensed by psychiatrists is little more than chemically induced ways of blocking experiences that may be better dealt with more sensibly, if not necessarily as cheaply, painlessly, or as quickly, but perhaps more knowingly, more effectively, and compassionately. The over-medicalization of culture is not a strictly American problem, though American culture is in the vanguard of employing this technology to both numb and manipulate our senses. The problem has become global, and probably always has been. Which, we may ask, is crazier: the use of drugs to approximate psychosis, or to block it when it occurs spontaneously? And what about the universal addiction to sedatives that has always been part of our nature? This is one of the reasons I'm not so sure that the "sobriety movement" initiated by AA is the most desirable alternative. Sobriety has its place in the scheme of things and should inform the way we work and think, but can it, or should it be, a way of *life*?

At the risk of repeating myself, I will say it again: falling in love, whether blessed or calamitous, always occasions, by definition, a loss in our capacity for judgment. It is loss of judgment that makes falling in love possible. When in love we overlook aspects of a person's personality that are obvious to everyone else, that would be obvious to us were we not in love with this person. Even in friendships, where the erotic component is not prominent or conscious, it nonetheless lurks beneath the surface and accounts for our lack of judgment among our closest friends. Yet, there are ways of loving that do not necessarily compromise our finer ability to judge, to determine what is the case. For example, one's relationships with patients. It is difficult, if not impossible, for analysts to fall in love with their patients. This is because analysts are so focused on the character traits that occasion their patients' neuroses they are incapable of falling under the spell of their charms, as others may. It would be like falling in love with a son or a daughter. When analysts do fall in love with a patient it is usually because the therapist is inconsolably unhappy, perhaps recently divorced, when self-esteem is at a low ebb and such therapists become especially vulnerable to the patients who find them most lovable. This doesn't mean that analysts do not ordinarily love their patients, but in other ways. The good ones, the ones who make themselves available, heart and soul, do. If this kind of love isn't eroticized, then what form of love is it? How can one love another person without the need to possess them, to have them for one's own? What about love that is not an edition or midwife to madness, but the kind of love that we equate with sanity, sobriety, and sympathy? What we aspire to in this context is a form of love that inspires sanity, the kind of sanity that enhances judgment rather than compromising it. Sanity, as we noted in Chapter One, enhances sanity and enriches our relationships with others. Its chief attribute is to help us perceive what is going on, in ourselves as well as in others.

Even if we allow that the principal feature of sanity is enhanced judgment in our affairs, the quality of that judgment and its reliability is never absolute, but relative. No one's judgment is immune from the turmoil brought on by the moods and emotions that lay at the foundation of our being in the world. At bottom, as Nietzsche suggested, humans are not rational creatures. This is because we are driven by passion, not reasons. It just isn't possible to lift ourselves out of our emotions, as in removing oneself from a swimming pool. As long as we are capable of feeling anything at all our emotions color the world in which we live and account for the decisions we make daily, however reasoned we try to convince ourselves that they are. Our desires, the principal vehicle of our passions, are so dominant there is virtually no time or place where they are not in play. So what can sanity possibly mean if we, for all intents and purposes, are desire-bound, irrational creatures?

So far I have been concerned with exploring the relation between love and madness, by asking in turn what it means to be mad and what it means to love, and how the two are related. The Greeks have a lot to say on the subject, and without them it is hard to imagine what Freud would have made of the human condition, let alone the vicissitudes of love. But what do the Greeks have to tell us about the relation between love and sanity, the converse of love and madness? We saw in their exploration of madness, that *Eros* was given the most prominent role in their conception of *mania*. This makes sense, for *Eros* is the form of love most prone to *mania*, the quintessential primogenitor of madness in Greek literature. In asking how the Greeks understood sanity we will have to look at the other editions of love in their nomenclature, the ones not specifically concerned with *Eros*.

Of the four types of divine madness, only the erotic touches on love, because it is the only form of divine madness governed by Aphrodite, the goddess of love. In turning our attention to a saner, less eroticized edition of love, we will find what we are looking for in the Greek concept of *agapé*. The Greeks had little to say about *agapé* specifically, so in order to enlighten ourselves about its nature we will need to look elsewhere, its Latin derivative and Christianized *caritas*. We touched on friendship in the preceding chapter (on the unobjectionable transference) so I won't repeat myself here. If, as noted earlier, friendship, or *philia*, is epitomized by a capacity for *forgiveness*, I want to suggest that the Greeks conceived *agapé*, or its Latin equivalent, *caritas*, as a singular capacity for *sympathy*. If sympathy, like other editions of love, is partially irrational, then it is a form of irrationality that is predominantly sane.

The word sympathy has been so plagiarized by greeting card companies that applying this term to the highest, most selfless love possible may appear trite. But when we take a closer look at the word and its shades of meaning I think you will agree there is no better word in the English language to depict it. Etymologically, sympathy derives from the Greek *pathe* (the same root that gave us "pathology"), which means to feel, or to suffer, or to experience something deeply. All three meanings are intimately intertwined. This implies that when we sympathize with someone we feel *with* them, that we somehow suffer their suffering, resonate with their experience. It also means we have an affinity for that person, to feel at one with them, to feel compassion for and in accord with them. In other words, I am in agreement with and of the same mind as him, by commiserating with this person on the deepest, emotional level. Freud was the first analyst to propose that the ideal attitude to adopt with one's patients is one of *sympathetic* understanding. Yet, sympathy is not an attitude one can literally *adopt*, for it cannot be accessed by will or volition. I don't choose to be sympathetic; I succumb to it, naturally and spontaneously. Like the divine interventions the Greeks speak of, sympathy, properly speaking, is a *gift of grace*: it comes over us and holds us firmly in its grip. We have no choice but to feel sympathy whenever it makes an appearance. Because we cannot resist it, neither can we beckon it to appear. Because it is a feeling, we cannot control it, yet it is anything but a blind emotion. Like all emotions, there is an intelligence at work, in this case an intelligence that recognizes something about the other person's situation, which in turn prompts us to resonate with that person. Sympathy visits us when we feel closest to someone, when we suffer that person's pain and predicament.

I may express a word of sympathy when someone tells me, for example, that his or her mother has died. But merely saying the words doesn't suggest that I *feel* sympathy. Yet psychotherapists, especially psychoanalysts, seem loath to use this word or even allude to it in their publications. Instead they prefer to talk about *empathy*, as though it is the same as, or even superior to, sympathy. I suspect I know why. The word empathy doesn't connote a feeling of love or anything remotely approximating it. To empathize with a patient is little more than a technique that can be cultivated and employed, like the act of interpretation. To empathize and sympathize are not the same thing. Empathy implies an ability to recognize what the other person is feeling, an act of the intellect, not of the heart. Its principal vehicle is identification, recognizing something of myself in the other person. I may sense that a patient is feeling sad, or heartbroken, or lost, but it doesn't necessarily follow that I am *commiserating* with what that person is feeling, that I suffer that person's pain, that I am affected by it, that it moves me to tears. To empathize is not an act of love, but sympathy is. That is the basic difference between them. This is why analysts are loath to employ it; they don't typically accept that loving one's patients is necessary, appropriate, or desirable. It probably violates one of the many boundaries that analysts erect between themselves and their patients. Some of them even think sympathy is dangerous. They tell themselves they are there to understand their patients and, perhaps, accept them, but it is not their mission to love them. I don't mean to say this is the case for all analysts. I know many who value sympathy, some of whom were my teachers, but they are in the minority. I don't believe you will ever take a course at a psychoanalytic institute that teaches you anything about sympathy, let alone the kinds of love that are suitable to feel for your patients. The very topic is unceremoniously avoided.

Love was a theme that absorbed Laing all his life,[10] especially its spiritual edition. Despite his preoccupation with the dark side of love, which he encountered in the intimate, familial affairs of his more psychotic patients, embodied in incidents of deception and subterfuge that occasioned their family dynamics, Laing believed there is an inherent goodness and decency most people aspire to in their relationships, even of a spiritual nature. One of the most prevalent features of Laing's relationship with spirituality was the capacity to love, epitomized by the Christian privileging of *caritas*.

Two of the books Laing recommended to me over the course of my relationship with him were Kierkegaard's *Works of Love* (1995) and *Purity of Heart Is to Will One Thing* (1956), a special little text that addresses Kierkegaard's notion of "double-mindedness." Kierkegaard believed that double-mindedness is a source of human suffering that derives from hypocrisy, but that its cure could be obtained by cultivating an aptitude for *caritas*. Laing was familiar with all the major religions and intimate with many, especially Chan and Tibetan Buddhism, Taoism, and other Asian disciplines. Chogyam Trungpa, the Tibetan sage who founded Naropa Institute in Boulder, Colorado, and later *Shambala*, was a close friend. Despite Laing's affinity for Eastern disciplines, it was Christianity with which he was perhaps most identified. For this reason Kierkegaard, who was both an existential philosopher and Christian adept, was especially important. Laing once told me that it was from Kierkegaard that he realized the sincerest expression of love is to not "trespass" against others, which is to say, never to encroach into another's personal space, but to do so cautiously, tenderly, and carefully. Though no relationship is free of encroachments – for we are all human and to be human, says Kierkegaard, is to sin – Laing believed that some people are able to achieve states of communion that are relatively free of transgression. At any rate, it is a facility everyone can aspire to, especially those of us in the so-called helping professions.

On occasion in his seminars, Laing would read from the Lord's Prayer, inspired, he said, by a book of Aldous Huxley where Huxley pored over each line of this famous prayer, rendering a more accessible contemporary interpretation of it. Laing was especially taken with the part of the prayer that speaks of *trespassing* against one's neighbors and the need to forgive those who trespass against oneself, but especially one's trespasses against them. Laing seemed particularly sensitive to crossing that line, when therapists, for example, may trespass into a space of vulnerability that is not necessarily therapeutic but injurious. Perhaps the one ineluctable conclusion that Laing arrived at over the course of his professional career was this: *mental and emotional anguish are more often than not the consequence of uncommonly subtle forms of violence perpetrated by persons in authority – be they parents, guardians, educators, psychiatrists, psychoanalysts – against persons, for one reason or another, who happen to be at their mercy, be they children, students, or patients in treatment.* He concluded that most of us are more callous in our everyday conduct with others than we readily admit to ourselves. Inspired by Foucault, Laing reckoned that those to whom we entrust ourselves when most vulnerable are oftentimes insensitive to the power they bring to bear when offering them help. In his research into families conducted at the Tavistock Institute (in the early 1960s), Laing learned that parents especially are often oblivious when they exercise such power in a less than benevolent manner, always "for the child's own good." Laing's most controversial message, the one that engendered most of his enemies, was his accusation that the very people who hold themselves out to be helpful – mental health professionals and the like – oftentimes make matters worse by the carelessness with which they treat their patients. What they typically lack, he suspected, is the requisite compassion, or *caritas*, with which to regard them. Instead of *caritas* their patients get "treatment," often of a brutal nature, masquerading as elixirs of hope.

Scheler also exerted a considerable influence on Laing's conception of the healthy and more spiritual component of love, epitomized by Scheler's conception of *sympathy*. Like Kierkegaard, Scheler was religious and much of his philosophical writing was concerned with comprehending our relationship to God. Unlike erotic love, which partially blinds us to the other person, sympathy, or *caritas*, reveals the other person as he or she is, in the most fundamental way possible, in his or her most acute state of vulnerability. Moreover, Scheler was convinced that the only way to truly know the other is via this special kind of regard. This means that love isn't merely something one feels but a metaphysical act that implicates every aspect of my being. This approximates Heidegger's conception of *Sorge*, or care. Heidegger never really talks about love, *per se*, and this has led some commentators, such as Binswanger,[11] to conclude that Heidegger lacked a conception of love in his philosophy. Heidegger himself disputed this and replied that what he had to say about love was contained in his conception of *Sorge*.

Heidegger's notion of *Sorge* is complex, as you would expect from a concept that is intended to characterize the most fundamental feature of what it means to be human. I haven't the space to do Heidegger's conception of *Sorge* justice, but it is useful to know that two important terms derive from Heidegger's usage of *Sorge*: concern (*Besorgen*) and solicitude (*Fürsorge*). Both terms are etymologically linked to *Sorge* in the German. Like Scheler, Heidegger views *Sorge* as a fundamental aspect of our being, that which makes human beings tick. It is closely linked to anxiety in that we can't help but care about where our lives are going, who we are in our individuality or "person," and what we mean to others, just as we can't help but care or be concerned about what others mean to us, how important they are in our lives, and how we should treat them. If I say, for example, "I don't care what you think of me because I don't love you anymore," or "I don't care what you do because you mean nothing to me," this is a lie because caring is *what* I am, through and through. I am no more capable of not caring than I can stop breathing. Hate or indifference are just as rooted in care as being in love. This is why my relationship to care (or love) says more about who I am as a person, than what I happen to be feeling on this or that occasion. What I care about and how readily I acknowledge the depths of my caring says more or less everything there is to know about the person I am.

The term that Heidegger employs for the way I care about other people is *Für-sorge*, or solicitude. We use the word solicitous in English to connote a sense of anxiety, or desire, as when I am solicitous of a baby in my care. It also describes that special kind of attention that therapists give their patients, and why Bion believed there is always an element of anxiety in every therapy session, experienced by patient and analyst alike. To care for or about someone also implies there is a reason I care and why I am solicitous, and the reason is that the other person *matters* to me. Some matter more, some matter less, but I am incapable of being indifferent to anyone who comes into my orbit, because to be in a relation with a person means that this person becomes a part of me, just as I become a part of that person. This is what people do: they get inside each other. I cannot help but care what that person means to me and me that person. Care is not an emotion: it the ontological foundation of what makes me human. Following Plato's example, Heidegger invented a Greek myth that he claimed explained how care brought humans into the world, in much the same manner that Plato, via Socrates, fabricated a myth that explains how love first entered the world (see pp. 149–151). According to Heidegger, the *Myth of Cura* goes something like this:

> Once when 'Care' was crossing a river, she saw some clay. Thoughtfully, she took up a piece and began to shape it. While she was meditating on what she had made, Jupiter came by. 'Care' asked him to give it spirit, and this he gladly granted. But when she wanted her name to be bestowed upon it, he forbade this, and demanded that it be given his name instead. As they were arguing, Earth arose and requested that her name be conferred on the creature, since she had given it a part of her body. They asked Saturn to be the judge, and he made the following seemingly just decision: "Since you, Jupiter, gave it spirit, you shall have that spirit at its death. Since you, Earth, gave it the gift of a body, you shall receive its body. But since 'Care' first shaped this creature, she shall possess it as long as it lives. But since there is a dispute among you about its name, let it be called 'homo,' for it is made of *humus* (earth)."
>
> *(1985, pp. 301–303)*

Heidegger goes on to explain that the myth suggests humans are rooted in care for as long as they live, and are released from it only when they die. He notes that the word for care in the New Testament is *sollicitidudo*, a technical term that can be found in the moral philosophy of the Stoic, Seneca. It's also worth noting that care is the etymological root of the word "cure," as the title of the fable suggests. This implies that the physician's greatest tool in his treatment of the sick is the care, devotion, and attentiveness he brings to bear with his patients, as noted in Chapter One. So what does this tell us about Scheler's conception of sympathy, and its relation to the most compassionate love possible, *caritas*? Basically, the kind of love that Scheler (1954) has in mind is the love that lets the other person *be*, in his or her beingness, without trespassing into or beyond that invisible line of vulnerability where we get into that person's head and have our way with him (or her), whether he is unaware of what we are doing, or whether he knows but is too helpless to protest. This is especially apt in the treatment of the so-called schizophrenic, the most vulnerable person on earth.

As we saw in Chapter Three, where I reviewed Scheler's interpretation of Nietzsche's concept of *ressentiment*, Scheler was acutely aware of the potential for deception and self-deception in our interpersonal relationships. He was especially sensitive to the self-deception we sometimes succumb to when professing sympathy for others. Let us take the psychoanalyst who is endeavoring to connect with his patient as an example. In one mode of self-deception the analyst listens as his patient tells him how terrible he feels, and the analyst tells him he knows how he feels, because he has been there himself. This is what I characterized earlier as *empathy*, a term typically used by therapists to connote their ability to identify, and thereby connect with, the pain their patients are alleged to be feeling. Scheler argues that what the analyst is really talking about in this example is his *own* suffering, not that of his patient, so the only person he is connecting with is himself. This is an incidence of narcissism, not sympathy. It may help the therapist feel better, but does little or nothing for the patient.

In another example of self-deception, the analyst addresses something that his patient shares or complains about. The analyst says something to the effect that, "Not to worry, you will be alright." The patient may respond positively, even appreciatively, for this act of apparent commiseration. But what is actually happening? Scheler suggests that the roles have been reversed. The patient is now reassuring the analyst that he, the patient, feels better, or relieved, or hopeful, that the future will be better than the present, so there is hope. What the analyst is really saying is that he doesn't want his patient to suffer and that he can't wait for him or her to get better, so that the *analyst* can feel better by not worrying that his patient may terminate the therapy if he isn't happy with how things are going. This is an example of what Freud termed *therapeutic ambition*, a term that has virtually disappeared from the psychoanalytic nomenclature. Freud knew only too well that some analysts aren't cut out for this work because they are either too neurotic to tolerate their patients' suffering, or that the analyst cannot accept the patient for who he is in his present condition, or that the analyst has no faith in the process.[12]

Being at the service of one's patients, giving them the kind of attention that no one else can or is willing to, and allowing them to be who they are without judgment, is not a technique that can be learned. Yes, it is a job, a job the therapist or analyst is paid to perform. But what we are being paid for is not to cheer our patients up, to promise a brighter future, or urge them to pull themselves together for their own good, or to track evidence of progress, like a good parent may to a child. The only way psychotherapists are able to put up with such relationships, with people who are neurotic or crazy, who are distressed and distressing to be with, is to accept them for who they are each step of the way. In effect, the analyst is being asked to care, to love them, not in the erotic sense of the term, but from a place of *caritas*, which is to say, genuine sympathy (the way Portland Road regarded Jerome in Chapter Five). Erotic love is useless in this context because, as Freud was aware, when you like a person too much you want that person to like you. That is when your tolerance of their pain diminishes. The kind of love that seems to help is the kind that *wants* nothing. This means being simply at their service, however frustrating, monotonous, or exasperating such service is. This is the kind of love Heidegger calls *Sorge*, Laing calls *caritas*, and Scheler christens *sympathy*, a modern word that has the advantage of asking us to ponder love from an altogether different angle. It is also a kind of love that each of us is capable of because, as Heidegger observed, it is an essential aspect of our nature. We have to ask how much we are able to access it, because it is the one kind of love that is most subtle.

Despite its elusiveness, our capacity for sympathy is readily abundant. It is one of those things we take for granted, like the water we drink or the air we breathe. Like water and air, we don't do so well without it. While most of our attention is focused on the more theatrical, passionate aspects of erotic love, the absence of sympathy would hamstring the therapeutic process, just as its absence would render marital relationships or friendships impossible. One of the remarkable phenomena I have witnessed among many of the couples I have worked with was the absence of sympathy in their marriage. One of the first signs that a marriage is finished is the lack of sympathy that either of the partners feels for the other's suffering and vulnerability. Each is so preoccupied with his or her own suffering that there is little if any sympathy for that of the partner's. In any close relationship, whether spouses, lovers, friends, or colleagues, each expects sympathy from the other, and is acutely aware when it is missing. Whenever we complain about our jobs, our health, even the weather, to another person, the first thing we look for is an expression of sympathetic understanding for what we have to put up with. It is the salve that keeps us going despite all the hardship we experience daily. It always improves our mood when we succeed in eliciting it, because its expression confirms that the person who offers it loves me, or at any rate regards me with a loving disposition. Yet, like sexual desire, sympathy cannot be aroused on command. You either feel it or you don't.

If sympathy is so important to us, if we crave and expect it in virtually all our relationships as a matter of course, then why does it break down? Why withhold it when it is asked of us, if it is so easy to offer? Why are we unable to *feel* sympathy, whenever we are called upon to offer it? There are many reasons, but one of the most pervasive is that the person soliciting sympathy is no longer *credible*. In order to arouse sympathy one must be credible to *me*, especially those relationships in which I am most intimately devoted. If I sense that your pain is genuine, for example, I am more likely to feel sympathy for you than if I sense it is not. If I suspect your expression of suffering is contrived, that you are orchestrating the pain you telegraph to me *in order* to elicit sympathy from me (e.g., hypochondriacs, hysterics), then you lose your credibility with me, and with that credibility you have lost my sympathy. I can love a person sympathetically only if and when that person is being genuine, or authentic, with me, which is to say, so long as I buy it. This is especially poignant in the psychoanalytic relationship. The therapist can be genuinely sympathetic only when his patient is most genuine and authentic with him. Otherwise it is contrived on both sides of the equation. If that is the case, then it is a therapy relationship that is only going through the motions, so it is going nowhere.

Every form of psychopathology, or madness, that we have explored thus far occasions a diminution in our capacity for loving, in one or other of the various editions of love, whether erotic, friendly, charitable, sympathetic. Sometimes erotic love is suppressed and sometimes, in its expression, it is just plain crazy. Our capacity for *philia*, or friendship, may also be compromised, as well as *caritas*, or mercy. How each is diminished or perverted in a given instance is unique to that person and that person alone. How we seek love or avoid it says more about the person we are than any pyschodiagnostic regimen ever could. Freud once offered that psychoanalysis is a "cure through love." This observation is easy to misconstrue, but he was right. Psychotherapy is a cure through love in a double sense. First, it is imperative that the patient comes to love the therapist, not erotically, but from the perspective of *philia*, like the crucial friend with whom one shares everything. Second, the analyst must also come to love the patient, but not, strictly speaking, as his or her friend. The analyst may be a friend to his patient, but the patient will never be a friend to his analyst, nor can he. Their relationship is too inequitable for a conventional friendship, rooted in reciprocity, to flourish. The kind of love analysts feel for their patients more aptly approximates *caritas*, a sympathetic and selfless giving over to the person who the patient is, a person whom the therapist cherishes as long as they work together. The love felt is selfless because therapists don't need their patient's love in the same way their patients need theirs. Patients need to be loved because that is what ultimately heals them, because that is what they are lacking, even when they least suspect it. The analyst's *caritas* for this or that patient is vital, because without it the therapist cannot tolerate the anguish he is unremittingly exposed to. Analysts who cannot love in this manner will eventually resent the uncompromising attention their patients require, and find a way to get rid of them.

I end this chapter with the question that is by now likely weighing on your mind. If analysts need to affect sympathy for their patients, then how do they cultivate this capacity? If the expression of sympathy is not a technique, then by what means does one come by it? Is it inborn, so that either you've got it or you don't, or is it nurtured? Why does it seem more accessible to some than to others? Why are most analysts capable of being more authentic, sympathetic, and sincere in their relationships with their patients than in their personal relationships? What is it about the analytic situation that invites us, even compels us, to be even more caring than we otherwise would or even could be? For the answer to these questions we will now turn our attention to the next and final chapter.

Notes

1 Freud believed that the obsessional neurotic tends to incline toward sublimating his need for love onto work activity because the outcome is easier to control. The fickle nature of love places him at intolerable risk.

2 See my "Happiness and Chance: A Reappraisal of the Psychoanalytic Conception of Suffering" (2004b), for more on the nature of happiness.

3 Though Klein and Lacan each adopted Freud's thesis of a death drive, their respective elaborations of it were so far removed from Freud's that they bear little resemblance to the original.

4 The fable that depicts his birth was apparently invented by Socrates. If this was indeed Socrates' invention it was one that came back to bite him. Socrates was eventually executed by the Athenian elders for the purported crimes of corrupting the youth and preaching false gods.

5 When Freud developed his dual instinct theory, naming one drive *Eros* and the other *Thanatos*, he separated the inherent duality of the Greek conception of *Eros* that was capable of both good and bad, not unlike the Christian decision to divide the Jewish God, who was both beneficent and cruel, into two entities, God and the devil.

6 The Greek word for happiness, *eudaimonia*, has at its core the word "*daimon*." The term literally means to *be with* your *daimon* spirit, such as *Eros* (one of many *daimon* spirits), who will bring you the happiness love provides, or ruin (the *daimon*, after Christianity, became *demon*). In other dialogues Plato presented alternative methods for obtaining happiness, by becoming virtuous, for example, or pursuing pleasure.

7 Freud believed that neuroses are not creative because they are designed to circumvent our intolerance of suffering. In order to be genuinely creative, Freud believed one must be willing to suffer, as all great artists have.

8 See my "*Logos* and Psychoanalysis: The Role of Truth and Creativity in Heidegger's Conception of Language" (2000), for a critique of Heidegger's conception of language in relation to creativity.

9 During the 1960s Laing in Great Britain, Timothy Leary in the United States, and Stanislav Grof in Czechoslovakia became famous for their respective experiments with LSD. Whereas Laing and Grof employed it in treating schizophrenia, Leary embarked on a disturbing mission to surreptitiously "turn on" the masses to the altered states that LSD induced, but without their awareness. Neither Laing nor Grof approved of what they perceived as Leary's reckless use of this extremely powerful and potentially dangerous drug.

10 See Stephen Gans, "Awakening to Love: R. D. Laing's Phenomenological Therapy" (2015), for more on Laing's views about love. See also Thompson, "A Road Less Traveled: The Dark Side of R. D. Laing's Conception of Authenticity" (2012).

11 For more on Heidegger's reaction to Binswanger's claim that Heidegger omitted love from his philosophy, see a discussion on this topic in Heidegger's *Zollikon Seminars* (2001, pp. 115–116).

12 Bion (1970) makes a similar point about the need to erase memory and desire in therapy, in order to elicit faith. What he means by "desire" in this context is what Freud meant by "therapeutic ambition," the need to look ahead and predict where things are headed in a patient's therapy, whether promising or depressing. Instead, Bion suggests that the therapist should stay in the present by not thinking about the past or the future. When one succeeds in doing this, the therapist accesses what Bion calls "faith," which I take to be what Scheler terms "sympathy."

References

Bergmann, M. (1987) *The anatomy of loving: The story of man's quest to know what love is.* New York: Columbia University Press.

Bion, W. R. (1970) *Attention and interpretation: A scientific approach to insight in psychoanalysis and groups.* London: Tavistock Publications.

Dodds, E. R. (1951) *The Greeks and the irrational.* Berkeley, Los Angeles and London: University of California Press.

Freud, S. (1953–1973) *The standard edition of the complete psychological works of Sigmund Freud.* 24 volumes. Edited and translated by J. Strachey. London: Hogarth Press. (Referred to in subsequent references as *Standard Edition.*)

Freud, S. (1905) *Three essays on sexuality. Standard Edition,* 7:125–245. London: Hogarth Press, 1953.

Freud, S. (1912) On the universal tendency to debasement in the sphere of love (Contributions to the psychology of love II). *Standard Edition,* 11:179–190. London: Hogarth Press, 1957.

Freud, S. (1914) On narcissism: An introduction. *Standard Edition,* 14:67–102. London: Hogarth Press, 1957.

Freud, S. (1915) Instincts and their vicissitudes. *Standard Edition,* 14:111–140. London: Hogarth Press, 1957.

Gans, S. (2015) Awakening to love: R. D. Laing's phenomenological therapy. In *The legacy of R. D. Laing: An appreciation of his contemporary relevance* (pp. 99–114) (Ed., M. Guy Thompson). London and New York: Routledge, 2015.

Hamilton, E. and Cairns, H. [Eds.] (1961) *The collected dialogues of Plato.* Translated by Michael Joyce, *The symposium.* (Bollingen Series). Princeton: Princeton University Press.

Heidegger, M. (1985) *History of the concept of time: Prolegomena.* Translated by Theodore Kisiel. Bloomington: Indiana University Press.

Heidegger, M. (2001) *Zollikon seminars: Protocols, conversations, letters.* Edited by Medard Boss and translated by Franz Mayr and Richard Askay. Evanston: Northwestern University Press.

Kierkegaard, S. (1956) *Purity of heart is to will one thing: Spiritual preparation for the office of confession.* Translated by Douglas V. Steere. New York: Harper Torchbooks.

Kierkegaard, S. (1995) *Works of love.* Translated by Howard V. Hong and Edna H. Hong. Princeton: Princeton University Press.

Laing, R. D. (1970) *Knots.* London: Tavistock Publications.

Laing, R. D. (1976) *Do you love me? An entertainment in conversation and verse.* London: Allen Lane.

Laing, R. D. (1979) *Sonnets.* London: Michael Joseph.

Lawrence, D. H. (2004) *Psychoanalysis and the unconscious and Fantasia of the unconscious* (The Cambridge Edition of the Works of D. H. Lawrence). Cambridge: Cambridge University Press.

Lewis, C. S. (1971) *The four loves.* (2nd ed.). New York: Mariner Books.

Nussbaum, M. (1986) *The fragility of goodness: Luck and ethics in Greek tragedy and philosophy.* Cambridge: Cambridge University Press.

Reik, T. (1975) *Of love and lust.* New York: Souvenir Press.

Santas, G. (1988) *Plato and Freud: Two theories of love.* London and New York: Basil Blackwell.

Scheler, M. (1954) *The nature of sympathy.* Translated by Peter Heath. London: Routledge and Kegan Paul.

Thompson, M. Guy (2000) *Logos* and psychoanalysis: The role of truth and creativity in Heidegger's conception of language. *Psychologist Psychoanalyst,* Vol. 20, No. 4:19–25.

Thompson, M. Guy (2004a) *The ethic of honesty: The fundamental rule of psychoanalysis.* Amsterdam and New York: Rodopi.

Thompson, M. Guy (2004b) Happiness and chance: A reappraisal of the psychoanalytic conception of suffering. *Psychoanalytic Psychology,* Vol. 21, No. 1:134–153.

Thompson, M. Guy (2012, February) A road less traveled: The dark side of R. D. Laing's conception of authenticity. *Psychotherapy in Australia,* Vol. 18, No. 2: 20–29.

8

ON SANITY

What is sanity? One would think that with all the attention we have paid to the notion of madness throughout human history that we would have a fairly clear idea of what it means to be sane. Sadly, this is not the case. As a topic in its own right it is seldom addressed, and when it is there is little insight into its nature.[1] Even Buddhism, with its emphasis on achieving a more enlightened manner of living, characterized by wisdom, rarely addresses the topic explicitly.[2] Is the enlightened person more sane than the unenlightened, or is happiness the determinant? Wisdom and happiness are arguably related, though not interchangeable, but what about sanity? Typically, psychiatry ignores the concept of sanity, which, in America, is a legal term, connoting the loss of responsibility. If sanity is invoked by psychiatrists at all it is commonly characterized as the opposite of insanity. It is hardly suggestive to allege that one thing is the absence of the other, especially when our notions about madness are hazy at best.

According to the O.E.D. the word sane comes from the Latin *sanus*, meaning healthy or sound, as in sound mind and body. Herein lies the problem. If sanity means health, is it any wonder we are so muddled as to what it entails, after we acknowledge we know just as little about health as we do about sanity. Medicine has traditionally defined health as the absence of disease or malady. This is the conceit of Western medicine, which endeavors to treat the illnesses it diagnoses with little awareness of the healthy condition it furthers. Unlike Chinese medicine, for example, which defines health as a state of wholeness and balance, Western medicine is content to treat illnesses by eradicating their symptoms, hoping for the best outcome. Western medicine has accomplished remarkable things in spite of this, but it also reminds us why it is ill-suited to "treat" what it (mistakenly) portrays as a "mental illness." Psychiatry's strategy in treating mental states is virtually the same as when treating the physical ones: locate what is wrong and neutralize it. *Health*, whatever it is, will take care of itself. We are finally beginning to realize the limitations of Western medicine by focusing more deliberately on what health is and cultivating it, intelligently. Isn't it about time we did the same for our minds?

What I want to look at in this, the final chapter, is the nature of sanity, what it is, and how to acquire it. My focus throughout this book has been on madness and what it means in all its maddening complexity. I have not altogether neglected sanity, but my allusions to it have for the most part been indirect, inviting you to decide how sanity is implicated in what it means to be crazy. Now I want to leave madness behind and focus explicitly on what it means to be sane. But in order to do that we will have to take a detour through the concept of authenticity, a term that on the surface may seem tangential to getting a better grip on sanity. I ask that you indulge me, because there is method in my madness. I hope in the end you will agree the two are not only related, but decisively so. But first, let's talk about the word, sanity, and what this word can tell us.

Although the standard definition of sanity – "health" – is relatively straightforward, its etymology is not so simple, but interesting nonetheless. According to Partridge (1966), the word sane is cognate with the words sanitary, sanitation, and sanitarium, words with which we are intimately familiar. We usually think of sanitary as related to cleanliness, and it is, but only indirectly. Sanitary literally means healthy, but because a dirty kitchen or surgical theater is deemed unhealthy, the terms health and cleanliness became synonymous. On the other hand, a sanitarium (or sanitorium, sanatorium) is a place crazy people go to in order to become sane, as in "mental sanitarium" (as distinct from sanitariums that segregated persons suffering from tuberculosis before the invention of antibiotics). Partridge tells us that the word sane is also akin to the Greek *iaino*, meaning "I heal," and cognate with the words health or healing. If sane, or sanity, means healthy or to heal, then what does health mean? Surely knowing this can help us get to the bottom of what it means to be sane. Partridge tells us that the words heal and health come from the word "whole," which in turn is derived from the Middle English *hole* and Old English *hal*, meaning sound, as in sound body or mind (as we noted above), or complete. Now it gets interesting. The word whole gives rise to wholesome, which we typically associate with health. It also gives rise to the word hail, as in hailing a taxi. The origin of this expression, however, was used as a simple greeting, when shouting out "hail!" to an acquaintance, as in "be well." It also means to make well, or to cure, so hail and heal are closely related.

To sum up, the word sane takes us back to the word health, which in turn takes us back further to the word whole, which among other things means sound or complete. Now we must wonder, what does it mean to be sound? There are three meanings for the word sound, two are nouns which connote a body of water or a noise. The other is an adjective, and that is the one we want to explore. Partridge tells us that sound comes from the Old English *sund* and is akin to the Latin *sanus*, meaning flawless or unharmed. The O.E.D. expands on this further, suggesting that a sound person is free from disease, infirmity, or injury. It also means to be unimpaired, in good condition, wholesome, of solid or ample character, morally good, honest, sincere, and of sober or solid judgment (one must be sober to judge effectively). With me so far? Now let's summarize what we have learned about the word sane and all its apparent meanings. Taken together via our etymological inventory, to be sane is to be healthy, to heal, to be whole, wholesome, or complete, to be sound, to be well, and to make well or to cure. It also means to be flawless, unharmed, unimpaired, of solid character, morally good, honest, sincere, and of sober judgment. If all that is entailed in being sane, I want some! It is worth noting at this juncture that the word wisdom, the objective of Buddhism, though not etymologically related, is nevertheless akin to sanity. The word wise derives from the word *vide*, which literally means to *see*. Derived from the Latin *uidere*, it is related to the Sanskrit words *Veda* and *Vedanta*, the Hindu word for knowledge. The word *vide* also gives us the words visa, envisage, visible, vision, visionary, visitor, advise, evidence, envy, interview, improvise, review, revise, supervise, survey, clairvoyant, wit, wizard, and, of course, wise and wisdom. The O.E.D. defines wisdom as a manner, custom, and course of action, as in *likewise* and *otherwise*. The wise person possesses and exercises sound judgment and discernment, having the ability to perceive and adopt the best means to accomplish an end, qualities we attributed earlier to sanity.

So, we have come full circle, when we recall that in Chapter One I suggested the principal goal of psychotherapy is to *improve one's judgment*. As we now see, sanity and judgment are inextricably linked. But we have also seen that there is more to sanity than judgment alone. One of the most common ways of characterizing a crazy person is that he or she is "split" or broken. The schizophrenic suffers from a broken mind, or heart. The paranoiac is literally "beside himself" (*para* = beside, *noos* = mind), split into two people or minds. Among psychoanalysts, splitting is embraced as the most prevalent symptom (or, if you wish, defense mechanism) of psychosis. If there is any truth to these assumptions, then it makes sense to think of sanity as the reverse of splitting, of becoming whole again, as in wholesome and solid, in effect, complete. But sanity is more complicated than simply becoming a whole, solid person who had fallen apart, had come apart at the seams and lost his or her bearings. It also implies the wherewithal of taking off the mask I was using to conceal myself from others, of coming out of the closet and becoming, perhaps for the first time, *who* I am, without fear of consequences. This is probably where the notion of honesty comes in and why that term is associated with becoming a sounder person. If pretending to be someone I am not is dishonest, then becoming who I am would entail becoming more honest, or more genuine with myself and with others. When I am honest I no longer need to affect the subterfuge that we often associate with madness.

As you probably suspected, we now come face to face with the problem of authenticity, what authenticity entails, and how becoming authentic can and may facilitate sanity, which is to say, a sane way of being with myself and with others. So what does authenticity entail, properly speaking? I will endeavor to answer that question by first turning our attention to the work of D. W. Winnicott and reviewing his conception of true and false self phenomena, and then comparing it with Laing's conception of the false self outlined in *The Divided Self* (1960). Winnicott never invoked the term authenticity specifically, but his conception of a false self enjoys important similarities. Moreover, Winnicott was one of his supervisors when Laing was undergoing his psychoanalytic training at the British Psychoanalytic Society in the late 1950s, during the period when both were developing their respective conceptions of the false self, Laing in *The Divided Self*, Winnicott most notably in his 1960 paper, "Ego Distortion in Terms of True and False Self," the same year Laing's book was published.

Winnicott believed that Freud's structural model of id, ego, and superego didn't adequately address the problem of selfhood and that it was impossible to locate a personal self in Freud's schema. Was the ego the self, as Freud implied, or was the entire tripartite structure the self, but a divided one, which Freud also inferred? Winnicott introduced the notion of a *self* to connote both a personal and technical term that was more or less superimposed onto Freud's structural model. This decision was slightly problematic because Winnicott didn't really integrate his model with Freud's but permitted them to exist side by side. Some have suggested this was a split in Winnicott's thinking. This was typical of Winnicott, a strategy he adopted when reconciling Melanie Klein's theories with his own, not entirely rejecting her theory but not integrating it with his, either. Be that as it may, though Winnicott's theory of a false self lacks theoretical cohesion, it does compensate for the lack of a self in Freud's model. Briefly, Winnicott posits a true self at the beginning of the child's development, while acknowledging that it shares similar qualities to Freud's conception of the id. Winnicott and Freud both believed that the child lacks an ego at this early stage and that the mother serves the function of an external ego for her baby, epitomized by Winnicott's unsettling statement that there is no such thing as "a baby" (without a mother to nurture it). The child begins to develop a "false" self after six months or so, as a normal part of its development, at exactly the same time that Freud avers that the ego begins to emerge from the id. Winnicott (1960, p. 140) admits that his conception of the true self shares similarities with the id, just as the false self shares similarities with the ego. However, at this juncture the similarities between Winnicott's and Freud's respective schemas stops. Though Winnicott held that the emergence of the false self is normative, he also stated that the baby may form its false self prematurely if the mother doesn't provide sufficient mothering (by intuitively grasping the baby's emotional needs). Should this happen (or rather, not happen) the baby has no recourse but to reverse roles and undertake to "mother" its own mother (or primary caretaker) to secure its welfare. This tactic, however, will result in grave consequences.

Winnicott envisioned the true self as a term that connotes the totality of our emotions, where our sense of being originates. It is not literally a "self" in the sense of a *second* self to the one that is false. There is really only *one* self, but with private and public functions and qualities. Likewise, the so-called false self is not nearly as ominous as it sounds. A better term might have been the social self, because that is effectively what it is. As envisioned by Winnicott, the false self more or less exercises the synthetic functions of Freud's ego: negotiating social space, learning appropriate social cues in its conduct of interpersonal relationships, devising and executing courses of action, and so on. We all need our false selves in order to deal with other people and compensate for our latent narcissism. It is the vehicle for our interpersonal relationships. However, if it takes over the function of navigating social space *before* the true self is able to flourish, the child will become compliant and eager to please at the expense of knowing what it desires from other people.

If a child isn't free to express its feelings to the mother, for example, who may be depressed or distracted, the child will instinctively hide its feelings and, in time, lose touch with them. This is the picture Freud posits as the function of the superego, but at a later stage of development. If the superego, for example, is too well developed moralistically it will compel the ego to repress the id's desires, painting the same picture as that of an over-developed false self. Unlike Freud, Winnicott didn't claim that a dominant false self would result in a typically repressed neurotic, but rather a person who is profoundly alienated from him- or herself, due to its occurrence at an earlier stage of development. This results in a person who develops an underlying schizoid personality, who has problems knowing who he is and what it is like to feel real, who has problems relating to others satisfactorily. This is why Winnicott never intended the true and false self concept to actually displace Freud's structural model. Whereas the structural model explains the etiology of neuroses (but in Freud's opinion, the psychoses as well), the true and false self dynamic introduced by Winnicott focuses on the etiology of schizoid or psychotic phenomena, and the terrible alienation this state occasions.

Though Winnicott and Laing each see the self as divided, they aren't suggesting there are literally *two* selves, one true and one false, the way that Freud conceives of *three* selves, one that houses passions (id), a second that determines rationality (ego), and yet a third that is responsible for conscience and guilt (superego).[3] Winnicott acknowledges that the true self is a fiction if it is taken to mean that one self is hidden beneath or inside the other. For Winnicott, the so-called true self is essentially my feelings, a private affair, whereas the so-called false self is my public face. One is more or less private, the other predominantly public. One pertains to *experiences* whereas the other pertains to *behavior*. Moreover, they are not necessarily nor always estranged from each other, though they may be, in which case the result is not good. In the healthy person they are not opposed but function in relative harmony. In such instances I express publicly what I feel privately and am at one with myself and my self-presentation. Those who engage in splitting harbor feelings so privately they have virtually lost touch with them. They are no longer sure what they feel about anything, but especially love. Alternately, I may know what I feel but dare not disclose it, for fear of rejection or humiliation. I keep my feelings and desires not merely private, but dark secrets.

Laing (1960) agrees with Winnicott that the schizoid condition is characterized by a crippling sense of alienation with one's self (noted in Chapter One). Though there are other important similarities between Winnicott's and Laing's respective conceptions of false self phenomena, there are significant differences. Winnicott follows the psychoanalytic custom of locating pathological phenomena inside neat developmental stages, so the false self is supposed to emerge as early as the preverbal stage in infancy. If the infant is able to get through the first year or two with a well-developed true self, then the child will have developed sufficient confidence to avoid the need for an overactive false self. Laing believed that the kind of false self Winnicott conceptualized doesn't necessarily develop as early as Winnicott assumed. Indeed, it may require the entirety of one's childhood, including adolescence.

Like Freud, Laing believed that children have first to acquire language in order to participate in the kind of sophisticated language games with parents that may result in the types of confusion and befuddlement we associate with schizoid phenomena. Another difference between Laing and Winnicott is how they each see the false self evolving. For Winnicott, infants who are unable to express their true feelings and form compliant selves to protect them, introject into their false selves the opinions of others in lieu of cultivating their own perspective. Laing partially agrees with this, but is more interested in how this is supposed to work. For example, Laing devotes an entire chapter in *The Divided Self* ("The False-Self System") to describing how some children learn to more or less *impersonate* the behavior and attitudes of one or more parents, effectively mimicking them, then integrating that mimicry into their own personality. Such children don't fashion their identity from their own experiences but adopt *as their own* the parents' self-identity. There is not only one false self that develops from this strategy, but a litany. This is such a painstaking and laborious process that it may require years to complete. Moreover, in Laing's schema the respective roles of the so-called true and false selves are not clear-cut. The true self may harbor pathological elements, for example, and the false self may "protect" such pathogenic elements from disclosure, compromising rather than furthering the self's interests. Additionally, Laing believed some parents may coerce their children into becoming the children the parents want them to be, by employing (unreflected) acts of deception and mystification (which Laing describes extensively in many of his writings).[4]

One may infer from this briefest of sketches how Winnicott's and Laing's respective notions of true and false self phenomena speak to an aspect of the individual's self-identity that is rarely noted in the psychoanalytic literature. They distinguish between a self that is genuine, confidant, and alive to its feelings and opinions, with a self so hidden from others it erects a mask, manufactured in order to "go along to get along" with others, but lacking a sense of self-agency and worth. In a word, a self that, on the one hand situates him- or herself in the world authentically while, on the other, living a double life, what we saw earlier that Kierkegaard characterized as *double-mindedness* (see below). Such a self is relatively false and fractured, broken and fundamentally confused, a typical scenario among persons diagnosed as schizoid or schizophrenic.

Despite Laing's close affiliation with Winnicott during the former's psychoanalytic training, and their common interests in teasing out the distinction between a genuine and compliant self-organization, Laing's views on the matter were not indebted to the psychoanalytic tradition, but to existential philosophy. Laing (1960) even adds in a footnote at the beginning of his chapter on "The False-Self System" that:

> The false self is one way of not being oneself. The following are a few of the more important studies within the existentialist tradition relevant to the

understanding of the false self, as one way of living inauthentically: Kierkeg-aard, *The Sickness Unto Death*; Heidegger, *Sein und Zeit*; Sartre's discussion on 'bad faith' in *Being and Nothingness*; Binswanger, *Drei Formen missgluckten* and 'The Case of Ellen West'; and Roland Kuhn, *La Phenomenologie de Masque.*

(p. 94)[5]

One can easily appreciate that because the psychoanalytic literature is so wanting in its dialogue with the Western philosophical tradition, and even hostile to the existential perspective in particular, Laing's immersion into that tradition prior to his psychoanalytic training resulted in a more sophisticated appreciation of what a compliant, or inauthentic, self looks like. To that end, we will now direct our attention to the existential tradition to glean from it what authenticity entails, in the context of sanity and madness.

Though authenticity is employed as a technical term in existential philosophy, psychology, and psychiatry, its origin is just as murky as the existential perspective. Some have traced it as far back as Socrates, symbolized by his decision to accept the death sentence passed on him by the Athenian Senate, rather than escape, which was what everyone (including those who passed the sentence on him) expected him to do. Socrates implied he would rather die a free man than live as a refugee, and so faced his death with remarkable courage and cool. These character traits are commonly taken to be emblematic for living one's life authentically. Not only in death, but in his life also, Socrates epitomized the kind of person who believed one must be true to oneself in order to live one's life honestly without guile. This is no doubt why Socrates became a very unpopular figure among the Athenian philosophical community, due to his penchant for engaging other philosophers in public dialogue. His mission was to crush their claims to the truth, roundly humiliating them in the process. Yet this is also commonly taken as Socrates' finest qualities as a person of principle. He was willing to stand up for his beliefs no matter how much enmity or ridicule it may cost him. One might argue that this even cost him his life, for it was his reputation as a troublemaker that resulted in his eventual trial and execution.

Socrates never actually invoked the term authenticity (or its Greek equivalent, *authentikos*) as far as we know, and no philosophical system embraced this concept as a cardinal principle before the modern existentialists. Kierkegaard is credited with initiating the modern existential perspective, and many of his books, especially *The Sickness Unto Death* (1980) and *Purity of Heart Is to Will One Thing* (1956), are devoted to describing the kind of trials entailed in living a life of integrity and authenticity. Kierkegaard was a pious philosopher who believed it is important to embrace your faith in such a manner that you remain true to *your* beliefs. More-over, in a manner that presaged the problems that we typically grapple with today, he thought that the Church as well as the nineteenth-century media of his day compromised individuals in such a way that it was easy to lose ones way. Both the Church and the media tend to coerce the populace into adhering to the truths of others, leaving little opportunity to think for oneself. He thought it is all too easy to accept the precepts of the Church passively without struggling with one's own faith, which he believed was the only way to become a "true" Christian. Kierkegaard argued that most Christians are hypnotized by the sermons they hear and treat church service as a social event instead of a moment of reckoning, even going so far as to exclaim, "I have met many pastors, but have yet to meet a true Christian!" He insisted that a person of faith must face up to the realities he values and take responsibility for his choices, wherever they lead him.

Like Socrates, Kierkegaard never actually invoked authenticity as a technical term, though his thinking on the matter is commonly assumed to have had a considerable impact on Heidegger's subsequent conception of it. Another important philosopher to be credited with epitomizing what authenticity entails is Nietzsche. Unlike Kierkegaard, Nietzsche was an atheist and rejected religion as a foil to living a life of integrity. As we saw in Chapter Three, Nietzsche (2002, 2003) believed that the Judeo-Christian tradition helped usher into the world a kind of "slave morality" rooted in weakness, envy, and resentment towards those in society who are more powerful. The latter epitomized a "master morality," men who were willing to put their life on the line in order to accomplish great things, with courage and fearlessness. Like Kierkegaard (whose philosophy Nietzsche was barely acquainted with), Nietzsche never actually invoked the term authenticity to depict his ideal personage, the *Übermensch* (or Superman, as it is frequently translated), though the entirety of his philosophy is arguably devoted to its features.

Because Nietzsche viewed the contemporary European society of his day as weak and hopelessly imbued with a "slave morality" (or inauthentic sensibility), he saw the ideal person as one who would one day emerge in the distant future, and *overcome* (hence, "overman") the challenges that his generation was incapable of facing. Unlike the common herd of Western society, the *Übermensch* would not refrain from grappling with the fundamental anxieties of living truthfully. Other qualities that the *Übermensch* embodied include an opposition to authority, that results in a fierce individualism; a perspectivism which holds that any truth is wedded to the perspective of the person promoting it, and not to fixed, immutable standards; and, most importantly, a moral relativism which holds that ethical standards are relative to a time and place, so they are neither eternal or objective but highly personal and fluid. To be authentic in Nietzsche's view means to live by your own rules while facing up to the consequences of advocating unpopular opinions. In effect, he saw *l'homme du ressentiment* that we examined in Chapter Three as the epitome of the inauthentic person, too weak-willed to take responsibility for his actions while blaming others for his limitations. Nietzsche's inauthentic person is too repressed to act in accordance with his or her desires and instead invests his or her efforts in legislating rules intended to reign in those who are passionate and ambitious. The inauthentic person in Nietzsche is one who lacks *the will to desire*.

Nietzsche's characterization of authenticity is imbued with a romanticism that Heidegger (1979, 1982, 1984, 1987), who wrote a four-volume work analyzing Nietzsche's philosophy, found excessive. For Nietzsche, it seems, there are people who are authentic and people who are not, with little room for anything in the middle. Yet, there is little doubt that both Kierkegaard and Nietzsche influenced Heidegger's conception of it. Heidegger was the first philosopher to invoke authenticity as a technical term and devoted more effort than any other to articulating what it entails.[6] As much as Heidegger appreciated Nietzsche's conception of authenticity, embodied in the latter's notion of the *Übermensch*, Heidegger believed there is no such personage as an *Übermensch*, the existential hero Nietzsche believed would rise out of the ashes of a collapsed civilization, heralding a new era in human affairs. Yet, like Nietzsche, Heidegger also suspected that the world is bound to experience a crushing collapse, brought about by the technologicalization of modern culture. Though Heidegger believed this may occur around the middle of the twenty-first century, he didn't associate this event with the emergence of a new kind of person, but perhaps a new era. Heidegger believed that all of us are inauthentic most of the time and that we need our inauthentic selves (akin to Winnicott's and Laing's respective conceptions of the false self) to navigate our social relations with others. This implies that behaving authentically isn't a process of cleansing ourselves of inauthentic character traits through a transformative religious or spiritual (or psychoanalytic) regimen. Though we are predominantly inauthentic in our daily affairs, we are also capable of behaving authentically when it counts, when something is at stake or on the line, so it is our ability to be authentic *in principle* that matters, not changing ourselves into a different kind of person than we already are. Because we are inauthentic through and through we cannot do anything to change our fundamental nature, but that doesn't mean we have to be captives of our inauthenticity. The point to remember is that each of us possesses the freedom to be resolutely genuine in our conduct with others, but we have to choose to do so. So what would behaving authentically look like?

Generally speaking, the common elements of authenticity to which Kierkegaard, Nietzsche, and Heidegger subscribed means that you live your life your own way rather than cowing to the expectations, or edicts, of others. This implies that you are able to distinguish between those things that are proper to you and your nature and the things that are not. This is why the notion of a "self" is so essential to any conception of authenticity. What is this true, or real, self to which I aspire to be true, the self that I embody in my actions and my understanding of the world?

All of us are perpetually consumed with the question of who we are and what others take us to be. Because this is never firmly established, however, who and what we are is always in process, and always a question. The self, in Heidegger's philosophy, is not nor can it ever be a fixed entity, like inanimate things are. The self is alive, and as such it is always projected into a future and in a process of becoming. So how can such a self, that is *not* what it is in a fixed or tangible way, make any sense in the context of being what it is, which is to say, being the self that I am? How can we be who we are if who we are is always happening and evolving, over time? This is the question Heidegger devoted the second half of his *magnum opus*, *Being and Time* (1962), to exploring, the most concerted investigation into the concept ever undertaken.

The very notion of authenticity drives postmodernists crazy. They reject the concept out of hand because they reject the idea of the self on which it relies. If there isn't a tangible, fixed entity called a self, or a subject, or an ego, then how can a conception of authenticity, which has at its core the need to become one's self in a genuine way, be grounded? The problem, as we will see, is not that authenticity depends on something called a self for its efficacy, but how we understand what the self is in the first place. Heidegger is critical of traditional conceptions of the self, conceptions that postmodernists are apparently still wedded to, and spends most of his time in Division Two of *Being and Time* critiquing these conceptions. Ironically, it was Heidegger's dismissal of the conventional notion of the self (to a large degree promulgated by Sartre) that helped inspire postmodernists in their conception of a de-centered self, developed by Lacan who more or less lifted it from Heidegger. In fact, Heidegger has very little to say about the self in a positive light. This is because he first needs to reject all the unsupportable notions of the self before he can get to what he regards as the one that is essential for understanding what human beings are, and what sets us apart from the other life forms in the world.

So what is it that the self is *not*? The self as Heidegger conceives it is not a self of *personal identity through time*, which endures throughout all the changes that we experience in our lives, which is the most popular conception of the self that we ordinarily embrace. As Heidegger puts it, "A gulf separates the selfsameness of the authentically existing self from the identity of that 'I' that maintains itself throughout its manifold experiences" (cited in Wrathall, 2015, p. 198). I may fashion various identities of myself, as an author, a psychoanalyst, a father, a husband, or a friend, for example, but none of these are necessarily fixed. Some may endure while others may fall away, only to be replaced by new ones. The various identities that I adopt are always evolving. Yet, none get to the core of *who I am*. Moreover, the self is not a subject, or a soul, or consciousness (Sartre), or even the "person" others take me to be. Neither is it located in the "sense of self" that Freud believed is situated in the body, nor the integration of body and mind. Our problem with identifying the self is compromised by treating it like other objects in the world, each with fixed attributes and characteristics that are for the most part unchanging. Naturally there is anxiety in not knowing exactly who or what we are and we no doubt endeavor to fix ourselves as such and such an entity in order to overcome that anxiety. This strategy, however, eventually backfires and produces even more anxiety, the kind that Laing alludes to when we become alienated from our "selves."

Yet, the greatest culprit that misleads us is the convention we all adopt when equating the self with the personal pronoun "I" that we invoke in conversation. This is the same idea that Heidegger shares with Nietzsche, that our very language misleads us into assuming that we are what our language games claim we are when we say, for example, "I am tired," or "Jane is delightful," or "Mark is untrustworthy," as though any of those things is *me*. Whenever we invoke the word "is" we employ it to *identify* someone or other *as* something or other, but just because we say it doesn't make it so. Freud's conception of psychoanalysis was predicated on the realization that language cannot be trusted, which is why patients in analysis (or similar therapies) spend so much of their time pondering what they are *really* trying to say. This is why analysts repeat back to their patients what they (the analysts) believe their patients are saying, but with *different words* than the patient employs. When I refer to myself with the personal pronoun, I am often characterizing myself as someone or something that I actually am *not*. What "I" typically refers to is what we assume is nearest to who we are. But it is usually the opposite, because "I" refers to what Heidegger calls a "fictitious" self. With me so far?

If I am not the "I" that I customarily associate with my *self*, then what is the self, if not my "I"? Basically, the self is more or less my *manner or way of existing*. According to Wrathall (2015), this amounts to evaporating the real core of human existence as we have historically conceived it. Whenever we use the word "I," we employ it at best as a kind of non-formal indicator at the moment it is invoked, while suspending any assumptions as to the veracity of how it is employed. This is the same attitude that the psychoanalyst endeavors to enlist his or her patient into adopting: to suspend all judgment about what one believes about oneself and others, what one is experiencing in the moment, and most importantly, who one really is. If the "I" is for the most part not who I am, then what is it? Basically, it is the inauthentic self, the self that has "fallen" (*Verfallenheit*) into this or that situation where I long to belong with others, perhaps the friends I keep or the colleagues I work with or the patients I treat. This doesn't mean that relationships, by their nature, are always inauthentic. It is also possible to be intimate with another person who takes care to respect the integrity and inherent mystery of who I am. Such a person, typically a spouse or best friend, refrains from making assumptions about me, and then judging me based on those assumptions, just as I, in turn, do for that person. Our closest and most treasured relationships are often of this nature. But most of our relationships are not like that, nor can they be. For the most part, we are capable of telling the difference, if we look closely. But sometimes we are not able to, when, for example, we are deceived by others or, more frequently, when we deceive ourselves. Because the crazier we are the less likely we can enjoy authentic relationships, some people don't experience genuinely intimate relationships with anyone, especially the so-called schizoid individual that Laing describes in *The Divided Self*.

Groups, however, are another matter. A preoccupying theme throughout Heidegger's work is the relationship between the individual and society and how it engenders a conflict that we can never resolve. This is because we are existentially isolated from others and in our loneliness we crave the comfort of feeling at one with the community that makes up our world, not unlike the *Oceanic* experience Freud describes in *Civilization and Its Discontents* (1930).[7] For Heidegger and Nietzsche alike, this sense of belonging is illusory. Though this quest is inconsolable, says Heidegger, the only way of approximating such a feeling is by denying an essential aspect of what we hold most precious, our personal integrity, and replacing it with "identities" that are impossible for us to ever be at one with, though they are often pleasing to others.

The person I take myself to be is basically an invention that I have a hand in creating, but the greater part of my self's authorship derives from what others make of me. In fact, I'm so obsessed with what others think about me and how they see me that I want to make myself into the person they expect me to be and, to a significant degree, that is who "I" am. This is why Heidegger calls the inauthentic self a "they-self," because its identity is rooted in what "they," others, make of me. This inauthentic self becomes an identity I cling to whenever I am loved by others, but sometimes even when I am hated by them, because in either case the identities others confer on me confirm that at least I am *somebody*. In Heidegger's view, we never really overcome this condition, and even when we least suspect it are looking to "them" to tell us what we should do and who we should be in order to ingratiate ourselves into that community. Our efforts to seek awards, accolades, the devotion of friends, even promotions and pay raises in our jobs, are often ways we typically seek to relieve the anxiety of never really knowing who we are, by holding onto whatever identity others give us. This is why Heidegger can insist that the self I typically take myself to be is not really me, but *others*.

When you think about it, we aren't literally capable of making a clear distinction between *our* selves and *other* selves. There is no obvious or reliable way of distinguishing between the person I take myself to be and the person I am with. Just as the young child introjects into itself aspects of its parents' views and personalities, in every human encounter we identify with others as a way of getting close to them, while unconsciously adopting views, habits, and ways of behaving that are actually *theirs*. But gradually, as if by magic, they eventually become *mine* and a part of who "I" am, just as the others do with my views and manner of being. We do this especially with whomever we love, but also with those who make an impression on us, who we seek to emulate. That is why our interpersonal relationships are not, strictly speaking, determined by straightforward communication between a distinct self and other, but rather by an ongoing unconscious process of replaceability and interchangeability, in which we inhabit a world together where the "who" that I am at any given moment could be anyone. It is, in fact, *they*.

For the most part, my self allows itself to be carried along by others while my relationship with them becomes incorporated into my sense of self. I lose myself in others and merge in and out of them, just as they lose themselves and merge in and out of me. This isn't an inherently bad thing; it is how we relate to one another as well as to ourselves, and how we generally feel "connected" to others. This is also the same process by which we become intimate with others in the marriages we cultivate and the friendships we hold dear. Yet, some marriages take us away from our authentic selves while others help us become more genuine. This is what makes relationships potentially rewarding or destructive. How can we know when one relationship furthers our true self and another compromises it? Are we able to tell the difference? This is why the problem that I face as a human being is not, as Husserl argued, how to establish a relationship with others, or whether others even exist (solipsism). I am already so enmeshed with others that my chief problem is one of becoming *my* own person, with *my* perspective, apart from what others, for the most part unwittingly, make me out to be. This is how most marriages find themselves on the rocks. Their relationship often falls in ruins because they tried to change each other into who they wanted them to be instead of accepting each for who they are and embracing that person in his or her fundamental "isness." All too often, they don't even know who they are talking to in their conversations with the other. It turns out that each is in relation with whom he or she imagines the other person is, but not with whom that person sees him- or herself.

So who is this self, my self, that I want the other person to embrace, and in so doing, accept? You have probably gathered by now that this isn't so easy to determine, no doubt why psychoanalytic therapy often takes a long time, why most marriages don't endure. After all, I may not be seeking to become who I am but somebody else. I may adopt a false self that I believe is preferable to who I "really" am and expect my friends or partner or analyst to embrace my impersonation, and pretend the person they embrace is me. Some of them may collude with this fiction, wittingly or unwittingly, but even if I succeed in passing myself off as someone I am not, this accomplishment can never be entirely satisfactory. In such situations, I am anxious of being found out, and eventually I will be, if I let others get close to me. When this happens in therapy I may feel recognized for the first time, or on the contrary, misunderstood. Alternately, I may have a pretty good sense of who I am and what I am about, but feel thwarted in finding relationships that complement the person I am, who accept me without judgment, even love. *The person who has a good sense of who he is and is content with it is typically less anxious in his dealings with others than the person who has something to hide.* The former's sense of self is marked by a kind of fluidity and spontaneity, even playfulness in his or her conduct with others (in the sense that Winnicott alludes to in *Playing and Reality* [1971]). This is a person who has committed him- or herself, not altogether consciously, but spontaneously and instinctively, to a broad range of possibilities that are open to him or her. When one door is closed he chooses another instead of demanding that the one that is locked must yield. He (or she) is flexible in his affairs and can acknowledge his failures and disappointments, without rancor.

Part of the problem in determining who I am authentically is that, when all is said and done, I am no one in particular or, as Heidegger puts it, I am *nothing*, a nullity. Basically, what I am is a person who lives on the cusp of possibilities, projected toward a future that is always on the horizon, never finally catching up with myself until I die, and then it doesn't matter who I am because I am dead, so I never come to know what that would feel like. Unlike Sartre, who claims that choices are always made deliberately and self-consciously, Heidegger argues that we can never get behind our actions and so we are always wondering what we are up to, *after* the fact. This is why psychoanalysis is regressive, not progressive. In order to discover who we are, we have to look back at where we have been, because we can never know precisely where we are going. The possibilities from which I plot the courses I choose in my life are sometimes chosen by me, but for the most part I stumble onto them, by happenstance. At other times I may discover via self-examination that I grew up with certain possibilities, but always in the background are the family I was born into, the schools I attended, the friendships I developed, the music I listened to. Because I am not nor can be a fixed entity that is what it is or what it is constructed to be, my identity can never do more than allude to possible ways of being, always becoming, amidst the temptations, distractions, and logjams that, together, comprise the repertoire of what my life has to work with. This sense of possibility is also what makes me feel alive, but it can just as easily be a source of intolerable anxiety when things don't go my way. Like a roller coaster that may be thrilling one moment and terrifying the next, my life goes along a course that can never be predicted, though I am always hoping that it inclines in a certain direction, the so-called plans I like to pretend I plot my life by. The depressed person has no such sense of possibility and feels dead. Sometimes he makes this feeling real by committing suicide, which is, ironically, a desperate attempt to feel alive, from death to rebirth. The manic person projects himself so far into the future that he gets too far ahead of himself to contain his experiences. This is when he spins off into psychosis. For the most part, we are able to manage the uncertainty of our situation and find ways to plot a course that takes us where we want to go to, with people we want to be with. But what determines the plans that I set for myself, the personality I adopt, and the person I become? Again, it is *no-thing*.

When I choose this path over that one, I kill off and place into abeyance the potential choices I acted against. In every decision I make and action I take, I nullify everything *except* the choice I opt to go with. My ability to turn away from the possibilities I abandon and commit to the ones I opt for is imbued with a sometimes exquisite, sometimes unnerving experience of freedom, without which none of my choices would be possible. The chronically ambivalent neurotic who cannot make decisions or commit to them denies this freedom and, in his or her way, clings to possibilities instead of killing them off. Even his ambivalence is a choice, the one that defines him as indecisive. The psychotic employs a more desperate strategy in order to avoid losing his or her possibilities. Unlike the ambivalent neurotic who sits on the fence or, having made a decision, is unable to wholeheartedly commit to or enjoy, the psychotic "splits" his decisions in two and proceeds to embrace *both*, relinquishing neither. The problem with this strategy is that the split he consigns himself to isn't rooted in reality, but illusion. The cost he pays for this choice is even greater than the neurotic's, but each rejects a crucial element of what makes us authentic, potentially happier, human beings: *the feeling of freedom we come to enjoy when we know that our life is what we make of it.*

Whether we acknowledge it or not, we are making "it" – the life we are living – all the time, every day, in every way, whether we embrace it or pretend that we are not free, but determined. Neurotics and psychotics both deny their freedom, but denying it doesn't make them any less free than the person who champions freedom and celebrates it. The act of becoming neurotic or mad, whether ambivalent or splitting, *are free choices*, because no one can force or coerce us into becoming neurotic or psychotic. Sartre mistakenly assumes that such choices are made deliberately and self-consciously, but for the most part our choices are made unconsciously, which is not to say "unknowingly." That doesn't make us any less responsible for the choices we make, nor does it mean that we can ever be in control of our lives, as though free choice makes us invincible. We are free, but the context in which we render our choices is not chosen, but given to us. This inexorable sense of freedom that we can never escape or control is what Heidegger terms "thrownness." It is a feeling of finding ourselves inserted or thrown into a world we neither created nor chose to be in, saddled with personality traits we don't necessarily want. But those traits are ours, comprising an ensemble of possibilities that make up each person's existence, for better or worse. The totality of our inheritance, traits, dispositions, and inclinations is what Wrathall (2015) terms our "initial disposedness," the milieu from which all our possibilities emerge. This is why Heidegger can say that each person:

> [C]onstantly lags *behind* its possibilities. It is never existent *before* its reason, but rather in each case it is existent only *from* it and as *this* reason. Being a reason accordingly means *never* having power over one's ownmost being from the ground up.
>
> *(cited in Wrathall, 2015, p. 204)*

This initial disposedness is the foundation for the plethora of possibilities from which I choose this over that, the things I discern that I like or dislike, and the singular way that I finally bring all my attention and capabilities to bear in determining who I am and what I will do with my life. What this means is that there are no "reasons" why I am compelled to make this choice instead of that one, nothing that "causes" me to be happy instead of sad, hopeful rather than bereft, schizophrenic or enlightened. Nothing can ultimately explain, for example, why I chose to be a psychoanalyst instead of an architect, a thinker instead of a surfer. There were influences, to be sure, both formative and accidental, but I cannot, nor will I ever be able to, explain *why* I chose the path that I have embarked upon, other than to say I did so freely, which is to say, unpredictably and, as Sartre might add, without excuse. Because there is no justification for my being the person I am, I cannot blame the shortcomings I have or the follies I commit on anyone else. This means there are no reasons *why* I am who I am, no matter how desperately I seek them, however painstakingly I look. When all is said and done, the choices I make, whether consciously or unconsciously, are not determined by me; rather *they* determine who I am.

This concept of freedom helps explain the common error that psychoanalysts often make, searching for the environmental influences that caused their patients to become neurotic or crazy, as though such causes exist in a specifically human, interpersonal context. Though analysts decry the inherent behaviorism practiced by cognitive behavioral therapists as simplistic, the search for unconscious reasons (as opposed to the conscious ones that CBT opts for) is no different. In such seeking analysts assume that one's family shaped the person each of us has become due in part to the "traumas" they inflict upon us. This is a perspective that Winnicott adhered to in his conception of a good-enough mother, which Laing rejected. In one of Freud's more brilliant moments he recognized that all families occasion trauma, because life itself is traumatic. How much so depends on how we experience it.[8] What we call trauma – experiences so painful that we become obsessed with them – is unavoidable. The issue is not how to avoid such traumas, but how to respond to and overcome them, by making them a part of who we are instead of fighting it. If some environments are more toxic than others it still doesn't mitigate the freedom each of us employs in figuring out what strategy to adopt in order to survive this or that toxic experience. Freedom isn't relative; we are free or we are not, but our choices are limited to the situations we find ourselves in. Otherwise freedom would be just another word for omnipotence. Sometimes the best choice we have available is to opt for psychotic disintegration, to get as far away from a painful reality as we can. Clinically speaking, the choices we make cannot be undone. We can't go back to where we were and do it over. Instead we are faced with new choices that we must act on *today*, which will have implications for the choices we make tomorrow, rooted in where we wish to go and who we want to be. No matter how deranged or confused I may be, I cannot *not* make those choices, each and every moment of my life.

One of the surprising consequences of this conception of the self is how it elicits guilt, not in the neurotic but the existential sense. Because there are no reasons why I act the way I do or opt for the choices I make, there is nothing to justify my actions. If, as Merleau-Ponty argues (1962, pp. 434–456), there were reasons for what I do, or compelling forces that coerced me this way or that, I could always say that my reasons, or external forces, "made" me do it, that I wasn't thinking, that I didn't realize what I was doing at the time.[9] Then I wouldn't really be responsible for my actions and I could simply plead ignorance, and so on. But if the being that I am always has a hand in my actions and deliberations, knowingly or not, then my actions are necessarily constituted by the fact that they are *my* actions, and no one else's. We saw in Chapter Six, for example, how psychoanalysts often invoke the concept of transference to argue that if I commit an act "unconsciously" or unknowingly, then I am not responsible for those actions and so am excused of culpability. But this is exactly what the inauthentic person is looking for, a way of blaming his actions on someone else, even his "unconscious," as though his unconscious were an alien force or puppeteer that coerces him, willy-nilly, into doing things *against* his will. What motivates inauthenticity is the desire to avoid the responsibility and consequent anxiety that derive from being answerable to myself and myself alone. The problem with the strategy of inauthenticity is that it also alienates us from ourselves, and the more we excuse our actions by resisting responsibility for them, the more we slide into neurotic guilt and the self-loathing it occasions. The authentic person assumes responsibility for his (or her) actions, conscious or unconscious, and resolutely owns up to who he is. He has no reasons why he acted this way, because *he* is the reason he acts this way or that. He doesn't determine his actions as much as his actions determine him, the person he is.

So what are the benefits of looking at ourselves in this fashion, as human beings who are responsible for our actions, whatever they are, whatever the consequences? For one thing, once I accept that I alone am responsible for who I am, I can stop looking for the justification of my actions in the social norms and standards of behavior that make up the world I live in. I can simply be who I am, and begin to accept myself accordingly: a person who isn't perfect, who makes mistakes and errors in judgment, but hopes to learn from them; a person who possesses (or is possessed by) character traits that are often sources of consternation, but even that can be forgiven. Perhaps most importantly, I can set out to fashion my self-identity, based not predominantly on what others would make of me, but on what I make of myself, based on my dispositions, not theirs. Unlike the *they-self*, which is often comprised of politically correct social norms that are usually arbitrary and often contradictory, the person acting from his or her authentic self will be more stable and consistent in their actions, and will be at one with themselves. That person may even come to love himself, for being who he is. The more we allow our authentic selves to take responsibility for our actions, the more we are able to accept who we are, and overcome the self-loathing that personifies neurotic guilt.

Those who committed themselves to living authentically have usually led unusual lives and often find themselves in opposition to cultural norms. The rise of the counterculture in the 1960s and 1970s in America and Europe was seen by many as an opportunity to live more authentically than was possible in "straight," conventional society.[10] The Beat era ushered in by the hip novelists, Jack Kerouac and Ken Kesey, epitomized many of the qualities that Kierkegaard, Nietzsche, Heidegger, and Sartre advocated.[11] Heidegger was especially drawn to the artistic temperament, arguing that the artists among us are committed to living their truth more authentically than the common person ordinarily dares to. According to Guignon (2004), the artist may have been the first person to concern himself with living his life in an authentic fashion. Some of this tendency probably goes back to the Enlightenment when Rousseau and other Romantics countered Descartes' identification of the self as rational (*cogito ergo sum*) with the notion of a self that is made up of non-rational feeling states, a perspective that became invaluable to artists, poets, and novelists. One of the implications of this argument is that subjective truth has precedence over objective, or scientific, truth, and that the artist is in a more advantageous position to obtain such truths than scientists are. Moreover, the kind of truths available were more open to debate. *Self*-discovery needed to be distinguished from, say, the discovery of new worlds across the oceans. For Rousseau, the most important task a man or woman could set for themselves was to discover who they were, because he recognized that we are opaque to ourselves and can only find ourselves through concerted effort and courage.

One may recognize something of both Nietzsche's and Heidegger's respective debts to the Romantic quest in their own rejection of the Enlightenment's privilege of rationality over more subtle forms of experience. The emergence of the artist as a new authentic figure no doubt influenced both Nietzsche's and Heidegger's identification with art over science. As Guignon (2004) points out, our contemporary notion of the artist as an uncompromising, morally free agent, so dedicated to his (or her) work and inner truth that he refuses to "sell out" for the sake of becoming rich or famous, is a recent phenomenon:

> The modern use of the word "artist" to refer to those engaged in the arts as we understand them first appears in English only in 1823 with the adoption

of the French term, *artiste*. The very idea that there is something that painters and musicians and architects and poets and chefs have in common – something called being an artist – is relatively new in Western experience.

(pp. 70–71)

The distinguishing feature of the so-called genuine artist when contrasted with the pretensions of the commercial variety rests on the idea that only the genuine article is authentic. The work each artist is faithful to contains a truth that is generated from somewhere "within," from an inner core of his or her being that cannot be accessed by skill or training. What makes art original isn't the skill employed in creating it, but rather some indefinable trial of suffering, *angst*, or unique something or other that belongs to this artist alone. By this reckoning, philosophers have not taught the artist how to be authentic; rather the artist has helped *them* learn something about the nature of authenticity in relation to our role in society and our relationship with ourselves.

Sartre was unusual among philosophers because he was also an artist, a highly acclaimed novelist and playwright who was awarded the Nobel Prize for literature. This may explain why his philosophy reads more like a "manifesto" on authenticity than a philosophical treatise, and why his work is so much more accessible than, say, Heidegger's or Kierkegaard's. Though profoundly indebted to Heidegger, Sartre was a unique thinker and drew from many other sources for his ideas. He championed the idea, no doubt borrowed from Nietzsche, of the existential hero who must singularly battle social convention, epitomized by the middle class, or *bourgeois*, sensibilities. Sartre was a radical politically, and so identified with Marxism that he fell out with his close friend and colleague, Maurice Merleau-Ponty, over politics. Sartre even refused to accept his Nobel Prize because he felt it would too closely align him with the West, thereby compromising his independence, claiming he would also refuse the Lenin Prize for literature were it offered to him. This fierce individualism and flair for the unconventional served to make Sartre by far the most famous existentialist philosopher, and many who are drawn to existentialism begin with Sartre, then move on to the more difficult expositors, such as Kierkegaard, Merleau-Ponty, and Heidegger.

This was also what drew Laing to Sartre, who, like me, began reading him in his youth. Though well-steeped in Heidegger, Laing was drawn to Sartre's interest in psychoanalysis and psychological issues generally, in a way that Heidegger was not. This made certain aspects of Sartre's thinking more relevant to Laing's work as a psychiatrist and psychoanalyst. Laing even wrote a book (Laing and Cooper, 1964), with David Cooper, summarizing Sartre's later philosophy, which was lauded by Sartre himself for Laing's "perfect understanding" of his thinking.

Laing was especially drawn to Sartre's version of inauthenticity, *mauvaise foi*, usually translated as bad faith or self-deception, which Sartre characterized as the refusal to take responsibility for oneself as a free agent. Though his take on authenticity was more or less lifted from Heidegger, Sartre was more interested in the nitty-gritty of interpersonal relationships and the commonplace deception among them, a theme elaborated in virtually all of Sartre's novels and plays. But what impressed Laing the most about Sartre was the latter's tenet of the ineluctable free agency that all human beings possess. For Sartre, we engage in self-deception in order to escape our responsibility as free agents, by treating ourselves and others as things. Because freedom is intrinsic to us, Sartre agreed with Laing that "mental illness" is not a medical condition or a product of one's environment, but a strategy to find a way out of an otherwise unlivable situation. No matter how alienated or crazed they become, the neurotic and psychotic alike always exercise a degree of choice. The task of "existential psychoanalysis," as Sartre conceived it, is to explore how the neurotic's *original and subsequent choices* contributed to their current predicaments and conflicts.

Sartre had an undeniable flair for a *Bohemian* lifestyle, hanging out in his favorite Parisian cafe where he wrote his novels and philosophical works, while engaged in intellectual conversations into the early morning with the intelligentsia of Parisian society. Though rich and famous, a rarity among artists, fame and fortune never went to Sartre's head. Sartre lived a modest life and was not remotely materialistic, qualities that impressed Laing enormously. Subsequent to publishing his first book, *The Divided Self*, Laing went on to write seven more books before the end of the decade, all devoted to teasing out the problem of authenticity (and lack thereof) in the psychiatric world. Like Sartre, Laing believed that the values of Western, *bourgeois* society are far too skewed toward consumerism, symptomatic of the blind ambition to fit in with prevailing social values. Laing was convinced that such hypocrisy engenders a form of cynical dishonesty and absence of moral scruples that filter their way into the bedrock of the nuclear family, the melting pot where all of our existential anxiety and madness are cooked up.

Laing's most controversial book, and the one that also made him famous, *The Politics of Experience* (1967), was for all intents and purposes an existential manifesto no less incendiary than Marx's *Communist Manifesto* and Breton's *Surrealistic Manifesto*. *The Politics of Experience* was an indictment against the mores of conventional society that epitomized Heidegger's conception of the anonymous "they," but to nightmarish proportions. Laing told me that both Nietzsche's *Thus Spoke Zarathustra* and Freud's *Civilization and Its Discontents* inspired it, both in style and content. Each took contemporary society to task for morphing into a kind of existential wasteland that makes living authentically highly problematic, if not altogether impossible.

The theme of deceptive practices between self and others was a central theme throughout Laing's writings. He was particularly interested in how being an agent as well as recipient of mystification eats at the heart of who we are. Like Sartre, Laing possessed an uncanny ability to ferret out such practices in the most intimate and seemingly innocent relationships we enjoy, including sexual, familial, marital, and social. All of Laing's early writings were focused on how the individual, whether "normal," schizoid, or schizophrenic, is alienated from himself due to his (or her) existential situation, compounded by mystifying patterns of communication that occasion all of our relationships. Though Laing dropped references to true and false self terminology in his later writings, inauthenticity occupied a key role in virtually all of them. One of his key discoveries in the research he and his colleague, Aaron

Esterson, engaged in at the Tavistock Institute in London was the commonplace acts of deception in all the families of schizophrenics they studied. Laing coined the term, *mystification* to pinpoint how we persuade loved ones to do our bidding, not through argument, *per se*, but by coercing them to see things our way, thus subverting their hold on reality. A child who is wide awake is told she is actually sleepy, and any protests to the contrary are further "proof" that the parent is right. Conflicts are avoided by effectively hypnotizing the people we love into perceiving reality as we see it, by convincing them they see it that way too.

Such ploys are innocent enough, and as Erickson (1981) pointed out, all of us engage in "hypnosis inducing" behavior with one another all the time, whenever we bring our influence to bear over someone we want to do our bidding. If a girlfriend notices me admiring another woman, for example, I may defensively insist she was "only imagining" what she (correctly) saw as a way of avoiding an unpleasant argument. Though such tactics are not liable to drive anyone crazy, Laing suspected that similar acts of mystification perpetrated by a parent against a young and vulnerable child may prove more sinister, and damaging. Laing discovered that many parents are eager to avoid conflicts with their children because the parents are so insecure they are convinced their children will stop loving them should they use their authority to compel their children to do as they say. A teenage daughter tells her mother she wants to pursue a relationship with a boy that her mother dislikes. Instead of the mother straightforwardly exercising her parental authority by saying, "I don't want you to date that boy" (thereby inciting an inevitable conflict with her daughter), she says instead, "I know you don't really want to date that boy, because *if* you did it would break your mother's heart . . . and I know you don't want to break your mother's heart, do you?". By avoiding a conflict between herself and her daughter, the mother effectively projects the implicit conflict between herself and her daughter "into" the daughter, who is now faced with a choice, albeit an impossible one: she can either obey her desire, which is to date this boy, but in so doing imply she does not love her mother, *or she can obey her mother's interpretation of her daughter's "real" desire*: that she is *not* interested in dating this boy, thereby confirming that she indeed loves her mother, as any "good" daughter would.

A more straightforward, and honest, prohibition would have placed the conflict where it belonged, between mother and daughter, in which case the daughter would have had to decide whether she wanted to obey her mother or alternately (perhaps surreptitiously) defy her mother and do as she pleased, as any healthy adolescent would. But because the mother wants to systematically avoid conflicts between herself and her daughter – which is to say, conflicts that will only serve to separate the daughter from her mother by allowing relationships with her peers – she chooses instead, via mystification, to hypnotize her daughter into doubting her own experience, thereby convincing her that she really wants, or doesn't want, what her mother wants her to want. This scheme wouldn't work, Laing admits, unless such tactics are employed regularly and relentlessly throughout the daughter's childhood, beginning in infancy. Laing and Esterson's book (1964) is replete with such examples in all the families they studied.

Laing never claimed, however, as he is often said to have, that mystification *causes* schizophrenia. Laing believed we will never know what causes us to become crazed or happy, mad or sane, but he nonetheless wondered what effect such stratagems may have on the unsuspecting or the gullible. In any case, no one can force another person to be mystified or hypnotized. The hypnotized person must *want* to be, as any hypnotist knows. If the daughter believes that the only way she can prove that she loves her mother is to believe what her mother tells her to believe, she will believe what her mother tells her to. But if the daughter believes that her mother will love her no matter what she does, or if the daughter doesn't care whether her mother believes that she loves her or doesn't, or if the daughter is too clever and un-compliant to be fooled by her mother's ploy, or if her mother lacks sufficient credibility in her daughter's eyes, the daughter will resist her mother's efforts or simply ignore her. Any of these options would serve to keep the daughter's sense of agency intact.

This is an example of how any one person, such as a parent, cannot actually *cause* another person, such as a daughter, to become crazy (in the same manner that a nail can cause a tire to go flat). The child must want, and so *choose* to be mystified (hypnotized) in order to develop the consequent false self that develops. In this context, the goal of therapy becomes one of "waking up" patients from the hypnotic trance that their families, or society at large, have induced in them.

In his efforts to explain what happens when a person falls prey to psychopathology, Freud distinguished between the etiology of neuroses and psychoses. With neurosis, says Freud (1924), there is a split between the id and the ego (i.e., between my impulses and my judgment), whereas with psychosis there is a split between the ego and the world, or reality. In the first the ego is dominant; in the second the id. Freud suggests that neurosis begins when the ego's defenses overpower my desires to the point of stifling my capacity to act on them. With psychosis the ego is unable to restrain the id's – or "my" – desires, so instead my relationship with reality becomes so savaged that I ignore the consequences of where I want my desires to take me, and then act on them anyway by ignoring (via denial) reality. There is no such symmetry in the true and false self equation offered by Laing. If there were, then the true self would be the instigator of psychoses and the false self would be the initiator of neuroses. We know this is not the case. Instead, the false self is responsible for virtually *all* forms of psychopathology, neuroses and psychoses alike. This means that the distinction between neuroses and psychoses is not as categorical as Freud believed, but a matter of degrees. Winnicott remained faithful to Freud's tripartite model of id, ego, and superego in order to explain the etiology of neuroses, reserving the true and false self paradigm to explain psychoses. Laing, like his Scottish compatriot, Fairbairn (1952), rejected the structural model entirely and situated both neuroses and psychoses within the framework of true and false self phenomena, including self-deception, mystification, bad faith, compliance, and all the other instruments of inauthenticity in action.

Laing implied that the journey to madness is initiated when the schizoid person's defenses fail to keep the (true) self vibrant and alive. The inner, or true, self fails to fashion a firm sense of identity, so when the outer (false, social) self collapses under the weight of, say, mystification, the true self re-emerges, this time finally expressing the existential truth about himself, but in a psychotic and incomprehensible manner that no one understands. Freud suspected that psychosis may be a feeble attempt at self-healing, a view that Laing shared, but such efforts may be thwarted by the conventional psychiatric practice of using "medication" and other devices to arrest the process. Whether the tools we alternately opt for are psychotherapy, or just taking a time-out from intolerable alienation, what needs to happen is an opportunity to finally *get to know oneself*, at the deepest, existential level. Not all versions of psychotherapy have this in mind. Cognitive therapies, for example, have as their aim shoring up the false self once more by trying to make it more viable, in tandem with psychopharmacology, which helps render the patient more compliant and susceptible to "hypnosis." (Ironically, the recent addition of "mindfulness" techniques to CBT and DBT are brought to bear to serve the same objective.)

Were the true self to rebel against its self-imposed compliance, the norm today is to simply crush the true self by empowering the (false) self into an even more compliant shell to act from, one that is representative of society's picture of normality. Laing's question, "Who is more crazy: the madman attempting to reclaim his lost freedom, or the society determined to crush him?", is apt. In a perfect world we are afforded the time and place to take a break, in order to nurture the true, authentic self into being, with the help of family, friends, and therapists committed to this endeavor.

If overcoming the dominance of our false, social, inauthentic selves (by devising a way of having it serve us rather than us serving it) is the way to a more authentic manner of living, then how does becoming more authentic put us on the road to sanity? How are authenticity and sanity related, even in an approximate way? After all, becoming mad may have been a more "sane" act than when dominated by a socially acceptable, compliant, but inherently false self, as Laing himself observed. Obviously, everything hangs on what one understands by the word *sanity*. We saw earlier that sanity implies honesty, sincerity, morally good and sound judgment. Everything rests on our capacity for judgment, because judgment alone allows us to know what is going on, in ourselves and in the world. If resorting to subterfuge, self-deception, and compliance compromises my capacity for sanity, then the truer I can be to myself, the saner I will be. I cannot judge what is the case if I am locked in a constant battle with myself, if I cannot or will not be honest with myself. Honesty and sanity are not synonymous, but they are mutually interdependent, and complementary.

Yet the tension between authentic and inauthentic modes of existing is constant. My relation with myself and my relation with others are never-ending efforts to find the right balance between what is optimal for myself and what is acceptable to others. When I get this balance right, both my self and my relationships are in harmony and flourish, in Aristotle's sense of the term. I am happy and all is well in the world. But for most people, this is seldom the case. For some it never is. They try to comply with what is expected, become hopelessly alienated from themselves, or they rebel against such compliance in ways that are not fortuitous, but self-destructive, futile, self-defeating. The so-called chronically "mentally ill" person, whether living on the street, in and out of treatment facilities, or resigned to a life on psychotropic medications that render him or her senseless, defeated, and alienated, is a problem of enormous scope in contemporary society. As a society, we simply don't know what to do about all the crazy people in our midst (and in ourselves), other than to segregate them, drug them, demean and condemn their mad ways. We say they frighten us, but what are we actually afraid of: the madness in the person deemed crazy, or the madness in us?

Throughout history (as we saw in Chapter One) the world has been intolerant of madness. There have been pockets of compassion, benevolence, and understanding here and there, now and then, but for the most part we have failed to understand it and accept it as an ever-present aspect of every one of us. I have argued throughout this book that madness is a perfectly ordinary component of what it means to be human. As Nietzsche observed, we acknowledge and celebrate the irrational in art, inebriation, and dance, but we aren't certain how much to permit, or what forms of madness we should advocate and which to avoid. When we look at the world today, it is impossible to deny that madness is everywhere. We find it in our penchant to kill or imprison those whose religions we do not share, whose intoxicants we condemn. In America, eighty percent of all the prison inmates (America has more convicts than any nation in the world) are there due to drug-related charges. We're talking about the drugs our society does *not* allow, because they are alleged to be more damaging than the ones we legitimize and administer to those who don't want them.

This kind of logic, a kind of madness in itself, is more insidious and pervasive than anything the so-called schizophrenic or street person could ever be accused of. We don't know if it has always been this way. We know it is now. I can't help but conclude that the crux of the problem is one of intolerance, *an intolerance we harbor toward anyone we perceive to be different from ourselves.* No one is more different from "us" than the person we label schizophrenic, our code word for anyone whose madness we have decided is beyond the pale. The only way of fixing this problem is to reverse it, by becoming more tolerant, more forgiving of those whose behavior and alleged state of mind we fear or have little sympathy for. This would amount to approaching the problem from a saner perspective.

If we insist on equating sanity with normality, or rationality, then our situation is hopeless. That is what we have been doing, and look where that has got us? We don't know why some of us are more insane than others, why some people get better and some people do not. But when you think about it, there isn't a person you know, including yourself, who doesn't fall prey to moments of madness, irrationality, or mania, now and then. For the most part we get away with it, because we are sufficiently strong and resourceful enough to recover, by healing the rift we fell prey to. Those who get treated by psychiatry, however, often lack such resources. They need help. When rallying to help them, whom are we trying to protect: the person so diagnosed, or the neighbor who simply wants the problem to go away? Yet intolerance is not exclusive to those who have the keys to the mental ward. We also meet intolerance among those who are stark raving mad. This is why, in the final analysis, living more authentically, which is to say, more astutely and responsibly, doesn't necessarily hang on whether I am crazy or sane. So what does it hang on?

Because we are all, to relative degrees, nut cases, there must be another standard that determines the difference between the person who is coping and the person who is not. Some people, including those that get diagnosed schizophrenic, are able to manage within their limits. Others don't. The person who does is able and no doubt willing to take responsibility for his craziness, his paranoid tendencies, his intolerance of anxiety, his manic episodes, his flirtation with omnipotence and grandiosity. This person more or less deals with the demands that society decrees, effectively and authentically. *The wherewithal to assume responsibility for the person one happens to be depicts a more authentic, and saner, way of being in the world.* The inauthentic person eschews this responsibility and blames his or her condition on others, no matter how crazy or sane that person is. Judgment, the benchmark for sanity, may be impaired, but not so compromised that we cannot locate and accept the responsibility we have to ourselves, and to others. The reason many people fear madness has something to do with the madness that lurks within. Others fear madness because of those who refuse to take responsibility for it, who won't take the bull by the horns and do something about it. Perhaps they embrace being crazy more than they like feeling sane? Maybe their suffering is simply too great, or the world is too scary to find a home in it? When that is the case they're liable to check out, for some intermittently, for others permanently.

A small fraction of these people take their anguish out on others. I'm referring to the few members of society who become a menace to others, who pose a threat and are capable of violence. Yet, far greater numbers of those who do pose a threat are allegedly saner than those who are crazy. We often have a hard time recognizing the madness that is staring us in the face. Who is crazier, the religious fanatic who murders innocents out of hatred, or the pilot in an airplane who kills himself and everyone else in it? The Mafiosi who murders for profit, or the general who sees enemies everywhere he looks? Some acts of violence are cold and calculated, others are desperate and nonsensical. Why do we fear the nonsensical, and why are we less tolerant of it than acts of violence we understand, and perhaps champion? Who is the judge in these matters, and how sound are those judgments being rendered? Who are we, or you, or I, to say?

If being more authentic means being truer to and more honest with yourself, by fessing up to and owning yourself, laying claim to who you are and what you stand for, then becoming more authentic will probably, even likely, result in more sanity. Though I can't find an etymological link to it, I like to think that sanity also suggests a greater sense of *serenity*, of being at peace with oneself and the world. This condition would appear to be the exact opposite of madness, and of violence. The Greeks called this form of serenity *ataraxia*,[12] the absence of havoc and a state of unperturbedness in the face of chaos and strife. Ironically, they characterized seren-ity as what follows when we have managed to *free* ourselves from judgment, not a consequence of it. Perhaps this leads to even deeper reservoirs of authenticity, by resisting the need to render judgment from places of intolerance, while pretending to know what we will never understand, including the parameters of madness. Perhaps this is what it means to be sane?

Notes

1 See Adam Phillips (2005), for an engaging treatment of how sparse the literature on sanity has been historically.
2 As far as I can tell, sanity is not a concept that Buddhism explicitly addresses. Its closest etymological connection to the Latin *sanus* (good health) and the Greek *iaino* (I heal) is the Sanskrit *isanyati*, meaning "he progresses." In its encounter with Western psychology, however, some Buddhists, such as Chogyam Trungpa, began to integrate Buddhist precepts into psychological concepts. Trungpa was especially intrigued with the many Western psychotherapists, such as R. D. Laing (who became close friends with Trungpa), who integrated Buddhist thinking into their work. In turn, Trungpa became fascinated with the Western psychotherapy tradition and began training psychotherapists himself. At this time he began to incorporate Western terms, such as "sanity," into his discourse, consistent with the Buddhist notion of enlightenment. See Trungpa's *The Sanity We Are Born With* (2005) for his views on Buddhist-inspired psychotherapy. See also Podvoll (2003).
3 Freud didn't actually designate his three agencies that comprise the structural model of the unconscious in Latin. This was a modification introduced by James Strachey when translating Freud's works from German into English. Instead, Freud used the colloquial German term *Es* which, when translated into English, becomes the everyday word, "it." In turn, he employed the German term *Ich* for the word "I" in English, and the German *Übermensch* for what should translate into English as "over-I." Strachey felt that translating the colloquial German terms employed by Freud into English would not sound sufficiently scientific to the English-speaking ear, so he chose their Latin equivalents instead. The "it" became Id, the "I" became Ego, and the "over-I" became Superego (in German, the word *Über* can mean either "over" or "super" in English; Nietzsche's employment of this term is usually translated into English as Superman rather than Overman). Although Freud's conception of the unconscious is more or less impersonal, it was never his intention to render these terms as impersonally as Strachey's translation suggests. Strachey exercised this option with other German terms that he found similarly problematic, resulting in more Latinizations such as *cathect* instead of invest, *cathexis* instead of investment, and so on.
4 See Laing and Esterson (1964), an extensive case study of families of schizophrenics conducted by them at the Tavistock Institute in the early 1960s, for more on how family dynamics may result in the development of a false self. See also Laing (1965), and Thompson (1996) for more on Laing's conception of mystification in relation to false self phenomena.
5 Note that Laing includes references to each of the books cited in this quotation, which I have omitted. As this book was written in 1960, several of the books cited were not at that time translated into English; for the most part they are now currently available in translation. For the citations omitted, see Laing (1960, p. 94).
6 The term Heidegger employs that is customarily translated into English as authenticity is not the German *Authentizitat*, but rather the term *Eigentlichkeit*, which literally means real, actual, or genuine. Heidegger, however, seizes on the adjective *eigen*, which means "own," to embody his unique interpretation of what authenticity properly entails. Hence, an even more literal translation of the German *Eigentlichkeit* would be something like *own-ness* or *owned-ness*. For Heidegger, the authentic person owns up to who he is and acts from that place of his own-most possibilities. Though this term is not the most common

one employed in German for this purpose, it is commonly accepted that this is the term Heidegger adopted for its English equivalent.

7 Freud believed that all of us aspire to feel "at one" with others throughout the course of our lives, and that this longing characterizes a quest for love that is impossible to fulfill, except in fleeting moments, as when falling in love. Freud believed this quest is rooted in an illusion, the wish to return to that experience, as infants, when suckling at the mother's breast (which we examined in Chapters Three, Five, and Seven). Freud implied that the goal of therapy is to disengage ourselves from such illusions and accept relationships for what they are: disappointing and complicated.

8 For more on the role of experience in the etiology of self-development, see Laing (1967, pp. 3–25), Thompson (2000a).

9 This is why Heidegger refused to apologize after the war for having been a Nazi. Nothing "made" him do it. He thought, at the time, that it was the right choice to make. Later he recognized that his brief collaboration with National Socialism was not an authentic choice, but inauthentic. He could no more apologize for the latter than he could for the former. The choice was his and he alone could take responsibility for it.

10 The person who was straight followed conventional norms; the person who was "cool" did not. The person who was straight wasn't interested in transformative experiences; the person who was cool was committed to them. And so on.

11 The tendency today to condemn the beat and hippy eras of the '60s and '70s due to their ultimate demise speaks to our tendency to decry any advocacy for independence of spirit and freedom of action. Freud's *Civilization and Its Discontents* (1930) as well as Laing's *The Politics of Experience* (1967) were intended to explain how society's principal function is to repress such instincts.

12 For more on *ataraxia*, or serenity, see Thompson (2000b, 2004).

References

Erickson, M. (1981) *Experiencing hypnosis: Therapeutic approaches to altered states*. New York: Irvington Publishers.

Fairbairn, W. R. (1952) *Psychoanalytic studies of the personality*. London: Routledge and Kegan Paul.

Freud, S. (1953–1973) *The standard edition of the complete psychological works of Sigmund Freud*. 24 volumes. Edited and translated by J. Strachey. London: Hogarth Press. (Referred to in subsequent references as *Standard Edition*.)

Freud, S. (1924) The loss of reality in neurosis and psychosis. *Standard Edition*, 19:173–182. London: The Hogarth Press, 1961.

Freud, S. (1930) *Civilization and its discontents*. *Standard Edition*, 21:59–145. London: The Hogarth Press, 1961.

Guignon, C. (2004) *Being authentic*. London and New York: Routledge.

Heidegger, M. (1962/1927) *Being and time*. Translated by J. Macquarrie and E. Robinson. New York: Harper and Row.

Heidegger, M. (1979/1961) *Nietzsche: Volume I, The will to power as art*. Translated by D. Krell. New York and London: Harper and Row, Publishers.

Heidegger, M. (1982/1961) *Nietzsche: Volume IV, Nihilism*. Translated by F. Capuzzi. New York and London: Harper and Row, Publishers.

Heidegger, M. (1984/1961) *Nietzsche: Volume II, The eternal recurrence of the same*. Translated by D. Krell. New York and London: Harper and Row, Publishers.

Heidegger, M. (1987/1961) *Nietzsche: Volume III, The will to power as knowledge and metaphysics*. Translated by J. Stambaugh, D. Krell, and F. Capuzzi. New York and London: Harper and Row, Publishers.

Kierkegaard, S. (1956) *Purity of heart is to will one thing.* Translated by Douglas Steere. New York: Harper Torchbooks.

Kierkegaard, S. (1980) *The sickness unto death: A Christian psychological exposition for upbuilding and awakening.* Edited and translated by H. Hong and E. Hong. Princeton, NJ: Princeton University Press.

Laing, R. D. (1960[1969]) *The divided self.* New York and London: Penguin Books.

Laing, R. D. (1965) Mystification, confusion, and conflict. In *Intensive family therapy: Theoretical and practical aspects* (pp. 343– 365) (Eds., I. Boszormenyi-Nagy and J. Framo). New York and London: Harper and Row, 1965.

Laing, R. D. (1967) *The politics of experience.* New York: Pantheon Books.

Laing, R. D. and Cooper, D. G. (1964) *Reason and violence: A decade of Sartre's philosophy 1950–1960.* London: Tavistock Publications.

Laing, R. D. and Esterson, A. (1964/1971) *Sanity, madness, and the family: Families of schizophrenics.* (2nd ed.). New York: Basic Books.

Merleau-Ponty, M. (1962) *Phenomenology of perception.* Translated by C. Smith. London: Routledge and Kegan Paul.

Nietzsche, F. (2002) *Beyond good and evil.* Translated by Judith Norman. Cambridge: Cambridge University Press.

Nietzsche, F. (2003) *Writing from the late notebooks.* Translated by K. Sturge. Cambridge: Cambridge University Press.

Nietzsche, F. (2006) *Thus spoke Zarathustra: A book for all and none.* (Adrian del Caro and Robert B. Pippin, Eds.) Translated by Adrian del Caro. Cambridge: Cambridge University Press.

Partridge, E. (1966) *Origins: A short etymological dictionary of modern English.* (4th ed.). London: Routledge and Kegan Paul.

Phillips, A. (2005) *Going sane.* New York and London: Harper Perennial.

Podvoll, E. (2003) *Recovering sanity: A compassionate approach to understanding and treating psychosis.* Boston and London: Shambhala Publications.

Thompson, M. Guy (1996) Deception, mystification, trauma: Laing and Freud. *The Psychoanalytic Review,* Vol. 83, No. 6:827–847.

Thompson, M. Guy (2000a) The crisis of experience in contemporary psychoanalysis. *Contemporary Psychoanalysis,* Vol. 36, No. 1:29–56.

Thompson, M. Guy (2000b) The sceptic dimension to psychoanalysis: Toward an ethic of experience. *Contemporary Psychoanalysis,* Vol. 36, No. 3:457–481.

Thompson, M. Guy (2004) Happiness and chance: A reappraisal of the psychoanalytic conception of suffering. *Psychoanalytic Psychology,* Vol. 21, No. 1:134–153.

Trungpa, C. (2005) *The sanity we are born with: A Buddhist approach to psychotherapy.* Boston and London: Shambhala Publications.

Winnicott, D. W. (1960) Ego distortion in terms of true and false self. In *The maturational processes and the facilitating environment: Studies in the theory of emotional development* (pp. 140–152). London: The Hogarth Press, 1976.

Winnicott, D. W. (1971) *Playing and reality.* London: Tavistock Publications.

Wrathall, M. (2015) Autonomy, authenticity, and the self. In *Heidegger, authenticity and the self: Themes from division two of* Being and Time (Ed., D. McManus) (pp. 193–214). London and New York: Routledge, 2015.

CONCLUDING POSTSCRIPT

At the end of the day, what *is* sanity? What *is* madness? These are the overarching questions that have guided this study. I am the first to admit that I have not answered them as satisfactorily as I would have liked. There are certain terms, seminal to be sure, that encapsulate our navigation of everyday reality, yet resist definition. Love, for example. How can one possibly define this term? All the more reason to think about it, discuss it, debate its gifts as well as its folly. That is what I have been attempting throughout this enquiry. I have taken you on a journey with me as we set about to ponder the meaning of sanity, madness, desire, mental distress, emotional jeopardy, resentment, jealousy, psychopathology. Sometimes, perhaps more often than we suppose, we must sneak up on a topic, via indirection, and follow whatever trajectory our minds lure us to. I hope you have enjoyed this journey as much as I have. It has been gratifying to discover that though I know less than I supposed, my curiosity has only increased.

I have tried to show that if we hope to get to the bottom of what sanity is, and what madness is, and what the kind of suffering that brings people to psychiatrists, psychologists, psychoanalysts, psychotherapists, and other mental health professionals is about, then we must come to terms with the basic drives, intentions, and motivations that guide us daily. In a word, we must come to terms with our desires and our ambiguous relationship with them. Because I view human beings as essentially the ensemble of their desires, I see madness in all its variety and permutations as the deadening or perversion of those desires. I have tried to show that sanity, in all its mystery and artifice, is only accessible to us the degree to which we are able to reconcile ourselves to our desires, and accept them.

A great deal of this book was devoted to determining what psychopathology, or madness, means, properly speaking, from a profoundly personal and human perspective. Other portions of the book were devoted to sanity. I don't believe that madness, neurosis, psychosis, is simply a consequence of our genetic code, but a manner of adapting to a world that is not of our choosing, a world where we are obliged to make ourselves at home, or perish. This is why our desires hold the key to understanding who we are, and what we are about. Because our desires make us vulnerable, they occasion the anxieties that hold us in their grip. I have tried to show that the burden of our desires and our attempts to find love through them account for our willingness to suppress those desires and even resent them.

I have also tried to show why every relationship we encounter, however fleeting or profound, will confront us with yet more opportunities to realize our desires or vanquish them. This is why the psychotherapy relationship is so loaded, and necessarily volatile. We therapists hold those who seek our help at our mercy. We had better be careful how we treat them, if we don't want to make matters worse. At the end of the day, our patients come to us for love, even when they hardly suspect this. If we are ever even partially successful in helping them, it is because love is what we give them, and all the sympathy and understanding that entails.

This book has also been a personal journey for me. In the first edition of this book, published thirty years ago, I left me out of it. This time I have tried to bring me into the picture. This book is a study, to be sure, but it is also a chronicle of my journey, undertaken some forty years ago, to find myself. I have Ronnie Laing, and Hugh Crawford, and all the fellow travelers I encountered there, to thank for the degree to which I did find myself, and re-found myself, again and again. Whoever you are, and for whatever reason you were prompted to read this book, I hope you have found it of value. Wherever you go, whatever sources of happiness you seek, I wish you a safe and electrifying journey.

INDEX

abstinence 131, 140n5
addicts, use of term 5
adolescence, and finding object of love 145, 146
affect, use of term 45
agapé (selfless love) 151, 152, 164–5
agitation 13, 14, 16
aim-inhibited love (Freud) 134, 137, 144, 151, 152
Alcoholics Anonymous (AA) 163
alienation 16, 56–7, 103–4, 178, 184
Alzheimer's disease 4
ambivalence 27–8, 56, 60–2, 73, 187
ambiverts 8
"Analysis Terminable and Interminable" (Freud) 34
analytic neutrality, defined 124–5; *see also* Freud, Sigmund
anger 57–9
anguish, origin of term 59
anti-psychiatry 1–2, 3, 9, 19n1
anxiety: and defense mechanisms 13, 14, 20n5, 47, 73; Kierkegaard on 22; neurotic 26–7, 43n4, 56; origin of term 59; due to repression 25–6; and somatic symptoms 78–9; as state of distress 74–5; types of 8; *see also* hysteria; mania
aphrodisiacs 163
Archway Community, London 103, 104, 119n2
Aristotle 23, 133, 151, 152, 195
artist, origin of term 190–1

artistic temperament 161–2, 172n7, 190–1, 196
asceticism 23
Asylum (documentary) 99–100, 119n2
atarxia 197
Augustine, Saint 133, 141n7
Austen Riggs, London 115
Ayahuasca 160, 163

behaviorism 48, 188
Being and Time (Heidegger) 182–3
being oneself *see* personal relationships with patients, and transference
benign neglect 114–15
Bergmann, M. 144, 147
Bethlem Royal Hospital, London 12
Beyond Good and Evil (Nietzsche) 49, 52
Binswanger, Ludwig xi, 167
Bion, W. R. 168, 172n12
bipolar disorder 3, 15, 89–90
bisexuality, Freud on 147
Blake, William 105
blaming others 65–6, 85, 197
Boss, Medard xi
Brenner, Charles 30
British Middle Group 82, 83
British Psychoanalytic Society 177
Buddhism: as complement to therapy 18–19; on desire 12, 23, 155; on life as suffering 74; on nonvirtue of privacy 104; on wisdom as related to sanity 174, 176, 198n2

"Building, Dwelling, Thinking" (Heidegger) 117

candor *see* honesty/candor, importance of
Canstatt, Karl Friedrich 81
caritas (charity) 152, 164–5, 166, 167–9, 171
castration anxiety (Freud) 78
"The Catalytic Role of Crucial Friendship in the Epistemology of Self-Experience" (Khan) 132
character, use of term 139–40
Charcot, Jean-Martin 33, 77
Chertok, L. 126
Chestnut Lodge, London 115
children, play therapy for 75
Christianity 154; belief in evil spirits 12; influence on Kierkegaard 166, 180–1; influence on Laing 166; influence on Scheler 56, 57; Jesus and prophetic madness 160; Nietzsche on 53, 55; *see also agapé* (selfless love); *caritas* (charity)
Civilization and Its Discontents (Freud) 184, 192
cognitive therapies 122, 125, 188, 195
compulsive behavior 75; *see also* obsessional neurotics
Confessions (Augustine) 133
confusion, state of 83, 85–7
Cooper, David 19n1, 100, 191
coping strategies (Haley) 29
Crawford, Hugh 162; comparison to Laing 104–5; as facilitator of Portland Road residence 100–1, 102, 104–5, 107–8, 109, 110, 111, 113, 114, 115, 117, 119n1; on Freud xi; periods at Welch farm of 111–12, 118
crazy, use of term 13; *see also* sanity and madness
crucial friendship (Khan) 135, 137, 171
cultural variance, in interpretation of sanity/madness 16, 17

daemon spirits 149–50, 152, 172n6
Dalí, Salvador 91, 161
De Anima (Aristotle) 23
deception: existentialist philosophers on 84; within family studies by Laing and Esterson 86–7, 192–3; Laing on 17, 85, 86–7, 179
defense mechanisms: and emotions 47; Laing on xi; for mitigation of anxiety 13, 14, 20n5, 47, 73; and sanity 16, 34
dementia 3
democracy, Nietzsche on 53–4

depression 34, 93–5, 187; *see also* suicidal depression
depressive position (Klein) 50
de Saussure, R. 126
Descartes, René 190
desire 21–44; and ambivalence 27–8; Buddhism on 12, 23, 155; and capacity for love 30, 36–42, 43n6, 43n8; distinguished from wishing 21–2, 38–9; Freud on *Libido* xii, xiv, 21–2, 36–7; Freud on third "magical" choice scenario 28–9, 47–8, 60–1, 73; and gratification delay 26–7; Hegel on xiv–xv; letting desires *be* 39–42; and mental anguish xii; as open wound 39; psychosis and inversion of 60–2; repression of 25–6, 36, 60; and self-deception 31–2; and self-inflicted symptoms 25–6, 28–9; Western philosophical views on 22–3; *see also* love and madness; Oedipus complex (Freud); resentment, and symptom formation
despots, power of 85, 86
Diagnostic and Statistical Manual (DSM) 3, 4, 87–8, 90–1
Dick (patient) 57–9
Diotima 149–51
The Divided Self (Laing) 2–3, 6, 7, 10, 14, 84, 88, 96n12, 109, 176–80
Dodds, E. R. 160–1
Don Juan Complex (Rank) 42
double-mindedness (Kierkegaard) xii, 93, 166, 179
Do You Love Me? (Laing) 161
dreams and dreaming: delusions/hallucinations in 4; Freud on 21–2, 38, 83; interpretation of 38; shared between roommates 111
drugs: abuse of 159; recreational 5, 172n9; use in personal transformation experiences 101, 102, 162–3, 172n9; and US prison population 196; *see also* medication
dual instinct theory (Freud) 149, 172n5
dwelling (Heidegger) 117
"The Dynamics of Transference" (Freud) 30–1

educational metaphor 18
"Ego Distortion in Terms of True and False Self" (Winnicott) 177
electro-convulsive therapy (ECT) 108
Ellis, Havelock 146
Elvis (Portland Road resident) 111
emotional, use of term ix–x

emotions: function of 47; impact on judgment 164; origin of term 45; as regulated by ego 149; *see also individual emotions*

empathy: distinguished from sympathy 165–6, 169; in therapeutic relationships 7, 16–17

engulfment 8–9

envy, distinguished from jealousy 50–2

Epicurean model 12, 23

Erickson, Erik 193

Eros (Plato) 149–51, 152–4, 156, 160, 164

erotic love 144, 167, 170, 171

Essais (Montaigne) 133

Esterson, Aaron 85–6, 100, 192–3

The Ethic of Honesty (Thompson) xi

existential factor 63

existentialists vs. analysts x–xii, xiv–xv, 7, 71–2

existential situations, as content of therapy sessions 7, 9, 34–5

extroverts vs. introverts 7–8

Fairbairn, W. R. 10–11, 194

"The False-Self System" (Laing) 179–80

femme fatale, in film noir 46–7

Ferenczi, Sándor 122–3, 128, 131

fibromyalgia 79

forced treatment 5–7, 13; *see also* mental hospitals

Foucault, Michel 11–13, 167

The Four Loves (Lewis) 152

Freud, Sigmund: ability to appreciate ambiguity 74; aim-inhibited love 134, 137, 144, 151, 152; analytic neutrality of 43n1, 70–2, 114, 134–5, 141n8; avoidance of standards for technical principles 130; on character 139–40; on constitutional factor 63; on counter-will (*Gegenwille*) 125–6; creates psychiatric interview format 70–1; on death drive 56; on desire (*libido*) xii, xiv, 21–2, 36–7; development of psychotherapy 73–4, 77–81, 96n9; displacement of erotic motive 151; on dreams and dreaming 21–2, 38, 83; dual instinct theory 149, 172n5; on ego-dystonic/ego-syntonic symptoms 79; on establishment of sexual orientation 145, 146–7; as existentialist xi–xii, 10; on finding object of love 144–9, 157, 158–9; friendship with Fliess 135–7; importance of honesty 43n1, 102, 139–40; Laing on behavioristic interpretations of xv–xvi; and medical model 17–18; on megalomania 146–7; narcissism theory 60–1, 146–7, 150–1; on neurosis xi, 24, 62–3, 77–8, 194; on neurosis as part of human condition 10, 34, 80–1; Nirvana Complex 23; Pleasure Principle 23, 43n11; on psychosis xi, 43n12, 60–1, 81, 83, 194, 195; on pursuit of happiness 34, 43n11, 64; Rat Man (patient) 34, 43n5, 56; on role of love in therapy relationship 24, 30–3, 43n1, 64, 137, 171; on sexual perversions 35–6; on sublimation 36, 151; on therapeutic ambition 169, 172n12; third "magical" choice scenario 28–9, 47–8, 60–1, 73; trains lay analysts 95n2; on transference 30–1, 124, 125–6, 128, 131, 132, 139–40; on unconscious 37, 72; on untrustworthiness of language 183–4; viewed as anti-psychiatrist 9, 71; on wish fulfillment 21–2, 38–9; Wolf Man (patient) 34, 56, 111; work with hysteria patients 32–4, 71, 77–80, 90; work with obsessional neurotics 33–4, 43n5, 80, 160; *see also* id/ego/superego (Freud); Oedipus complex (Freud); *individual writings of*

friendship: Aristotle on 133; Freud on 137; Khan on 135–6; loss of judgment amidst 163; Montaigne on 133–5, 136; *philia* (love of family/friend) 151–2, 165, 171; and sympathy 170; *see also* personal relationships with patients, and transference

Fromm-Reichmann, Frieda 10–11, 35, 118

frustration: during childhood 26–7; endurance of 72–3, 137; in neurosis/psychosis 81; *see also* resentment, and symptom formation

genetics 16

Golden Rule 17

"good-enough" mother theory (Winnicott) 82–5, 188

gratification delay 26–7

Great Britain, licensure in 18

Greene, Graham 32

Greenson, Ralph 128

Grof, Stanislav 172n9

Group Psychology and the Analysis of the Ego (journal) 137

Guignon, C. 190–1

guilt *see* neurotic guilt

Haley, Jay 29

happiness, xii, 15, 34, 43, 47, 57, 60–66, 70, 85, 93, 99, 133, 144–155, 162, 172, 174

hatred: origin of term 59–60; and
    resentment 55–60
Haynal, A. 123
health, origin of term 174, 175
Heaton, John 100
Hegel, G.W.F. xiv–xv, 39, 55, 85
Heidegger, Martin 191; on authenticity
    181–2, 190, 198n6; on dwelling 117; on
    fear of non-existence 78; on language as
    given 162; on love/caring 167–9; on self
    as evolving identities/nothing 181–3, 186;
    on *Sorge* 167–8, 170; on they-self and
    groups 184–5, 190, 192; on thrownness
    188; *see also individual writings of*
Hemingway, Ernest 14
Hinduism: and desire 23; sane/sanity, origin
    of terms 176
Hippocrates 12
Hippocratic oath 17
Hoffman, I. 123–4, 125
homelessness 117–18
home offices 122
Homer 53
honesty/candor, importance of 11, 74,
    102–3, 139–40, 176, 195; *see also* true/
    false self concepts
hospital, origin of term 115, 119n4
Hubbard, L. Ron 158, 160
hubris (condition of excess) 153–5, 162
Hume, David 23
Husserl, Edmund 185
Huxley, Aldous 166
Huxley, Francis 100
hypomania 90–1, 93, 94; *see also* mania
hysteria: Freud's work with patients 32–4,
    71, 77–80, 90; origin of term 33, 77; and
    somatic symptoms 78–9

"I," use of term 183–4
id/ego/superego (Freud) 23, 56–7, 81, 83,
    96n11, 126, 154, 177–8, 194, 198n3
The Iliad (Homer) 53
implosion 8
initial disposedness (Wrathall) 188
insatiability of human beings 9–10, 22, 150
Instincts and Their Vicissitudes (Freud) 149
The Interpretation of Dreams (Freud) 38

Jack (patient) 40–1
Janet, Pierre 33
Jason (Portland Road resident) 102
Jaspers, Karl 33, 70, 71
jealousy: distinguished from envy 50–2;
    leading to resentment 57; as motive

for murder 159; and Oedipus complex
    49–50, 159; and psychosis 50, 51
Jerome (Portland Road resident) 108–19,
    154, 170
Jesus *see* Christianity
Jones, Jim 158
judgment, use of: and manic episodes
    156–8; and sanity 13–16, 163–4, 176,
    197–8
Jung, Carl 35

Kafka, Franz 91
Keats, John 114
Kerouac, Jack 190
Kesey, Ken 190
Khan, Masud 132, 135–6, 138
Kierkegaard, Søren 190, 191; on anxiety
    22, 78; influence of Christianity
    on 166, 180–1; influence on Laing
    84; on integrity and authenticity
    180–2; on *ressentiment* 49; *see also* double-
    mindedness (Kierkegaard); *individual
    writings of*
Kingsley Hall, London 2, 99–100, 103,
    115, 116, 117, 162; *see also* madness and
    unconditional acceptance, Portland Road
Klein, Melanie 35, 50–2, 65, 83, 149, 177
Knots (Laing) 161
Kojeve, Alexandre 39
Kraepelin, E. 81

La Boétie, Etienne de 132–3, 135, 136
Lacan, Jacques xv–xvi, 36, 39, 52, 149, 183
Laing, R. D.: on behavioristic interpretations
    of Freud xv–xvi; on broken heartedness
    31, 64, 83–4; comparison to Crawford
    104–5; comparison to Szasz 2; on
    deception 17, 85, 86–7, 179, 192–3; on
    defense mechanisms xi; depression of
    95; on diagnosis of mental disorders 4, 7;
    false self concept 176–80, 183; on Golden
    Rule 17; influence of Kierkegaard on 84;
    influence of Marx on 85; influence of
    religions on 166–7; influence of Sartre
    on 84, 86, 191–2; influence on author xi,
    xii, 99–100, 101; influence on Nietzsche
    on 84; journey through madness with
    91–2; loss of writing Muse 161–2; on
    mystification 85–7, 179, 192–5; on
    ontological security/insecurity 7–8,
    14; personality of 103; on psychiatry 1,
    2–4; quotations of 1; rejects Winnicott's
    "good-enough" mother theory 188;
    on relationship with patients 10–11;

on schizophrenia 1–3, 7, 8–9, 13, 81, 83–7; therapy, use of term 74; on trespass concept and violence by authority figures 166–7; true/false self concepts 176–80, 183, 194; on untying of knots approach 119; on use of diagnostic manuals 3; use of Sandoz acid in therapy 162, 172*n*9; work with psychotic patients 35; writings on authenticity 192; *see also* Kingsley Hall, London; madness and unconditional acceptance, Portland Road; *individual writings of*
Last Chance Clinic Helps Those In Need (article) 115–16
Lawrence, D. H. 162
Lear, Jonathan 30
Leary, Timothy 172*n*9
Lester, Muriel 100
Lewis, C. S. 152
Libido (Freud) xii, xiv, 21–2, 36–7
life coaching 18
Lithium 91
Losey, Joseph 55
loss and mourning 94–5
love, healing power of *see* love and madness; madness and unconditional acceptance, Portland Road
love, in therapy relationship (Freud) 24, 30–3, 43*n*1, 64, 137, 171; *see also* personal relationships with patients, and transference
love and madness 143–73; *agapé* (selfless love) 151, 152, 164–5; *caritas* (charity) 152, 164–5, 166, 167–9, 171; and divine madness 153–4, 160–2; falling in love and merger with ego ideal 148, 154, 155, 156–9; Freud on finding object of love 144–9, 157, 158–9; Freud's narcissism theory 60–1, 146–7, 150–1; Heidegger on love/caring 167–9; *hubris* (condition of excess) 153–5, 162; love/caring for patient by therapist 169–70; obsession with lost love 159–60; *philia* (love of family/ friend) 151–2, 165, 171; Plato's birth fable of *Eros* 149–51, 152–4, 156, 160, 164; and possession 143, 152, 154, 155, 159–61; self-deception by therapist 169–70; and sexual orientation 146–7; and sympathetic understanding 165, 170–1; tension between ego and ego ideal 147–8
LSD 101, 102, 172*n*9
Lunatic Asylums 12, 13

mad, use of term 59
madness and unconditional acceptance, Portland Road 98–120; admittance process 102–3; capacity for benign neglect 114–15; Crawford as facilitator of 100–1, 102, 104–5, 107–8, 109, 110, 111, 113, 114, 115, 117, 119*n*1; dangers of 105–8; Elvis (schizophrenic resident) 111; healing power of love 115, 118–19; importance of honesty 102–3; Jason (schizophrenic resident) 102; Jerome (schizophrenic resident) 108–19, 154, 170; Laing's consultations regarding Jerome 110, 111; Laing's establishment of household communities 99–101, 104; living together vs. therapize approach 115, 117–19; Mary (schizophrenic resident) 106–8; mixture of personalities in 105; newspaper article on and court case 115–16; periods at Crawford's Welch farm 111–12, 118; vigils 101
mania: and capacity for intimacy 93–4; comparison to falling in love 148; *DSM* categorization of 90–1; imperviousness to self-enquiry during 92; origin of term 90; in Plato's *Phaedrus* 153–4; states of 14–15; and suddenness of behavior 156–8; *see also* bipolar disorder; hypomania; megalomania
manic depression *see* bipolar disorder
manic depressive insanity (Kraepelin) 81
manic depressive psychosis 35
marital relationships 134, 135, 144, 151, 155, 156, 170, 185–6
Maroda, Karen 122
The Marriage of Heaven and Hell (Blake) 105
Marx, Karl 85, 86
Mary (Portland Road resident) 106–8
master morality *see* Nietzsche
medical metaphor: comparison to Chinese medicine 174–5; influence of Hippocrates on 12; as initiated by Freud 17–18; pervasiveness of ix–x; and suffering 35; usefulness of 18–19
medication: cultural over-medicalization 163; in forced treatment 6, 13; for grief 94–5; as hindrance to self-healing 195; for mania 91; for mental disorders x, 4–6, 19, 75–6
megalomania 146–7, 148, 158, 160
Menninger Clinic 115
mental, use of term ix–x
mental anguish, Epicurean model on 12

mental hospitals 6, 7, 115, 118, 119n4; *see also* forced treatment

mental illness, myth of 1–20; attempts to define sanity and madness 13–18; diagnosis 3–4, 7; early historical views and treatment 11–13; and ethical obligations 17; Foucault on 11–13; Freud on 9–10; and genetic theory 16; and medical metaphor ix–x, 12, 17–19; ontological security/insecurity 7–8, 14; psychopathology, origin of term 2–3; Szasz on 2; on therapist/patient relationships 7, 10–11, 16–17; use of medication 4–6, 13, 19; *see also individual theorists and philosophers*

Merleau-Ponty, Maurice 189, 191

Mill, John Stuart 23

Montaigne, Michel de 132–5, 136, 141n7

moods, use of term 45

Moore, G. E. 23

morality *see* Nietzsche

Moses 160

Muses 161–2

mystification (Laing) 85–7, 179, 192–5

Myth of Cura (Heidegger) 168–9

The Myth of Mental Illness (Szasz) 2

narcissism theory (Freud) 60–1, 146–7, 150–1; *see also* psychosis

negative capability (Keats) 114

neurosis: and ambivalence 27–8; and capacity for love 43n8, 64; as free choice 187–9, 192; Freud on xi, 24, 62–3, 77–8, 194; and Freud's *Libido* 36–7; incidence of treatment for 88–9; lack of overarching theory on 23–4; as mitigation of pain 29, 73; origin of term 33; as part of human condition 10, 24, 34, 80–1, 83; and wishing vs. desire 22, 38–9; *see also* hysteria; obsessional neurotics

neurotic conflicts 24, 26–7, 39, 56–7, 71, 73, 75, 145–6

neurotic guilt 56–7, 189–90

Nicomachean Ethics (Aristotle) 133

Nietzsche 23, 91, 190, 191, 196; criticism of 60; on humans as driven by passion 164; on illusion of group belonging 184; influence on Laing 84; manic episodes of 158; on master/slave morality 52–4, 55, 56, 58, 60, 61, 66, 181; on *ressentiment* 49, 66, 84, 181; on spite 55; *Übermensch* 181–2; *see also individual writings of*

Nirvana Complex (Freud) 23

No Exit (Sartre) 85

Nussbaum, M. 152–3

"Observations on Transference-Love" (Freud) 30–1, 124

obsessional neurotics 33–4, 43n5, 80, 160

obsessive compulsive disorder 90

Oedipus complex (Freud): child's interpretation of 64; desire and wish fulfillment 21–6; and jealousy 49–50, 159; Klein on 50–2; vs. Oedipal victor 43n3; and resentment 47, 49–51, 54, 55; sexual nature of desire xii, xiv, 29–30, 144–5, 151; and unrequited love in childhood 9–10, 82, 83

On the Genealogy of Morality (Nietzsche) 49

On the History of the Psychoanalytic Movement (Freud) 24

ontological security/insecurity (Laing) 7–8, 14; *see also* true/false self concepts

oral sex 145

paranoia 3, 8–9, 13, 35, 52, 83, 158

paranoid-schizoid position (Dlein) 50

passion: defined 45; as madness 153; Nietzsche on 164; origin of term 45, 156; vs. reason 22–3; *see also* emotions

patient: as agent 32, 75; use of term 69

Paul (patient) 41–2

penis envy (Freud) 78

persona, origin of term 127

personal relationships with patients, and transference 121–42; and analytic neutrality 124–5; as confidante/ friendship relationship 132–8; connectedness as transformational component of so-called transference 131–2; and countertransference 127–8; existentialist approach to 138; Ferenczi on 122–3, 128, 131; Freud on 124, 125–6, 128, 131, 132, 139–40; Greenson on 128; Haynal on 123; Hoffman on 123–4, 125; Renik on 128–9; spontaneous conversations 130–1; Stone on 124; theorists' support for relational authenticity 122, 123; therapists' behavior as technique 128–30, 138; transference interpretations 124, 125; and unconscious phenomenon 125–8

perversions *see* Freud, Sigmund

Peter (patient) 155–6

petrification 8

Phaedrus (Plato) 22, 149, 152–4

phenomenological tradition xiv–xv, 1, 86

Philadelphia Association (PA) 100, 101, 102, 116, 119*n*1; *see also* Kingsley Hall, London; madness and unconditional acceptance, Portland Road
philia (love of family/friend) 151–2, 165, 171
philosophical metaphor 18
Pinel, Philippe 12–13
placebo effect 76, 77
Plath, Sylvia 161
Plato 22–3, 42, 43*n*11, 96*n*11, 144, 158; *see also* Eros (Plato); *individual writings of*
Platonic love 152
Pleasure Principle (Freud) 23, 43*n*11
Poe, Edgar Allen 161
poetic madness 160–1, 162
The Politics of Experience (Laing) 1–2, 192
Pollock, Jackson 91
Portland Road residence (PA) *see* madness and unconditional acceptance, Portland Road
Pound, Ezra 161
privacy 104, 114
prophetic madness 158, 160, 162
The Protagoras (Plato) 23, 43*n*11
psychiatry: birth of 10–13, 70–1; diagnosis 4; forced treatment 6–7; ineffectiveness of 9–10, 19; Laing on 1, 2–4; medical metaphor in 174; origin of term 70; reliance on medication 4–5; on schizophrenia as incurable 87–8; *see also* anti-psychiatry; personal relationships with patients, and transference
psychic phenomena 45–6
psychoanalysis: function of xii, xiv–xvi; regressive nature of 186; as temporary solution 34; treatment relationship in 10–11; *see also* personal relationships with patients, and transference
psychopathology, deciphering of 69–97; absence of medical context for 71, 73–4, 76, 96*n*5; defined xv; depression 93–5; DSM categorization of schizophrenia 87–9; and existential aspects of suffering 71–3; Freud on xi, 9–10, 81, 83; Freud's development of psychotherapy 77–81, 96*n*9; Laing's work with schizophrenia 81, 83–7; mania 89–93; origin and use of term ix–x, 2–3, 70; *pathos* 69; and patient as agent 75; and placebo effect 76, 77; *psyche* 70, 74, 81; psychosis, origin of term 81; state of distress 73–5; therapy, origin of term 74; trauma, use of term 82–3; use of deception to elicit love 84–5; *see also* mental illness, myth of

The Psychopathology of Everyday Life (Freud) 34
psychopharmacology *see* medication
psychosis: de-inversion of inverted values 65; as free choice 187–9, 192; Freud on xi, 43*n*12, 60–1, 81, 83, 194, 195; incidence of treatment for 88–9; and jealousy 50, 51; mental hospitals for 115; origin of term 81; and possession 156; resentment and symptom formation 50, 51, 60–2, 64–5; splitting 176, 178, 187; tension between ego and ego ideal 147–8; types of 35; views on therapy for 75; *see also* schizophrenia
psychotherapy: coerced participation in 75; Freud's development of 77–81, 96*n*9; function of xi, xii; motives of therapists 9; origin and use of term 3, 74; *see also* personal relationships with patients, and transference
Purity of Heart Is to Will One Thing (Kierkegaard) 166, 180

Rank, Otto 42
Redler, Leon 100, 119*n*2
Reik, Theodore 158
relational vs. classical analysts 122–3, 127–9, 131, 138; *see also individual analysts*
Renik, O. 128–9
repression, Freud on 25–6, 36, 60
The Republic (Plato) 22–3
resentment, and symptom formation 45–68; alienation from desire 56–7; ambivalence as purgatory of desire 60–2; blaming others 65–6; and death of desire 54, 55–61; distinguished from self-pity 54; distinguished from spite 54–5; and emotions 45–52; Freud's superego 56–7; Freud's third "magical" choice scenario 47–8; hatred as consequence of 60; and internalized parental prohibitions 56–7; and irresponsibility 63; and jealousy/envy 49–52, 57; Klein on 50–2; Nietzsche on master/slave morality 52–4, 55, 56, 58, 60, 61, 66; and power of anger 57–9; and psychosis 50, 51, 60–2, 64–5; as reaction to thwarted desire 54, 57, 58, 60; Sartre on 48, 51; Scheler on 49, 55–7, 58, 59, 60, 62; and sense of vulnerability 54–5
ressentiment: Nietzsche on 49, 66, 84, 181; use of term 49
Ressentiment (Scheler) 55
ritual madness 160–1, 162
Robinson, Peter 99–100, 119*n*2
Rousseau, Jean-Jacques 190

Sam Spade (film character) 46–7
sane/sanity, origin of terms 174, 175–6
Sanity, Madness and the Family (Laing and
  Esterson) 85–6, 193
sanity and authenticity 174–200; and artistic
  temperament 190–1, 196; and freedom
  as taking responsibility 187–92, 197;
  health sense of self 186; Heidegger on
  authenticity 181–2, 198n6; Heidegger on
  self as evolving identities/nothing 181–3,
  186; Heidegger on they-self and groups
  184–5, 190, 192; "I," use of term 183–4;
  Kierkegaard on 181–3; Laing's writings
  on 192–4; in marital relationships 185–6;
  Nietzsche on *Übermensch* 181; in relation
  to judgment 176; sane/sanity, origin of
  terms 174, 175–6; and serenity 197–8;
  tolerance of differences 196–8; true/false
  self concepts 176–80, 183, 194; Wrathall
  on 184
sanity and madness: attempts to define
  13–18; and defense mechanisms xi, 13,
  14, 16, 20n5, 34; and extreme anger
  59–60; use of terms ix–x; variance in
  cultural interpretation of 16, 17; *see also*
  resentment, and symptom formation
Santas, G. 151, 153–4
Sartre, Jean-Paul 51, 190; as artist and
  philosopher 191; on choices as deliberate
  186, 187–8; on emotions 47, 48; on
  heartbreak of relationship 85; influence
  on Laing 84, 86, 191–2; on schizoid
  person 9; on self-deception 191–2;
  see also individual writings of
Scheler, Max 49, 55–7, 58, 59, 60, 62, 167,
  169, 172n12
schizoaffective disorders 87–8
schizoid personality/condition: as alienation
  103–4, 178, 184; challenges of diagnosis
  88; comparison to mania 92, 93; language
  acquisition as prerequisite 179; as normal
  condition 9; use of term 7, 84; *see also The
  Divided Self* (Laing); psychosis
schizophrenia: and alienation 16;
  comparison to mania 92; and
  dependency on family 65; diagnosis of
  4; *DSM* categorization of 87–9; false self
  concept 179; Laing on 1–3, 7, 8–9, 13, 81,
  83–7; and need for *caritas* 169–70; origin
  of term 83–4; views on therapy for 35,
  75; *see also* madness and unconditional
  acceptance, Portland Road
schizophreniform disorders 87–8
Schopenhauer, A. 144

Scientology 158, 160
seduction theory *see* Oedipus complex
  (Freud)
self-deception *see* Sartre, Jean-Paul
self-disclosure (Renik) 128–9
self-pity 54, 63
serenity 197–8
The Servant (film) 55
sex addicts 93
sex life discussion, as taboo 36–7
sexual orientation 145, 146–7
sexual relationships 134, 137, 160; *see also*
  love and madness; marital relationships
shamanism 11–12, 160, 162
The Sickness Unto Death (Kierkegaard) 180
Sketch for a Theory of the Emotions (Sartre) 48
slave morality *see* Nietzsche
sobriety movement 163
sociopathy 108
Socrates 18, 149–50, 152–4, 180
sollicitidudo (care) 168–9
somatic symptoms 33, 35, 78–9
Sonnets (Laing) 161
Sorge (Heidegger) 167–8, 170
sound, defined 175–6
spiritual anguish, Epicurean model on 12
spiritual crisis metaphor 18–19
splitting *see* psychosis
spontaneous conversations *see* personal
  relationships with patients, and
  transference
Stone, Leo 122, 123, 124
Strachey, James 198n3
sublimation *see* Freud, Sigmund
suckling, as originary love (Freud) 144–5,
  146
suffering, as existential phenomena 35,
  71–3, 74
suicidal depression 5–6, 15, 94–5
suicide 55, 159, 187
Sullivan, Harry Stack 7, 10–11, 20n5, 118
support groups 60
sympathy: capacity for 169, 170–1;
  distinguished from empathy 165–7, 169;
  as gift of grace 165; origin of term 165;
  Scheler on 167, 169, 170, 172n12
Symposium (Plato) 149–50, 152, 155, 158
symptom, use of term 29, 38–9
Szasz, Thomas 2, 6, 11, 91, 126

Tavistock Institute for Human Relations 86,
  167, 192–3
testosterone 36
Therapeutae 11

therapeutic alliance *see* personal
relationships with patients, and
transference
therapeutic ambition (Freud) 169, 172*n*12
therapy, origin of term 11
they-self *see* Heidegger, Martin
third "magical" choice scenario *see* Freud,
Sigmund
Thompson, Clara 118
Thompson, M. Guy: becomes aware of
Laing 99; biographical experiences of
46–7, 101, 102, 106–7, 154, 162–3;
Crawford as analyst for 105; influence of
phenomenological tradition on xiv–xv, 1;
Laing's influence on xi, xii, 99–100, 101;
psychoanalysis training at PA 105; *see also*
madness and unconditional acceptance,
Portland Road
Three Essays on Sexuality (Freud) 144
thrownness *see* Heidegger, Martin
Thus Spoke Zarathustra (Nietzsche) 192
tough love 28
transference: and anger 58; defined 30;
within PA household communities
103; and placebo effect 76, 77; and
technical principles 122; and unconscious
phenomenon 30, 125–8, 189; *see also*
personal relationships with patients, and
transference
transpersonal movement 19
trauma, use of term 82–3
trauma theory 188–9; *see also* Oedipus
complex (Freud)
treat, origin of term 115
A Treatise on Human Nature (Hume) 23

treatment, use of term 115
trespass concept 166–7, 169
true/false self concepts 176–80, 182, 194
Trungpa, Chogyam 166, 198*n*2
The Truth About Freud's Technique
(Thompson) xi

Übermensch (Nietzsche) 181–3
unconscious: and creativity 162;
depersonalization of 10, 20*n*5, 126–8;
and fantasies 38–9; inability to take
responsibility for 48–9; and self-inflicted
symptoms 28–9; and transference 30,
125–8, 189; *see also* id/ego/superego
(Freud)
United States, licensure requirements
18–19
unobjectionable transference *see* personal
relationships with patients, and
transference

Valéry, Paul 21
Van Gogh, Vincent 161
violence 106–8, 166–7, 197

Will, Otto Allen, Jr. 118, 130
Will to Power (Nietzsche) 52
Winnicott, D. W. 10–11, 35, 118, 130; on
The Divided Self 96*n*12; "good-enough"
mother theory 82–5, 188; true/false self
concepts 176–80, 183, 194
wisdom, defined 176
workaholics 9, 147, 172*n*1
Works of Love (Kierkegaard) 166
Wrathall, M. 184, 188